THE BACKBONE

Harriot Slessor in old age

Colonel John Henry Slessor,
35th Regiment of Foot, c.1817

Lieutenant Henry Thomas
Slessor, R.N., 1803

THE BACKBONE

*Diaries of a Military Family in the
Napoleonic Wars*

edited by
ALETHEA HAYTER

The Pentland Press Limited
Edinburgh · Cambridge · Durham

Other Books by Alethea Hayter

Mrs Browning: A Poet's Work and its Setting (1962)
A Sultry Month: Scenes of London Literary Life in 1846 (1965)
Opium and the Romantic Imagination (1968)
Horatio's Version (1972)
A Voyage in Vain: Coleridge's Journey to Malta in 1804 (1975)
*Portrait of a Friendship: Drawn from New Letters of James Russell Lowell
to Sybella Lyttelton, 1881–1891* (1990)

© Alethea Hayter 1993

First published in 1993 by
The Pentland Press Ltd.
1 Hutton Close
South Church
Bishop Auckland
Durham

ISBN 1 85821 069 0

Typeset by Elite Typesetting Techniques, Southampton.
Printed and bound by Antony Rowe Ltd., Chippenham.

Contents

Contents

FOREWORD

The substance of this narrative of events in the Napoleonic Wars between Britain and France consists of the diaries of my great-grandfather Major-General John Henry Slessor (1777–1850) and of his mother Harriot Slessor (1748–1834), with some letters of her husband John Slessor, Governor of Oporto, and of her other two sons William and Henry, and some passages from the diary of her second daughter Harriot Amelia. John Henry Slessor, as a much-travelled serving officer, was an eye-witness at many actions and campaigns on the fringes of the main theatres of the war. Harriot was able to describe at first hand what it was like to be a civilian in an occupied, and then liberated, country. Between them, the Slessor family were involved in the struggle with France in Ireland, the Channel Islands, Gibraltar, Syria, Egypt, Calabria, Portugal, the Ionian Islands, the Northern Adriatic, Northern Italy, Belgium and France, and their records of their experiences reveal aspects of the peripheral events in the long war which have not been much described by other contemporary witnesses.

Both John Henry's and Harriot's diaries are partly daily-kept jottings, recording genuinely contemporary reactions, and partly retrospective memoirs. Sometimes a month's or a year's events are summarized, and it is clear from internal evidence that both diarists did a fair amount of later editing; some of the passages of foreboding comment on the probable turn of political and military events are in fact hindsight, inserted later. Both of them inserted copies of letters, proclamations and newspaper reports in their diaries, and made what are obviously addresses to the reader, though both denied that they expected their diaries to be read by anyone. Harriot, and to a lesser extent John Henry, included flashbacks on the earlier history of their lives and of the other members of the family.

John Henry writes briskly and factually. 'I like your laconic, short-sentence style,' his father commented on his letters from Ireland, and he himself, twenty years later, described his own method as 'the short-sentenced style of a soldier's narrative'. Harriot's style is less spontaneous, more thoughtful and

studied, given to double negatives, full of moralising and speculation on political developments. She has a large vocabulary and a fluent pen, but her
spelling is wildly inaccurate. She always, for instance, spells 'trifling' – one of
her favourite adjectives – with two f's. Her shots at spelling French and
Spanish names are often weirdly phonetic guesses, as when the French generals
Thomières and Brennier appear as Tonnieurs and Berimer. Even the frequently
mentioned Junot sometimes loses his final t and turns into a Roman goddess.
She dropped the last letters of English names quite often too; Sir John Moore
and Colonel Browne always appear without their final e's. John Henry's spelling is much more reliable, though he too made some strange guesses at Italian
and Greek place-names. I have decided with some reluctance to correct their
spelling mistakes; they give a rather attractive idiosyncrasy to the diaries, but
would probably irritate any meticulous reader. I have also referred to John
Henry throughout by both his Christian names, in order to avoid an otherwise
inevitable confusion with his father; though in reality his family always addressed him simply as 'John'. Extracts from John Henry's and Harriot's diaries
are marked JHS and HS; those from the letters of John Slessor and his second
son William are marked JS and WS; Louisa Canavaro's and Harriot Amelia's
diary entries are marked LC and HAS.

John Henry's and Harriot's characters – his sociable, shrewd, observant,
matter-of-fact, with a certain dry humour and self-mockery; hers strong-willed,
apt to strike attitudes and indulge in heavy irony and sharp-edged portraits of
those around her – emerge in mainly unconscious self-revelation in their diaries. Both were children of their time in their assumptions about the world they
lived in. They could have sung the second verse of 'Rule Britannia' with
untroubled conviction.

> The nations not so blest as thee
> Shall in their turn to tyrants fall,
> While thou shalt flourish great and free,
> The dread and envy of them all.

This serene confidence, however exasperating to other 'not so blest' nations,
must have been a comfortable – and in some ways a beneficial – feeling for
Britannia's sons; if it made them insensitive and unadaptable, it also made them
unselfconscious, and aware of their responsibilities.

The diaries have remained in the possession of Harriot's and John Henry's
descendants, and are now the property of John Henry's great-great-grandson
George Slessor Burnett-Stuart, by whose permission they are published. At the
beginning of this century John Henry's grandson, Major Arthur Kerr Slessor,
did considerable research, using the diaries as his starting-point, into the ancestry of John Slessor, and published some of it in an article in *Blackwood's* of
June 1902 on 'The Scottish Artillery', and the information he there supplied
found its way into Charles Dalton's *English Army Lists and Commission*

Registers, 1661–1714 (p.227) as established fact. But Arthur Slessor's later research brought to light contemporary evidence about John Slessor's immediate Scottish ancestry, and caused him to revise the conclusions he had published in *Blackwood's*. The manuscript notebooks in which he recorded the progress of his researches are the property of his grandson Group Captain John Slessor, by whose permission I have quoted from them.

No other material deriving from the diaries has been published before, but the genealogical researches of John Gordon-Clark (whose wife was a great-grand-daughter of John Henry), Peter Hadley (whose wife is a connection of John Henry's daughter-in-law) and Colonel Hervé Patoureau (great-great-great-grandson of Harriot) have established the wide-spreading ramifications of the Slessor family tree. Neville and Mark Girardot, whose forbears intermarried with the Slessors in the eighteenth century, have also helped me to disentangle the intertwined branches of the family tree. I am grateful to Dr Hector Macdonald of the National Library of Scotland, Mr Peter Vasey of the National Register of Archives (Scotland) and Mr Keith Cavers, for help over the Slessors' Scottish ancestry; to Miss C. Wright, of the National Army Museum, for information about the first John Slessor's brief career in the British Army; to Mrs David Francis for giving me access to her late husband's research notes on the Portuguese army in the eighteenth century; to Mrs Fleetwood, of South Australia, for bringing to light the link between her ancestress Maria Natalizia and the Slessors; to Senhor Pedro Canavaro (great-great-great-great-grandson of John and Harriot Slessor) and Mr John Delaforce for information about the Slessors in Oporto.

A list of printed sources consulted is given at the end of this book. Of the more recently published works in that list, the books by Elizabeth Longford, Rose Macaulay, Piers Mackesy, Carola Oman, Thomas Pakenham and R.J. Rath have been particularly helpful.

London 1992.

PART I

**A Military Family
1669–1798**

1

All Slessors like to be on the move. A mixture of chance and choice sends them off to work in, travel through, escape from, countries other than their own. It was perhaps their mixed ancestry that made them nomads. It becomes less surprising to find that quintessentially British couple, John and Harriot Slessor, living in a remote village in North Portugal in the late eighteenth century when we know that John, though a Scot from Aberdeenshire, was descended from a German who settled in Scotland a century earlier, and that, if Harriot's father came from a line of Norfolk squires, her mother was descended from Huguenot refugees who fled to London from France.

Here, then, we first meet the family, in the Portuguese village of San Pedro on an autumn day in the 1780s. John has ridden to the nearby garrison town where his cavalry regiment is stationed; Harriot is setting out with their six children to spend a day in the vineyards – each child has a basket to fill with grapes, and expects to be a great help to the vintagers. Kind Louisa, sturdy John Henry, sentimental pouting Harriot Amelia, sulky William, taciturn Henry, pretty engaging Sophia – they and their parents have many strange and sad events ahead of them in the next thirty years, a microscopic cross-section of the strange and sad calamities that were to engulf all Europe for most of those years. Half choice, half chance had wafted John Slessor to Portugal; chance and choice were to blow his wife and children far and wide in Europe, Asia and Africa.

'My father was a Scotsman by birth, altho' originally of a noble family from Silesia' wrote his son John Henry Slessor the diarist. His father always maintained that his surname was of German origin, and that he was descended from the German artillery officer, John Slezer, author of *Theatrum Scotiae*, a book of engravings of Scottish castles and palaces celebrated in its day. John Slezer visited Scotland for the first time in 1669, 'being upon my travels' as he said. He may previously have joined the Scottish Brigade of the Dutch Army, which included German officers in the mid-seventeeth century; he must somewhere have acquired military experience as an engineer and artillery officer, since in 1671 he returned to Edinburgh and was appointed Chief Engineer, Scotland, and six years later Lieutenant to the Artillery, Scotland. In 1677 he married a Scottish woman, Jean Straiton. In 1681 he was sent on an official visit to

3

Holland, to recruit artillerymen and buy guns. He was briefly imprisoned in 1689 when he at first refused to take the oath of fidelity to William III, but made his peace with the new regime and was re-appointed Captain of the Artillery and Surveyor of Magazines for Scotland. (His commissions referred to him as 'John Abraham Schlezer, German' and other contemporary documents labelled him 'High German'.) Three years later he published his noble *Theatrum Scotiae*, but fell on evil times because both the official subsidy accorded to him for its publication, and his expenses for equipping his artillerymen, remained unpaid, and he had to spend thirteen years in the debtors' sanctuary of Holyroodhouse. He died in 1717. He had three sons, John, Charles and David. John died in 1699, David was still alive in 1708, but was dead by 1723. Charles seems the most likely to have left issue. He was commissioned as an ensign in the Earl of Orkney's Regiment of Foot (the Royal Scots) and served in Marlborough's campaigns in Flanders, and was later stationed in Ireland.

An interesting and appropriate ancestry for a family tree of serving officers stretching on for nearly another three centuries. But so far not a provable one, though the Slessor family tradition of descent from John Slezer is strong. It is possible that Charles Slezer decided to change his surname to the well-known Scottish one of Slessor because of the constant mis-spellings of Slezer. His father John Slezer is referred to as Sletcher, Sletsher, Schlezer, Schleiser, Slazer and Sledzer in contemporary documents, and Charles Slezer is listed as Sletcher in the 1708 Army List (though correctly as Slezer in the 1715 one). Charles's parents married in 1677, so he may have been born in 1679 or 1680, in which case he would have been quite old enough, before he was commissioned into the Army in 1708 and went on foreign service, to have fathered a son in Scotland. But here we reach a gap so far unbridgeable: was Charles Slezer the father of Thomas Slessor of Bridgend by Auchlee, in the parish of Longside in Aberdeenshire, who is known to have been the diarist's grandfather?

The diarist's father, John Slessor, was born in 1735, the son of Thomas Slessor, owner or tenant of the farm of Bridgend by Auchlee, and of his wife Elspeth. She had been previously married to Charles Robb, by whom she had had one daughter, Janet; her maiden name had been Moir. Young John Slessor was at first educated in the Parish School at Longside, and then went to the University of Aberdeen. He intended to become a doctor, and was apprenticed to Dr Livingstone of Aberdeen.

This account of his childhood and youth was supplied by two of his contemporaries, the physician Sir Walter Farquhar and his sister, both of whom had known John Slessor as a boy. Miss Farquhar remembered that when she was a schoolgirl John Slessor had been brought to Aberdeen, to enter the University, by his father Thomas, 'a very respectable-looking man'. Walter Farquhar, who also started his medical career as apprentice to an Aberdeen doctor, became a lifelong friend of John Slessor's, and told his son the diarist that he 'would have made I have no doubt an excellent Practitioner, had not an old and mutual friend General Fraser induced him to change his line of life and become a soldier.'

Farquhar, who was reminiscing nearly sixty years after the event, must have been wrong in thinking that it was General Fraser who persuaded John Slessor to go into the army. Fraser and Slessor were indeed old friends, and relatives as well – they married sisters. But it seems very improbable that they could have met in the 1750s when John Slessor was a student at Aberdeen University, and then a doctor's apprentice there. The Hon. Simon Fraser of Lovat, son of the notorious Lord Lovat who was executed after the 1745 Rebellion, was eight years older than John Slessor, and by the 1750s, having taken part in the 1745 Rebellion, been imprisoned after Culloden and been pardoned, he had been called to the Scottish and English Bars, become MP for Inverness, raised a regiment from his own clan, and fought in America and Canada. He is variously described as 'straightforward, honourable and independent' or as having, under a pleasing exterior, a hard heart and rapacious greed. He was to enter John Slessor's life in the 1760s and to remain a friend till his death in 1782. But it must have been some other tempting friend, or John Slessor's own ambition for wider horizons, that inspired him to throw up his medical apprenticeship and join the Army.

In April 1762 he broke off his ties with home, and was commissioned as an ensign in the 64th Regiment of Foot, then stationed in Ireland. His Scottish relations almost lost track of his subsequent career. Once he did get in touch again with the children of his half-sister Janet, who married Andrew Sangster and died young, as did her husband, leaving their five children in poor circumstances, so that the daughters had to become domestic servants and the son a baker. That son remembered John Slessor coming to see the orphaned children and 'expressing himself most affectionately with regard to our Mother, and said that he would do something for us, but the distance being so great betwixt us I do not recall seeing him again.' John Slessor's Scottish connections are never mentioned in his wife's or son's diaries. The geographical and class gap had opened too widely.

It is rather surprising that John Slessor was able to secure a commission as ensign; commissions were then mostly won by purchase or influence, neither of which would seem obviously available to a doctor's apprentice whose father was a farmer. His appointment, specially to a regiment stationed in Ireland, may strengthen the possibility of his descent from Charles Slezer, whose much grander regiment had been in Ireland twenty years earlier. The 64th, to which he was gazetted as an ensign on 19th April 1762, had recently returned from the West Indies, and was later to be in America during the War of Independence.

Soon after John Slessor joined the 64th in Ireland, his first encounter with major historical events changed the course of his career. In the Seven Years War, England's opponent France, allied under the Family Compact with Spain, issued an ultimatum to Portugal to join them against her ancient ally England. When the King of Portugal refused to renounce his alliance with England, the Spaniards invaded Portugal in April 1762. The Portuguese Chief Minister, the Marques de Pombal, had anticipated the Spanish move by appealing to England for reinforcements of troops and money, and for British officers to command the disorganised Portuguese army in the defence of Portugal against the invaders. According to Pombal, the Portuguese army was then 30,000 strong, with 5,000 cavalry; in fact it consisted of a maximum of 17,000, most of them raw recruits, without arms, tents, stores or transport.

All British military observers in the eighteenth century agreed that the Portuguese rank and file, when properly led, were brave, long-enduring, biddable, ready to live on basic rations, to march barefoot and disregard hardships. But they were not properly led; the majority of their officers were idle and corrupt. 'They knew nothing and they refused to learn; the generals huddled together in one place because it was the custom, and obstinately rejected any proposal to split into brigades'; they preferred to live a city life apart from, and unconcerned with, their troops. The corrupt system under which colonels contracted with the Government for their regiments, and then could fill their muster-roll with absentees or non-existent men whose pay they could then draw and pocket, ensured that battalions were depleted, and made up of half-drilled, ill-equipped, poorly disciplined troops.

The British response to Pombal's request was to send seven regiments of British troops, 8,000 men, from England, Ireland and Belle Isle, to Portugal. The two regiments from Ireland did not include the 64th – John Slessor's move to Portugal was to be an individual one, as part of the scheme by which British officers were to be offered posts in the Portuguese army. The British forces sent to Portugal were commanded by Lord Loudon, under whom were Generals Burgoyne and George (later Viscount) Townshend. The combined British and Portuguese forces were under the command of a German aristocrat, Count Schaumberg-Lippe-Buckenberg. British officers, mostly already colonels or upwards, sent at this time to take over commands in the Portuguese army, included General Fraser, a Scottish officer John Forbes of Skelleter – who was to spend the rest of his career in Portugal, ending up as one of its most senior generals – McDonell, Rainsford, Smith, Maclean and others.

The campaign of 1762 in Portugal was soon over; it lasted only four months and ended with the withdrawal of the Spanish forces and a peace treaty, and by April 1763 the British regiments had left Portugal. The British officers who remained behind attached to the Portuguese army included, intermittently at least, Simon Fraser, who was made Governor of the Minho and Tras os Montes, and Colonel Smith, who commanded the Chaves cavalry regiment.

It is not clear exactly when John Slessor went to Portugal. His wife and son, in their diaries, give accounts which do not establish the date of his move. Harriot Slessor says

HS My husband came early in life into it, in the reign of the Marques de Pombal. Then English officers were much in request. He was one among the many that offered their services. All got double pay and rapid promotion. At the peace, having only the rank of Ensign in his own country, and that of Captain in this, he remained.

The 'reign' of Pombal lasted till 1777; the 'peace' may have been the end of the Seven Years War in 1763. Harriot goes on to say that her husband, who died in 1800, had 'between 30 and 40 years' service' in the Portuguese army. From her account it can only be said that John Slessor joined the Portuguese army some time in the 1760s. John Henry's diary is more precise, but no less confusing. He says of his father that

JHS He, as also many other young officers, viz. Fraser, Forbes, McDonnel etc. were offered terms too advantageous to refuse. They retired on British half-pay, and accepted commissions in the Portuguese service, in the time of Lord Townshend.

This sounds as though John Slessor must have joined the Portuguese army in 1762, when Townshend was commanding the British troops in Northern Portugal. But John Slessor only joined the 64th in Ireland in April 1762, and is hardly likely to have abandoned it for the Portuguese service within months, and in fact the 1767 Army List shows him as still on the strength of the 64th as an Ensign. It is not till the 1768 Army List that he appears as a half-pay ensign in the disbanded 123rd (Pomeroy's) Regiment of Foot; while serving in the Portuguese army, he remained on the Irish Half-Pay List for the rest of his life, drawing an ensign's half-pay, which at that time would have been about two shillings a day in a foot regiment.

Perhaps he heard of the opportunities in Portugal from friends in the two British regiments which returned to Ireland after the 1762 campaign. At any rate, some time before 1768 he had accepted a commission, with promotion to Captain, in the Portuguese army. British officers who took this offer were given double the pay of their Portuguese opposite numbers, and had better chances of promotion; it was 'too advantageous to refuse', as John Slessor's son said.

The Portuguese army, when John Slessor joined it, was in a much better state. Count Lippe, who remained in Portugal till 1764, reorganised the army into thirty-nine regiments, twenty-four line, twelve cavalry and three artillery, with a permanent footing of 30,000 men, and much improved morale and discipline. A British observer in 1765 considered the Portuguese army well-clothed, regularly paid, and of good appearance. John Slessor joined the Chaves cavalry regiment, which under Colonel Smith had achieved a high state of order and efficiency.

This prosperous state of affairs did not last long. Deterioration began soon after Lippe left Portugal, and accelerated when King Joseph I died in 1777 and Pombal fell from power. The new monarch, Queen Maria I, and her husband and uncle Don Pedro were more concerned with religious affairs than with military efficiency. Army pay was frequently in arrears, so that the common soldiers were often reduced to begging, the officers to taking menial jobs on the side. The reforms and discipline imposed by Lippe had broken down by the end of the 1770s; a British officer visiting Portugal in the 1780s considered that the army was in such a hopeless state as to be incapable of serious resistance to any invasion.

In such conditions, the position of many of the British officers in the Portuguese army became increasingly disagreeable. Part of the trouble was that the Portuguese officers were not unnaturally jealous of their British opposite numbers who received double pay (when pay was forthcoming at all, which it frequently was not). A Portuguese colonel was paid only £114 a year; a British colonel in the Portuguese army, drawing double that sum, was paid nearly £30 a year more than a colonel in the British army. Jealousy over pay led to intrigues against British officers, aided and abetted by the Portuguese Court unless the British were prepared to turn, or to pretend to turn, Catholic. A graphic, though one-sided, description of their plight was given by an Irishman, Arthur William Costigan, who visited Portugal in 1778 and met Forbes, Maclean and other British officers in the Portuguese service, including a Colonel Bagot whom he describes as 'one of those few unhappy English officers, who has remained in the Portuguese service ever since the campaign of 1762 in this country, of which he now heartily repents', but who had been 'seduced by the whistling of a name, the prospect of high rank, and the flattering behaviour of the Court to him at the beginning.' The subsequent treatment of him and other British officers had been such that many had left, although a few of 'capacity and merit' had stuck it out, though often on resentful terms with their Portuguese fellow officers. Some of these latter succeeded, by intrigues and string-pulling, in getting themselves reinstated even when they had been cashiered for inefficiency, or worse. In one case, British officers found themselves compelled to share a mess table once more with a Portuguese colonel who had been convicted of incest, murder and seducing nuns, and had fled to Spain. Embezzlers, rapists, even murderers all secured pardon and reinstatement, according to Costigan.

He and other British visitors to Portugal, keenly collecting horror stories to include in books about their travels, perhaps did not see the whole situation in perspective. Costigan was a bigoted Irishman who had served in the Irish Brigade of the Spanish army, had imbibed anti-Portuguese prejudices from his Spanish colleagues, and clearly enjoyed what Rose Macaulay calls 'the pleasures of disapproval'. It is hardly surprising that British officers who were determined to condemn everything in Portugal were not popular with, and consequently not well treated by, their Portuguese colleagues. One such pig-headed officer, Captain Gaynor, was well described to Costigan by Colonel Bagot, who was himself a sufferer from, and complainer of, his treatment in Portugal, but who seems to have been dimly aware that there might be faults on both sides. 'This poor fellow Gaynor is the worthiest fellow alive, and so full of uprightness and honesty, that these virtues . . . have literally been his ruin in the service . . . He cannot put up with the smallest appearance of disingenuity or dissimulation, and is entirely incapable of that share of prudence in dealing with people of different manners and nations, which is perfectly compatible with the character of a man of probity and honour everywhere; he revolts at the smallest departure from the rules of propriety and truth, in such a manner that he cannot help by some exterior act or gesture expressing his displeasure and disgust; and, as he hardly meets in this country with anything but duplicity and deceit, it is no wonder the natives here should look upon him as a rude, surly, dissatisfied being . . . an English savage, totally void of manners and good breeding.' It is a chilling picture of the harm done, and offence given, world-wide and over centuries, by conscientious but fatally rigid Colonel Blimps. Some traces of this disposition will be found in the diaries of Harriot and John Henry Slessor, but modified by humour, curiosity and sociability.

Costigan's atrocity stories about disgruntled British officers in Portugal give a distorted picture of the general situation. Several of the best British officers in Portugal did willingly, or at any rate resignedly, stay on, and John Slessor was among them. He perhaps took a less jingoistic, more sympathetic view of the majority of his Portuguese fellow-officers (many years later his eldest daughter was to marry a distinguished Portuguese general very different from the mur-derous and incestuous colonel described by Costigan), and he seems to have been very popular with his own Portuguese cavalry regiment. He was a genial, tolerant man, with too much integrity to be easy-going, but keen to elicit the best in other people, and he brought this hopeful tolerance to the military milieu in which he spent the last thirty-five years of his life. He enjoyed steady if not spectacular advancement in his career; he was a lieutenant colonel in command of the Chaves cavalry regiment by 1774, a major-general by 1795, and he ended up as Military Governor of Oporto. His contented existence was centred on his happy family life.

There is no record of how and where John Slessor first met Harriot Bristow, but it was almost certainly in Portugal. The Bristow family were Norfolk squires of some standing, and Harriot's father John was a Member of Parliament and a Director of the South Sea Company, with large financial interests in Portugal, where his nephew, another John Bristow, was a member of the British Factory in Lisbon. John Bristow the elder married Ann Judith Foissin, of a Huguenot family, and they had three sons and eight daughters, of whom Harriot was the youngest but one. The terrible Lisbon earthquake of 1755 crippled John

Bristow's fortunes; he lost more than £100,000 in unpaid debts from Portuguese traders ruined by the earthquake, and was compelled to sell the family estate at Quidenham in Norfolk for £20,000. In 1763 he went to Lisbon with his family in a vain attempt to reclaim his debts, and they stayed there till his death in 1768. John Slessor may therefore have met Harriot with her parents in Lisbon. He might also have met her through William Henry Lord Lyttelton, who was British Minister in Lisbon from 1768 to 1771, and who later married Harriot Bristow's sister Caroline. But the most likely person to have brought John and Harriot together was Simon Fraser, who was a lieutenant general in the Portuguese army and Governor of Tras os Montes when John Slessor was with the cavalry regiment at Chaves in Fraser's area. Fraser married another of the Bristow sisters, Catherine; Slessor and Fraser are known to have been friends of long standing; and Harriot may well have stayed with the Frasers in Tras os Montes and met her brother-in-law's friend there.

Wherever they first met, John Slessor and Harriot Bristow were married in England, on 2nd August 1773 in St James's Church, Piccadilly. It is possible that Harriot's marriage to a Scottish officer in the Portuguese army, thirteen years older than her, with no private means and no family distinction, may have been regarded as a *mésalliance* by her family. Four of her elder sisters were married to the Hon. Henry Hobart, MP for Norwich, to the Hon. Simon Fraser of Lovat, to Sir Richard Neave, Bt., Governor of the Bank of England, and to Lord Lyttelton. After she married, Harriot kept in touch with her mother (her father had died five years before her marriage) and with some of her married sisters, but the sister to whom she was closest, and the only one to whom she felt she could confidently turn for help with her sons' school holidays, was Louisa, who had made a comparatively modest marriage to her second cousin Tillieux Girardot, a wealthy London merchant. In fact Harriot's Neave, Hobart and Fraser relations were all hospitable to members of the Slessor family when they were in England. But the Slessors had mainly to depend on their own exertions. Harriot had thrown in her lot with an isolated man in a foreign exile, and there they made a home and a happiness which shine through the conventional and sometimes sententious phrases of their and their sons' diaries and letters.

John Slessor's regiment was stationed at Chaves, in the province of Tras os Montes in the north of Portugal, and the Slessors lived in the village of San Pedro nearby. The austere simplicity of their way of life in their remote province in the 1780s was very unlike the luxuriant ease which most English visitors to Portugal in those years remembered as their chief impressions of Lisbon and Cintra: the sumptuous aristocratic hospitality, voluptuous Church music and intricate Court intrigues that Beckford enjoyed, the well-stocked libraries and picnics among lush verdure in which Southey revelled, the convivial diplomatic parties at which William Hickey and his Charlotte were such a success. Later, when the Slessors were living in Oporto, they were to see rather more of social life, but the fashionable Portugal beloved of so many English tourists – men of letters, consumptives, Royal dukes, wealthy widows – was always beyond the Slessors' range. They were not quite continuously at San Pedro; John Slessor took his regiment to the Algarve for a time in 1774, soon after their marriage; they visited Oporto occasionally for the christening of their children in the English church there; but the first fifteen years of their married life were mainly spent in the isolated well-loved quiet of San Pedro.

They had seven children, first a son who died in infancy, then Louisa, then the diarist John Henry, born in 1777, then Harriot Amelia, William Edward, Henry Thomas, and Sophia Matilda. Forty years later Harriot addressed to her son what she called a 'triffling picture' of the life at San Pedro.

HS The rural scene of your youth when every little grief was momentary to your innocent minds, and every insignificant amusement pleasure. It may be somewhat out of place for me to be spouting romantic ideas, when old age is too visibly marked on my brow. Yet I can, with some success, I think, describe passed scenes of rural pleasures, when blessed with an amiable, truly good and sensible companion. Altho' sequester'd from the world, we were happy in each other. Many years elapsed, and a growing family made our union more interesting. With three sons and three daughters I counted myself rich indeed, and even imagin'd I could not be possessed of too many such blessings. I will likewise own to you, that I fancy'd you all such pretty perfect creatures, that I was even surprised if those who beheld them did not see them in the same light with me. This weakness of a mother's fondness, to do myself justice, was but transient; for as you in succession grew out of infancy, my delight and pleasure was to instruct you in the little I was mistress of.

Here I must observe, and you know it to be a fact, we were fixed in a distant province of Portugal, where there were no persons as masters of any kind, so that necessity forced me to exertion. What could I do better than devote my time to you? I should have merited to be condemned by all, had I done otherwise. My first attempt alarmed me with the fear I was not equal to such a task, it being so perfectly new to me. I was always very fond of children, but only for amusement, and never thought I had patience or ability in my nature to turn school-mistress, as in fact I did. Marriage, and becoming a Mother, sometimes acts like magic on a character that in youth may appear light and giddy. I will not say that for certain I was not thought so, but in some measure I retrieved my character by setting hard to work, and really found that in teaching you all I improved myself, which gave me good hopes that my labour would not be lost with regard to you. And you can say how far I succeeded. One thing I can with confidence affirm, that you had nothing but good example to follow, and as soon as your innocent minds opened to reason you were taught, that truth should ever be a reigning maxim, deceit a crime. Your hours of study never interfered with those of recreation. They were suited for health, and much pleasure.

You were little acquainted with the confinement of a town house. From the time your eyes opened upon life, rural scenes presented themselves to your view. At an age when thought and curiosity begin to vie with each other, every scene is a source of delight to innocent minds. The different seasons procured us plenty and a variety of amusements. In particular the vintage was a delightful time for you all, and most pleasing to me, when I sallied forth with my playful train, full of life and spirits, and gambol'd away to the luxuriant vineyard, each with their basket under their arm to join the country people in their day's labour, who received us with a cheerful song. You imagined you helped the good people greatly. If you did not, it was sufficient you thought you did, and you were all happy.

Those who pass their lives in indolence and ease, and in the dissipation of fashionable thoughtlessness, so fascinating to the giddy and gay . . . may laugh at the like notions of felicity, and pronounce those who enjoy them mighty stupid beings. I have been young and full of spirits; liked society, and like it still. Circumstanced as I was, I prefer'd retirement to society that did not please us. In our retirement I experienced that solitude is no enemy to contentment, and of course happiness not out of the question. There is one danger that I fear for persons that live secluded from the world, which is, that they insensibly form too severe an opinion of the actions of those employed in the busy scenes of life. It is surprising how quickly we learn to have a better opinion of our own actions than those of others, particularly in retirement; romantic ideas intrude of too great perfection.

John Henry's briefer account of his father in the years at San Pedro was:

JHS United to an amiable and loving wife, year after year rolled over their heads in uninterrupted happiness, until a growing family warned them that a village in the north of Portugal afforded but poor means of education.

It was decided that the two elder sons must be sent to school in England, and so followed the first break-up of this self-sufficient family unit, whose members were never to meet all together again.

2

Up to 1788, the lives and fortunes of the Slessor family have had to be pieced together from later flashbacks in their diaries, but from the time when the eleven-year-old John Henry and his nine-year-old brother William were taken to school in England, John Henry and his mother and father tell their own chronological story in their diaries and letters. Recalling to John Henry the decision about the departure for England, Harriot strikes one of her noble attitudes.

HS You and William were come to an age for school to be thought of; then began my anxiety. Your father could not be spared from his regiment; he proposed my taking you to England. I did not hesitate, having your good so much at heart, How to reconcile the act of separation – it had never been seriously thought of, till from reason we were convinced such a step was most proper. You may remember the parting scenes on board a ship. What would it have been, had we been told, tho' we were then separating with the hopes of some future happy meeting all together, Alas! that meeting never, no never, was to arrive. 'Tis well we are not allowed to look into the book of fate! Cruel events were in reserve for me.

John Henry's account is less histrionic, though it includes the manly tears of which no-one was then ashamed; the stiff upper lip came in much later, in the nineteenth century.

JHS My Mother undertook to bring William and myself to England. My sister Louisa accompanied us; Harriot, Henry and Sophy were left with our Father. We embraced and kissed them with abundance of tears; took leave of the faithful nurse, Francisca, servants, villagers, etc; bade a final adieu to our rabbits, pigeons, gardens, etc; thus quitted the village of St Pedro and started on our journey to Oporto, where we took shipping for England. Our young, flexible minds were easily diverted by the novel scenes of such a country, where we landed after a favourable voyage: repaired to Putney to the home of my Uncle and Aunt Girardot: were received most kindly. A few months quickly passed, and we parted from our dear Mother and Sister, who got back safe to Portugal.

John Henry and William were placed at a school in Kensington run by a Dr Thompson, which their cousin Richard Neave also attended. It had been warmly recommended by a friend of John Slessor's, Sir William Fordyce. Harriot believed that it was a thoroughly satisfactory establishment, she was impressed by Dr Thompson's pleasing manners and conversation when she took her boys to settle them in the school, and in her letters about it to her husband in Portugal she drew a flattering picture of the headmaster as both good and clever, and likely to treat the Slessor boys with paternal kindness. On hearing this, John Slessor wrote a long affectionate letter to his two boys, advising them about their conduct towards such an admirable master. It was the first letter John Henry had ever received from his father. As he wrote later, 'Many letters did I afterwards receive from the best of Fathers, and often and often regretted not having stored them up. The few I possess are here faithfully copied.'

JS   Chaves. April 1st 1788

My dear John

The greatest happiness I have had since we parted has been, as you may well believe, that of receiving letters from you all, and knowing that you were all well and happy in England. It is true we were all happy enough together at St Pedro, but that was only good for you whilst you were all children, and you will soon find out that England is the only country for you to grow men in, be clever and learn to know the world. You will soon come to like it better than Portugal. For this reason it is that Mama and I gave up all the pleasure we had in your being with us, & for your good forced ourselves to live without you, with so many *Saudades* [remembrances] and at so great a distance from you. I know very well that you will always have great *saudades* for us too, but the many new things that you will see, & the occupations that will engage your time and attention, between learning and play in your school life, will make you think much less of us after some time than we shall of you; because everything that we see about us must be for ever putting us in mind of you. Therefore, as William said in his letter to Mr Wrey, you must write to us often not to forget us. We all know your loving and affectionate nature, and are sure that it will be your greatest pleasure to make us happy, by letting us know very often by your letters that you and William are well and happy too.

Your going to school now, puts me so much in mind of the time I was sent to school myself, when I was about your age, that I am thinking continually about it, and wishing it were possible for me to return to that happy time and to have it pass over again. But alas! that is gone for ever for me, but you have it all before you, & I hope you enjoy it well. You will remember me telling you at St Pedro, that it had been the happiest of my life, altho' I did not think so then; for boys are always wishing to be men, thinking that they shall then be happier; but when they get to be men, then they would wish to be boys again. Everybody will tell you this, and you will find it yourself to be true; because, at school, if you follow what is good, fly from what is bad, & apply care and patience to your lessons, you can have nothing to make you unhappy. Your Master, Dr Thompson, is the best man in the world, much cleverer and knows a good deal more than either Mama or I. All you have to do therefore is to look up to him and behave to him as if he was your only Father & Mother, and never forget anything he tells you; by which means he will not only be your friend and protector against all bad boys in the school, but finding that you shew love for him, he will also be kind to you & love you as if you were his son. And here, my friend William, I must turn to you, to tell you how well pleased I have been with you since you have been in England. Mama writes me that you have always behaved exceedingly well, which I assure you makes me love you very much. You know that when you were here you had a trick of behaving sometimes in a sulky manner, but your having quite left off that foolish custom, shows that you are getting a clever boy. Francisca is very happy to hear so much good of you, and so is Brigadier and Mrs Wrey. Your letter to Mrs Wrey was a very good one and pleased her very much and made us all laugh. You will read what I have written to John in regard to your conduct at school and everything else, as it is meant equally for you as for him; and remember always it comes from your Papa, who loves you the best that anyone can except Mama, who loves you just the same. When you receive this letter the time will be drawing near when Mama and Louisa will be thinking of taking leave of you to return to pay us a visit here, which you know is but fair, as they have been a long time away from us. I know you will all be sorry enough at parting, but it cannot be helped, we must have patience, and comfort ourselves with the hopes that we are all to meet again, some time or other, because when your education is finished, if we are not already gone to England, you and John will come and pay us a visit in Portugal.

In the meantime we shall always be wanting to know how you both do, & how you go on in your learning; for which reason it will be necessary that one of you write to some of us every week, which will be a letter apiece that we shall receive every fortnight by the ships that come to Portugal. Mama will settle how you are to send them, & some one of you must write a letter besides the beginning of every month to be sent by the packet, that we may not be too long without hearing from you. And now, having written you both so long a letter, let me finish by desiring that for the sakes of all that you love best, for your own sakes, & for that of your own happiness, you will on all occasions be kind, obliging, forgiving & loving to each other, and then you will always be happy, and everybody will love and admire you. You, John, I know will do so, because it is your nature to be gentle and good-tempered, & William, I make no doubt, will follow your example, & always love you on that account, and be equally affectionate and good-humoured to you. This above all things will show to everybody that you are good boys and must be clever men. Let me also recommend you not to forget your Portuguese, but to talk it always together when you are by yourselves. Francisca also desires this, that it may keep you in mind of her; otherwise she is afraid you may forget her too. We are all very well here, and no news but what I write to Mama. Little Sophia runs about & talks a good deal; she is very pretty. Many kisses and *saudades* from all. I am always, dear boys,

your affectionate Father

J. Slessor

Harriot and her daughter Louisa remained in England for nine months, staying mostly with her mother, who was now eighty-one and was to die before the end of that year. It was a consolation to Harriot that she had been in time to see her mother once more.

HS I had the satisfaction, while in England, to be with my aged Mother, and to be a comfort to her the last year of her life. She was very fond of Louisa, that came with us, and much pleased with your and William's good-humoured, pleasing manner. Again a painful separation was to take place. The business of settling you both at school, as I flattered myself, much to my satisfaction, was effected. I had then to turn my thoughts towards Portugal, to join again a Husband and three children, that called for my presence. I left behind two equally beloved. After passing near nine months in England I settled my departure, with Louisa, and took our passage for Porto in the same ship that brought us. When the Captain came to desire I would be on board in two or three days, my poor Mother fell to scolding the Captain at a great rate, and crying told him, it was a shame he should have given me so little warning. Her distress moved to tears a few persons present. In reality I had had full notice, and our baggage had been on board above a fortnight. The day arrived too soon for our departure. You were both old enough to be aware of the importance of such a separation. You knew all the good you had enjoy'd; but when I was gone, you could not tell where were the friends you were to look to, that might be inclined to supply my place.

You will not have forgot the distress of parting with my Mother, and how difficult it was to tear ourselves from her last embrace, particularly so with regard to Louisa, whom she held so fast in her aged arms that we had not the courage to tear her from her. She lamented that she would never see us more. You showed more resolution than I was mistress of. I was ashamed of myself to see a boy of ten years old have more command over his grief than I could, for you was much afflicted. You entreated me to leave the melancholy scene at once. What was the good of such delay? Go we must. You reasoned well, and we left my poor Mother. I think I see her, altho' so many years ago, sitting in her wheelchair, with a little black bonnet pulled over her eyes grown dim with age, to hide her tears, for she was crying bitterly. So thus we parted, and for ever. She had completed her 81 years; very few weeks after was no more. She could not resist the death of a favourite daughter, that happened just after my departure. It may be said for certain that my Mother died of grief. It was hard at so advanced an age.

From my Mother's we went to good Mrs Fraser's, to meet and to take leave of your Aunt Girardot, and after a hasty dinner to depart. My sister Fraser, on seeing I was unhappy at the thoughts of making my journey alone to Gravesend, where we were to embark, determined to see us safe there in her own carriage, and not leave us till we were on board a ship. Mrs Girardot was the only sister I might venture to hope might take you home for the holydays. During my stay in England I had never ventur'd to give a hint to her how much my mind was oppressed at the idea of leaving you without a certainty that some one of my family might take an interest in you. I knew too well the fear that in general is imbibed for schoolboys. You had been well lectured on that subject, during the time we were at your Grandmother's and had both behaved well: so that I hoped for the same in your future conduct. The chaise was at the door to take us away. I could not resist the impulse. We were both crying in each other's arms. I exclaimed 'Look at my dear boys. Can you have the heart to neglect them? Do but say you will be kind to them. If you knew the pang I feel at parting with them, you will not refuse some comfort by the answer I so anxiously wish for'. Mrs Girardot seem'd as much afflicted as I was. She promised all that was kind, that she would act as a Mother towards you, and you know how strictly she kept her word. For many years during your schooling both her and Mr Girardot were as kind as possible to you. It is impossible ever to forget such kindness.

While Harriot and Louisa were on their way back to Portugal, John Slessor wrote again to John Henry:

JS   St Pedro 20th May 1788

My Dear John

As I must suppose that your Mama and Sister Louisa will have set out for Portugal before this letter reaches London, I now begin my correspondence with you and William, and hope this may find you well and happy. We often think here of the cruel circumstances of your dear Mama being obliged to take leave of you for so long a time to come to us, and of the melancholy scene of parting which must have been something like that on the bar of Porto the day we left you in the cabin, which I am sure, none of us will ever forget. But it is a comfort to us to think that you are near so many good friends & relations, and above all, that you are left to the care of so good a guardian and protector as Doctor Thompson, in whom, if you deserve of him as well as I think you will, you may be sure of finding a second Father, as well as a kind affectionate Master. And to be completely happy all you will want, I am sure, will only be that we should all be nearer to you. That is what we wish for as much as you can do, but as it cannot be yet awhile, we have patience until Providence shall grant us that happiness . . . You will be glad to hear that we are all well here; poor little Sophy was a little sickly for some days, but is now in perfect health again, and the prettiest engaging little girl that can be. Henry is growing a fine stout boy, and begins to read in Charles's book. I suppose he must go to you in a year or two. Harriot also is grown much taller since you saw her, and has quite left off her pouting way that she used to have sometimes, and grows very clever and agreeable. Francisca loves you just as much as ever, and cries at the sight of everything that puts her in mind of you. They all join with me in love and a thousand *saudades* to you & our dear William and hope you will not forget us. You must give my best compliments to Doctor Thompson & love to your Uncles and Aunts, when you see them. Mama will have left you instructions about writing to us. Adieu, my dear John. I promise myself much pleasure from our correspondence. Many blessings from

> your affectionate Father
> J. Slessor

Harriot and Louisa got safely back to San Pedro, and found all well with John and the three smaller children, Harriot Amelia, Henry and Sophia, now aged nine, six and two. A year later, John Slessor was still writing confidently to his sons about their progress and happiness at Dr Thompson's school.

JS   Chaves Janry 26th 1790

My dear boy

I have been a long time a letter in your debt, and fear you will have set me down as a bad correspondent; but as you have not the same cause of complaint of your Mama and Sisters, I hope you will the more readily attribute my want of punctuality to the true motive, which is that of being always very busy, and not suppose it to proceed from my not thinking of you enough. Indeed I do, my dear John, quite enough, and if I were certain that you remember me as well as I do you, I should be perfectly satisfied; but that I can hardly expect, because I have many things here to put me for ever in mind of you and former times, whereas you can have but few there to put you in mind of me. Here our longing thoughts turn very naturally towards the happy country where you now are; but yours between business and amusement must generally be too much engaged to allow them to wander into the mountains of Portugal.

It is now near six weeks, which appears to us a little age, since we last had the pleasure of hearing from you, and how and where you and William passed your Xmas holydays. If your good Aunt Girardot's health will have permitted her to have you at Putney, we are well assured of her and Mr Girardot's kindness, as well as Mrs Mary Girardot's. Pray God send us good accounts of you all. You will not fail to remember us affectionately to them, as well as to your kind Aunt Fraser. And now let me have the pleasure to tell you that your letters for some time past have been much approved of. Your last pretty one to Louisa in French was answered three weeks ago by three different people, viz, herself, Mama and Don José. I should have added a few words too, but was not very well at the time. We shall be glad to know that you received that letter. What William wrote on the other side of your paper was also very acceptable, and was acknowledged at the same time. I must further express the pleasure and satisfaction it is to us to receive such good accounts as we have lately done from Doctor Thompson himself, and from other people who are your friends, of your improvement in learning, application and manliness, as well as of your agreeable, engaging manners, and attentive behaviour wherever you go. These, my dear John, are the great and useful lessons at your time of life, that alone can qualify you for becoming men of the world, which the more you grow up the more you will experience the advantage of, and be sensible how much your present and future happiness depends on them. And although as to myself, declining age like a thief comes stealing on me, yet I cannot but look forward with pleasure to the time when you are to reap and enjoy the fruits of your present diligence, in acquiring those early and invaluable accomplishments. Latin in the beginning to be sure must appear a dry kind of study to you, but it lays the foundation for so many other useful and agreeable ones that it cannot be left behind; there is no doing without it, and it has one good thing, which is that, as you advance in the knowledge of it, the more easy and pleasant the studying of it becomes; that with these considerations, & the kind attention and assistance of your good Master, you will I hope be induced to look upon this part of your education, not as a task imposed upon you, but as one that you would choose to impose upon yourself. Pray let me know if General Smith has been to enquire for you, or has desired to carry you to his house. He is a very old & good friend of mine, and can give you much good advice, if he finds you well disposed to receive it; but it will be fit that you should seek for it, rather than that he should force it upon you. William you know is his godson. I came in from St Pedro this morning, and left them all well . . .

The section of this letter that referred to Dr Thompson's good reports must have been read with bitter smiles by John Henry and William. Soon after it was written, news was to reach the Slessor parents at San Pedro that Dr Thompson and his school, seemingly so satisfactory, were a very unfortunate choice for the education of their sons, as John Henry grimly recalls.

JHS Two years did my brother William and I idle away at Kensington with Dr Thompson. Fortunately our cousin Richard Neave was at the same school, much our senior. He mentioned his suspicions to Uncle and Aunt Girardot. On being examined we were found very backward, considering the time we had been there; out of above 100 boys, it was afterwards proved that we were not the only ones neglected; shamefully so, and what boy will learn without coercion? I could fill sheets were I to tell all the tricks, immoralities, vicious habits of the big boys, to which the younger ones, as fags, were witness.

Harriot was appalled that she could have been so much deceived when she had taken all reasonable precautions when choosing her sons' school.

HS Some time after my return, we got a most distressing letter from my Sister, that I had been entirely mistaken in the character of your Schoolmaster; that for some time they had observed a great change in you for the worse; and that you appeared perfectly unhappy when the time came for your return to school. Instead of being improved in your learning, they found on examination you had been perfectly neglected; not only in that, but in every respect equally so. It is not usual to venture at telling tales of what passes in School. Bad usage was quite strange to you. You pined in secret, but would not complain, till the truth was forced from you. When your Master was reproach'd for such cruel usage, his answer was, with all the composure in the world, that others had made the like complaint, and had taken their sons from the school. Of course you were not allowed to remain any longer with such a man.

It might be thought that I too lightly inquired into the fame of this school. On the contrary I had the most flattering recommendation of it, and in particular from your father's great friend, Sir William Fordyce, who declared to me, that if he had an only son, he would prefer that school to any other, having such an opinion of the Master. My nephew, R. Neave, being at the same school was a great inducement to me for placing you there, but he left it soon after you went there. This same person was Doctor of Divinity – the more shame to him – of very polite pleasing manners. From his conversation could only be formed a good opinion of his heart and understanding. To hear him talk of you both I should have supposed you to be the greatest favourites. The truth is, that he was grown rich, and too fine a Gentleman to do his duty, and mind his boys; so that among above a hundred, unless with proper tutors, many must be neglected, particularly the younger ones. We heard that soon after he gave up the school. Such behaviour was cruel and shameful. While you were neglected, both in your learning and in every other respect, your Father received repeated letters from your Master, praising you both, saying what fine boys you were, and that he was quite satisfied with your improvement with your masters. Such deceit rendered him doubly guilty.

As soon as John and Harriot Slessor heard from the Neaves and the Girardots what a Dotheboys Hall they had consigned their sons to, the boys were taken away and sent to a newly-founded school in Middlesex, of which John Henry gives a very reassuring account.

JHS We were speedily removed to Dr Moore at Sunbury, where the number of boys was limited, and to whom every attention was paid, and every care taken of. William and I soon made up for lost time, and looked back with horror to the treatment received at Kensington. Our studies were made agreeable to us, much emulation, and the Usher, Mr Lamphore, combined the companion with the Master; all the boys appeared happy, and the fame of the school gained ground.

Here his father wrote to him a year later, full of enquiries about his studies and of renewed confidence that he was making progress. He told his sons that their handwriting had improved, that they made only occasional spelling mistakes in their letters, that they had had a good conduct report from the Girardots on their latest stay at Putney, and that he had also heard well of 'your school studies and improvement, regaining lost time, and being healthy and happy under Mr and Mrs Moore's good care'. He asked for detailed progress reports.

JS Pray let me know in your next how you both stand in arithmetic and how Greek goes on. It is the language of science and taste, highly becoming the gentleman, and indispensably necessary to the scholar. Tell me also how many boys are in your class, and of these how many are above you and William. As you were among Mr Moore's first scholars, I suppose your class may be the highest in the school.

All the family at San Pedro were well, and Henry was distinguishing himself by his skill in drawing cocks and mules. The old nurse Francisca, who by her 'tender and ever watchful care' had saved the children's lives in infant illnesses, should always be sent messages of remembrance in the boys' letters. John Slessor was now in his late fifties, rather gouty, and inclined to prose on with his admonitions and reminders and messages to aunts and uncles, but his warm-heartedness glows through his long uneventful letters to his far-off little boys, and it is not surprising that John Henry kept them all his life.

3

'Uncle and Aunt Girardot', Harriot's sister Louisa and her husband, played an important role in the lives of the Slessor family. The childless couple received the Slessor boys at their house in Putney for the school holidays, kept their parents in Portugal informed about their health and conduct, put up any member of the Slessor family visiting England, and finally bequeathed to the Slessors their family portraits and miniatures, their silver, and a complete dinner service of the rare Peking Tobacco Leaf porcelain; these have remained in the possession of the family ever since.

This well-to-do, often ailing, couple were very kind to the Slessor boys, but perhaps rather fussy. John Slessor often reminded his sons of the need to write proper bread-and-butter letters: 'your Aunt Girardot has taken much notice of your not writing to her, and you will stand much in your own way, my dear John and William, if you neglect her; for she has a sincere love for you both, and you well know what you owe to her and Mr Girardot's kindness.' After her husband's death in 1793, Louisa Girardot went to live at Marlborough Buildings in Bath, and there too Harriot Slessor and her children frequently stayed.

Louisa and her husband were second cousins, and thus doubly connected with the Slessors. The history of the Girardot family in England starts with Paul Girardot of Château Chinon, a Huguenot who emigrated to England in 1699 and became a London merchant and an esteemed member of the community centred on the Huguenot church in Threadneedle Street.

The Girardots used the Christian names Paul, André, Jean, Marie-Louise and Jeanne again and again in each generation; one Marie-Louise, moreover, married a man whose *surname* was André; many of them were married twice, as often as not to a cousin; both the Girardots and the Bristows intermarried several times with the Dashwood family; so a family tree illustrating the Slessor/Girardot relationship is a nightmare of complexity. The connection starts with two daughters of the original Paul Girardot.

Through his daughter Louise he was Harriot Slessor's great-grandfather. Louise Girardot married Paul Foissin, and their daughter Ann Judith Foissin was Harriot Slessor's mother.

Another daughter of Paul Girardot, Jeanne, married at the age of fifteen her cousin Jean Girardot of Chancourt, as his second wife. Their fifth son, another Jean Girardot, also married a cousin, Jeanne Girardot Duperron, and they had five children, the eldest of whom, Tillieux, married his second cousin, Louisa Bristow.

Tillieux's uncle, his father's eldest brother Paul, lived in Paris and had a daughter, Marie-Louise, who married Antonin André, a merchant of Genevese origin who lived in London and traded to the Levant. And here these tangled and somewhat tedious genealogical explanations impinge on historical events, for the son of Antonin and Marie-Louise André was the celebrated Major John André, hanged as a spy by the Americans in the War of Independence.

John André was born in 1751 at the Manor House at Clapton in Middlesex, which his father had bought when he partly retired from business. Three daughters and another son followed. Antonin André died in 1769. John André was a young man of great charm and many accomplishments, well-read, a fine linguist, a musician, poet and painter; he was a close friend of the Lichfield poetess Anna Seward, whose ward Honora Sneyd he vainly hoped to be allowed to marry. He was commissioned in the Army in 1771, and was sent to America in 1775, and was so highly thought of by his superiors that he was made Adjutant General of the British forces in America, though still only in his twenties.

The tragic story that followed is well known. During the War of Independence, André was sent on a secret mission behind the American lines to negotiate with the American traitor (or, from the British point of view, loyalist) General Benedict Arnold, for the handing over of West Point to the British. André was wearing his army uniform when he was taken up the Hudson River in the sloop *Vulture*. He met Arnold, who gave him plans and troop numbers for West Point, which André hid in his boots. But from then on, the plot went wrong; the *Vulture* was not at hand as agreed to take him back, he was obliged to hide in a farmhouse and to disguise his uniform with a civilian greatcoat, and when he was making his way on foot back to the British lines, he was captured by some American soldiers. Arnold, meanwhile, had safely escaped to the British in New York. To get their hands on Arnold, the Americans would willingly have exchanged André for him, but the British Commander General Clinton could not do so even to save the life of André, who was a personal friend. André, who had had a written safe-conduct from Arnold when he undertook his mission, expected at first that the Americans would respect this and send him back; then, when he was brought before a Court of Enquiry, he supposed that he would be treated as a prisoner of war or, at the very worst, would die a soldier's death by firing-squad. But the Court found him guilty of spying, and in spite of appeals from André and from some on the American side, Washington gave orders for him to be hanged as a spy. He went to his death with a serene courage which excited the admiration and pity of all the American troops present at the execution; he was 'lamented even by his foes', as his epitaph records.

British reaction to his murder, as it was considered, was one of violent indignation and grief. The whole British army in America wore black armbands in mourning for him. A monument to him was put up in Westminster Abbey, adorned with a sort of marble strip-cartoon showing the events of his last days, and his body – which had been buried in an unmarked grave at Tappan, near New York, the place of his execution – was later brought back and buried in the Abbey. Anna Seward wrote a furious *Monody on Major André* in which she abused George Washington as 'Thou cool determin'd murderer of the brave!' and demanded to know why, if Washington could not set aside the Court-martial's decision, he could not at least have allowed Major André to be shot, not hanged like a felon, thus cruelly wounding 'the sensibility of an intrepid spirit'.

Major André in his will and last letters expressed the hope that the value of his commission could be made over to his mother and three sisters, whose income had been much reduced by the loss of a West Indian fortune. His grateful and indignant country did better than that; they awarded a pension of £300 to his mother, and gave his younger brother, Captain William André, a baronetcy. After bequests to his sisters, André left the residue of his effects to his brother William. But William died without issue in 1802, and by the time the Slessors became close friends of the André family, its only survivors were the three unmarried sisters, Louisa Catherine, Mary Hannah and Anne.

Harriot before her marriage presumably had met her second cousin John André, whose uncle had married her sister; but at the time of his execution in 1780, all the Slessors were still at home in their remote village in Portugal. Their later friendship with the André sisters – referred to by Harriot as 'our ever good and dear friends' and by Henry Slessor as 'those worthy persons and true friends' – was cemented when the André sisters were living in Bath in companionship with their aunt Louisa Girardot. They showed their friendship with the Slessors by bestowing on them some of Major André's possessions, a diamond ring and two cases of volumes of the English poets; these also are still in the family's possession.

It has seemed worth while to enlarge on the Slessors' connection with the Girardots and the Andrés, because this side of their genetic inheritance explains something sturdy yet keen-edged, something of Huguenot resource, resolution and clannishness, which runs through the diaries of Harriot and her son.

When John Slessor came to England in 1792, bringing his third son Henry who was to go to school in England like his elder brothers, his first action was to collect John Henry and William from their school at Sunbury and take the whole party to stay at the Girardots. John Henry records the happy holidays that followed.

JHS We were not aware of his arrival, and suddenly one morning they made their appearance at Sunbury. Judge of our surprise, our joy on recognising our good and dear Father, with what sincere parental love and affection did

he embrace us. It was settled we were to leave Mr Moore, as he was
unwilling to keep boys after a certain age. I shall ever with gratitude bear
in remembrance the days I spent at Sunbury under his kind care and
tuition. To Mr Lamphore I also felt very much indebted. He and I for some
time afterwards kept up a correspondence in Latin. We repaired in the first
instance to pay a visit to our kind Uncle and Aunt Girardot, and my Father
seemed to be really happy with his three boys. He then took up his abode in
Jermyn Street in London where lodged the Honble Henry Hobart, member
of Parliament for the city of Norwich; he had married a Miss Bristow, one
of my Aunts. The short time my Father could stay in England rapidly fled.
He made us very happy by shewing us everything he could in and about
London; took us out to Dagenham, Sir Richard Neave's, etc etc. He now
resolved we should be placed under the care of a private tutor, a Mr
Freeman at Peterboro' who was to be our future guardian (he was a canon
of the Cathedral), that is William and myself; Henry went to a small
school; our situation pleased us.

Nine years later William Slessor told his sister Louisa that this time of his
father's visit to England was the happiest that he had ever known, happier even
than their childhood together at San Pedro, when he had not yet experienced
what it was to be separated from his family for years and then to feel the bliss of
seeing his father again.

   John Slessor stayed in England from November 1792 to February 1793. He
went to Peterborough to see Canon Freeman, the tutor with whom John Henry
and William had now been placed, and where they were well taught and well
pleased, with a fair amount of social life including their first ball, for which
their father solicitously chose and sent them stockings and shoe-buckles. He
also sent John Henry his first gun, and hyacinth bulbs to grow in the garden at
Peterborough. Most of John Slessor's time was spent in London, staying at first
in his brother-in-law Henry Hobart's house in Jermyn Street, and then in
Albemarle Street near his wife's nephew Richard Neave. He went several times
to Court.

JS   I was yesterday at the Levée, and today at the drawingroom; had the
     honour of being presented and kissing hands, as also of being graciously
     spoken to by both their Majesties. But they have so strangely tortured my
     poor German name in the spelling, that if you see it in any of the newspa-
     pers among the presentations, you will not know it again. In one I have
     seen it Sleesden, in another Sleesor, another Slaucher, etc. I am quite
     angry with the dogs of Printers, who I suppose only ask people's names of
     the footmen and chairman at St James'; perhaps in some of them I may get
     rectified.

He visited Cambridge, where he received 'very flattering civilities' from various acquaintances, and wrote rather wistfully to John Henry describing his experiences.

JS When you ask me if I would wish to be a young man again, and go and study at Cambridge, I believe you could guess pretty well at my answer, but as that wish is but vain, I can only anticipate the pleasure I shall share with you and William, should it be your lot to go there. I often thought of what Mr Freeman told me, that a young man well disposed, who attended to his studies, could be nowhere and at no period of his life happier than at Cambridge, and I am now quite convinced of the truth of it. I had a very pleasant, altho' solitary journey, having travelled mostly alone, a circumstance I by no means dislike when I cannot choose my company. I will own, however, that I felt alone here, having been used to your and William's chattering.

During his time in Cambridge, and later in London, he scoured libraries and bookshops for 'Our Ancestor's *Theatrum Scotiae*', but he failed to find a complete copy, so he did not buy one. This is the only clue in the Slessor papers to their claim that their German ancestry was through John Slezer, author of *Theatrum Scotiae*.

John Slessor clearly had a happy time renewing friendships and leading a social life in the great world of England after his many years of exile in a remote corner of Portugal. But letters from his wife back in San Pedro were complaining of his absence, and European events were at last beginning to impinge on the private life of the Slessor family. Till now, there had been no mention in any of their letters or diaries of the fearful events in France – the outbreak of revolution in 1789, the overthrow of the monarchy, the Terror of 1792. But in January 1793 Louis XVI was executed and England joined the First Coalition with Prussia and Austria, and was at war with France, and the Slessors' carefree sea crossings from Portugal to England and back no longer seemed so much a matter of course. War regulations began to affect ordinary life in England; the French emigré Chevalier d'Estimanville who was to have gone to Peterborough to teach French, German, mathematics and drawing to Canon Freeman's pupils was detained in London by a proclamation requiring aliens to register, and John Slessor had to intervene with the Secretary of State to help get him a passport. That John Slessor was in a position to do this, and to be well received at Court, shows that he was by now regarded as a man of some standing, associating as an equal with his wife's Hobart and Neave relations, and this was to be further confirmed by events after his return to Portugal. He was needed back there, but would he get there safely? Waiting for a ship at Falmouth in February 1793, he speculated:

JS   If we are taken by these mad Frenchmen, which there may be some danger of, it is hard to say where you will have to direct to me next, perhaps to the other world, for they show themselves now no better than ferocious savages at sea.

Held up till March 4th by contrary winds, he finally got away a few days later, leaving Henry at school in Devonshire and John Henry and William at Peterborough. Neither John Henry nor William ever saw him again, as John Henry sadly recorded.

JHS He bade us, alas! adieu for ever. My Father's amiable manners and disposition, his excellent character as a Father, Husband and Christian, his accomplishments as a perfect gentleman and man of honour, gained him friends and esteem wherever he went.

4

John Slessor got back to Portugal safely, after a squally nine-day passage from Falmouth to Lisbon on which they saw no sign of any French ships. From March to October 1793 he was detained in Lisbon, unable to join his family in San Pedro because Portugal was in danger of being drawn into the European war, and her military forces were being mobilised and shifted.

JS This country is all in a bustle too, and most of the troops in motion to the sea-coasts. My regiment has not moved, but has orders to be in readiness. There is a very pretty squadron in the Tagus, ready to join Great Britain, six sail of the line and eight frigates . . . War will probably be very soon declared by France against this country. A Minister from the Convention is on his way hither; he came thro' Spain, where he was arrested for some time, and is now travelling thro' Portugal, with an escort of cavalry to protect him from the people, who would otherwise probably put him to death, so great is the odium of the populace against all Frenchmen. It is probable he will be worse treated in this country even than Chauvelin was in London. His papers were seized on the frontiers, the consequence of which must be an immediate declaration of war. I write you this news, as I suppose you are all politicians.

In October, still in Lisbon, he told John Henry:

JS Our troops, about 5000 in number, sailed from here the 21st ulto for Catalonia. I hope they will not let themselves be beaten as the Spaniards were. These bad Frenchmen still fight but too well.

He reported too that communications between England and Portugal were endangered, French privateers were chasing British mail packets which sometimes only escaped by taking refuge in Cork harbour. On the personal side, he had good news to send to his sons in England; all the family at San Pedro were well, he had had good reports from Canon Freeman about John Henry's and William's conduct and progress in Greek and other studies, and his enforced and unwelcome wait in Lisbon had been enlivened by royal celebrations and by news of his own promotion.

29

JS   The birth of a Princess Hereditary, heiress to the throne, has been cele-
     brated with extraordinary demonstrations of joy. Oh Henry, if you had
     been here, what wonderful fireworks and illuminations you would have
     seen. They far exceeded those in London on the King's recovery . . . I must
     also tell you, that I was made a Major-General on this occasion, but for the
     present it is only the rank, without any additional pay, so do not suppose
     me the richer for it; on the contrary so much the poorer by being obliged to
     make up expensive uniforms etc; but I keep my Regt.

While he kicked his heels in Lisbon, John Slessor turned his thoughts to the
decisions that must soon be made about his sons' future careers. John Henry
was now sixteen, William was nearly fourteen, it was time to consider what was
to follow their schooling at Peterborough. While he was still in England, their
father had spoken of their possible future occupations as 'military, civil or
ecclesiastic'; the Services, the Law or the Church were then conventionally the
obvious choice in the upper middle class to which the Slessors could be said to
belong. Now from Lisbon he wrote to ask John Henry squarely what he wanted
to do.

JS   Dear John, time flies fast away from us; I am growing old, and you are
     growing a man. You are endowed with a sufficient share of forethought
     and reason, for your age. Have you turned in your mind or formed any
     choice of the line of life you would prefer to go through the World in? I
     need not tell you, I am sure, that few objects in it lie so near my heart as
     your happiness and well-doing in whatever line of life it may be your
     destination to embark. It is therefore well that we should familiarize our
     ideas together on that subject; it is an important one to both, but in the
     natural order of things most so to you, who are in the morning of life,
     while I am drawing towards the setting sun. For instance, should we be
     ultimately disappointed in the East India views you know of, tell me if you
     would prefer a military life? In short, tell me all you feel in that respect,
     having first consulted thoroughly with yourself and your own inclinations.

The 'East India views' were the offer of a civilian post in India, a Writer's
appointment to Madras, which John Henry apparently refused. His parents
scarcely regretted this; they wanted a military career for him, as Harriot related.

HS   Yours and your brother's education being at an end, the most material
     point was to be settled; what was to be your destination in life was the
     point. Those born to little or no fortune must early learn to shift for
     themselves. Such was your case; and your conduct in life we hoped would
     be no bad recommendation in whatever station you might be placed. I own
     I did not like the idea of the counting-house. Your Father was military. We

inclin'd to the profession of arms; you none of you seemed averse to it. With the good help of a friend you got into the Irish Artillery, and soon went off for Ireland, at a very early age, to shift for yourself as well as you could.

From this point, the start of his military career, John Henry's diary is full and continuous, and must have been conscientiously kept, probably as a result of his father's recent suggestion that he should experiment with keeping a journal for the benefit of his distant family:

JS   a task we must require of you, seeing your former letters were lost; that is a kind of journal, to the best of your remembrance, beginning with General Smith's letter inviting you to Dover, journey to London, proceedings thence to Dover, reception and proceedings there, and so on to the date of your said letter of the 20th September. You will think this a troublesome requisition, but I am certain if you could imagine how interesting it will be to us, and what a pleasure to know every particular, in regard to your movements and at your first starting, you would not grudge the work of an hour or two, to give us that satisfaction.

John Henry's diary contains some private reflections, such as those on the superficiality of the teaching of the Chevalier d'Estimanville whom his father had so strongly recommended, which he would not have sent off to Portugal for family reading, but on the whole it is a straightforward, shrewd, unaffected account of his actions and feelings.

JHS In June 1794 I obtained a commission in the Royal Irish Artillery. General Edward Smith, Uncle to Sir Sidney Smith, was the person who interested himself in my favour. He ordered me to repair without loss of time to Kent. Mr Freeman lost no time in preparing me for my journey, and in a few days I made my first start in the World, proud of my appointment, and happy in the idea of being my own master. Still I acknowledge that I left Peterboro' with regret, and not without a silent tear trickling down my cheeks, for Mr Freeman had indeed acted the part of a Father, as well as a tutor to me; nor was Mr Loftus less kind to me, for I felt that I had made good progress in my learning. The Chevalier's instructions and lessons were superficial. The fact is that among the numerous French Emigrés that inundated England at this time, many professed to teach more than they were capable of. I affectionately embraced my dear Brothers, little thinking that William I should never see again; for not many months after he himself was called upon to act his part upon the stage of the wide World, being appointed a Cadet in the East India Company's service, and embarked for India . . .

I bid all my kind friends at Peterboro' Adieu, and set off in the Coach
for London, where I saw Mr Neave, and then on to Hythe camp, which was
commanded by General Smith. He received me very cordially, gave me
abundance of good advice, and put me under the care of an artillery officer.
I slept in a tent, dined at the Mess, attended the parades, etc, and was
delighted with the bustle, shew, etc, etc, of a military life. I remained here
but a short time, when I was ordered to join my regiment in Ireland. (At
this epoch the English and Irish Artillery were distinct Regiments.) In
travelling from Dover to London I met with an Irish *gentleman* who borrowed two guineas from me, which he faithfully promised to pay me on
arriving at our journey's end; but I saw nothing more of him or my money
afterwards, a useful lesson to a young beginner, which put me on my
guard. Paid a farewell visit to Mr T. Neave, my Aunts Fraser and Girardot.
Received the good wishes of all. So proceeded on my journey to Ireland,
by the way of Chester and Parkgate. No adventure. After a tedious passage
of 4 days landed at the Pigeon House, Dublin; was struck with the beautiful and splendid appearance of the Wicklow Mountains, and the Bay of
Dublin. I was, however, on landing too much hurried, and my ideas confused, to make many observations, and lost no time in going out to
Chapelizod, the Head-quarters of the Irish Artillery. Uniform, books, etc,
etc, were soon obtained, and the early principles of military duties easily
learnt; but the great point was resolution to abstain from, and prudence to
resist the temptations of pleasure, particularly in this Country, where the
hospitality, disposition, and natural lively convivial manners of its inhabitants are so fascinating to a youthful mind. However, I indulged with
caution, and wished to apply myself to the study of artillery in all its
branches, conscious of the necessity of doing so, and the benefits arising
from such a determination; feeling also the superiority I should possess
over many of my brother officers, who never troubled their heads over any
but the practical part of the profession . . .

Owing to an augmentation in our regiment, and the death of some
officers in the West Indies, my promotion was rapid. I almost immediately
was appointed 1st Lieutenant, and in little more than 12 months was
gazetted Captain-Lieutenant. In the Artillery advancement goes by senior-
ity, so that no one is put above your head. My most sanguine expectations
were exceeded, and I naturally thought myself a very lucky fellow. Having
gone the routine of drills, gun, mortar, and Howitzer practice, and attendance in the Laboratory, I was ordered on detachment; quartered at Clonmel
for near a year: encamped in the neighbourhood; received much attention
from the families of Bagwell, O'Nials, etc. There is some woollen trade
here. The Suir is a beautiful river. For some months I was stationed at
Cork, Speke Island, etc., a description of which would fill a volume. The
river down to Cove, views, etc, very fine: a populous and trading city; the

Cove would hold the British fleet in safety. I every where was most hospitably treated. After my return to Head Quarters I was ordered to Belfast, a borough and seaport in the County of Antrim, a large, commercial City, very populous, with different manufactories.

I prefer the North to the South of Ireland. In the former the people in general are more enlightened, more industrious and cleaner, which I attribute mainly to the difference in religion, public schools, linen trade, etc. We recruited all our men for the Artillery from the Northern Counties. They made excellent soldiers, combining the steadiness of the Scotch with the spirit of the Irish.

Between 1794 and 1797 John Henry received six long letters from his father; he included them all in his diary.

JHS I deeply regret that here ends the collection of my dear and good Father's letters. Would I had preserved more, for I am confident that whoever peruses them will agree with me as to their worth

wrote John Henry many years later when he was editing his diary. Anyone perusing them in full now would probably agree as to the worthiness of the man who wrote them, but not perhaps to their worth as readable history or literature. Family messages, introductions to useful friends in Ireland, reproaches for infrequent letter-writing, arrangements for allowance payments, make up much of the letters. There are plenty of admonitions about regularity of conduct and attention to duty, though these are often softened by a deprecating 'Here ends my lecture' or – as when he was advising his son not to get drunk at convivial Irish parties, or to risk his health by 'sacrificing at the altar of Venus' – by the addition of 'I do not expect you to be a saint'. His pride and gratification at John Henry's rapid promotion to Lieutenant and then Captain-Lieutenant are warmly expressed, though he wonders whether John Henry would still need to draw his £30-a-year allowance from his father's Irish half-pay when promoted to Captain-Lieutenant:

JS Now with your five shillings a day I suppose you will think yourself a rich fellow, and above accepting anything out of the puny pittance of an Ensign's half-pay.

In the 1790s an Ensign in a foot regiment got four shillings and eight pence a day, so John Slessor's half-pay would have been two shillings and four pence – a pittance indeed.

Apart from complaints about the loss of long-hoped-for letters because of the war at sea, John Slessor makes curiously few allusions in these letters to the war with France. He comments briefly on the signing of the Franco-Portuguese peace treaty in 1797, and with concern on the capture of Admiral Sir Sidney Smith by the French and his imprisonment in Paris, but this last was chiefly on personal grounds of the anxiety it would cause to Sidney Smith's uncle and John Slessor's friend, General Edward Smith, who had served with Wolfe at Quebec, and was Colonel of the 43rd Regiment. John Slessor makes no mention of the great War events of the late 1790s: the break-up of the First Coalition when Prussia and Spain, and then Austria, made peace with France, the French expulsion of the British forces under the Duke of York from the Netherlands, the French conquest of Italy, Nelson's victory in the Battle of the Nile. Even the raising of the French siege of St Jean d'Acre, in which his own son Henry took part as a midshipman, or the British naval victory at the Battle of St Vincent, so near and important to Portugal, have no place in John Slessor's letters to his son during these years. This may have been for fear of possible interception or censorship of letters. Asking John Henry to go on including reports on 'the real state of Ireland' in his letters home, his father added that he could do it 'without committing yourself in a political light, nor would it be necessary to sign your name'.

Another surprising omission is that in none of the surviving letters does John Slessor mention his appointment as Military Governor of Oporto, where the Slessor family then removed from San Pedro. Harriot's description of the society they enjoyed after their establishment in Oporto – a rather intolerant but lively picture of the city in the 1790s – will appear later, in her diary for 1807. The Slessors made more friends among the Portuguese than among the British families attached to the English Factory at Oporto, on whose homely manners Harriot rather snobbishly looked down; her chief English friends were the family of the British Consul Mr Whitehead. In Oporto she and her daughters Louisa, Harriot Amelia and Sophia, now aged twenty-one, eighteen and ten, enjoyed a bustling social life very different from the secluded calm of remote San Pedro; now they lived in the Military Governor's quarters in the centre of Oporto. John Slessor was not with them all the time; his military duties (he was still in command of his cavalry regiment) called him back to Tras os Montes from time to time, and it was from there that he wrote in a rather melancholy mood in a letter of March 1796, worth quoting at some length as the last sound of a voice – nostalgic for his own part, but affectionately forward-looking for his sons – to be heard in these family records. 'John, my dear fellow,' he begins, dating his letter from San Pedro, where the Slessors had kept on their house after their move to Oporto.

JS You see how strangely we are dispersed about the World. I here behind the Black Mountains, Your Mother and Sisters at Oporto, you in Ireland, Henry at Peterboro', and William gone to the other side of the globe. This reflection, – finding myself here alone, seeing the beds you were used to sleep in, the same trees you used to climb, in short every object that presents itself recalling to mind those former happy times, (of which you can have a much fainter remembrance) when we were all together, – I think you will allow must be sufficient to inspire melancholy, and therefore will not wonder if this letter is in the style of a solitary philosopher. However you may be inclined to laugh at it, as the mercury in your thermometer may not stand so low as in mine, which I think is about the same pitch it stood at when sitting alone by the fire, – as I am now, – in the parlour of the Inn at Alconbury Hill, after our last parting that gloomy evening at Peterboro'. Whether you may have forgotten it I cannot tell; I am sure I never shall. There John, I have just stopped to read your letter, and feel my spirits the better for it. *Elle me plait.* I like your laconic short-sentence style, as long as it gives us a satisfactory account of your sweet person, as you call it, (I hope you do not perfume,) and all your proceedings, amusements, studies, circumstances and manner of passing your time. *A propos* to this I must quote you some lines from General Smith's last letter to me *sur votre sujet*; perhaps your Mother gave you some hint about it already. He says, 'If our Artillery-man does not read, write, draw, in short if he does not work like a day-labourer, hang him, he is a commissioned goose. I placed him there to lead, not to follow. By what you can observe of his manner of writing to you, you will be able to judge what he is about, and if he is likely to be anything'. These are as nearly as I can recollect the General's words, so you see he will not be content with ordinary spirit. He looks upon you as his own, and would have you a Sir Sidney if possible. Now my dear John, I hope the cap does not fit, or the shoe pinch in any respect; if you feel it does somewhere, look to it, for I know he has an eye upon you when you least think it. Write to him frequently in confidence, and consult him as your friend and patron in everything, under whose direction and guidance you wish to go on. Nothing will please him more than this, and your informing him of everything concerning yourself, and you may find your account in doing so. In regard to books and instruments pray write to me soon, and tell me those you have got, or such you may be in particular want of, that I may see if I can assist you with any of mine, which I can now do without, as I am growing old and cannot read much. Yours is the age for that and every other exertion which youthful ambition in well-formed minds should inspire. You are but a short way from the bottom of the ladder, although few young men of your age have the good fortune to climb so many steps in so short a time. *C'est un bon augur* that you feed your hopes and redouble your efforts in the arduous career of glory. Youth is the time, the happy and precious time, to look to the top of the ladder. A philosophic reasoner has said, that let a man say to himself in his early life, I will be this or I will be that, by perseverance he may certainly obtain his object. As to the tender passion and your soft nonsense, it is to be warily managed indeed. Should matrimony turn up trumps in the game, with £20,000 at least, it is all very well; nothing under to be thought of at your time of life and your situation; such a connection without advantageous means, however amiable the object, would only be entailing a life of difficulty and distress to both. Herein is my sermon. Despise it not, oh young man; read and mark the words of the preacher, chapter verse etc. A visit from you, whether at Lisbon or Oporto, you may well suppose would be highly gratifying to us all, but I fear much the continuance of the War may stand in the way of your obtaining leave of absence, or even the propriety of your asking it, at least until the campaign is over. Leave for less than six months is not worth crossing a sea for. Should it happen in war time a good neutral ship to Lisbon would be best.

There was no chance that John Henry could get leave and visit Portugal again. By 1796, when that letter was written, dark and dangerous shadows were spreading from the war with France across the Irish scene, and the British forces in Ireland would soon be fully engaged.

PART II

Campaigns in Ireland and the Mediterranean
1798–1807

5

Captain-Lieutenant John Henry Slessor was now twenty-one. His early success had made him slightly smug about his devotion to his military duties and his superiority to his idler brother officers. He was capable of 'soft nonsense' about pretty Irish girls, but prudent enough to follow his father's advice not to risk early marriage if no heiresses were available. Everything was going well for him, he had not yet encountered the griefs, disappointments and dangers which in a few years' time would mature him into a man of weight.

He had been in Ireland for four years with the Royal Irish Artillery, first at Chapelizod, then at Clonmel, then at Cork, and finally at Belfast. He had studied the techniques of warfare, but there had been no occasion to put them into action. But no young officer who moved about Ireland on duty and on leave, and whose own troops were Ulstermen, could fail to notice the critical state of popular feeling in Ireland.

JHS Quiet times were on the eve of being succeeded by broils and discord, religious feuds and civil war. Belfast was the focus of rebellion. Not all the vigilance of Government could fathom the conspiracies that were going on. Associations of United Irishmen became universal: fabrication of pikes, etc, were clandestinely carried on; the names of many citizens of good families, even of Nobility, were in the list of Rebels: the Irish Militia were tainted. On the other hand, Government sent over Fencible and English Militia regiments, formed Yeomanry and Volunteer corps, and the Protestants swore allegiance to the King and constitution, Church and State, under the name of Orangemen.

In the Spring of 1798 open rebellion broke out South of Dublin. Wexford was the scene of much bloodshed, and horrible atrocities, particularly on the bridge, where many Protestants were piked and thrown into the river: at Vinegar Hill, Ross, etc, fighting. At Scullabogue a Captain Swayne and his company of Militia were overpowered by numbers and burnt in a barn. Hosts of armed men rose, at it were, from the bogs and mountains. They faced boldly the King's troops, but were always defeated in open warfare. Towards the Protestants the Catholics shewed inveterate enmity. One of their oaths was to annihilate them. So savage were they that on one occasion they cut off a Protestant's ears, put them in whiskey punch, and drank it.

John Henry's hearsay report of the first months of the Irish Rebellion in the south from March to May 1798 is compressed and confused, and contains the usual rumours of atrocity acts by the enemy side. Some of these were true. On the events in the Irish Rebellion at which he was actually present he was, as will be seen, a fair and impartial witness; of what went before, he formed a simplified but not vindictive judgment based on the information available to a junior British officer in Belfast. To set this in perspective, some summary of the early history of the Rebellion is necessary.

The Dublin leaders of the United Irish associations which aimed at freeing Ireland from British rule – the barrister Thomas Emmet, the doctor William McNevin, Arthur O'Connor, Lord Edward Fitzgerald – had planned a rising which would encircle Dublin, and, in preparation for this, pikes were being forged and stock-piled all over the country, in spite of frequent searches and seizures by the British army. The United Irish leaders Emmet and McNevin were arrested in early March, and Fitzgerald in May; martial law was proclaimed on 30th March, and the surrender of United Irish pikes was enforced by 'free quarters' (commandeering of free food for the army), floggings, and in a few cases by a horrible form of torture known as 'pitch-capping'. Only some of the British army leaders, including General Lake, the Commander of the Northern District, were in favour of such severity. Sir Ralph Abercromby, the Commander-in-Chief of the British army in Ireland, had a low opinion of his own forces whom he described as 'formidable to everybody but the enemy', a remark which cost him his job – he was forced to resign.

The trouble came to a head in the last week in May. The planned rising then was immediately preceded by an incident which John Henry mentions in his diary, though he confuses it with another rebel atrocity. A Captain Swayne, in command of a detachment of thirty-five militia-men from Cork at the town of Prosperous, had a prisoner tortured to make him reveal where arms had been hidden. That night a force of 500 rebels piked and shot the militia-men, burst into Swayne's bedroom and shot him, and then set fire to the barracks, burning more men in their beds, and paraded Swayne's body which they then burnt in a barrel. A fortnight later the rebels shot and burnt a group of loyalists, including women and children, in a barn at Scullabogue. These two horror stories have been conflated in John Henry's narrative.

The rising round Dublin planned for 24th May failed to come off, but the United Irish in Kildare rose, massacring the passengers on a mail coach from Dublin, and soon Carlow, Kildare and Wicklow were in revolt. A few days later a successful attack on the garrison at Wexford delivered it into the hands of the rebels, and when after three weeks it was menaced with recapture by Government troops, the rebels piked to death ninety-seven loyalist prisoners on Wexford bridge.

These were the events in southern Ireland of which John Henry, in the so-far-untroubled north, heard sometimes garbled accounts. It was a time of horrible misery from which neither side emerged with honour. In that last week of May 1798 houses were set on fire, men and boys hanged, flogged, piked, by both sides, as towns and villages were successively terrorised by bands of Orangemen, by the rebels, by the scattered army garrisons fighting for their lives or inflicting revenge when they recaptured rebel centres. Often the very men – Catholic priests, Protestant clergymen, doctors – who tried to mediate and restrain were the first to be murdered. But the most piteous victims were the completely innocent bystanders, massacred by both sides. Mobs of Protestant loyalists at New Ross, Catholic rebels in Kildare, tortured and piked to death old men, halfwits, fourteen-year-old girls, only because they belonged to the opposite religion.

For the first fortnight of the rebellion in the south, Northern Ireland remained quiet, but the Government forces there were watchful, and ready to move when in the first days of June the Ulster United Irish rose and attacked Ballymena and Randalstown, broke down the bridge at Toome, and marched on Antrim.

JHS In the North we were kept on the alert, every moment expecting the storm to burst. Not long in suspense: for on the morning of the 5th June (we had been stationed for some time with the infantry at Blairs in wooden huts, 12 miles from Belfast and near Hillsborough) at ten minutes' warning we received orders to march towards the town of Antrim ten miles off. I had under my command two 4½ inch Howitzers and was attached to a Battalion of Light Infantry and the 64th Regt, under the command of Colonel Clavering. On approaching the town we saw the rebels in great numbers, and met a party of the 22nd Light Dragoons and artillery retreating, with some wounded, among them Col Lumley, their commander, on a car. He had gallantly charged into the town with two guns, Yeomanry and his Dragoons: they behaved nobly, but the rebels were very numerous; had possessions of the houses, walls etc, from which they kept up a destructive fire. One Cornet was killed, and about 40 men killed and wounded. A little less impetuosity, and patience until other corps came up, would have been more prudent perhaps. Lord O'Neill, with some Yeomanry, had also entered the town: he was killed, 'twas said brutally piked, by his own tenantry. ('Twas a singular circumstance that this Nobleman and Lord Mountjoy, who was killed in the South, were both strenuous advocates in the Catholic question of Emancipation).

From the Belfast side a simultaneous movement with ours had been made by Col Durham, at the head of 2000 men. We now attacked at all points, and in about an hour got possession of the town, dispersing the unfortunate, deluded rebels in all directions, and taking no prisoners. In this second affair we did not lose a man. About 300 of the rebels were left dead. All firing having ceased Col Durham returned to Belfast, and Col Clavering's detachment took up their position at Shane's Castle, the beautiful family mansion of Lord O'Neill, situated at Lough Neagh, two miles from Antrim. This was my first trial, my début, and I must say, that after the thirst of blood was over, cool reflection did not much reconcile to my feelings such a horrible carnage of our own countrymen; but it was self-defence.

It is not certain how Lord O'Neill met his death. He had come into Antrim to attend a magistrates' meeting, and was caught alone in the street when the rebels marched in. One story is that he fired at them first, the other that he was attacked by his own lodge-keeper; he undoubtedly died from a pike-thrust in the back. John Henry is honest enough to distinguish between what ''twas said' and what he saw with his own eyes, as in his vivid account of the battle for Antrim, and its dismal aftermath.

JHS *8th June.* Sent a party to throw the dead bodies into the lake. A large detachment went out reconnoitring as far as the village of Randalstown: saw some rebels on the hills: but they took care to keep out of reach of shot: three were taken prisoners, and we were on the point of hanging them, when it was thought more prudent not, they having in their possession two Yeomanry Officers, whom they had taken prisoners in a smart skirmish the day before.

9th. Martial law was now proclaimed thro'out the Kingdom. Col Clavering received orders to burn Randalstown. We marched to it this morning, and it fell to my lot to set fire to it, which was soon effectually done by sending artillerymen in different directions with port-fires. The houses being mostly thatch were soon in a blaze. Only those who witness such distressing scenes can form any idea of them. How far such measures are politic Government ought best to know. With the greatest difficulty could the officers restrain the men from plundering and committing all kinds of excesses. This painful duty being performed, we returned to the castle. At eleven o'clock this night we marched to Toome 9 miles, there to meet General Knox, as we had information of the rebels being in numbers. When we arrived they had plundered the village, broke a beautiful arch across the river Bann, which prevented our junction for the time; they frequently cut trenches across the roads to impede our Cavalry and Artillery.

10th. Early this morning returned to quarters.

11th. Marched to Ballymena: got possession of a quantity of pikes and arms: again disappointed, happy disappointment: the people are beginning to see their error, and ask for pardon: returned in the evening. In the county of Down, at Saintfield and Ballynahinch there have been two severe actions: Monroe and Dickey, active leaders, hanged.

12th. We remained quiet at Shane's Castle for some days.

18th. Rode over to Blairs: attended the trial of a Dr Birch, a presbyterian priest, for high treason; he was transported, and prosecuted by his own brother, who was in the Yeomanry: to such a pitch was party spirit carried, and so horrid are the evils of a civil war.

19th. Returned to my post.

22nd. Lord O'Neill was buried in the family vault with military honours: he was a nobleman of most excellent character, good landlord and friend to his country. He has left two sons, minors at Oxford; fine young men: they attended the melancholy ceremony.

23rd. Received orders to march to Broughshane, three miles from Ballymena, where we encamped: wet and unpleasant weather. We constantly inflict martial law on the country people, flogging and even hanging. There is a nice race course here, where the Rebels used to hold their nightly meetings; the inhabitants speak a mixed dialect of Scotch and English.

July 1st. The spirit of Rebellion appears to die away. Chiefs, and their plans, detected: French not having arrived at the time expected. Still the country is far from quiet: though large bodies do not assemble, yet partial frays take place, and long nights are coming on.

23rd. We remained near a month very miserably under canvas, the weather became so bad, that we broke up, and went into quarters at Ballymena: bad enough, but under shelter. Three miles from hence, is a settlement of a sect of people, called Moravians, somewhat resembling Quakers, composed of different nations, clean, industrious, religious and 'tis said loyal.

August 1st. Ordered back to our old quarters, wooden huts at Blairs. Quiet was generally restored, and the people returned to their usual occupations.

6

The collapse of the Irish rebellion was partly due to the non-arrival of the expected help from France. In December 1796 a French fleet with 15,000 soldiers on board had actually threatened Bantry Bay, but had failed to land the troops. All through 1797 and the early months of 1798, Wolfe Tone and Edward Leiris were in Paris negotiating with the Directory, and then with Napoleon, for a French invasion of Ireland in support of the planned rebellion which would, it was argued, seriously hamper the English war effort against France. In February 1798 a force of 50,000 men, with horses, artillery, supplies and a fleet of transports, was assembled in the Channel ports to be launched against Ireland. Wolfe Tone and Edward Fitzgerald confidently believed that when the Irish rebellion started in May 1798, the French would redeem their promises and launch a supporting invasion. But May, June and July passed, and there was no sign of a French invading fleet. By mid-August Wexford had been recaptured, the last rebel forces in Kildare had surrendered, the ringleaders McCracken, Monroe and the Sheares brothers had been captured and condemned to death, and Lord Cornwallis, who had succeeded Lord Camden as Viceroy of Ireland, had offered a general pardon to the rank and file of the rebels if they surrendered their arms and took the oath of allegiance.

Suddenly, when it was too late to help the Irish rebels, the French invaded Ireland after all. On 23rd August a force of 1,100 men under General Humbert landed at Killala in Co. Mayo, and four days later they attacked the British forces at Castlebar, part of whom, the contingents of Irish militia, threw down their arms and ran away when confronted by the French. This defeat of the Government forces put most of Co. Mayo under French control, many Irishmen now joining Humbert's force, and he marched north-eastwards towards Sligo. Here John Henry Slessor re-enters the course of events.

JHS *27th August*. Sudden and unexpected indeed: An express arrived that the French had landed at Killala in the county of Mayo. At ten o'clock at night Col Ennis of the 64th Regt was ordered to march with his regiment, the light battalion and two Curricle Guns which I command. We proceed with little intermission day and night, thro' Lurgan, Armagh, Monaghan, Clondess, Enniskillen, Manor Hamilton, until we reach Sligo, where I halted. The next day the Infantry moved on to join Lord Cornwallis. I was much disappointed at being left behind, but obey was the word. General Nugent commanded here, our force consisted of six field pieces, the City of Limerick Militia, Essex Fencibles, a few of the 23rd Light Dragons, and some Yeomanry. The reports of the French General Humbert's force were various and contradictory. Our troops had been beaten at Castlebar, owing to the bad conduct of two regiments of Irish Militia, and the enemy were advancing rapidly into the interior joined by rebels.

Sept 3rd. General Nugent was called away: the command devolved upon Col Vereker, C. L. Militia. We had our pickets and patrols out: doubtful even of the inhabitants, whether friends or foes.

5th. This morning about five o'clock, a cavalry picket was driven in, after exchanging shots with the French, whom they reported to be advancing on Sligo. I was immediately ordered out with my two curricle guns, 250 of the Limerick Militia, a few of the Essex Fencibles, and some Yeomanry. Col Vereker marched out at our head. About four miles off, on approaching the village of Colooney, we discovered the French strongly posted. They began a smart fire, which we as quickly returned, and for about an hour we appeared to have rather the advantage, but their force was far superior. One of our officers being killed, some wounded, men also, the Infantry began to give way: the enemy annoyed us much by their sharp-shooters, at which kind of warfare they are very expert, and had kept up a hot fire. To our right we had a craggy mountain: on our left a river. The men behaved uncommonly well, particularly when we take into consideration that this was the first time the troops had been opposed to a regular force. We were overpowered and forced to retreat, some to ford the river. I lost one gunner killed, also a horse; was slightly wounded in the head by the graze of a rifle ball, and my hat shot through, a wonderful escape. We returned to Sligo not quite in such good spirits as when we sallied out. Had our whole force been brought into action, I believed we should have finished Monsieur Humbert's career. The enemy did not attempt to follow us. Humbert said that large towns were like rat traps, and his object was to get into the interior, where he expected a rising of the people in his favour: hitherto but few had joined him. He spoke highly in praise of Col Vereker's detachment at Colooney: the check we gave him obliged him to move with caution, and delayed him for three hours: which greatly favoured General Lake, who was in pursuit.

The Battle of Colooney was not much more than a skirmish from which the British, after holding up the French for a few hours, had to retreat, but it had an effect which in contemporary eyes magnified it into a strategic turning-point of great importance. Humbert, who had expected the Sligo garrison to be as easy a push-over as the Castlebar one had been, met with more resistance than he bargained for, and concluded that the force which he had driven back must be

the advance guard of the main British army. He therefore marched east and
south, in the direction of Dublin, avoiding Sligo. A week later he was confronted by the main British forces which he had believed he was out-flanking;
Cornwallis and Lake, with 10,000 men, forced the small French force, after a
brief battle, to surrender at Ballinamuck.

The Battle of Coloney was therefore celebrated at the time as a splendid feat
of British arms. Colonel Vereker, who was severely wounded in the action, was
hailed as the Irish Leonidas, awarded a sword of honour by the city of Limerick, given the thanks of the Irish Parliament, and accorded the right to add the
motto 'Coloney' to the coat of arms of the viscountcy of Gort to which he later
succeeded.

For John Henry Slessor, Coloney was his first taste of battle against the
French, to be followed by many other peripheral clashes with the forces of
France and her allies in Europe and the Middle East for the rest of his life on
active service. In all the advances and retreats, the landings and captures of the
seventeen years still to come of his share in the Napoleonic Wars, he received
only one more slight wound in the leg after the graze on the head he suffered at
Coloney. He was brave, but also lucky – a survivor, unlike his less fortunate
brothers.

He and his contingent spent the rest of 1798 in mopping-up operations.

JHS *7th Sept*. This day the French surrendered at Ballynamuck. No mercy was
shown to the Irish who had joined their standard, but is it not strange that a
body of French, not exceeding 1000 men, should have so long held their
ground.

We marched to Ballyshannon, where General Champagny commanded.
(A famous salmon fishing here). We were at this time always billeted on
the inhabitants, churches, chapels, etc. were converted into barracks and
stables: provisions taken by force: such are the melancholy consequences
of rebellion. The Limerick Militia returned to Sligo, and after a few days I
was ordered with my brigade of guns to Enniskillen, a handsome City with
good barracks, situated on an island in Lough Erne, a pass of great importance between the North and South of Ireland, with two strong Forts. Near
here is the seat of Lord Belmore, reckoned one of the handsomest houses
in Ireland.

I passed the remainder of September here pleasantly enough. My old
friends the Light Battalion (I ought to have said they were composed of
light companies of Militia regiments) marched through bearing a French
standard and other trophies.

Early in October I was ordered to Charlemont Fort, a depot of Artillery
for the Northern district. Here we were brigaded off in heavy and light
brigades; I was appointed to a light one and ordered off to Coleraine,
where I arrived on the 17th Oct. well pleased with my station. The Manx

Fencibles (Lord Henry Murray Colonel) are quartered here: I had met them before.

20th Oct. Lieut Tisdale arrived, with orders to take half my brigade (two guns) to Ballymena, 25 miles off, to be attached to the 1st Foot, the Royals. Coleraine, being so far North, is no thoro'fare: a neat town, situated on the river Bann which discharges itself into the sea four miles off: good hunting and shooting, and famous for its salmon fishing: provisions abundant and cheap; salmon three halfpence per pound, and rabbits 3*d* per couple: they tell you that servants stipulate that they are only to have these articles twice a week. I have already been shown much attention by the respectable inhabitants of the town and neighbourhood, Lisles, Cromies, McCauslands, Hills, etc.

About this time Sir T.B. Warren fell in with and captured a French fleet off the coast of Donegal, having troops on board for the invasion of Ireland. An Irish barrister, T.W. Tone, was on board, bearing a French commission. He was quickly identified among the prisoners by Sir George Hill, soon after which he cut his throat. It appeared three expeditions had left France about the same time; this one, Gen Humbert's, and a third which put back by stress of weather. Had the three succeeded in landing, we should have had enough to do. The names of Lord Edward Fitzgerald, Arthur O'Connor, Emmett, Tone, Sheares, McNevin etc shone conspicuous; they will be handed to posterity as traitors to their country. What blind infatuation to suppose that Ireland can belong to any other country but England; much less can she be an independent State. The misguided people are generally returning to their homes and peaceful occupations.

John Henry had no doubts about the rights and wrongs of that year's conflict. In his simple conviction, Ireland belonged to England; Irish independence was an infatuated fantasy. The leaders of the Irish rebellion were traitors, in league with the French enemy against whom England was fighting for her life, and whom the Irish revolutionaries had invited to invade Ireland and stab England in the side. He had no condonation, no sympathy, for Lord Edward Fitzgerald, for the Sheares brothers, Wolfe Tone, Emmett, O'Connor; to his mind they all deserved to pay the penalty of treason. He believed, too, what he learnt from hearsay, that the savage cruelties – the massacre on the bridge at Wexford, the burning alive of Captain Swayne's men and the loyalists at Scullabogue, the mutilations and pikings, the murder of Lord O'Neill by his own servant – were all on one side.

But when the time came for him to see the fighting and its aftermath with his own eyes, he realised that the cruel necessities of war dragged down both sides into outrage. Ordered to kill all rebels and take no prisoners at Antrim, to set fire to the poor hovels at Randalstown, he obeyed, but with reluctance and pity for the wretched peasants misled by illusory hopes into a rebellion in which they were to be the greatest sufferers. Sent to round up rebels for execution at Ballymena, but finding them ready to sue for pardon, he found it a 'happy disappointment'.

7

John Henry's military experience got off to a dashing start with the Battle of Coloney, but it was to be nine years before he was in action again, though the war with France continued through eight of those nine years. He spent the two years after the Rebellion of 1798 in a superficially pacified Ireland, on garrison duties varied by firing *feux-de-joie* to celebrate royal birthdays and good news of the war, and by sight-seeing and visits to hospitable Irish families. He heard much discussion about the proposed Legislative Union of Ireland with England, which when it was carried in 1800 was to have an unexpected side-effect on his career. But Irish events no longer dominated his diary; for the period from February 1799 to September 1800 it is much fuller than before of comments on the progress of the war with France, some of them clearly retrospective entries made later. That period saw the formation of the Second Coalition, of England, Austria and Russia, against France; a French army locked up in Egypt by Nelson's victory in the Battle of the Nile; the expulsion of the French from Italy by the Russian General Suvorov; the disastrously unsuccessful landing in the Netherlands by the Duke of York's forces; Napoleon's escape back to France from Egypt, his proclamation as First Consul, and his recapture of Italy after his victory at Marengo; and the break-up of the Second Coalition. Although John Henry's diary shows that he had begun to take a more mature interest in world affairs outside his own concerns, he was not satisfied with his own development so far, as he looked back on what he had achieved and what he had neglected in the six years he had spent in the army in Ireland.

JHS *1799. 1st Febry*. Severe weather, much snow and frost.
    17th. Brigadier-General Dunn reviewed the troops and expressed his appreciation of their appearance. I rode with him to the Giants Causeway. This grand phenomenon of nature, the uniformity of the stones, convex and concave, fitted as it were by art into each other, mathematically cut, as it were, into many sides as octagons, is wonderful: the coast is bold, fine and romantic, affording ample scope for the naturalist.
    12th March. The Yeomanry called out, and general orders issued for the troops to be ready to turn out at the shortest notice. A large fleet has left Brest.
    1st May. All quiet: time flies. I often receive letters from Portugal: my

Mother and Sisters well, but my valuable and dear Father, I fear, is breaking fast. My brother William is doing well in the East. Henry must get over the drudgery of a midshipman's life before he can come into play.

18th. The Manx Fencibles have been relieved by the Aberdeen, Col. Leith.

29th. The French fleet gone up the Mediterranean.

4th June. King's birthday: fired a *feu-de-joie.*

16th June. Lieut Tisdall joined with his half Brigade.

10th August. An expedition under Sir R. Abercromby sailed for the coast of Holland.

30th. Dutch Fleet in the Texel surrendered to Admiral Mitchell, our troops landed and stormed the Helder, great exertions made by Government to reinforce our army, and an act of Parliament passed to allow the Militia to volunteer into line Regiments, hope of restoring the Stadholder, the Duke of York has taken the command in Holland, a body of Russians under Suvorov joined him.

Sept 1st. Long before this period Bonaparte had landed in Egypt with an army of 40,000 men, and beat the Turks making themselves complete masters of that country, their ultimate views on our East Indian possessions. At St Jean d'Acre Sir Sidney Smith (whose singular escape from the Temple at Paris I need not mention) displayed great gallantry and skill. My brother Henry was then a Midshipman on board the *Tigre* and present.

19th. Hard fighting in Holland: the cause weakly upheld by the Dutch themselves.

21st. What wonderful islanders we are: at work in all quarters. In India our people distinguished themselves at the storming of Seringapatam, when Tippoo Sahib was slain, and his two sons made prisoners by Genl Harris.

4th October. Fired a *feu-de-joie* in consequence of good news from Holland.

11th. Lord Cornwallis arrived here, from public report feeling his way and canvassing for the Union. This great measure, it is to be hoped, will prove advantageous to the United Kingdoms, and consolidate the British Empire by indissoluble ties.

20th. Our affairs in Holland wear an unfavourable aspect.

24th. Bad news from Switzerland. These confounded French are setting the whole world in a flame. General Hotze killed.

28th Oct. A treaty concluded in Holland between the Duke of York and the French General: our army re-embarked: some vessels and men lost: thus ends, after the greatest waste of money and sacrifice of lives, an expedition badly planned, and no better executed.

1st Nov. About this time Bonaparte abandoned his army in Egypt, and was made first consul.

1800. 1st Janry. Union the topic of conversation. Bonaparte addresses the King of England, and receives a clever answer, signed Grenville.

1st Febry. Another expedition talked of.

1st April. The *Queen Charlotte* blew up: 800 souls perished. Malta closely blockaded by Lord Nelson: our expedition gone up the Mediterranean.

10th. An attempt made on the King's life at the theatre by a maniac.

1st June. The Union carried.

30th. Bonaparte gains the Battle of Marengo, and returns to Paris crowned with laurels. An armistice on the Continent: report of peace.

1st July. A French frigate cut out of Dunkirk roads by Capt Campbell in a most gallant manner.

1st Aug. Sir R. Abercromby and the Expedition rendezvous at Minorca.

15th. This day set out on a little expedition with Captain Hill of the Navy and a Mr McCausland along the Coast, to visit Fair Head, Island of Rathlin, etc. We sailed from Fort Rush, a little fishing town five miles from Coleraine: in about three hours reached Rathlin, and were most hospitably received by Mr E. Gage, the Laird and proprietor. His house is in fact the only decent one. He is an agreeable old man with a wife and family. The Island is about five miles long, and forms part of the County of Antrim. During the rebellion the inhabitants mostly took the oath of United Irishmen, but by Mr Gage's exertions and by banishing the priest, tranquillity and fidelity was restored. The Islanders principally pay their rent by kelp, and their leases are renewed from year to year. They catch an abundance of fish: and the mutton, tho' small, is sweet. The morals of the inhabitants appeared good, and Mr Gage cannot inflict a more severe punishment than banishing a subject to Ireland, which they call the Continent. We enjoyed the hospitality of this good family for three days, when we crossed over to Ballyshannon and dined with Capt Boyd. Next day visited the Head, collieries etc: descended several hundred yards underground: there are fine veins of coal here.

20th. Dined with Mr Staples, M.P. He has a large and pleasant family.

21st. Returned by land to my quarters; crossed the nervous bridge of Carrickarade; admired the wild scenery and bold coast.

1st Sept. General Kleber appointed in Egypt.

Artillery officers from the nature of their detached services are in general taken more notice of than those of the Infantry Regiments, which are so numerous. I felt grateful for the friendly attentions I received while in Coleraine where I had passed many happy months. I had been in Ireland since 94, and when I take a retrospective view of the past, wish I could say I was satisfied with myself. (But where is the person who can?) My application to study did not keep time with my promotion, nor had the most fatherly, the most affectionate letters that influence they required. An early separation from my parents in some degree alienated those filial affections it was my duty to cherish and observe. Thus was I left without a Mentor at my elbow. It is true I never felt myself inferior to my brother officers, either as a gentleman or officer; but emulation and ambition ought to have made me soar far above many who had not had the same advantages I had.

In October 1800 he received news from Portugal that his father, of whose health he had heard bad reports as far back as May 1799, was now dangerously ill.

JHS Now, alas! a melancholy occasion called me away, no less than a most alarming account of the state of my dear Father's health. I quickly obtained leave of absence and on the 7th October I mounted my horse at six in the morning for Belfast, where I was detained five days waiting for a passage to Liverpool, and after a stormy passage of 30 hours landed there on the 14th. From Liverpool I made the best of my way to Bath, where I called on my uncle, William Bristow, and Aunt Girardot. The latter first gave me the doleful intelligence of my Father's death, whom I really may say, was a man, take him for all in all, you may not look on his like again.

John Slessor had died a month earlier, on September 8th. Harriot describes the event with her special mixture of strong sincere emotion and dramatic heightening.

HS I had been dreading his death for some time before it happened. It was not the less a cruel loss to me, and to you all. He died at St John's, near Porto, the 8th of September 1800. It was a night fit for the awful melancholy scene. The rain poured down in torrents. The wind blew furious. Thunder and lightning was excessive. It seemed as if the elements were in anger that death should deprive the world of so good a man . . . a most valuable friend, a most affectionate good Father, and in his profession was esteemed and beloved by all. The soldiers of his regiment looked up to him as their protector, as their father, and in his last illnes, when he was obliged to leave them, it was a general lamentation throughout the regiment.

His eldest daughter Louisa recorded her father's death in more detail in a note written many years later in her sister Harriot Amelia's diary.

LC My father (General Slessor) died at S. Joao Macetos near Oporto the 8th of Sept 1800, having lingered for a long time, universally respected, lamented and regretted, by all around him, and all who served under his orders, valiant, generous and honourable, a good Husband, a good Father, and a true Friend, aged 63, buried in the English burying ground of Oporto.

Even when every allowance is made for the contemporary conventions of filial sorrow, the real grief and sense of loss of John Slessor's family when he died pierce through the stilted phrases in which they expressed their feelings. William Slessor, far away in India, did not hear the news of his father's death for nearly a year. The letter he wrote to his sister Louisa a few days after the news reached him is a tangle of confused double negatives and awkwardly manipulated platitudes, but a real unmistakable desolation and shock lie behind it. The 'happy ignorance' in which he had slumbered all these past months, while his family in Portugal were already mourning their loss, seems a comfortless irony to him now. He tries to reach out to his distant family with consolation, and to muster resignation and good sense, but does not feel 'the feeble resources of my own mind' equal to the task. Nine years before, when he last saw his father, he was a schoolboy of thirteen, but not too young to remember with 'reverence and gratitude' what a kind affectionate father John Slessor had always been, how liberally he had provided for his sons' education, how he 'commanded the respect and esteem of all who saw him, and were happy enough to be acquainted with him.' He was 'the best of parents Heaven ever blessed children with.'

8

John Henry's diary of his reunion with his mourning family in Portugal, and his sad memories of past happiness at San Pedro, are veined with grief but, unlike poor lonely William in India, he had the comfort of renewing his links with his mother and sisters, whom he had not seen for more than a decade, and the interest of seeing Portugal again with changed eyes. After hearing from his Aunt Girardot the news of his father's death, he hastened from Bath to Falmouth and caught a packet boat to Lisbon.

JHS *27th Oct.* Landed at Lisbon, having made a journey by land and by water, of about 1500 miles in 14 days. I lived with General Fraser, who commanded the troops in the pay of England. From him and from Messrs Mayne and Brown I received every attention. The entrance of the Tagus and up to Lisbon is splendid, but on landing I was much disgusted with the filth: dogs innumerable, stinking fish, etc. As to the superstition, it is incredible. My time was limited: I could see but little: I panted to reach Oporto.

3rd Nov. Set off for Oporto on a coach drawn by six mules. The driver tied himself on the box: three Portuguese gentlemen, bundled up in their Capotas were my travelling companions. I understood not a word of the language, and they spoke no other. However, altho' extremely loquacious among themselves, they were very civil to me. We traversed a wild and romantic country. The verdure of the valleys, the variety of foliage, shades of green, orange, cork and olive trees, attracted my attention, so different from the cold country I had just left. We stopt to sleep one night, and fared better than I had expected. The next evening arrived at Coimbra, where is a magnificent Cathedral, and University. Here this public conveyance ceases, for the road is no longer passable for a carriage. We stopped in the middle of the street, where the passengers alight. Fortunately for me a servant had been sent to meet me from Oporto. He immediately seized me by the knees, according to the custom of the country. He was an old faithful domestic; conducted me to a dirty Inn, where a fowl was speedily killed and boiled to rags; this, with some indifferent wine, bread and fruit, formed my supper. I then lay down in my cloathes, but could not sleep. At three in the morning old Manuel called me: I soon mounted my horse and compressed my thighs in a country saddle, the stirrups like small coal boxes. We travelled over dreary wastes and through woods or forests for six leagues, when we halted for breakfast, composed of fresh eggs, good bread and fish fried in oil. I was hungry and ate heartily, though my bones were bruised; after which we again started; but you must never attempt in this country to go fast, for a certain time is allowed for a given distance. Manuel rigidly adhered to this, for I sometimes attempted to push on; but he kept to his own pace; so that when I came to a cross road, I was obliged to wait for him. We slept this night at a miserable Albergo, full of Muleteers and their mules, jingling their bells all night.

6th. Reached home: I must call it so now: but the sensation I felt is not so easily described. My Mother and Sisters in deep mourning: we were strangers to each other: after the melancholy scene they had just witnessed, my arrival seemed as it were to revive their grief. Our meeting was naturally of the most moving and tender kind: mixt sorrow and at the same time gratification at renewing our acquaintance after a separation of 14 years. Only those who experience such scenes can form an idea of their force.

1801. 1st Jan. It was some time before I got reconciled to this country, but Oporto is a delightful place, both with regard to climate, society, etc. The English Factory are a most liberal, hospitable class of gentlemen: I have every reason to say so. My family I plainly saw were universally esteemed, and the death of my Father as generally lamented. Our ideas soon familiarized, and I now felt that I now had a kind Mother and Sisters. As yet commerce flourished and peace reigned in this quarter; but French influence gained ground, and war with that country was strongly apprehended.

14th. The Millbrook Schooner (Lt Smith) gallantly beat off a Spanish Privateer of very superior force off the bar of Oporto.

I went one day to see a beautiful girl take the veil, a truly painful ceremony to an Englishman. Still the young victim's feelings are worked upon to such a pitch, that they wish to make you believe the act is voluntary.

The troops, more particularly the Infantry, appear to be in a very wretched, disorganized state; but I am informed that if well officered, they are good stuff; but the Government is imbecile and corrupt, eat up with bigotry and superstition.

I made an expedition up the Douro with Mr Warre, the Consul, to what is called the Wine country. At this season of the year the merchants go up to purchase wines; it is two days journey. The Country is wild and romantic, the river beautifully winding, and the numerous boats gently moving along with their white sails have a pretty effect. The banks for many miles on each side of the river are covered with vines, low walls in gradation to the top supporting the soil, the workings of which, pruning, and making the wine, gives ample employment to the proprietor. As to roads, you can hardly say there are any; narrow lanes, scarcely wide enough for two mules to pass. We went one evening to a ball, but I was nearly suffocated with dust, and glad to get away. Some of the company were good subjects for Hogarth. On Sunday morning I paid a visit, when I found the family busily employed playing at cards, a favourite game called Boston, in complete deshabille, capotes, slippers, hair uncombed, with a large pan of charcoal under the table. I joined this grotesque party for a time, and was not a little astonished at their freedom of speech.

25th. Having travelled thus far, I thought I might just as well see a little more, so ordered my mules. Mr P. Garby, an entertaining young man accompanied me. Went as far as Villa Real, where we dined with a Portuguese family. From thence to Villa Pauca: slept in a miserable place, but merry enough. The next day rode an easy stage to the once known village of San Pedro. Near this, at Chaves, (an old fortified town, the key into the North of Portugal), my ever to be lamented Father had his Regiment, and here his halcyon days were spent. No pair could be happier, no people, in private or in public, more beloved, altho' in a wild and retired part of the Kingdom, no person within 20 miles but adored them. Here the revolving seasons rapidly passed in all that innocent happiness and pure state, so little known in capitals and public places to the higher classes, until six children, whose education my Mother had hitherto principally conducted, were to be introduced into the World and competent Masters obtained. But oh! what a theme was here, how much scope for the purest, the most refined ideas. Oh that my pen could do justice to this dear place! My heart bled when I entered the house my Father had built. (It was sold at his death.) I burst into tears and went into every room, recalling my infant past times. Every object which I thought I recollected added a melancholy, tho' pleasing reflection. But, Oh deserted village, hadst thou, Goldsmith, visited this once blessed retirement, thy muse would have inspired thee afresh! The corroding hand of time seemed here to delight in waste and ruin, for everything looked decaying. The remnants of furniture, the gardens overgrown with weeds, every thing in short tended to overcloud my mind, and but for my companion I should have departed immediately.

We frequently rode to Chaves, and dined with the officers, who appeared glad to see me, and lavish in their praise of their late Commander. The Spa waters of Chaves are worth visiting, bubbling up as if boiling, almost too hot to bear your hand in.

3rd Feb. Bid adieu for ever to San Pedro, and set off for Oporto by way of Braga (Garby started off the day before by a different route) where I found a very tolerable Inn. Dined in a Convent with two nuns; that is there was a strong grating between us, rather a novel entertainment. They were Sisters, and a third had taken the veil. What an unnatural and wretched existence! They were pleased at seeing me, as I brought them good accounts from their families, and left a present of tea, sugar etc. On the third day reached Oporto in safety, but nearly killed one of the mules by riding too hard. These useful and hardy animals will go uncommonly safe and perform long journeys, but must not be put out of their usual pace. They live often to the age of 50 or 60 years.

The political horizon began now to darken. The Spaniards at the instigation of France declared war against Portugal. The Galicians, a class of people laborious and industrious, and the principal hard-working fellows in Lisbon and Oporto, (most families have one as a servant) were ordered, under the severest penalties, to return to their country.

Developments in England and in Europe in these early months of 1801 were soon to propel John Henry out of his elegiac wanderings in Northern Portugal, back into professional anxieties and decisions. One of the effects of the Act of Union of Ireland with England was that Irish regiments were incorporated with their English counterparts. The Royal Irish Artillery became the 7th Battalion of the Royal Artillery *tout court*. By 1801, John Henry Slessor's name had reached the head of the list of Captain-Lieutenants in the Royal Irish Artillery's section of the Army List, and his chances of early promotion to full Captain should have been good. But after the Royal Irish Artillery was incorporated with the main body, the 1802 Army List shows John Henry's name far down in a big group of Captain-Lieutenants, and the likelihood of his promotion had receded much farther into the future.

Partly foreseeing these difficulties, he felt in March 1801 that he must leave Portugal and his family, and return to his regiment in Ireland.

JHS *1st March*. The time for my departure approached, and ignorant of the fate of the Irish Artillery, on the measure of the Union being carried, I was rather anxious to return to Ireland. Altho' my Father died without a will, family affairs were easily arranged; for indeed so much unanimity existed among us, that there was no danger of any litigation.

17th. At 5 o'clock this morning I left my Mother's house, and shall never forget my dear and warm-hearted Sister Louisa. She thought I was averse to the painful task of bidding farewell, and watched for me long before the hour of parting arrived. The morning was beautiful, and we took several turns in the garden, which commanded a view of the river. All was bustle, above 100 sail getting under weigh, anxious to cross the Bar, which is always dangerous, and laden with 27,000 pipes of wine. The uncertain state of affairs in Portugal made me very uneasy on account of my dear Mother and Sisters, whom I should have been most happy to have seen embark with me for old England before the storm broke out. I obtained my passage on board the *Maidstone* Frigate, Capt Donelly, and passed four weeks in a very different manner, amongst a noisy, rattling set of gentlemen, witnessing the novel scene of the discipline of a British Man-of-War, the unbounded and arbitrary power of the Commander, strict obedience to orders, duties, cleanliness, working the ship, etc – a little World in miniature.

9

While John Henry was lingering nostalgically at San Pedro, the Austrians, shaken by their defeats at Marengo and Hohenlinden, made peace with France. While he was on board HMS *Maidstone* on his way back to England, the Tsar Paul I, architect of the League of Armed Neutrality between Russia, Prussia, Sweden and Denmark – formed against the British exercise of the right of search of neutral vessels for contraband of war – was assassinated, and the League broke up. When John Henry landed in England, he was greeted by the news of Nelson's victory over the Danish fleet at the Battle of Copenhagen. Meanwhile in the Mediterranean a British force under Sir Ralph Abercromby had been sent to Egypt in March to dispose of the French army which Napoleon had left marooned there. It was in support of this operation that John Henry's company of the Royal Irish Artillery, on the verge of losing its separate regimental identity, was suddenly sent off to the Mediterranean, only two months after he had rejoined it.

JHS *13th April*. Made the Isle of Wight. Saw some Privateers on our voyage.

   14th. Went on shore at Portsmouth: visited the block manufactory; splendid invention: walked round the works, etc: heard the first news of Lord Nelson's action in the Baltic.

   16th. Arrived in the great Capital: slept at the house of my good friend and cousin Mr Thomas Neave: got my leave of absence renewed until regimental affairs were settled. My time passed very pleasantly in London, until the 10th of May, when it was finally settled that the Irish Artillery should be incorporated with the British. I lost no time in preparing to start for Dublin: and fortunately, having called on Mr James Warre, met an amiable young lady, Miss Ellen Lyle, whose family I had been intimate with at Coleraine. She with an elderly lady was going to Ireland, so we joined, and had a very pleasant journey and passages, via Parkgate.

   On arriving in Dublin, I found to my grief that instead of being a full Captain, as I expected, I stood only the 65th Capt-Lieutenant, according to my comparative standing and length of service with the British officers. This at first appeared rather hard, but our promotion had been very rapid. Still the measure was founded on just principles. I had my option to remain or retire with my rank on full pay of seven shillings a day. I had made up my mind to the latter, when a company was ordered to embark for Egypt. However, being the first for duty, I immediately set off for Cork, between which City and Speke Island we waited some time for a transport. While at the island I had some very fine fishing on a turbot bank with a Doctor Rogers, who lived near Cove; he was very kind and hospitable. Some of the Baltic fleet came into this beautiful harbour, as also Indiamen. The latter had been five months on the passage home. What a time to be at sea: *12th July*. At last the transport appeared, a large cut down Man of War, armed *en flute*. Embarked without loss of time, and set sail with a fair breeze.

13th. A calm.

14th. A breeze: off Scilly.

15th. Came to an anchor at Falmouth: idle for some days: dined with Sir William Lemon: a pretty seat a few miles from the town: visited Pendennis Castle, etc. In addition to the Company I commanded, two Lieutenants and eighty men, we received on board a melange of Officers and men, 350 of different regiments. Hitherto we had been very comfortable, but now commenced a scene of confusion, riot and irregularity. Col Nepean commanded, a good kind of family man, but I should say not much of a soldier, and led much by a hot-headed Welshman, a Major Davis. We had frequent Courts martial and flogging. In the ward-room the company was by no means select or agreeable, so that we formed ourselves into different messes.

1st Sept. Set sail in company with the *Hind* Frigate but obliged to put into Torbay by contrary winds: a large fleet wind-bound.

13th. Sailed: it was a beautiful sight: between two and three hundred vessels got under weigh, and the next morning, each convoy steering to its destination.

30th. Must make the best of a bad bargain: becalmed off Cape Spartel.

7th Oct. Passed thro' the Straits.

8th. At anchor before the Mole of Gibraltar. We had been told off to our respective quarters, the artillery to the guns, where we had been the whole of the preceding night, expecting to be attacked by the Spanish Gun-boats from Algeciras, which in a calm or mild weather are very daring.

9th. Landed, and happy indeed to be quit of the Pandour Transport. During our voyage I had been greatly annoyed. There are, it is true, many allurements and fascinations in a military life, but still many moments of trial and vexation. The different dispositions of men; whims, caprices, tempers etc of commanding officers; discipline, climate, separation from those nearest and dearest to you; these combined often tend to damp a young man's ardour in the profession. Nor was I much enamoured with the Scotch manners of the Commanding Officer of Artillery; so made up my mind to retire. We had a very pleasant Mess, and Gentlemanlike Officers, both Engineers and Artillery. The Garrison is very weak at present; principally composed of Fencible Regiments. General O'Hara, the Governor, is on his death-bed.

The unpleasant voyage to Gibraltar had enhanced John Henry's temporary disillusion with military life, and a month after his arrival in Gibraltar, the war news seemed to indicate that there would be little chance of seeing action. The Egyptian campaign, to take part in which the company had been sent from Ireland, was over, and a general peace between England and France began to seem probable.

JHS *20th Nov.* News arrived of the surrender of Alexandria, and the total expulsion of the French from that quarter of the Globe. Never was there fought a more glorious action in the Bay of Aboukir than Lord Nelson's; and never did the British army display more valour than on their landing in Egypt on the 8th of March, and the two subsequent actions on the 13th and 21st, when brave old Abercromby was killed.

24th. The game is up. Troop-ships come in daily, with wounded and ophthalmia subjects: peace confidently spoken of.

1st Dec. Communication with Spain opened; but as yet the Garrison are only allowed to go on the Neutral Ground, that is, the Isthmus which separates the Rock from the Mainland. The Plague having raged in Barbary, provisions have been extremely dear. I will not attempt to describe this bulwark of nature, and now made impregnable by art; yet still the Engineers carry on their excavations, bomb-proofs etc. There is a splendid Garrison Library, a great resource. A few partridges and rabbits, but strict orders not to shoot them. The short tail monkey, or baboon abound, and in severe weather are very daring.

10th. Sir James Saumarez, who fought two gallant actions some time ago, one in sight of the Garrison, having followed the enemy into Algeciras, was this day installed Knight of the Bath.

I went into Spain twice, and the Spaniards came freely to us, highly delighted at the cessation of the hostilities. I wished to have visited Barbary, but could not accomplish it. I now fully determined to quit the Artillery, not doubting that I should be allowed my full pay of Capt-Lieut; so applied accordingly. Thus my career as an Artillery Officer draws to a conclusion. Committing to paper these notes occupies an idle moment. Short-sentenced and methodical as they may appear, they may at some future date amuse me. Probably the routine of a military life, early habits of discipline, regular hours and dependence, rather curbs or controls an Officer in an expansion of ideas. Still on the other hand, he ought to gain great general information from the advantage he derives from mixing in society in the four quarters of the Globe.

1802. 1st Febry. Pax. The Fencible Regiments ordered to be disbanded. My leave to retire notified to me. Struck off duty, and put on a plain coat. Your most obedient humble servant.

John Henry Slessor was now twenty-five, a retired Captain-Lieutenant with a pension of seven shillings a day, and he had to decide what to do with himself. In the next few months he showed an impulsive recklessness and irresponsibility not characteristic of him. He had gone straight into the army from his tutor's at the age of seventeen, and for the next eight years had been 'your obedient humble servant', his life regulated by military discipline and the gentle pressure of his father's admonitory letters. Now he was free, adult, his own man, and ready perhaps for a brief spell of dare-devilry.

JHS My head now planned a hundred schemes. One day I proposed visiting Malta where I expected to meet my dear brother Henry. Another, I thought of going overland through Spain. Ultimately I met some officers of the 26th Foot. They were bound for Ireland, and I took my passage. Adieu, ye scorching Rock of Gibraltar, ye gamblers, drunken barracks, and cheating Jews.

29th. Got under weigh. We were eight Officers in the cabin; laid in a good stock of provisions, and promised ourselves a pleasant voyage. One officer was delirious owing to a *coup-de-soleil* in Egypt. However he recovered. Beguiled the time as best we could, until the 22nd March, when we made Cape Clear, the most Southern part of Ireland.

23rd March. Got into Cork Harbour. Before we had anchored, were put into quarantine, and the transport was ordered to Plymouth. Capt Pratt of the 5th as well as myself wanted to land, but the quarantine officers said 'twas impossible. However we manoeuvred so well that we bargained with a boat to come out to sea at night. The quarantine people saw us clear out of the harbour, when we hoisted a lantern, the signal agreed upon, and our boat was soon after alongside. Shook hands with the 26th friends, and silently stole along shore, conscious of our guilty act. The boatmen ran the same risk as ourselves, so we were safe. The night was dark; after much labour, and as may be supposed constant fear, and apprehension, we passed all the guard boats, and pulled for 16 miles up a river. At length, about one o'clock in the morning, reached a miserable village, where with considerable difficulty we got admittance into a dirty Inn. After some refreshment lay down to rest. Our boatmen got drunk, and valiantly set at defiance all the Quarantine Officers in Ireland. A discovery of so flagrant a breach of the law would have been attended with serious consequences, altho' there were no sick on board the transport. So early on the morning of the 24th Pratt went off to his friends, I with my servant made the best of my way to Cork, where I remained but a few days.

8th April. Started by the mail for Dublin. Peace proclaimed, the definitive treaty being signed.

The Treaty of Amiens between England and France had been concluded on 27th March, while John Henry was in Cork. In that brief interval of peace in the twenty-two-year war, John Henry roamed about Ireland through the summer of 1802, staying with friends and making his final shrewd and not unsympathetic assessment of the country where he had spent the first years of his manhood, and which he was not to see again for another twelve years.

JHS Here I am once more among the Sons of Erin, the Emerald Isle; a country rich in soil, rich in produce and resources, fine harbours; climate more mild than England or Scotland, but more subject to wet and damp; still ever unfortunate, inhabitants restless and difficult to be governed; indolent yet shrewd and indiscreet, impetuous, brave, impatient and improvident; thoughtlessly generous, quick to resent and forgive offences, to form and renounce friendships, they forgive injury rather than insult; the country's good they seldom, their own they carelessly pursue, but the Honour of both they eagerly vindicate. Oppression they have long borne, insolence never; with genius they are profusely gifted, with judgment rather sparingly; vain, lively and witty, inclined to exaggerate, studying rather enjoyment and society than neatness and economy; hence profusion precedes dilapidation, and few estates remain long unmortgaged. The English merchant and tradesman will still plod on, the latter still stand behind his counter, and maybe give his daughter 5 or 10,000 pounds. The Irish on the contrary, turns gentleman, keeps hounds, and in a few years ruins himself. Should not England learn how to govern her sister country, (without which she cannot exist), improve her morals, give her the same laws and rights, assist her manufactories, her trade, agriculture, etc, she will ever be a thorn in her side.

10

On 23rd February 1802 Louisa Slessor married General Pedro Antonio Machado Pinto de Sousa Canavaro, Baron Vila Pouca de Aguiar and Arcossa. The Slessor family's reaction to this eligible and prolific marriage, from which many distinguished scions in nineteenth and twentieth century Portugal are descended, was surprising. Harriot seems already to have dreaded the prospect of this marriage at the time of her husband's death.

HS   After this severe loss I had little satisfaction, with the fear of an event that did take place too soon for my happiness, Louisa's marriage. You will know my opinion on this subject, which can never alter. By such a marriage she has given up her family, and I have lost a daughter, that was once perhaps too great a favourite.

John Henry's comment on his sister's marriage is more balanced, but he too foresaw a complete separation between Louisa and her family.

JHS Louisa was already married to a Portuguese Officer of excellent character and good family; now totally alienated from her family and relations. May she be happy is my fervent prayer.

The only explanation of this strange hostility is a religious one. The Slessors' Huguenot heritage made them violently anti-Papist. Both Harriot's and John Henry's diaries are full of contemptuous references to what they regarded as the superstition and flummery of Roman Catholic institutions and practices. They seem to have felt that Louisa's marriage into a Catholic family must inevitably cut her off from her own relations for ever. Happily, this foreboding proved unfounded; before many years had passed, the family links were renewed, and Harriot's Portuguese and English descendants have remained in friendly contact ever since.

When John Henry returned to England after his visit to Portugal in the winter of 1800-1801, he was very uneasy at having to leave his widowed mother and his sisters in Portugal; he would have preferred them to have accompanied him back to England before the storm broke over Portugal. Spain, at French instigation, had again declared war on Portugal, and it was hard to say whether it would be more dangerous for the women of the Slessor family to remain in Portugal, threatened by invasion, or to take ship for England on a voyage menaced by French privateers. But on 27th March 1802 the Treaty of Amiens temporarily ended war between England and France, and it was safe for Harriot and her two younger daughters to take ship for England. One of those daughters, Sophia, was soon to follow her elder sister into matrimony. John Henry ended the family entries in his 1802 diary with news of her engagement.

JHS Sophia the youngest was about to enter the married state, having formed an attachment to Mr J Walsh, whose family I was well acquainted with in Ireland.

The seventeen-year-old Sophia's fiancé was James Walsh, of an Irish family from Stedalt, near Balbriggan, whose ancestors were said to have originated in Brittany, and to have followed Henry II to Ireland and Richard Coeur de Lion on his crusade. But unlike the elder branch of their family – who sided with the Jacobites and emigrated to France in 1682 – the Walshes of Stedalt stayed in Ireland and became Protestants. James Walsh met Sophia Slessor when he went to Portugal for his health, as so many of his compatriots then did; Lisbon and Cintra were full of English invalids, many of them consumptive. James and Sophia were married on 5th November 1803, and Harriot and the young couple set up house together on their return to Portugal. Sophia rapidly produced three sons, William Henry in 1804, John in 1806, Henry George in 1807, outdoing her elder sister Louisa, whose two elder sons, Joao and Frank, were born in 1804 and 1807. (The constant reappearance in successive generations of the Slessor family of the Christian names John, William and Henry must have made for a good deal of confusion.) The Walshes and their children were from now on to be at the centre of Harriot's life and of her diary about it. Everybody loved Sophia Walsh, from her childhood when her father called her 'the prettiest engaging little girl that can be' to her later years in France when she was described as affectionate and 'exquisitely affable', very fond of children, charitable to the poor and, in spite of her constant Anglican faith, loved and sought after by all the Catholic gentry of the neighbourhood. James Walsh was a less open character; in later life he was described as having 'the icy manner and rigid temper of the typical Puritan', but in his early married years in Portugal he seemed, at least in the eyes of his mother-in-law, to have a faintly ridiculous dexterity in avoiding danger and pursuing the main chance.

11

Harriot and her daughters Harriot Amelia and Sophia had spent the winter of 1802-3 in Bath, in the company of Harriot's sister Louisa Girardot and their cousins, John André's three middle-aged sisters (their younger brother, Sir William André died in Hampshire that autumn). For part of her time in Bath, Harriot had the happiness of being joined by two of her sons. John Henry came over from Ireland after his summer of visits there, and Henry was on leave from his frigate. He was still only twenty, but he had already seen much more of the world and the war than his elder brother John Henry had, and he had some exciting adventures to describe to the family whom he had not seen for five years.

When Henry was six, he was left behind in San Pedro with his father and sisters while his mother took John Henry and William to school in England. His indulgent father described him in letters to his wife as 'a fine stout boy' with a considerable talent for drawing, but his mother, in the record of his life which she sadly compiled, draws a less hearty picture.

HS Henry even from childhood had a something in his nature that endeared him to all; that gained him friends and the good will of everyone. Tho' not a lively child, nor in learning, as a youth, did he show much quickness; rather the contrary; we had a few battles on that score. Yet he had a steadiness in his nature, and way of settling points that interested him in a manner that gave no bad judgement for future good sense; and to tell you the truth, I flatter'd myself that tho' he might not turn out a great scholar, the many amiable qualities that were developing in him, might serve him to better purpose. It is certain that my ardent wishes were fully gratified, for this dear son did me honour . . . The expressive, rather melancholy character of his countenance made it impossible not to take an interest in a youth whose good qualities were painted in every feature. He was gentle, affectionate, full of sensibility, but without weakness; for he was brave – if it is allowed the expression – almost to excess. The school he was nurtured in from a boy, gave him the example, and he caught the flavour with all the ardour of youth. Altho' I have said so much in his favour, it is not to be supposed that he had not his faults. There is not such a thing in nature as all perfection. The few fleeting months that I enjoyed in his company left but good impression. 'Twas all I knew of him from the time he left me to go to school. A good report of him I ever had. I will observe one thing, that as a boy he was by nature shy and reserved, and I believe, that when he attained to manhood he retained somewhat of that disposition, and likely did not cast off that reserve till he was sure of the persons he had to deal with.

In 1792, when he was ten, his father took him to England and left him at a small school in Devonshire. Later he was moved to Peterborough, to Canon Freeman who had tutored John Henry and William. By 1796 his parents were already concerned about his future career. They had hoped to get him into the Navy, through the influence of John Slessor's friend General Edward Smith and his nephew Admiral Sir Sidney Smith, but that year Sidney Smith was captured at sea by the French and imprisoned in the Temple in Paris, where he was to remain till he escaped two years later. On 24th June 1796 John Slessor wrote:

JS I have not heard from General Smith. He must be in great anxiety for poor Sir Sidney, and so am I till I hear what has been his fate. But for his misfortune, Henry would probably have been at sea with him by this time.

Although the powerful influence of the Smith family was not available to launch Henry's career, he got into the Navy all the same as a midshipman of fourteen, and a year later we hear of him at sea off Lisbon in a frigate commanded by Captain Wells, and doing well. 'He seems to like the life, and Capt Wells speaks much in his favour, and they seem to like each other,' reported his father. But this happy state of affairs did not last long, as Captain Wells shortly gave up his command. Harriot now takes up the tale.

HS Lord St Vincent was at Lisbon, at the time, in the Ville de Paris. Captain Wells presented Harry, before he went to England, to Lord St Vincent, who took him on board, but only for a fortnight. His Lordship said that in so large a ship Henry could not learn so well to be a good seaman, and put him into a Frigate then in the Tagus, recommending him particularly to the Captain. When he took leave of Lord St Vincent he told him that, tho' he parted with him then, he should not forget him, but ever look on him as belonging to him. Lord St Vincent declared, that in his walk of life, he had not seen a more promising youth.

At this time Henry paid us a visit in Porto. His stay was short. Even so he succeeded in persuading his Father to get him exchanged, from the Frigate he was serving in, to serve under Sir Sidney Smith. He knew that his Father had a promise from Sir Sidney that, if he should ever have a son he wished to be in the Navy, to send him to him, and he would accept him. I own we should not so easily have listen'd to what might be called the fancies of a boy. He said, his Captain might be a good seaman, and might be master of his profession, but that he had nothing of the gentleman in him, and that he hardly knew how to write, and was very severe and rough with his Officers, as well as often abusive to them; that he was equally savage with his messmates the Midshipmen. We asked him if he had any complaint against the Captain as to himself. His answer was no and added, that he was aware, that he was acting contrary to what was right in asking the favour of his Father, but that he could not bear to see his companions treated for ever with such harsh language. Should his turn come, he could not answer how he might behave, and what command he might have over himself. He said, he well knew the consequences of an improper reply to his Captain; therefore requested his Father to grant his request, which he did, by giving him a letter to Sir Sidney Smith. This Henry delivered on his arrival in England, and was received most kindly by Sir S.S. Before he opened the letter, he said he guessed at the contents of it; accepted him as a Midshipman and set him down in his books.

Henry was delighted at the idea of being accepted by a Commander even at that early age he had the highest opinion of, and his likewise looking upon him as a friend of his father's was a great consideration for him. It was necessary to explain to Lord St Vincent the reasons for such conduct in your father. Tho' we could not but admire that kind of spirit, and such sentiments in Henry, yet he was much too young to be allowed to judge for himself. Your father's plea with his Lordship was, that the Frigate Henry was in, as soon as they arrived in England, was to be put into dock for repairs, (which was the case), and that he might not remain idle for some months he had availed himself of an old offer of Sir Sidney Smith's, etc. We feared the answer, as certainly Lord St Vincent could not be pleased. It was a short one. His Lordship expressed in strong terms his disapprobation at the very ill-judged step we had taken by removing Henry from the Frigate he had placed him in, Notwithstanding he declared that we might on any future occasion depend on his being ready to use his interest for his advancement in his profession. Here was a little reproof, but at the same time much satisfaction to reflect that our young Midshipman might look upon Lord St Vincent as no trifling friend and patron, and he ever proved a steady one. Henry delighted to be placed as he wished. It made us happy to see him so. We only looked forward to an increase of content in the future brave conduct of this dear son, not venturing a thought to intrude, how many are the dangers that a military life is exposed to, more particularly so the Navy.

When he was in Porto with us, Henry was only 14 years old. Glory was his theme. From that time till the year 1803, we never met, when it was in England at Bath.

Henry's sceptical elder brother's comment in his diary on the affair of the brutal frigate captain was:

JHS Henry must get over the drudgery of a midshipman's life before he can come into play.

Henry's posting to HMS *Tigre* under Admiral Sir Sidney Smith did indeed bring his capacity into play, though he was still to remain a midshipman for some years. At first, his shyness and reserve stood in his way, as his mother reported.

HS Henry talked little. On his first serving with Sir Sidney Smith, Sir Sidney complained to your Father that he could not get acquainted at all with him; he was so silent. Those silent fits wore off as he grew older, and Sir Sidney then declared that he was just the kind of young man he would wish to have to do with.

Soon Henry was involved in stirring events which strengthened and matured his character. In 1798 the 80-gun HMS *Tigre*, with Sidney Smith in command, was ordered to the Mediterranean. Sidney Smith, though nominally under the command of Lord St Vincent, was appointed Joint Minister Plenipotentiary, with his brother Spencer Smith, to the Court of the Ottoman Emperor at Constantinople, and regarded himself as having a free hand in the Eastern Mediterranean. Napoleon had subjugated Egypt, but had been locked up there with his army by Nelson's naval victory at the Battle of the Nile in 1798. Napoleon turned his attention to Palestine, capturing Gaza and Jaffa. In March 1799 he called on the Turkish Governor of St Jean d'Acre to surrender. Sidney Smith meanwhile had taken the *Tigre* to Constantinople, and signed a treaty with the Turkish Government. Now when St Jean d'Acre was threatened by Napoleon's siege, Sidney Smith rushed keenly to the rescue.

The raising of the siege of St Jean d'Acre was a spectacular success against Napoleon, as Sir Sidney Smith never allowed anyone to forget. Sixteen years later at the Congress of Vienna, he was still boring everyone with his lengthy boasts about his exploits at St Jean d'Acre, causing the sharp-tongued old Prince de Ligne to nickname him 'Long Acre'. The exploit had made him a hero to the British public at the time; he was one of those war-time commanders who are more admired by the general public than they are by their own colleagues. Napoleon and his forces appeared before the town on 17th March, and for two months they made repeated assaults on the town and the Turkish garrison. Smith, who sailed from Alexandria on 3rd March in the *Tigre*, accompanied by HMS *Theseus*, captured at sea the French gun-boats, artillery and siege train which Napoleon had destined for the siege. Anchoring off Acre, Smith used the captured gun-boats to pour a devastating fire against the French besiegers,

while further out to sea the *Tigre* and the *Theseus* pounded the French positions
with their heavy guns. Midshipmen from the *Tigre* were in charge of the gun-
boats, whose crews, even after many days of incessant rowing and firing,
refused to be relieved. Parties from the ship, including midshipmen, were also
landed to help hold the town's breached defences and repel French assaults.
Faced with this ferocious resistance, and with the arrival of Turkish reinforcements, Napoleon – after one more determined attack on the town – abandoned
the siege on 20th May and withdrew.

Henry Slessor was in the thick of it, as he was able proudly to tell his family
when they at last met again, three years later.

HS   He had much to relate, having been in constant active service. He was with
     Sir S. Smith at the taking of St Jean d'Acre. On that occasion the Midship-
     men had their command of gun-boats, and were exposed to many a shot; at
     times balls on all sides of him flying about, and even into the boat. But his
     time was not yet come, and no harm came to him.

Later, while still serving in the *Tigre*, he survived another alarming adventure.

HS   On another occasion Sir Sidney gave Henry the command of an insignifi-
     cant prize. In this small vessel, in a violent storm, he and his brave crew
     were thrown on the coast of Barbary. The vessel was dashed to pieces, but
     no lives were lost. They had no sooner got clear of the raging sea, and
     escaped a watery death than they were beset by the natives. Henry under-
     stood enough of their language to find out their intention was nothing less
     than to murder them all, taking them for Frenchmen. He made out as well
     as he could his pathetic tale to move them to compassion; told them they
     were their good friends, Englishmen, and not French. This alone had so
     good an effect, that instead of effecting their first cruel intentions, they left
     them, but not till they had put them into a perfect state of nature; and in
     this state Henry and his poor fellow-sufferers had to walk some miles thro'
     burning sand, and an intensely hot sun. At length they arrived at a Turkish
     town nearly exhausted, and met with kind treatment and clothing, such as
     they were. Even so, poor Henry was most thankful. They remained with
     these people, till they had an opportunity of getting out to sea. When they
     did, they were buffeting the waves many days before the Admiral's ship
     appeared to their longing eyes. What joy this was, to Henry and his
     handful of men, when they found themselves once more on board, and
     received with every mark of kindness from Sir Sidney, and attention to the
     miserable state in every respect in which they appeared. Henry soon
     thought no more of dangers passed, in the true style of a seaman.

The *Tigre* remained in the Eastern Mediterranean for two years, taking part in the Turkish landing at Aboukir Bay, and supporting the British forces under General Abercromby which defeated the French in Egypt in 1801, and forced them to evacuate Egypt. In February 1802 when John Henry was in Gibraltar, having been halted *en route* to Egypt by the news of Abercromby's victory, he thought of going to Malta to see Henry, whom he believed to be there at that moment. But the project came to nothing, and he was not to see Henry till he returned to England after his years in the Mediterreanean. His return coincided with the arrival from Portugal of Harriot and her daughters, but it was some months before they could meet.

HS In the year 1803 Sir Sidney Smith was at home in England on account of bad health. Henry arrived there just before we did, in the same year, and went to pay his respects to his patron. His Lordship received him with his usual kindness, shook him by the hand, and asked him what he wanted with him. After paying the proper compliments, he told Lord St Vincent that he was idling at home, which was never his wish to be, and wish'd to avail himself of his Lordship's goodness to him, and entreated to be sent to sea. Lord St Vincent asked him if he had not almost completed his time as Midshipman. He said he wanted three months. 'Then go your ways', – and named the Frigate he might go on board, that was ready to sail. Henry ventured to give a hint if he could be allowed only a few days, just to see his Mother and sisters, that he was hourly expecting from abroad. Lord St Vincent seemed amused at the idea, and told him: 'Never mind your Mother and sisters. Put off seeing them till you return, which you have my leave to do. Then get clear of your examination, after which come to me, and we will see what we can do for you'.

Of course after this he posted off to the Frigate, whose Captain received him mighty cool, not being known to him. He did not like to have a Midshipman put upon him, as he thought with so little ceremony. He took no notice of him, and never asked him once to dinner, during the three months. Henry was perfectly indifferent on the subject, his intention being to leave this proud gentleman as soon as the three months were elapsed. Which he did, and well for him it was, for this same Frigate was ship-wrecked shortly, it was said entirely from the obstinacy of the Captain.

At length we met in Bath, on Henry's return. You joined us. We passed some happy weeks together, which only served to endear us the more to him. I had never thought of having any of my children's pictures drawn. We seemed unanimous in wishing to have Henry's. So it was. We all attended the sittings, to see that justice was done him, and in particular our ever good and dear friends, Miss Andrés, were consulted, as being the best judges by far of the party. We little thought that a very good likeness would be all that we should ever possess of him again.

After this we soon parted. Henry was yet only a Midshipman, and of course not much troubled with cash. I gave him a bank note, which he would not accept; but as I was as positive as he was, he took it, to put an end to the contest. On the morning that he left Bath, I found on my table the bank note, with a few expressive words: – 'Henry is young; has the world before him, and must shift for himself'. Henry was of too generous a nature to be interested. His first thought was, that it would distress me, the giving him money at a time that he knew I had been obliged to lay out much money; and likewise we were on the eve of our departure for Portugal. I was vexed at his refusal, and rather reproached him for not keeping the note, in a letter to him. His answer was

'Dear Mother

Unfortunate indeed, dear beloved Mother, have I been in doing what has displeased you. But you well know my motives, which is all I can offer for a misdemeanour my conscience cannot reproach me with. I considered the step before I took it, and a certain something told me, You have already received too much from the hands of a dear and benevolent parent. Heaven bless her with happiness. You are young, and have a fair prospect of doing as well as is requisite, therefore have nothing to do but to confide in your own integrity, perseverance, and upright behaviour. Your letter was of the greatest comfort to me. It came while I was at a solitary breakfast, ruminating on past occurrences . . . How sensibly did I feel the too affectionate sentiments of such sisters and brother. 'Twas too much for my heart to bear, without paying the tribute due to the irresistible torrent of such reciprocal love. You, dear Mother, condemn it, – call it want of fortitude. I cannot agree with you in that point. Nor can I be angry with myself for giving way to it, especially when we have read of the greatest characters being susceptible to it. Enough. While I remain in town, shall be indefatigable in your service.

Adieu, dearest and most valuable of parents, to render himself worthy of whom shall ever be the first consideration of

your dutiful son H.T.S.'

Henry soon after he had undergone his examination was promoted to Lieuf't. He was beginning to be impatient, thinking that Lord St Vincent had forgot his promise; so ventured to write to him, rather in strong terms, lamenting that he should lose such flattering hopes in so kind a patron as his Lordship had been to him. Lady St Vincent answered the letter, saying he had been promoted to Lieutenant some months before the date of Henry's letter. He being at sea, by some mischance the news of his promotion had not reached him. This was the last favour he received from Lord St Vincent.

The miniature of Henry executed in Bath on this occasion still exists. It shows a shy and rather melancholy young man with black curly hair, in naval uniform. His emotional and faintly absurd letter to his mother (with whom he shared a rather histrionic style, as did William – but not John Henry) reveals a self-conscious and somehow awkward character. Henry was brave, generous, and devoted to his profession, popular with his fellow officers and highly thought of by most of his superiors; but he was also impatient, tactless and obstinate, apt to annoy as well as impress those who were trying to help him. He had little of the born survivor's resilience which carried John Henry unscathed through twenty years of war.

The two brothers did not overlap for long in Bath, but it was long enough for John Henry to carry away an affectionate impression of the younger brother whom he had not seen for more than ten years.

JHS Am happy to say that I enjoyed the society of my dear brother Henry for some days while at Bath, but he could not stay long absent from his ship. He was a fine amiable young man, and very promising officer.

12

John Henry saw his mother and sisters on board the packet at Falmouth on their return to Portugal. He had then to turn his attention to his own affairs and future, and how they would be affected by the breakdown of the brief Peace of Amiens with France.

JHS The small patrimony I inherited, added to my pay, was not sufficient to live upon with any degree of comfort in such an extravagant country as England, where it is a crime to be poor. I therefore determined to get employed again. War declared! And thus is the World to be involved in all its horrors; '*Bella, horrida bella*'. The treaty of Amiens promised no durability of peace; the sword once more drawn; adieu to all social and domestic comfort. Ambitious Bonaparte at the head of our restless neighbours the French cannot remain quiet. He has begun by detaining as prisoners all the English families, males and females. On the other hand, France complains that we have broken our faith by not giving up Malta. Thus for the pride and caprice of monarchs is the human race to butcher each other. Proud and powerful England, what will you come to at last! The community must suffer, and John Bull pay the piper; taxes, subsidies, foreign troops etc. But our little Island is tight, loyal, rich, brave and generous, the envy and admiration of other countries, although our national manners and hauteur often excite the jealousy and dislike of foreigners.

The Peace of Amiens came to an end in March 1803 because the British Government, fearing French designs on Egypt and India, had refused to evacuate Malta, essential to the defence against the French of the Mediterranean route to the East, although the terms of the treaty called for its evacuation. War was declared again between England and France, and Napoleon began assembling at Boulogne the vast 'Army of England' which was intended to be launched in a massive and decisive invasion.

In face of this threat, the British Government set about reorganising its armed forces, which were then in no state to repel a formidable invasion. On paper there were 40,000 infantry and 12,000 cavalry of the Regular Army in Britain, Ireland and the Channel Islands, but most of the efficient full-strength regiments were in Ireland, and the rest had many under-strength battalions, some of

74

them of only 400 men, and many of the men were in poor condition after years of unhealthy service in the East and West Indies. The old militia and fencible regiments had been disbanded, so there was little back-up for the Regular Army.

The Government's first measure was to recall the disbanded Militia, which by June 1803 had again been built up to over 40,000 men, most of whom had already served for nine years, earlier in the war, and were therefore experienced and efficient. To strengthen the Regular Army, an Army of Reserve Act was passed in July 1803. Under this scheme, 22,000 volunteers joined the Army of Reserve by September 1803, and with conscripts the Army of Reserve was built up to 50,000. Soldiers in the Army of Reserve were permitted to enlist for general service in the Regular Army, and the real intention of the Army of Reserve Act was that they should be formed into second battalions of regular line regiments whose second battalions had been skeleton forces or non-existent. They were trained by experienced officers and sergeants at training camps in Essex, Kent and Sussex, the most important of which was at Shorncliffe, near Hythe.

It was this procedure which gave John Henry Slessor an opportunity to return to a military career, at first only in the Army of Reserve.

JHS In October I left Bath for London . . . All is bustle. The French Ambassador has received his passports and embarked for Calais. Our Navy and Army are immediately to be augmented; the Militia called out, new loans, fresh taxes, etc. The Admiralty and Horse Guards are crowded with applicants for employment. Some of our countrymen have succeeded in escaping from France. Mr Fox has been at Paris, several times at Bonaparte's Court, evidently averse to war, which he and the Whigs think might be avoided without committing either the honour or safety of the British Empire. France had fitted out armaments which they said were for her colonies; we in confidence had reduced our War Establishment.

I now got appointed to a company in a Reserve Battn. This was supposed to be an effective way of recruiting the regiments of the line; rather a compulsory act in the first instance, whereby each county was obliged to furnish a quota of men for home service, who after a while, were permitted, with the temptation of an additional bounty, to volunteer into Regular Regiments. The consequence was that all our best men left us. Our Head Quarters (1st Battn) were at Jersey. We received men from Middlesex and I was on that duty in London for some time, after which I was ordered to superintend the embarkation of recruits at Weymouth. From hence the packets sail to Guernsey and Jersey twice a week. My time passed pleasantly enough here, altho' a dull season for a watering place. Near this is the isle or rather Peninsula of Portland, famous for building stone. A delicious little bird, called a wheatear, is caught in great numbers in

Portland. Admiral Christian's fleet, with a convoy, outward bound, suffered dreadfully by shipwreck on this coast; many ships and lives were lost.

1804. On the 21st of April I was ordered to join, and took the packet. Sailed in the evening. Next morning, after touching at Guernsey, landed at St Helier's. The regiment was quartered four miles off in wooden barracks at Grouville Bay, near Arganil Castle, from which you can distinctly see the French coast. I soon established myself, but on looking about had little reason to be satisfied; the Battalion very ineffective, and a queer set of officers; no chance of active service with such a Corps.

The Island is extremely pretty, highly cultivated and fertile; the inhabitants not very agreeable in general; few handsome women. Sometimes an English Officer marries and settles here, as living is very reasonable, being a free port. The laws are very summary; administered by the Jurats. Inhabitants apparently attached to England, but at the same time exceedingly tenacious of their rights. They are reckoned brave; can muster four Regiments of Militia. They speak bad English, and worse French. The women work a good deal out of doors, and are otherwise equally industrious. Houses bad; cattle better; cows give an abundance of rich milk; sheep small. Island divided into 12 parishes; a Church and spire to each; roads bad and narrow. The principal persons are the Duke of Bouillon and Sir John Dumaresque; a regular correspondence is carried on with the Chouans in Normandy. Climate mild; trade with Newfoundland; much cider made; Property divided, enclosed and wooded. The last time the French attempted to take Jersey, the gallant Major Pearson was killed in the square of St Helier's. We are frequently under arms all night but I apprehend no regular invasion. The Governor, Lieut-General Gordon, is in a very declining state of health.

1st Dec. I now command the Regt, but hope soon to be disbanded.

20th. Napoleon crowned Emperor; the Pope ordered to repair to Paris; and we may now, I think, expect some still more wonderful operations, at the expense of millions of money and thousands of lives, to mark the career of so wonderful a man. The French nation are blindfolded, but they like novelty in any shape.

After nearly a year in Jersey with his miscellaneous Reserve Battalion, John Henry found his way back to a more professional and worthwhile appointment in the Regular Army. He took his 'motley crew' back to England (hearing on the way through Portland of the loss of the Indiaman *Abergavenny* in Weymouth Bay, whose captain John Wordsworth, brother of the poet, went down with his ship).

JHS *1805. 14th Feb*. All Reserve Battalions are to be reduced and consolidated into three regiments.

14th March. I embarked at St Aubyn's with my motley crew, 160 men; sailed the next morning for Guernsey, but did not reach St Pierre until the morning of the 17th. Wind-bound here for four days; of course went on shore and saw the lions. Privateers fitted out from Guernsey, and much smuggling going on. A sociable place. Sir James Saumarez is the Admiral on the station, General Doyle the Governor; both popular characters. I was sorry my stay was not longer, as I had a letter to Lady Saumarez.

22nd. Got under weigh, and with much ado made Portland, the next day, when we came to an anchor. An Indiaman lost in the Bay of Weymouth; 300 souls perished.

27th. Landed at Portsmouth, thank God; made my report to General Oakes, and immediately marched to Hillsea barracks. Spithead was full of transports with troops, destination not known. My party had not taken off their clothes for 14 days. To attempt a description of Portsmouth would fill a volume. To me, altho' I had seen it before, it had no attraction; on the contrary I thought it a most unpleasant place. Being such a rendezvous for our navy, there is an amazing circulation of money; bustle eternal. A sailor full of prize money, thoughtlessly throwing it away in all directions, is more welcome than a soldier, vulgarly called a boiled lobster.

3rd April. Received a route for Sheerness, a long march; got on very well, considering all things, having only one officer to help me. Passed thro' Deptford: visited the Powder Mills; well satisfied to reach my destination, and get rid of my detachment. Sheerness is a small fortified town. The Island is famous for sheep. That most alarming epoch, when the Fleet at the Nore mutinied, fresh in everyone's recollection, cannot be looked back to without horror.

I soon got tired of an inactive life, and the monotony of a garrison town, so went up to Town on leave, attended at the Horse Guards, and in May was gazetted to a company in the 35th Regt of Foot, (General Lennox Colonel), a new Battalion just raised by volunteers from the Militia, a new system, most annoying to Colonels of Militia.

The 35th (or Sussex) Regiment of Foot, to whose second battalion John Henry was gazetted, had distinguished itself in the American war of Independence, at the Battles of Bunkers Hill and Brooklyn, had helped to recapture the Island of Dominica in the West Indies from the French in 1778, and had taken part in the disastrous British expedition to Holland in 1799, where 350 men of its first battalion were taken prisoner. In this estimable regiment John Henry, now twenty-nine and a captain, was to find his home and – apart from occasional cravings to be transferred to more spectacular theatres of war – his *raison d'être* for the rest of his working life.

JHS Joined at Winchester in June. The moment we were clothed and armed,
ordered to camp near Weymouth on King's duty. Here we dangled attendance on Royalty; passed a pleasant time; frequently at balls at the Lodge;
turned the Princesses in the dance. They in the most gracious manner did
away with the shyness one naturally felt on such an occasion. The good old
King, George III, frequently addressed himself to Officers of all ranks,
rather in a hurried tone, and would answer the question himself. Ambassadors, Ministers, and all the branches of the Royal family, with the
Household, etc, made Weymouth very gay, different indeed from when I
was first there. In October the Camp broke up. We marched back to
Winchester; then to Lewes. We have some chance of going on service
now.

18th Nov. Great rejoicings for the Battle of Trafalgar, tho' a victory dearly
purchased by the death of the immortal Nelson. His memory must ever be
dear to an Englishman. Two other great public characters died about this
time, Mr Pitt and Lord Cornwallis. A change of administration; Fox came
in. Troops sent to Hanover; most of the Line Regiments under orders for
service. Our time passed pleasantly enough at Lewes; a short distance from
London, near Brighton etc. Great changes on the Continent; the French
everywhere victorious by land; Bonaparte out-generals both Austrians and
Russians, enters Vienna. Our troops return to England; suffer by shipwreck.

The 'changes on the Continent' had been great indeed. In March 1805 the
French fleet under Admiral Villeneuve had escaped from Nelson's watch on
Toulon, made for the West Indies to destroy the British forces there but had
been chased back by Nelson. In August the Third Coalition of Russia, Austria
and Britain was formed, but in October Napoleon defeated the Austrians at the
Battle of Ulm. One day later Nelson and the British fleet vanquished the French
at the Battle of Trafalgar, and British supremacy at sea was ensured for the rest
of the war. But French supremacy on land was again demonstrated a month
later by Napoleon's defeat of the Austrians and Russians at Austerlitz. The
destruction of the French fleet at Trafalgar had nullified the threat of Napoleon's 'Army of England' at Boulogne; there would now be no sufficient French
naval force to make an invasion of England possible. The scenes of action were
to shift elsewhere, and John Henry's regiment and many others were now
poised for service overseas.

13

In April 1806 John Henry and the Second Battalion of the 35th had their orders to embark for Sicily. Since the renewal of the war in 1803 the French had re-occupied most of Italy, and by the autumn of 1805 they were threatening the Kingdom of Naples. In November 1805 British forces from Sicily under General Craig (including the First Battalion of the 35th, which was already in the Mediterranean) had, jointly with a Russian force, landed in Naples to support the Bourbon King Ferdinand IV of Naples and his dominating Hapsburg wife Maria Carolina. But in February 1806 the British withdrew to Sicily, the Russians to the Adriatic. The King and Queen of Naples fled to Palermo from the approaching French forces under Napoleon's brother Joseph Bonaparte. Naples surrendered to the French, and Joseph was made King of Naples by Napoleon. By May 1806, when John Henry's convoy was in the Atlantic *en route* for Sicily, French forces under General Reynier had occupied the Calabrian coast opposite Sicily, confronting the British army which, with the agreement of the Neapolitan Court at Palermo, was now encamped and fortified on the other side of the Straits of Messina.

Major General Sir John Stuart now commanded the British army in Sicily, succeeding the seriously ill General Craig. The Commander in Chief of the British Navy in the Mediterranean was Admiral Collingwood, but in April the flamboyant Admiral Sir Sidney Smith, the deliverer of St Jean d'Acre (as he never tired of telling anyone who would listen) had been given command of the naval forces in the Central Mediterranean. His brief was to prevent a French invasion of Sicily, but that was not how he saw his mission; he had selected a more romantic role. Spurred on by Queen Maria Carolina, who was burning to recover her lost Neapolitan kingdom, Sidney Smith spent his time cruising up and down the Calabrian coast, attacking French batteries and landing arms and supplies to the Calabrian guerrillas, or 'Masse', who were more likely to use them for settling old scores between themselves than against the French. Smith's showing-off activities were regarded with exasperation by the British generals in Sicily under whose command John Henry was shortly to be. His diary logs the voyage out from Portsmouth.

JHS *April*. Under orders for embarkation. The Regt marched for Portsmouth; route Brighton, Arundel, Chichester, etc. Quartered at Cumberland Fort; 300 convicts are generally kept at work here.

May. Embarked for the Mediterranean. Adieu old England once more. The 21st, 27th, 31st also embarked.

12th. Put into Falmouth by contrary winds.

14th. Sailed. Gentle breezes; went about five knots. We have an excellent transport, and pleasant lot of officers. Major Moore commands. A ship full of men presents a curious scene, and when obliged at all hours in a crowded cabin to associate with the same people, every individual character is soon developed.

21st. Off the coast of Portugal; got some fresh fish from a Viana boat.

30th. Came to anchor in the Bay of Gibraltar. Nothing very new at the Rock. A very good understanding exists between the Governor and the Spaniards. We replenished our stock. I frequently went on shore, but the Devil's Tongue, St Michael's Cave etc were no novelty to me.

6th June. The fleet got under weigh with a fair breeze, and cleared the Rock.

7th. Becalmed: lowered a boat, and exercised ourselves rowing: bought a turtle from a Maltese Galliot: the small pox on board: committed a man to the deep. The weather now became exceedingly warm, and we experienced constant calms, and light breezes. Our fresh provisions getting low: every precaution taken to keep the ship healthy: no man allowed to sleep in the sun or at night on deck, on account of the dew. 'Tis customary to divide the troops into three watches, one of which at night is always on deck: in the day time generally all hands: bedding brought up and scrubbing etc going on between decks. In calm weather swimming was allowed and a boat out to catch turtle, which afforded us much amusement and variety at the Mess table.

30th. Another man died.

9th July. Made Sardinia.

10th. A fair breeze.

They were still at sea, becalmed between Gibraltar and Sardinia, when the British army of Sicily briefly regained the offensive against the French. General Stuart landed a force on the Calabrian coast and on 4th July won a pitched battle against the French under General Reynier on the plateau of Maida. A light company of the 35th First Battalion took part in the battle, its 'flankers' successfully driving back the French at the height of the action. At the end of July Stuart and his army returned to Sicily, having achieved the object of his campaign by capturing all the batteries and supplies assembled in Calabria by the French for the invasion of Sicily.

John Henry was much disappointed that he just missed the chance of taking part in this brilliant feat, in which the First Battalion of his regiment had distinguished itself. It was eight days after the Battle of Maida that his convoy finally reached Palermo, after a voyage of two months from Falmouth.

JHS *12th July*. At anchor in the Bay of Palermo, to our great joy, after so tedious a voyage, but mortified at not having shared the laurels of the glorious Battle of Maida, under Sir John Stuart. Part of the 1st Battn were present. This is a beautiful city: streets and buildings regular, full of people, with an air of affluence and gaiety. The fête of Santa Rosalia is now celebrating, so that we are lucky in witnessing so novel a scene. The Royal Family show much attention to the English army: many Officers introduced at Court. The King is but a poor creature: the Queen appears to hold the reins. We could only find one Hotel and that very indifferent. The approaches to the city are fine, the four gates splendid. The Marina is a delightful walk, crowded all night with carriages and company: fireworks beautiful. The horse races were ridiculous, for there were no riders, but trained to gallop at full speed thro' a line of people in a long street having bladders knocking against their sides, with a sharp spur fastened to them, so that the faster they galloped, the harder the horses are spurred. Flora gardens are laid out with great taste, and well illuminated, which had at night a brilliant effect. The Madre Chiesa is a fine Gothic building. Rode out to Monreale: saw a handsome rich Church, with some valuable paintings: also visited the famous Capuchin Convent, remarkable for the cemetery, subterraneous apartments with large galleries, hollow places in the sides of the walls. These are occupied by dead bodies embalmed, set upright, several hundreds, dressed up in the clothes they wore when they were alive: the greater part in admirable preservation, but those in part decomposed a disgusting memento of our frailty. We regretted leaving Palermo. I understood but little Italian, but there was much fascination in the novelty of all we saw.

18th. Sailed for Messina. Passed near the Lipari Islands, and as a volcano is a rare and novel sight, all hands were on deck to see Stromboli, a Lighthouse (if you may so call it) placed by nature in these seas as a warning to mariners. It is an isolated rock, with liquid fire constantly pouring down its sides, boldly rising from the bosom of the sea. The spectacle is striking.

19th. Passed thro' the Straits or Faro of Messina, the ancient Scylla and Charybdis.

20th. Alongside the Marino of Messina, a beautiful harbour, depth of water sufficient for Men of War to make their cables fast to the shore, altho' 'tis often difficult from the currents to enter it; but when once in this fine bason, you are perfectly safe. The situation of this city is indeed beautiful, the views from the hills in the vicinity enchanting: picturesque ravines and fumaries, rich groves of orange, lemon and olive trees. It extends along the sea, and up to the base of the mountains. Vines hang in tangled festoons from tree to tree: fields and gardens luxuriantly rich in fruit and vegetables. From the Convent of Saint Gregorio the view is splendid. You look over the whole extent of the Straits and see the wild and rugged coast of Calabria to great distance. The Marina is a magnificent drive, but still in a deplorable state of dilapidation, the effects of the earthquake of 1743. But there is a new plan of rebuilding it, which they say will soon be entered upon. Still what security can there be against another similar catastrophe?

Our troops are returning from Calabria. The Division of the British Army who beat a superior French force at Maida have covered themselves with glory; a great many sick.

26th. The Light Companies (I from the beginning had the Light Company of the 2nd Battn) ordered to land. The Battalion also ordered to disembark and march to Milazzo, 25 miles. We went to Contessa, 3 miles off, where was formed a Light Battalion from different Regiments under the command of Colonel Kempt. The weather was now intensely hot; no moving out in the middle of the day, particularly when the Siroc blows. Providentially there is always ice to be had, which is a great luxury, and very conducive to health. Provisions are reasonable: beef and mutton not in general good: fruit and vegetables abundant: wine very cheap: the Sicilian cooking much in the style of the Portuguese, with oil and garlic. As far as I have seen of the inhabitants, they are dirty, immoral and effeminate, irreligiously religious, not scrupulously honest, bad sailors and worse soldiers. Assassinations are common, but less so since the arrival of the English. Our brave tars suffered much at first, owing to their surly behaviour and drunkenness.

The British forces on the east coast of Sicily had now been built up to a sizable army, reinforced by the four battalions of infantry, the 35th, 21st, 27th and 31st, 2,400 strong in all, who had just arrived at Messina from England. The military historian Sir John Fortescue says slightingly that the second battalion of the 35th was 'very weak and composed of the indifferent material which had been collected under the Army of Reserve Act'. Although this does to some extent apply to John Henry, he would certainly have resented such an aspersion. He felt that he had returned to his proper sphere. After the years of unemployment, and then of training raw recruits in dull garrison towns, he was back in a theatre of war among professional soldiers, and he soon found congenial friends. His mind was expanding as he experienced this new world of colour and brilliance. Like the many other foreign soldiers – Greek, Roman, Byzantine, Arab, Norman, Angevin, Spanish – who had occupied Sicily over the last two thousand years, he was enthralled by the beauty, fertility and strangeness of the island, by its volcanoes and hanging vines, its lemon groves and blue mountains and shimmering seas. He was an ardent sight-seer, though not a very cultivated one; he called the wonderful Monreale mosaics 'pictures', and – like so many other tourists in Palermo – he gave more time and attention to the grisly mummies in the Capuchin catacombs than to all the glories of the

Martorana and the Palatine Chapel. He was more interested in natural wonders and in local customs and characteristics, observant but making up his mind with a too rapid intolerance about the Sicilian way of life. He was eager to explore the island, and was soon setting off to Taormina and Mount Etna.

JHS *1st Oct.* I obtained leave to visit Mt Etna. We made a party of five: hired mules for the occasion. The roads in this country are only carriageable in and about the large towns: litters or mules are generally used to go a journey: women ride astride. To an observant and classic traveller food for the mind is to be had in all parts of Sicily, but I leave all learned and flowing descriptions to wiser heads. The sea coast is rich and beautiful; the sides of the mountains highly luxuriant and cultivated: corn, wine, oil, vegetables, fruit in abundance: on the summits the Churches, villages and Convents afford a picturesque and romantic appearance. We reached Taormina to dinner, and were well entertained at the Mess of the 8th Regt quartered there. The ascent to this ancient City is rather difficult.

2nd. Walked about: saw the Amphitheatre, ancient walls, convents etc; then proceeded on our journey thro' Giodini to Catania, where we found a decent Inn. This is a beautiful City, and as often as an earthquake destroys it, or an eruption of Etna lays it waste, as quickly is it rebuilt, and with additional elegance. Its situation is immediately, I must say, at the foot of this great volcano. We got a profusion of dishes for supper, then retired to clean beds, without curtains.

3rd. Visited the Prince of Biscari's Museum, valuable from the many antiques. The Convent of Benedictine Monks is an immense building: a fine organ, some good paintings, and sumptuous apartments, wealthy, but in an unfinished state. What good a set of lazy Friars do, I am at a loss to conjecture. They were exceedingly polite, shewed us their museum, gardens etc. The inhabitants tell you that Catania is one of the most ancient Cities in the World, and of course affords many remains and relics of antiquity. They place much superstitious credulity in their tutelar Saint Agatha. There is no harbour but for boats: a quantity of amber, jet and coral was offered for sale.

4th. This morning felt a slight shock of Earthquake. We now prepared to ascend the Mountain, providing ourselves with warm clothing, eatables and spirits, both of which are indispensably necessary. There are three distinct regions, *La regione culta*, or fertile region, *La regione sylvosa* or woody region, *La regione deserta*, or barren region. Our first stage was to Nicolosi, a dreadful bad road; the heat quite oppressive. But as we ascended to the woody region, the air became cooler and refreshing. The appearance of these parts is very fine, awfully so, for many places or gulphs that once vomited fire are now in a luxuriant state of vegetation, producing fruit, flowers etc. About four o'clock in the evening we halted in a thick part of the wood at a shed. Our first care was to forage for wood and make a fire, which was quickly done. Our guide and muleteers being well accustomed to these expeditions are very expert. Our mules were picketed and fed, a good fire kindled, and provisions spread out. We brought even water with us. Close by was a large Cave, called Spelanca dei Capri. We certainly cut a very grotesque appearance, rather a savage one, as the night approached; collected plenty of leaves for bedding; wrapped ourselves well up in cloaks, and lay down to sleep.

5th. Three hours before day-light our Cyclops roused up all hands. The grand object is to reach the summit before the sun rises. Our guide led us through paths where it appeared that no human foot had ever trod; now through gloomy forests of majestic oak; at other times over lava and precipices that you appreciated a false step of the trusty mule will launch you into eternity. At intervals heard the awful roaring of the Mountain, enough to deter one from prosecuting the expedition. The cold now became excessive, but with the aid of our flasks, we arrived safe at a pile of stones, called the Philosopher's Tower, some time before the sun rose. The cold was intense; brandy flasks hugged repeatedly. Here is the foot of the great crater of Etna, and you ride no further. It is impossible to describe or picture the glorious, the magnificent scene that opens to the view as the sun rises. The morning by degrees advancing, dispels darkness and shades. The heavens brighten; the stars disappear; the dark and black forests gradually, and with varying tints, display their form and colours, the volcano at times howling and roaring with terrific grandeur, the glorious luminary rising from the Ocean. You look down upon the whole of Sicily, Calabria and the neighbouring Isles. All appears sublime enchantment, as if you were removed from the Earth.

We now walked up to the edge of the crater, which they tell you is three miles in circumference. As you pass the dense lava, you traverse many little eruptions of smoke. One of our party could not get on, and it was with difficulty the guide could be persuaded to ascend as far as the brink. However some of us went to the very verge. At the moment the Mountain was roaring hellishly and vomiting fire and stones, which rose perpendicularly and fell in of course again. If Hell can be pictured on Earth, here you must see it. We were glad to get down again, and after contemplating for some time this magic sight, began our descent and returned to Catania, where we arrived highly gratified and astonished in the evening, safe and sound, but much fagged.

6th. Visited the bay of Ulysses etc: went in the evening to a *conversazione*. I now began to pick up a little Italian.

7th. We were very politely treated at Catania, and fared well. Started this morning for our quarters, but took a different route, in order to see a famous chestnut tree, called the Castagna de Cente Cavalli, but was much disappointed. The trunk is spacious and appeared to be of more than one tree; the branches shade over a great deal of ground. They tell you it once held or sheltered 100 horses. Some of the trees are of a noble size and we passed thro' forests growing out of the lava.

9th. Reached Contessa. I soon got acquainted with some Sicilian families. They are animated in their manners and conversation, fond of equipages and horses, musical, addicted to gambling, but effeminate and revengeful in general: by no means tidy: speak a corrupt Italian: indifferent troops: sailors rather better. About here they appear to be well affected to the English. The country eat up with priests and monks.

Changes were taking place in the army command in Sicily. General Fox, brother of Charles James Fox who was then Prime Minister but was to die in September, arrived to take over as Commander in Chief and as Minister to the Neapolitan Court at Palermo. General Stuart went home in a huff at being superseded after his gallant exploit at Maida. General Sir John Moore was appointed second in command to Fox, whom he dominated by his quietly forceful advice. Moore decided to establish the main camp for the British forces at Milazzo, twenty-three miles from Messina, where only a garrison would be left. John Henry, who had enjoyed his quarters at Contessa, was not enthusiastic about this new plan.

JHS General Fox arrived about this time and took the command. Sir John Stuart went home. Our time passed at Contessa pleasantly enough.

1st Nov. Sir John Moore is arrived. A new General as a matter of course always introduces some new order of things, and finds fault with the last. We were now annoyed with marches, new steps etc.

20th. Marched to Milazzo, in order to save Government money, I suppose, as also to accustom the troops to bivouac or build their own barracks, (the idea taken from the French). Whole Regiments were employed erecting huts; parties sent to the Mountains in order to fell trees, etc: while others, knee-deep, cut rushes. We had a great deal of wet weather, so that these duties were very harassing. The Light Battalion was cantoned in the neighbouring village, called Pozzo de Gotto, where we formed a tolerable good Mess. Excellent shooting, and a pleasant set of Officers, so that notwithstanding, the time passed pleasantly.

14

John Henry's autumn in Sicily did not all pass so pleasantly. His diary records:

JHS In September I received the melancholy tidings of the untimely fate of my dear and valued brother Henry.

Henry had moved to the Mediterranean almost at the same time as John Henry had. In January 1806 Sidney Smith, now a Rear-Admiral, had been given a detached command in the Mediterranean, and had hoisted his flag in the 80-gun ship of the line, HMS *Pompée*. This event was to decide Henry Slessor's fate, as Harriot records:

HS On Sir Sidney recovering his health he was appointed to the *Pompée*. He had the liberty of naming his officers. Those that had served under Sir Sidney flock'd to him, Henry among the number. On this occasion he expressed himself in a letter to me of the highest content, at being once more under the command of a person that he ever thought preferable to any other.

To join the *Pompée*, he left a Captain with whom he was very happy, and would willingly have remained with, (I will add) but for such infatuation. It is almost enough to convert the least bigoted into predestination. Every part of Henry's conduct seemed to be actuated with the probable idea of what might be his fate. Therefore he left nothing to be settled before he went on board the *Pompée*. He mentioned in his letter, that 'he had been busy with Pinkett; had settled all his worldly affairs, for fear of accidents, and have completely cleared up all accounts, and laid everything upon a fair scale previous to going aboard; what every young man ought to do, and what I am confident of having done; for to my knowledge I do not owe a farthing to any man, and that is a great comfort'.

Such sentiments in so young a man are worthy of imitation. I fondly looked forward to a future happy meeting, but instead of that, death put an end to his fair prospects.

Just before he joined the *Pompée*, Henry wrote what was to be his last letter to his eldest brother.

HS Dear brother John

I have been most anxiously expecting you in this part of the World, but from your long delay have concluded that you could not get sufficient leave of absence to make the excursion you had in your last letter given me reason to expect. I myself propose asking a fortnight's leave after the service now in contemplation, and before I join the *Pompée*, and also provided the said service does not leave me a head shorter. But this is the fortune of war, the possibility of which persons of the bravest cast too must silently reflect upon before they enter into action; and when there, with shot flying overhead, that thought must not be admitted. I believe I shall be among the thick of it, Sir S. Smith having appropriated a rowing Gunboat to my command. This being the case and our departure from the Downs being momentarily expected, I shall defer, of course, sending you this letter until the result of the service may be known, and my safety. Now I think it time for me to be serious, and think of making a few arrangements before I proceed in a service that may prove desperate and fatal to many. Consequently everyone in the same situation, having relations he tenderly loves, should think of them in his last moments, and his own last letter be the account of such an event; which must certainly be a more satisfactory manner of disclosing his fate to his relations than by the hand of a stranger, or by the public papers. If I fall, 'tis God's will; my time is come, and with a conscience that cannot accuse me of ever having knowingly done a dishonorable or wicked act. Commend me, dearest brother, to my excellent Mother, and Sisters, and brother, and all my other relations. Some, I believe, had a regard for me, and all persons who had not, I most heartily forgive.

My small property in this world I leave all to my Mother that she dispose of hereafter as her judgement may direct. Consequently I must beg of you this my last request, you will settle these affairs according to my wish. To the Neaves you will most gratefully remember me, telling them that their goodness to me had made too strong an impression in my breast to be forgotten in my last moments. To them I am indebted for the greater share of happiness in England, and when so distant from the best of parents. To my Aunts Girardot and Fraser in the like manner. To you, dear brother, I leave the two cases of books that contain the English Poets, given to me by those worthy persons and true friends, the Andrés. This momento is the only one in my possession worthy your acceptance. I beg you will receive it, as the last testimony of my love and esteem for the best of brothers.

Henry presumably left this letter with his man of business, to be delivered to John Henry in the event of his death. The two cases of books which he left to his brother were a handsome set of 108 volumes of Bell's edition of *The Poets of Great Britain, Complete from Chaucer to Churchill*, published in 1777. They had originally belonged to the well-read Major André; on his death, they went to his siblings with the rest of his property, and his sisters gave them to Henry Slessor. They are still in the possession of John Henry's great-great-grandson. Major André simply wrote 'J.L. André' on the end-paper of each volume. To this, Henry added:

> By whose worthy and much esteemed Sisters, these Books were to me given, and are deemed of inestimable value
>
> H. Slessor

Below this, in every single one of the 108 volumes, John Henry Slessor laboriously wrote

> By my ever to be lamented Brother these books were to me given, and their value enhanced as having once been his property. He fell when Lieutenant on board Sir Sidney Smith's ship the *Pompée* in the flower of youth, an untimely sacrifice in his country's cause, a rising ornament to his profession, brave, mild and affectionate, beloved and esteemed by all who knew him.
>
> John Slessor

The *Pompée* sailed for Cadiz, where Smith was instructed by Admiral Collingwood, Naval Commander in Chief in the Mediterranean, to proceed to Palermo to secure Sicily against the threatened French invasion. The *Pompée* arrived at Palermo on 21st April, and Sidney Smith was soon, in collusion with Queen Maria Carolina, planning a far more active role, to support guerilla activity against the occupying French army in the Kingdom of Naples, with a view of regaining it for its Bourbon King and Queen. The *Pompée* landed supplies for the town of Gaeta, which under the Prince of Hesse was holding out against the French, and in May took part in the action which temporarily ejected the French from Capri. Sidney Smith then cruised up and down the Calabrian coast, attacking French batteries and landing arms for the guerrillas. At intervals he reappeared at Palermo or Messina, but his movements were so erratic that the Army Command at Messina never knew where he was. Just after the British victory at Maida, Sidney Smith, who had been at Palermo intriguing with the Neapolitan Court, unexpectedly turned up in the *Pompée* in the Gulf of St Eufemia, and that evening General Stuart, the victor of Maida, dined with Smith on board the *Pompée*, as did Henry Bunbury, who was on the staff at Messina and who, many years later, wrote the brilliantly readable *Some Passages in the Great War with France, 1799-1810*. Bunbury's description of the dinner on board the *Pompée* that night is unforgettable. Sir John Stuart, who might have been expected to be congratulated on his fine victory earlier in the day, was instead made to listen to Smith 'treating us, as was his usual custom, to the whole history of the Siege of Acre', and the evening ended by Smith 'taking one of the many shawls with which his cabin was hung, and instructing Sir John in the art of wreathing it, and putting on the turban after the fashion of the most refined Turkish ladies'.

Smith did, however, promise Stuart that next day he would sail north to aid in the defence of Gaeta. Instead, he sailed south, achieving cheap successes by firing on isolated French batteries and detachments which Stuart's forces could much more easily mop up from the landward side.

It is not surprising that Smith was not much loved by the Army Command at Messina, who wanted the Navy to concentrate on its proper and appointed task of guarding Sicily from invasion, and not to waste men and supplies on showy amphibian attacks on the Calabrian coast. They had no belief in the usefulness of arming the Calabrian guerrillas, who were simply bandits fighting among themselves and terrorising their compatriots rather than the French. Sidney Smith, the Army leaders felt, had been flattered into this mistaken and mischievous policy by the treacherous and malign Queen Maria Carolina. The verdicts on Sidney Smith, both of his army contemporaries and of later military historians, are excoriating. 'He could talk of no subject but himself; he worked chiefly if not entirely for his own hand and his own distinction; he would flaunt himself like a peacock in any company; he had a pestilent love of displaying his name and exploits in the newspapers; and, worst of all, he was most docile even to servility when concerned with crowned heads. In a word, he was utterly unfit for supreme command,' wrote Sir John Fortescue. Sir John Moore bitterly criticised Smith's activities with the Calabrian guerrillas. 'In his imagination he is directing the operation of armies, but in reality he is only encouraging murder and rapine, and keeping up among that unhappy people, whom we have no intention to support, a spirit of revolt which will bring upon them the more severe vengeance of the French Government.' Most glacially deadly of all, because it acknowledged Sidney Smith's good qualities, but showed how inadequate they were to offset his failings, was Bunbury's portrait: 'an enthusiast, always panting for distinction; restlessly active, but desultory in his views; extravagantly vain; daring, quick-sighted, and fertile in those resources which benefit a partisan leader; but he possessed no great depth of judgement, nor any fixity of purpose, save that of persuading mankind, as he was fully persuaded himself, that Sidney Smith was the most brilliant of chevaliers.'

There is of course another side to the story. Some of Smith's biographers regard his operations off the Calabrian coast as spirited and judicious in execution, if not well-judged in policy; and defenders of the Neapolitan Court like Harold Acton, who see Maria Carolina as 'a glowing centre of resistance' for the gallant guerrillas who were effectively harassing the French occupying forces, are inclined to view the criticisms of Moore and Bunbury as just a blimpish reaction of the conventional officer who considers it *infra dig* to

associate with guerrillas. Such opposition – between regular military commanders and maverick leaders who believe in arming and cooperating with guerrillas in enemy-occupied territory – has been not unknown in more recent wars.
No doubt there was some tinge of jealousy of Sidney Smith's celebrity among
the admirals and generals who criticised him so heartily. It should be remembered that the crews of Sidney Smith's ships were apt to give him three hearty
cheers, and that whatever his senior officers thought of him, young men like
Henry Slessor competed to serve under his command. Excitement and publicity
were the fiery element in which he lived, and which attracted others to him.

But when all allowances have been made, Sidney Smith's conduct during and
after the action in which Henry Slessor was killed remains indefensible. The
most reliable account of it is given by Bunbury, who heard of it from indignant
eye-witnesses only twenty-four hours after the event. Bunbury had gone with
Sir John Moore on a cruise of inspection up the Calabrian coast in the frigate
Apollo. 'We fell in with his fine ship, the *Pompée*, of eighty-four guns, in the
Bay of Policastro, crippled and torn by shot. These shot had been received the
day before from an old watch tower on which one gun was mounted. The story
told by the officers of the *Pompée* was this: Sir Sidney, coasting along, as was
his wont, having the *Hydra* and another frigate in company, and looking out for
brigands to receive his muskets and his orders, espied a French flag flying on
this tower of ancient days. He simply gave orders that the ships should run in
and drive the enemy out of their little fortress by cannon shot; and these orders
given, the Admiral went quietly to his cabin to write his letters. The *Pompée*
drew near and opened her fire; the one gun then responded; the broadsides of the
man of war were returned for half an hour by this solitary but unerring gun; at
length the Captain found it necessary to interrupt the Admiral's correspondence
by informing him that Lieut. Slessor and a midshipman and several men were
killed, many more wounded, and the ship seriously damaged. Sir Sidney looked
surprised, but gave order that the boats should be lowered and the marines sent
ashore to reduce these obstinate Frenchmen. As soon as the boats touched the
beach, some thirty Corsicans ran from the tower to meet them, waving a white
handkerchief, and telling the officers that they had been longing to desert to the
British, but as the ship fired on them instead of inviting them to surrender, they
had no choice but to use their gun to the best of their ability. We went on our
way, leaving the *Pompée*'s crew employed in repairing her damages and in
burying the poor fellows whose lives had been thus idly thrown away.'

It is clear that Smith's own officers took a very poor view of this day's work,
and indeed the picture of the Admiral, snug in his shawl-hung cabin peacefully
writing one of his immensely long self-glorifying letters, while his men were
being mown down on the deck over his head, is a sickening one. He must soon
have realised this, and have ordered an edited version of the event to be put out.
The news was communicated to Henry's brother in a letter from the Captain of
the *Pompée*, in which marines from the *Pompée* are now said to have landed

before the cannonade from the fort which killed Henry; but the Captain's real feeling about the affair is revealed in his comment about the Admiral and 'this contemptible place'. As Harriot pointed out, the letter 'will too well expose in what light was seen by all on board such an attack'. The Captain's letter, dated from the *Pompée* at Palermo on 13th August, reads:

JHS 'When we first arrived here, I intended to have written to you, on the very melancholy subject of your brother's death; but from a want of your address it was not until the moment I received your letter that I found myself enabled to do so. Did I not most sincerely sympathise with you on this mournful occasion, my duty to him alone as a messmate would have impelled me to undertake the task. I assure you, Sir, altho' any reflection on so deplorable an event must give me the deepest pain, yet it gives me great pleasure to tell you how much your excellent brother was beloved. His death has been the cause of the most unfeigned lamentations. In obedience to your request I shall describe the unfortunate affair as well as I am able.

On the 13th of August, in the evening, the Admiral determined on attacking a battery of two guns, which is on Point Licosa, near the entrance of the Gulf of Salerno. As it could not immediately be carried in the rear by assault on account of a strong tower which completely covered it, it was deemed necessary to anchor the ship before it, which was done. While the Marines and a party of the Neapolitan Insurgents invested it in the land side, Henry Slessor was mortally wounded by a splinter. He lingered about an hour and a half, and expired in less pain than could have been expected, since the wound was in the bowels. In this sacrifice there fell six other victims, besides thirty-six wounded. It is best known to the Admiral what importance was attached to this contemptible place.

Your brother was buried, according to custom, in the deep, the next day, with military honours. The eyes of all present were suffused with tears, which were shed a just tribute to his memory. All his effects, except his sword, watch, books, etc etc, were sold according to the general rules and regulations of the Naval Service. The things which were reserved shall be safely conveyed into your hands when we arrive at Messina, which will be in a few days. We then all promise ourselves the pleasure of seeing you, when I shall have the opportunity of giving you a more circumstantial account.'

Further editing was done in Sidney Smith's despatch of 21st August:

JHS 'H.M. Ship *Pompée*, off Point Licosa, 21st August 1806.
I hoisted a flag of truce intending to summon the place, but it was answered by a shot, and I consequently lost not a moment in making a regular

attack upon the post. It was not reduced without considerable trouble and loss: during upwards of three hours and a half firing, every shot except four, struck the *Pompée*. I have to regret a most gallant and in every respect an excellent Officer, Lieutenant Slessor, with a promising Midshipman, five seamen killed, and thirty-four wounded. The musquetry from the Royalists at length drove the enemy from their guns into the tower. The Commandant, with a body of French troops and peasantry of their party, made an attempt to relieve the place, but were repulsed with loss. It was not until the next night, the 14th, after some correspondence, that the Garrison surrendered prisoners of war by capitulation.'

We now hear for the first time of a flag of truce having been hoisted before the *Pompée* fired on the tower; if Bunbury's account is true, this must be a fabrication. The Corsican garrison of the tower, who were only too ready to surrender, would, if they had seen a flag of truce, have given up the tower before a shot had been fired on either side. It was only the *Pompée*'s attack on them without warning which provoked them into returning the fire with the deadly accuracy which killed Henry Slessor and the others. Moreover we now hear of a hard-fought action on land (in which the favoured guerrillas, 'the Royalists', suddenly make a hitherto unmentioned appearance) to capture the fort, very unlike Bunbury's account of the instant surrender of its defenders the moment the party from the *Pompée* landed. To conceal the truth still more, Sidney Smith lumped together the deaths of Henry Slessor and the others in a casualty list for several weeks of minor operations off the Calabrian coast. It was a thorough attempt at a cover-up, but Henry Slessor's family was no more deceived than Smith's military opposite numbers were. Harriot Slessor wrote bitterly:

HS   What made the loss still more severe to me, and to dwell long on my afflicted mind, was the manner in which poor Henry's life was sacrificed, and that he fell in executing an obscure and unprofitable service.

John Henry, who had been not many miles away from his brother for two months – John Henry at Palermo and Messina, Henry at Palermo and off the Calabrian coast – without ever managing to meet him, was well aware of the uselessness of the operation in which Henry's life had been sacrificed.

JHS   This desultory warfare tended but little to promote general interest. Both Officers and men of the *Pompée* condemned such an unnecessary sacrifice of life. My good Mother and all of us will long mourn the fate of a dutiful Son and affectionate Brother. Would my pen could do justice to his worth.

15

In February 1807 John Henry entered in his diary:

JHS The two Light Companies of the 35th and 31st Regts were ordered to
embark at Milazzo for Messina. Colonel Kempt shewed much regret at
parting with these three companies, as their quitting nearly broke up a
Battalion, in the command of which he prided himself not a little.
1st March. Reached Messina in safety, and joined our Regiments.

John Henry's commanding officer, described by the rather haughty HQ staff at
Messina as 'Little Kempt, quietest and smallest of brigadiers' was an able and
popular officer who had taken part in the Battle of Maida, and whom his
subordinates at Milazzo evidently much respected. John Henry and the 35th
were about to embark on an operation as futile as the one in which Henry
Slessor was killed, but a far larger and more costly one. It had been ordered by
the Foreign Secretary, Castlereagh, and the British Government at home,
against the advice of the military command in Sicily. It was motivated by the
increasing hostility of Turkey, formerly an ally against the French, towards
Russia and Britain. French forces in Dalmatia, which Austria had been forced
to cede to France, were now threatening both Russian power in the Adriatic and
the Turkish territories in the Balkans. The Turks feared Russia's intentions
more than the French ones, so they accepted an alliance with France and
declared war on Britain's ally Russia. The British response was a double one: to
send a British fleet to demonstrate off Constantinople – ineffectually in the
event, chiefly because of contrary winds – and to send a force of 5,000 men
from Sicily to occupy Alexandria, in order to forestall any French attempt, in
agreement with Turkey, to regain their foothold in Egypt and to threaten the
route to India. As a means of frightening the Turks out of their French alliance,
the British expedition to Egypt was not efficacious; the Turks cared little for the
fate of their distant Egyptian province compared with the threat much nearer
home from Russia. Even Britain's ally Russia was not grateful; she suspected
British ambitions for a sphere of influence in the Eastern Mediterranean, and
would have preferred British help to take the form of action against the French
in the Adriatic.

However orders were sent to General Fox in Sicily to despatch a force to Egypt to seize Alexandria from the Turks, and 5,000 troops, including both battalions of the 35th, set sail from Messina on 6th March 1807.

JHS Early in this month sailed with an Expedition of about 5000 men, ignorant of our destination, but had not been long at sea, before we ascertained it to be Egypt. General Mackenzie Fraser commanded. Off Candia we had stormy weather, and the fleet, consisting of 36 sail, parted. On the 16th came to an anchor to the Westward of Alexandria.

Henry Bunbury, who did not accompany the expedition to Egypt, but wrote a detailed account of it evidently culled from those who did, on their return to Sicily, paints a condescending picture of the man in charge of the British forces, General Mackenzie Fraser, as 'an open, generous, honourable Highland chieftain. A man of very good plain sense, but one who had never studied the higher branches either of politics or of military science. Everyone in the army loved Mackenzie Fraser, but no one deemed him qualified for a separate and difficult command.' His second in command General Wauchope was no more than a 'brave, hard-working regimental officer'. This weak leadership was ominous for the success of the expedition, which was unlucky from the start. The convoy of thirty-three transports under the protection of the 84-gun HMS *Tigre*, Captain Hallowell, and the frigate *Apollo* encountered such storms that it parted company. The *Tigre* with 16 transports with 2,000 men aboard (including John Henry and the 35th) arrived off Alexandria on 16th March; the *Apollo* and the rest of the convoy only caught up with them four days later.

The campaign began well, and rapidly achieved its planned objective, the capture of Alexandria. The first half of the force, which had arrived on 16th March, landed next day through heavy surf to the west of Alexandria. John Henry's diary relates the sequel.

JHS *On the 17th* landed to the Eastward of Marabout. The Turks were weak and unprepared. Major Misset our Consul gave us every information and advice. He earnestly recommended an immediate attack. We quickly stormed a palisaded entrenchment, then moved towards Aboukir: sent a party to take possession of the Castle, and the cut between the lakes Maadi and Mareotis.
On the 19th, so as to prevent reinforcements getting into Alexandria, the rest of the Expedition anchored in Aboukir Bay. The enemy appeared determined to make every resistance, but after an interchange of flags of truce, a capitulation was arranged. By this the town of Alexandria and much bloodshed spared.
On the 21st of March, the anniversary of a day memorable in this country, (when the gallant Abercromby fell, and the French were driven out of

Egypt) we took possession of the town, forts, batteries, shipping, etc. The Turkish garrison consisted of about 500 men. Our loss was too trifling to be mentioned, tho' the service for the time was arduous, particularly the landing.

The subsequent events were directed not by Mackenzie Fraser, but by the man whose advice he had been instructed to follow, the British Resident in Egypt, Major Misset. Misset was a wily intriguer, a cripple who could not move about Egypt but relied on a web of informers. He had been in Egypt since 1801 and had convinced himself that Cairo and all Egypt could be secured for Britain if the Mamelukes, the powerful Circassian militia, could be won over to oppose the Turkish Viceroy Mehmet Ali. Misset was determined to get the British forces to advance further into Egypt, not just to remain in Alexandria; only an advance towards Cairo would sufficiently impress the Mamelukes to induce them to change sides. He therefore told Mackenzie Fraser that supplies of food in Alexandria were so low that the British must capture more territory if they and the inhabitants of Alexandria were not to starve. Such a move was contrary to Mackenzie Fraser's instructions, but he reluctantly agreed to detach 1,400 men under General Wauchope to occupy Rosetta and Rahmanieh. John Henry and the 35th were not involved in this movement, but he gives a vivid account in his diary of its disastrous outcome.

JHS Our situation rather critical as regards provisions, for Major Misset represented on the part of the inhabitants their fears of starvation in case Rosetta was not taken possession of. This undertaking was supposed to be easy. In consequence the 31st and Chasseurs Britanniques Regts, with two guns and a few Dragoons, under the command of General Wauchope, were detached on this service. After gaining the Heights of Abamandour, which commanded the town, he incautiously marched into Rosetta, and soon had cause to lament his rashness; for the Turks opened a galling fire from the loop-holes, windows and tops of the houses, which caused an immediate retreat. Every house in this country is in some degree a fort in itself. Gen Wauchope was killed, Gen Meade wounded, total 400 Officers and men killed and wounded. However, the remainder effected a regular retreat to the Caravanserai, and arrived at Alexandria, altho' not covered with laurels.

The second attempt to capture Rosetta was even more disastrous, and this time John Henry's diary gives an eye-witness account throughout, for his company of the 35th was included in the force of 2,500 men, under Brigadier Generals Stewart and Oswald, which set out on 3rd April along the shore towards Rosetta, dragging their guns with difficulty through the heavy sand.

JHS With a view of retrieving our failure a second force of about 2500 men was
marched off under the command of Gen the Hon William Stewart. We
moved with caution; but the Turks had evidently gained confidence, and
most likely received reinforcements. The first night we bivouacked at
Aboukir Wells, the men literally fighting for water. In the morning at
daybreak crossed the Caravanserai, passed by Edko, and reached El
Hamed, very hot and tired; drank a great quantity of buffalo's milk; the
Arabs set up a hideous shriek; saw some Turkish horse flying about. Next
morning invested Rosetta, after taking the necessary precautions with
respect to Guards, Outposts, etc. Our next care was to send out fatigue
parties to bury the headless corpses, that lay about the sands, in a shocking
putrid state. Such a sight had a great effect on the men, who swore they
would never be taken alive. We learned that the Turkish Chief put a
premium of so many dollars on the head of a Christian. Captain Hallowell
of the Navy cooperated with us in the most cordial and zealous manner.
Guns were brought up, batteries erected during the night, shells thrown
into the town. We tried terms of capitulation; our flags of truce were fired
at. At last an Arab was bribed to go into Rosetta with proposals, but he was
heard of no more; his head most likely paid the forfeit. The howling during
the night in the town was most horrible. The enemy sometimes made
sorties, but were as often driven back. We daily lost men by their fire, and
saw no prospect of our barbarous warfare and hardships ending. Much
rather storm and come to a general action and have done with it. We suffer
much from the scorching heat by day and the excessive dew by night. A
few branches of the date tree shelter us a little. We lay on the ground with
a blanket or great coat; often nothing but rations of salt provisions, sea
biscuit and burning *acqua dente*, with soft Nile water. This kind of warfare
lasted nearly three weeks; no one was ever safe a minute, and it was cruel
to see a brave fellow knocked down in such a manner.

On the 20th April Col Macleod of the 78th had been detached with some
companies of the 35th, 78th, and De Rolls to El Hamed. Next day at
daylight he saw a large fleet of germs coming down the Nile full of troops.
He was soon after attacked, overpowered by numbers, killed, after a most
gallant and desperate resistance, and his whole party *hors-de-combat*. All
our hopes now vanished. We immediately broke up, destroyed what you
could not bring away, got our camels, with the wounded, provisions,
ammunition etc into the plain, and commenced our retreat in square. The
Turks in crowds soon sallied out of the town: our Light troops constantly
skirmishing, and hard work I found it: inglorious fight, against a barbarous
enemy. As often as they pressed upon us, the Square halted, and our field
pieces opened fire and drove them off. The manoeuvre was beautiful and
well executed.

We at first directed our march towards El Hamed, anxiously and eagerly looking out for our ill-fated comrades, but alas! in vain. All firing had long ceased, and the enemy strong in that quarter, and elated with victory. So we gained Edko, about two o'clock in the morning, the Turks keeping a respectable distance, and indeed giving up the pursuit.

Next morning crossed to Aboukir Wells, and blew up the Caravanserai. We lost about 50 men in this retreat. Thus had a second Expedition returned, with far greater loss and worse success than the first. Why this war was declared or waged against the Turks, I know not. We have made enemies of a savage, brutal nation, which I wish with all my heart were driven out of Europe, but a nation with which we had always been at peace, who had been our faithful ally, and respected us, but now boast of beating both our Army and Navy.

It had indeed been a costly catastrophe. Colonel Macleod (whom John Henry phonetically spells Macloud) and all his men, including the Light Company of the first battalion of the 35th, had been killed or captured, and the main force had to retreat to Alexandria with heavy losses. John Henry was slightly wounded in the leg; his company of the 35th distinguished itself. Bunbury paid a warm tribute to the steadfastness of the 35th under General Oswald in protecting the main column retreating from Rosetta against the Albanian and Turkish troops who poured out of Rosetta to attack the retreating British. 'On the 35th the fight fell . . . heavily, for the long fire-arms of the Albanians told upon their ranks; but the steady and well-supported fire of the battalion, the good service of our 6-pounders, and the flanking fire of the light companies, baffled every attempt to disorder the retreat'.

The diminished force got back to Alexandria late in April, and dug in there for the summer. Misset's warning about the shortage of supplies proved to be completely untrue; food of all kinds was plentiful, as John Henry reports in his account of the idle disagreeable summer which the British troops spent in Alexandria.

JHS We now thought of strengthening our original lines and positions, and having received reinforcements from Sicily felt quite secure. We wanted for nothing; the Arabs brought abundance to our Camp and quarters; and speculators soon found their way to Alexandria with all kinds of things. At one time I was encamped at Aboukir, another on Eastern Heights, latterly in ruins outside the town. We now began to suffer much from Ophthalmia: the heat in June and July excessive: quantity of vermin, and flies so numerous that we with difficulty could eat our meals. Safe in our stronghold, and inactive as to any military operation. Our poor fellows who survived the woeful affair at El Hamed are prisoners at Cairo, some slaves. Only sixteen out of eighty of the 35th 1st Battn Light Company survived, and out of these five alone were not wounded. They fought like lions; the Turks must have lost a great many. The 35th Regt, so honourably mentioned in Gen Stewart's despatches, have been the greatest sufferers. I thank my God for having escaped: four Captains of ours were killed.

Alexandria has nothing of antiquity but the name. Around a mass of misery and horror lie the remains and ruins of one of the most celebrated Cities of the World, and the most precious monuments of Art. The inhabitants appear to be a set of beings taking events as they occur, surprised at nothing, dreaming away the time squatted before their doors with pipe in mouth. Their exterior is imposing: strongly marked physiognomies: the women wrap themselves in a piece of cloth, which passes over the head, and descends in front to the eyebrows. The poorer sort cover the whole of their face with linen, leaving only two small apertures for the eyes, so that they look like so many hobgoblins. A burning sky, sands, arid deserts form a melancholy contrast with our green fields. Water bad and scarce: a few date trees scattered here and there about the country, and the date is a melancholy tree. Such is the coast of this country, so fertile in the interior – and where the age of Alexander and the Ptolemies will never be revived. The streets are not paved, and the image of desolation is rendered more striking by being within view of two objects that have passed thro' the lapse of ages uninjured, that has devoured every living thing around them, Pompey's column and Cleopatra's needle. The inhabitants are calculated to be under 10,000. Alexandria when approached by water looks best. It appears as if rising from the sea; all this coast is very flat. I was struck with the number of Arabs with only one eye, so that the ophthalmia is not confined to strangers alone. A traveller in search for antiquities may here find field for study and employment, Cleopatra's needle, baths, etc: Pompey's Pillar, subterraneous vaults, cisterns etc afford ample scope. There is one good street principally occupied by merchants. The square or rather parade ground is spacious, but I suppose the town has been much modernised, commencing with the arrival of Bonaparte.

Not mixing with the natives, we knew nothing of their mode of living, but they appear to prefer apathy and indolence to industry. Filthy in their persons and houses: richly clad: in general well made and robust: smoking and drinking coffee: they are early taught a contempt of all nations who do not believe in the Koran. I used to listen with pleasure to a fellow chanting with a musical stentorian voice from the top of a mosque, a hymn calling the people to prayers at sunrise and sunset. I was much astonished at the tameness of birds, both in the town and the environs; the Turks never fire at them; the doves feed about tamer than pigeons with us. It is now (September) the season for quail, caught in thousands by the Arabs, and delicious eating. Saw a great variety of foxes and jackals, and many species of serpents, lizards, etc; the chameleon the soldiers used to pet.

The Turks do not admit dogs in their houses, but protect them out of doors, where they are wild and savage, not easily tamed. The hog is loathed: wine forbid: opium used to excess. In warm baths the Turk indulges. His beautiful horse he highly values, and rides boldly on a most awkward saddle and stirrups, and a most severe bit. I saw the Mamelukes display great adroitness in throwing a javelin. The Bedouin Arabs are the great breeders, and in general mounted on beautiful mares, for which they ask a high price.

Some of the Dardanelles Fleet came into Harbour. I went on board the *Windsor Castle*, where I saw an immense granite ball, thrown from the Turkish Battery. We daily expect to evacuate the country. A treaty going on about our prisoners. The poor Arabs dread much the vengeance of the Turks on our departure.

Back in Sicily, Sir John Moore passed a severe judgement on the expedition and Mackenzie Fraser's leadership. 'The disasters which have befallen were owing to the bad measures he adopted, and to the worse manner in which they were executed . . . Neither Rosetta nor Rahmanieh are posts which can be held by inferior numbers, and therefore, to hold them it was necessary to command Egypt. This, with 5000 men, was out of the question . . . Deceived by Misset as to the enemy's force, and the military character of the country, he employed detachments to take Rosetta, which detachments were ill-conducted, and they were cut up . . . It is difficult to see what advantage arises from holding the port of Alexandria independent of Egypt – and thus locking up a body of 5000 troops. I always thought the Expedition an absurd one, and that it marked ignorance of the state of affairs in the Mediterranean.'

By the late autumn of 1807 the British Government had come to agree with the uselessness of holding onto Alexandria with troops now needed elsewhere, and orders were given for its evacuation and the return of the troops to Sicily. The alignment of European powers had again changed. The French had defeated the Russians at the Battle of Friedland in June, and in July the Franco-Russian Treaty of Tilsit was signed, under which Russia agreed to exclude British trade from Europe and to cede the Ionian Islands to France. This shift of the Mediterranean balance of power endangered Britain's position in Sicily, and there was another looming French threat further west in the Iberian peninsula. So on 19th September the evacuation of Alexandria was begun, and ten days later John Henry was delighted to find himself on his way back to Sicily.

JHS *1st Oct*. Orders arrived for embarkation: joyful tidings. (I should have liked much to see the Delta and Upper Egypt). All is bustle. I had bought a beautiful mare, but could not get her a passage in a transport. Other Officers were in the same predicament, so we agreed to hire a Greek ship, into which we put sixteen horses. I also purchased a fine milk cow. Her I managed to embark on board of our own transport; she afforded us a quantity of milk, no little luxury on our voyage. In a few days all hands, sick, stores, etc were afloat, but we left some beautiful brass guns behind us. The fleet rendezvoused in Aboukir Bay: here the prisoners joined us, grotesque figures, some of them. Judge of their joy at finding themselves clear out of the hands of their late savage Masters, the sad remnants of a brave set of fellows, but alas! when an Expedition fails, gallantly as the troops may behave, no credit is given them. This one must have cost a great sum of money, and a cruel sacrifice of lives.

While at anchor our boats watered from the Nile water, which discharges itself into the sea near Rosetta, and does not impregnate with salt water for some distance from the shore; at least a surface of some feet is free. Every arrangement being made, the fleet weighed, and we bade Adieu to the burning sands of Egypt. On our passage to Messina nothing extraordinary happened, except the rascally Greek with our horses having disappeared; we never heard more of the vessel.

Two months before the expedition returned from Alexandria, Sir John Moore in Sicily had received secret instructions to embark with 8,000 troops from the British garrison of Sicily and make for Gibraltar, where he would receive further instructions, but he was not to embark till the force from Alexandria got back to Sicily. It reached Messina on 17th October, and soon afterwards Moore set sail for Gibraltar in a convoy of fifty-six ships with 7,058 men on board, the main strength of seven regiments described as 'the flower of the army' in Sicily, and including the second battalion of the 35th. John Henry did not even have time to go ashore at Messina before the sailing to Gibraltar.

JHS On arriving in Sicily, an armament was preparing for Portugal, under Sir John Moore. Our Battn formed part, and we remained on board; the 1st Battn landed. Recruited our stock of provisions etc, and sold my cow. In November sailed once more. Our force I should say amounted to about 7,000 men.

When the convoy reached Gibraltar at the beginning of December, Moore was informed that a threatened French invasion of Portugal might require him to land forces in Lisbon, in cooperation with a planned manoeuvre by Sir Sidney Smith who was then cruising off the Portuguese coast. But a few days later, news arrived of the sudden turn of events in Portugal (to be more fully described in a later chapter) which ruled out any British landing in Lisbon at this stage. Moore, relieved at least not to be required to act in concert with Sidney Smith, therefore followed his alternative instructions, to take the main body of his forces back to England, where they arrived on 1st January 1808. It was tantalising for John Henry to come so near to a landing in Portugal, where his mother and sisters were living, but his account of the events of that autumn is laconic.

JHS Three Regiments were told off for Madeira, in case we met with Sir S. Smith in a certain latitude. However, this did not happen, and we put into Gibraltar, and in a few days started again for Lisbon. But the French got the start of us, and we bore up for old England.

PART III

War in Portugal
1807–9

16

While John Henry was spending a sweltering summer in dusty fly-ridden Alexandria, his mother was enjoying an excursion among romantic wooded mountains in the temperate delicious weather of a Portuguese June. For the last four years she had been living in Oporto with the Walshes. Now she at last made up her mind to visit her eldest daughter Louisa, who was living with her husband and two children (the second son, Frank, had just been born, in March 1807) at the Villa Pouca de Aguiar, near Vila Real in Tras os Montes. Harriot's description of this visit, written some years later for John Henry's benefit and addressed to him, reflects her own surprise that she had allowed herself to give up her determination not to be reconciled with Louisa.

HS The summer of the same year that the English Factory were obliged to quit Porto, I was coaxed into making a journey, which I had professed I never would perform. How often, when at one time we are positive no persuasions can gain consent, a moment of weakness overturns such appearance of firmness. I can give it no other appellation, and cannot but condemn those who shew so little firmness and constancy; that take a resolution at one time, and act quite the contrary of that determination another.

Your sister Louisa for a long time had exerted all the eloquence she was mistress of, in many letters, to recede and reverse my No to Yes. At last she succeeded, and I agreed to pay her a visit, to her no trifling content. It might appear to superstitious minds that I had in the performance of this visit a foreboding of what came to pass some months after, as it proved to be a long farewell one, our separation being so circumstanced that can give little or no chance of our meeting again, Louisa's situation in Portugal being such that she is not likely to have it in her power to quit it. Nor can I have an idea of ever returning to Portugal.

Harriot's relenting was perhaps influenced by a wish to draw together her links with her surviving children after Henry's death in the previous year. It had taken some time for the sad news to reach her. Henry was killed in August 1806, but in September of that year his mother, still in ignorance of his death, was busily pulling strings to secure his promotion.

HS Lord St Vincent was at Lisbon, with his squadron, in September 1806.
Henry was then no more, and I still living in happy ignorance. For many
weeks after the event we did not get the news, and I was taking measures in
hopes of forwarding Henry's promotion. I had written to a friend in Lisbon
to see what could be done by speaking to Lord St Vincent. The answer,
tho' not favourable, was most flattering. It is from a great friend of your
Father's, who had on different occasions been very kind to Henry. This
letter says:

'I deferred acknowledging the receipt of your letter until I had dined with
Lord St Vincent, and had mentioned your son to him. Your son is perfectly
well known to his Lordship, and all that is handsome to be said of an
aspiring young man His Lordship in a public manner repeated aloud in his
favour at table, regretting at the same time that it was out of his power at
present to help him towards promotion. Lord St Vincent said the powerful
interest that was used for Henry by Sir R. Neave and others, would indeed
have induced him long ago to have served him, if he had had an opportunity. But his Lordship had no doubt in his own mind, he says, that Sir
Sidney Smith will forward his promotion as well as any man, knowing that
Henry stands high in his estimation; and if a good opportunity offers, he
will certainly meet promotion. It would have afforded me the greatest of
all satisfactions if I could have given a lift, as the sailors say, to my young
friend, towards promotion. But after what I have heard drop from his
Lordship, I am afraid there is little chance of doing anything for him thro'
Lord St Vincent at present. I was determined to hear what his Lordship had
to say about Henry, and still, altho' the point of promotion was arrested, I
give you my word the very handsome manner in which Lord St Vincent
spoke of my young friend afforded me most singular pleasure. I could not
delay a moment giving you this account of my application in favour of
Henry; and notwithstanding the little success it has been attended with, I
feel a pride in having interested myself of a young man whom I esteem,
and who is esteemed by the highest characters in his own profession'.

Henry's Admiral did promote him to some purpose. When this kind and
respectable friend was interesting himself with so much ardour for his
young friend's advancement, he little thought that he would never see him
more. Thus was the fate of a beloved son and brother irrevocably settled. It
is time for me to leave a subject that I could dwell on for ever. It has been
a pleasing, tho' truly melancholy subject to me, as I have indulged in
recalling every particular that could picture to you a brother in the most
flattering light; and I must think that you will agree with me that it is a just
one. Henry was not much more than 22 years old when he met his fate; full
of health, and fair prospects; at a crisis that he, with every just reason,
might look forward with satisfaction, to speedy promotion. But his sun is

set, and he is no more. But not his image. That will, as long as I exist, remain fresh in my memory.

In the spring of 1807 Harriot's situation was not cheerful. She had lost one son, another was so far away and cut off in India that letters to and from him took a year to arrive, her eldest son was involved in a dangerous campaign in Egypt; the progress of the war with France was increasingly threatening Portugal. It is not surprising that the mother and daughters of the Slessor family, marooned in Portugal, should have felt an urge to draw together.

So in June 1807 Harriot Slessor and her unmarried daughter Harriot Amelia set off with a friend and a considerable train of lady's-maids and muleteers from Oporto. In spite of griefs and forebodings, Harriot seems to have thoroughly enjoyed her adventurous holiday, which she describes in a style obviously borrowed from Mrs Radcliffe's novels; the party evidently saw themselves in the role of Emily St Aubert travelling through the Apennines towards the remote Castle of Udolpho, enraptured by the wild landscape of crags and precipices and hanging woods. 'No heroine of Romance could have been more transported with delight,' Harriot records, making the source of her inspiration quite clear.

HS My consent once obtained, every disposition for this great undertaking was very quickly settled, and the day soon named for departure. It is no bad advice for those that are disposed to make a journey in Portugal, before they set off, to lay aside all refined ideas, and go armed with a spirit truly philosophical, to bear with Christian patience the many inconveniences that are inevitable in such journeys. I was well acquainted with them from experience, and for my self fear'd not. But we had in our party Miss Hardy, in a delicate state of health, that was only acquainted with the comforts of travelling in England. But she quieted my fears on her account, assuring me she had not the least apprehension of threatened dangers; that she was above allowing reflections of the kind to intrude on her fortitude, and even declared she was in the expectation of receiving amusement from the novel distresses we were preparing her to encounter.

We set off for our journey in high glee, and no insignificant escort; Miss Hardy, Harriot Slessor, myself, two Abigails, and a few pedestrian attendants. Travelling in chaises being perfectly out of the question, two litters supplied their place, two little sure-footed ponies, to mount when we were weary of jogging on, at a foot's pace, in the litters, and a mule, loaded with turkey, fowls, etc, etc, not the least necessary on this expedition, as no dependence can be laid for any kind of provisions on the miserable habitations we were to halt at. Plenty, it is true, crowned our board, but how to settle for the night was a comfortless thought. As the determination was to take all in good part, at the close of our day's journey, we enter'd with decent composure a forlorn habitation, and took possession of a large bare room, the black walls of which had certainly never been white-washed, or even the cobwebs brushed off; a window without an idea of a sash, with lumbering shutters that let in plenty of fresh air; and a floor black with dirt, and a comfortable number of holes, that served for perfume from the stables below. The bedroom and eating parlour were all comprised in this one apartment, with furniture of the same doleful description.

Here we were to rest our weary heads after a long day's journey. The first care was to settle Miss Hardy in her own little tent bed, that travel'd with her. As for us stout ones, we thought ourselves greatly off, in getting plenty of fresh straw, piled high from the floor, covered with our own sheets and good warm cloaks. Such were our beds. This is a true description of a Portuguese Inn, as you go to the North. They are better towards Lisbon, but not to be compared with those in England.

In this journey, the scenes of the day amply made amends for the night inconveniences. We had chosen the most beautiful time of the year for travelling in Portugal, the very beginning of June, when in general the weather is temperate, delightfully fine without heat; and when dreary winter has cast off its dark appearance, and in its place nature revives, displaying its beauties in its most lively colours. Our friend has a touch of the romantic in her nature. The country we travel'd through was of a perfectly novel nature to her, and not the less pleasing. The further you go to the North of Portugal, the more wild and majestic the scene is, displayed to your wondering sight. No heroine of Romance could have been more transported with delight than Miss Hardy was. When mounted on our little ponies, steering our course up the steep hills; the morning beautifully mild, and the sun rising in all his glory; we soon forgot the hardships of the night, and had only eyes and mind to contemplate the varied scene that presented itself to our view.

My friend had never beheld such high mountains. Here in succession they rise one above another, that they appear almost to touch the heavens. This part of Portugal is called Tras os Montes, behind the Mountains, it being so surrounded with mountains that not even a peephole can be discover'd to see what is beyond them. Some display a most fantastic appearance, as if tossed one above the other, in wild and rugged forms. Some of a dark and dreary hue, others adorned with beautiful heath, of a variety of kinds, covered with flowers of different colours. The Arbutus and Myrtle likewise flourish in these mountains. In short nature, with the Spring revived in full perfection, and we mortals had nothing to do but admire, except when our fears were awakened when travelling on the verge of a precipice. And even then the mind was hurried from the idea of fear, the sight involuntarily being attracted viewing the scenes in the depth below, where cascades formed by nature, and the water with tremendous roar dashes from rock to rock of no insignificant height into a river at the bottom, where it drives all before it. The mountains on the opposite shore, of an immense height, are adorned with fine verdure, with plenty of beautiful oaks and chestnut trees.

Good luck attended us in the whole of this journey of two days and a half; the weather constantly mild and fine. The last day's journey Miss Hardy and myself were upset in our litter, from the inattention of the muleteer. It was a very laughable scene. We were no sooner down than I jumped out at the window, leaving both shoes behind me. It was not so easy a matter to extricate Miss Hardy, she measuring at least six feet in height, and could not move till the litter was raised from the ground. The man not being in a hurry to do that, first fell to beating the mules in great rage, to punish them for such bad behaviour, when he was the one in fault. After waiting the litter man's leisure, all was set to rights again, and in a few hours after we arrived safe at Villa Pouca, where you may suppose our reception was most cordial.

Louisa Canavaro, whose house, Villa Pouca de Aguiar, was near Vila Real in Tras os Montes, was delighted to be reunited with her mother and sister, whom she had not seen for five years.

HS   All poor Louisa's fear was, for she was overjoyed to have us, that we should not stay long enough. We did, too long for Miss Hardy. The first three months she was uncommonly well, taking her rides, enjoying them and the beautiful romantic country. But this was not to last. When we were planning a pleasant tour on our return home, she was taken desperately ill, that put us in fear this would be the last of the many trials she had already had. But nature still held out and conquer'd, but not for many weeks had we hopes for her recovery . . . I must relate a trifling circumstance with regard to her during our residence with Louisa, which shows the ignorance and rusticity of the people in those parts. It is well known that in old times, Portugal was often a prey to the Romans and Moors. History relates the valorous feats of the Heroes of that country, who after many a well fought battle free'd their country from such rude intruders. Roman bridges are still standing in Portugal. I am well acquainted with one that had the Roman Arms but the Portuguese have been savage enough to efface them, and put in their place the Portuguese Arms. There are likewise in many parts of the country, ruins of castles erected by the Moors.

Carrying on the Gothick novel mode, Harriot describes at some length a visit to a ruined Moorish castle perched on a mountain-top, only to be reached by scrambling through thorns and thistles up a rocky goat-path, where she was shown underground hiding-places and heard tales of buried treasures of gold coins, and where a huge boulder had hurtled down the mountain-side, uprooting trees and terrifying the surrounding villages with a thunderous sound which seemed to portent the end of the world, or at least an earthquake.

HS   This digression from what I had to relate of poor sick Miss Hardy may be excused, it having something to do with the antiquities of the country. In our romantic rides together our attention was attracted by two ancient pillars, placed on the top of a mountain that overlooks the principal street in the town. These pillars by the oldest inhabitants are supposed without a doubt to have been erected on that spot by the Romans, and no one had ever ventured to remove them. The wish to do it, and see what was under those stones, was irresistible. One of the pillars has a Latin inscription, distinctly to be made out. 'Here lies interred' with a Roman name, the remainder of the inscription is effaced. In many parts of Portugal coffins have been dug up, and when opened bodies have been found in them in a perfect state of preservation.

I was prepossessed with the idea that under these stones there must rest some Roman Chief, or Hero, and could not rest till my curiosity was gratified. If I was to be disappointed in the beholding a well preserved hero, I hoped at least to be rewarded for our pains with the discovery of a plentiful treasure of coins. Miss Hardy's servant was the only idle one in the family. I distinguished him from the rest for so honourable an under-taking. This was a delightful party for my little grandchildren. They took care to provide a basketful of good things, to satisfy good appetites, expecting many hours to be employed in this laudable undertaking. Taking leave of our friends at home (which to say the truth, were much disposed to laugh, and doubt of the success of our attempt), we set off merrily, the servant taking axe and spade. To work he went in all ardour, and certainly did his duty, digging and more digging the best part of the day. But alas no coffin appeared, no treasure, nothing but earth; of that we had enough. It was with reluctance that we could determine to replace the pillars as we found them, tho' I was convinced it was vain to dig more.

While this work was going on I had no suspicion that the people in the street were watching us and attending to the whole business, but had not formed an idea of the real motive. Theirs was that Miss Hardy had died, and that the servant was digging her grave; and what could be more cruel, they observed, than for her friend to make her own servant dig the grave where she was to be buried, and what appears still more ungrateful to his late mistress, that the servant should not have refused doing it. The people were so persuaded of the truth of this strange story, that their imagination wandered so far, as to describe the dress Miss Hardy was to be buried in. It was to be all in white, and she was to be taken out of the house in the dead of the night, and then laid in the grave that was prepared for her in the morning. We were much surprised, as soon as it was dark, to find a crowd had taken their station round the house door, nor would they be prevailed upon to quit it for many hours, in expectation of seeing the poor dead lady conveyed out of the house. It was with the greatest difficulty that a friend of the family could prevail on such rusticks, to believe Miss Hardy was still living.

Soon after this rather surprising archeological escapade, Harriot had to return to Oporto, to be with Sophia Walsh whose third child was due that autumn. The still ailing Miss Hardy had to be left behind in the care of Louisa and Harriot Amelia.

HS As Sophia was expecting to be confined, I left Harriot with Miss Hardy, and went to Porto. They followed as soon as Miss Hardy could bear the fatigue of the journey, and very soon after her arrival in Porto we got her safe on board a ship for England.

The two Harriots and the Walshes were thus together again in Oporto in the autumn of 1807 when the thunderclouds of war which had been looming ever nearer to Portugal finally burst overhead.

17

Portugal had now become important to Napoleon because the Battle of Trafalgar had established British supremacy at sea, so the isolation of Britain from Europe could only be secured by conquering or dominating all Britain's allies on the Continent. Prussia and Austria had gone down before Napoleon in 1806; in July 1807 Russia had renounced her alliance with Britain when she accepted the Treaty of Tilsit. All Italy and much of the Adriatic were under French control; Turkey was now allied with France. Spain had been in league with France, under the influence of its principal minister Godoy, for the last decade, and had been forced in 1804 to declare war on Britain. The destruction of most of the Spanish fleet at Trafalgar had temporarily diminished Spanish importance to either France or Britain, but it was still more or less in Napoleon's pocket in 1807. Britain's only remaining ally on the European mainland was Portugal, and it was to Portugal that Napoleon now turned his attention.

On 12th August 1807 the French and Spanish Ambassadors in Lisbon delivered to the Prince Regent of Portugal notes demanding that he should declare war on England, join his fleet to those of France and Spain, confiscate all British goods in Portuguese harbours, and arrest all British citizens in Portugal. The Prince Regent reluctantly agreed to break off diplomatic relations with Britain and to close Portuguese ports against British ships, but not to seize British merchants in Portugal or their property.

In face of this threat to her oldest ally, and her last on the European mainland, Britain began – but too late – to make plans to land troops in Portugal to support the Portuguese against the threat of French and Spanish invasion. Sir John Moore was warned to hold himself in readiness to take a force of 8,000 men from Sicily – as soon as the Alexandrian garrison got back to hold the fort in Messina – to Gibraltar, where instructions would await him to go on to a landing in Lisbon. Sidney Smith was also sent to cruise off Portugal and await the turn of events.

This was the ominous crisis to which Harriot Slessor returned after her agreeable three months in Tras os Montes with Louisa from June to August 1807. It was now that she decided to keep a regular diary recording the events of the rapidly deteriorating situation. When she arranged the diary six years later for the benefit of John Henry, she gave it a resounding title:

HS Observations on events in Portugal, passed in the year 1807 and what followed in the year 1808; with a political review of events passed within those two years, in the way of journal, to refresh the memory of the individual much interested in such events.

She explained to her son how it had occurred to her to keep such a record. All the other English residents in Oporto had left for England, and she and her family were left alone, with no possibility of writing to or hearing from their friends in England, and with the threat of French and Spanish invasion hanging over their heads. In these dismal circumstances, 'Time seemed to linger. By way of diversion, it seemed to me no bad idea to write something like a journal, in that way in some measure to help on the heavy hours. There was full subject for such occupation. The pity is that an abler hand did not undertake the task.'

Harriot evidently felt that mock modesty was the appropriate stance for a female diarist, but in fact she embarked with confident fluency on her journal.

HS *Porto, August 7, 1807.*
The following matter of fact relation most certainly is written without an idea of its being perused by anyone: but solely for my amusement, or rather to possess a memento of events as they pass along, so full of wonder and dismay. Although it cannot cure, complaint relieves, and may be called a melancholy pleasure: I must indulge it. There is a gloom spread over my future prospects and fond hopes, alarming to a degree. The storm is gathering fast. How far I and mine are likely to be sufferers time only can disclose. Old age for certain cannot be the crisis to encounter the rubs of fortune, and to be exposed to tyranny and oppression. How often has it been presented to my mind in too lively colours, the difference between these times and happy ones that procured me many a contented day, with pleasure and satisfaction. These times seem to me to have flown away like a dream, and have left many a melancholy thought behind. The scene is totally changed. We have much to fear, and little good to hope for.

Poor Portugal, you are sick indeed! In what quarter of the globe are you to look for aid? I much fear you will be left to your fate. The scene of action to every appearance is now to be in Portugal. Napoleon having succeeded to the full of his expectations and ambitious views in Italy etc., seems inclined to turn his longing eyes towards this fine country, and see how far he may venture in the attempt to join it in the train of his former conquests.

The political events of the present time are so far beyond what is recorded in history, therefore so extraordinary, that the strongest minds can hardly resist the impulse of fear, and exclaim with the general voice 'In what is all this to end?'. We do not doubt that there is a ruling power that all look up to for mercy, and that directs every event for the best. This religion teaches us, as well as to bear with philosophy the ill inflicted on us, and not to repine at the will of Heaven. But as the power of reflection is given, particularly to thinking minds, let it be sacrilegious or not, such minds will not, cannot, remain dormant. They will involuntarily repine and wonder, that thousands are suffering to satisfy the ambition of one once most insignificant mortal; that he should be chosen out, above all, to give the law to nations, and attempt to ruin with despotic power. Individuals cannot fail to lament, to reason on the past, and tremble at the prospect of future events.

Bonaparte is not yet satisfied. Ambition is a monster not easily satiated. It is no unpleasant pastime, to give Kingdoms, and when it suits, to take them away again. Portugal has thought herself lucky to have been suffered to remain neutral, although on the hard conditions of paying immense sums at repeated periods, for the enjoyment of peace, when war was raging throughout Europe. Her treasury is empty, and she has a fearful prospect before her. That is all she seems for the present to gain.

While Lord St Vincent was last year in the Tagus with his Squadron, this Government had little reason to be at their ease with regard to French plans for the pretended future good of Portugal. She will now I fear be made to pay dear for her constant and time immemorial alliance, which she has ever kept true to, with her good friends the English. Early in the Spring the storm was gathering and the evil day fast approaching. But as hope is ever at hand, to soothe and to flatter, and too often to deceive, likewise it is not the first time this country had been thought on the brink of destruction, but has reared her head against the threatened storm. Those deeply concerned in the event, because they ardently wish it, flatter themselves it may again blow off. Alas, appearances are not for certain in favour of so desirable an event.

A week after this first entry, the Franco-Spanish ultimatum was delivered to the Portuguese Prince Regent, and thereafter the pace of events accelerated, as Harriot's next two diary entries record.

HS *September 1807.* All hopes are vanished. For some weeks negotiations have been going on between France and this country, and are now finally concluded. The French insisting on all British subjects being turned out of Portugal, and their property to be confiscated. The Prince Regent's answer to this is that he will sooner risk the loss of his Kingdom than act so treacherous a part against such a friend and ally as England has ever been to Portugal. Besides these hard terms, Bonaparte will come to no less agreement than Portugal for the future looking upon the English as enemies, and shutting her ports to every description of English Vessels. This sentence did not come unexpected. The Consul in Lisbon, previous to this, had warned our Consul here, that Government had declared to the British Envoy, that after a certain period given, it would not be in their power to protect the English, that quitting Portugal would be the only alternative: therefore advised them as soon as possible to settle their concerns, and embark for their native country.

This information did not come unexpected either, yet put the members of the Factory in the utmost dismay and confusion. They have little time to lose, and much to settle, of most important business. Shortly after this information a manifesto is published, in which the Prince informs his loving subjects, that for the sake of humanity, and to save the shedding of blood, he has entered into an alliance with the French, and had consented to sending the English out of the country, and to shut his ports against that nation. At the same time it is given the English to understand that they will be allowed time to get away, with their families etc. Of course those that do remain must take the consequences. This conduct from Government towards the English is much praised. Every one may make their reflections the way they think proper. It is too true this country is in such a state that resistance seems vain against such an enemy ready to overpower them. I do not see how or where the remedy is to be found without foreign assistance. We might look towards England for help, but it does not appear that she thinks this the crisis to send troops to fight our battles; for it is most probable we may expect to see the French march into the country more as enemies than friends, and a few thousand Englishmen might alarm those invaders.

Our poor countrymen, seeing no alternative, are preparing with their families, and with very heavy hearts, for their departure. Some are already gone. A convoy is waiting to guard them safe to England. The Consul will be the last to depart. He guides himself by the Envoy and Consul at Lisbon. Till they embark he is safe.

As the Englishmen of the British Factory in Oporto prepared to leave, Harriot's diary sets the scene by a flashback to the Portuguese and British society of Oporto as she had observed them during her years in Portugal. The Mr W—d and Mr W. to whom she refers in the following entry were John Whitehead and Willliam Warre. The celebrated and universally liked John Whitehead was British Consul in Oporto for nearly fifty years, and designed the splendid British Factory House there. He was kind, hospitable, learned, eccentric but not reclusive, a comfortable bachelor who owned a rich and varied library. His portrait in the Factory House was actually painted after his death, but shows him as a middle-aged man with a chubby but strong face and keen eyes.

His sister Elizabeth married a member of the Warre firm of wine shippers in Oporto, and their son William Warre succeeded his uncle John Whitehead as British Consul when Whitehead died in 1802. Harriot's sharp-tongued and rather snobbish comments on the habits of both the Portuguese and English inhabitants of Oporto, and on William Warre, suggest that she may not have been very popular in Oporto society in general.

HS I must take a little review of our departed friends, the English, and then lose sight of them.

I may be supposed to be pretty well acquainted with Porto and its inhabitants. The first visit I paid is it nearly forty years ago, and altho' it is only of later years that we have entirely taken up our residence here, we have occasionally passed many months at a time in a very pleasant manner at the Consul's. Porto now, and Porto formerly bear very little resemblance to what it was. There is no end to the new buildings; some are handsome. The old streets are very ugly, and bad for a carriage, and in old times none but litters were to be seen. Now no such thing appears. The numerous new houses in the outlets of the town are in general beautifully situated, commanding a fine view of the river with its shipping, with the addition of the rising hills on the opposite shore, interspersed with wood and houses, as well as convents, that forms a most majestic appearance.

When we first determined on living in Porto, our society was a good deal among the Portuguese. The women are lively, full of trifling chat, and very noisy. Both men and women are strangely ignorant, and seldom look into a book. It seems impossible to me to form anything like a friendship with a Portuguese family. Their manners and customs are so perfectly different from ours. If any individual among them chances to please by her manners and sprightly conversation, for the enjoyment of her society you must bear more than you wish to do, from the motley assemblage of persons you are constantly obliged to endure. There is likewise a want of order and cleanliness in their houses, most uncomfortable, and often disgusting. These have long been my sentiments, which till now, I have not felt the least inclination to vary, so that by degrees I have managed to keep clear of such parties, and visits on both sides are confined to very few in the course of the year.

The above account certainly does not speak much in favour of Portuguese society. The English and French mode of dress have long been adopted. We shall see, if the French remain in the country, how far the manners of that nation will prevail.

I must retract and contradict myself upon the score of friendship, with the recollection that we really did form a friendship when living in the North of Portugal with an Officer in General Slessor's regiment, a Portuguese, who is very clever, well informed, and has an excellent library that did not serve him only for show. For he has made good use of it, and while in the regiment we never wanted for books. But we did not long enjoy the agreeable and good company of this friend, as his merit, great fortune, and family connections soon destined him for the diplomatic line. He was well chosen, and certainly is one among the few that has done honour to his country. We lost him and his library, and so ended all ideas of friendship in the mountains of Portugal.

The English factory in Porto has undergone a total change within my memory. The members of it were ever noted for their hospitality and hearty welcome to strangers, in which good inclination for sociableness they kept up to the last of their residence in the country. Not much can be said in praise of the families in general, with regard to their polished manners, in days of yore. But everything has a beginning, nor is it necessary to enquire too minutely what rank of life most of the good ladies that then figured could boast of, before their good husbands preferred them as companions for life. Good eating was one of the first considerations, and those homely dames were perfect in the art of cookery. If they did not study to cover the table with nice little delicate dishes such as would suit the appetite of an epicure of these modern times, they made up for refinement in that respect by presenting their guest with hearty good will all that was solid. The want of refinement was made up by the tempting appearance of fine turbots, large plump turkeys etc. To be sure these feasts were rather overcharged, and to a nice stomach might take away the inclination to eat. It looked something like cramming to fatten. Yet these feasts in those times were not flung away, for I have seen the guests fall to with no little credit to a good appetite, and to do honour to the hostess. What was the least pleasant in these entertainments was, after the first feasting, a supper followed in as plentiful as the dinner.

Time and death, that took off many of the old members of the families, likewise produced a more polished set, so that the society by degrees began to form itself into something like, or at least an attempt was made at something like, the appearance of gentility. Old stupid families were replaced by young men, many of them with pretty wives. The Consul, Mr W—d, was a clever man, somewhat of a character, but very comical and entertaining. It was not easy to be dull in his company. He had a sister married to a man as old again as herself. She was nothing of the fine lady, but a friendly pleasant sensible woman. They lived in a beautiful Quinta, within a walk of Porto. Our chief society was with this family. It was a large one, and they had a set of sons, that gave life to the party. Besides every pleasant guest was in the custom of making this old lady's the rendezvous at night. In course of time many changes took place, and paved the way for the loss of this old lady for ever. One son married, and settled with his wife and family at the Quinta. She was a great addition to the family party. Mrs W. was blessed with plenty of grandchildren; like all grandmothers she thought them models of perfection. They were her delight, and her wish was certainly to have ended her days in her little

Paradise, where it may be said she had reigned Queen of it without control
from her early youth, and governed those under her dominion in a manner
to gain the love and goodwill of all around her. But she had an only
daughter, and that daughter, in the bloom of youth and beauty, elegant and
amiable, full of accomplishments, grew sick and pined to go to England,
and to England the mother went, with this object of her affections. It was a
cruel parting for Mrs W. She left Porto as if she was quitting her existence,
and in reality she did, not long after her arrival in England.

The society most congenial to my taste was at an end by the departure of
the old lady's married son with his family. They were a sad loss. The
Consul lived to a very old age. At his death his nephew, Mr W. was
appointed Consul in his place, by the unanimous voice of the Factory. No
great parts are required to make a Consul in Porto. Mr W. suits them well.
It is not likely that such a Consul as the late will appear again in a hurry.
He managed the business with a masterly hand. The English were attached
to him, and the Portuguese had a high opinion of his understanding and
learning. He was certainly a man of parts; had read a great deal and had an
excellent memory. The present Consul in his family was ever looked up to
as the Beau and fine gentleman. Since he became sole possessor of the
sweet Quinta, he had lived in ease and luxury; was the Bon Vivant, the
Epicure. He could boast of having the best cook in Porto, of giving dinners
quite in style, his table exhibiting delicacies of every nature to invite the
appetite. His guests were not always as choice as his table. Too open to
adulation and flattery, he was courted by all, and some that certainly
should not have found so easy admittance to his particular society.

Mr W. cannot be pronounced a man of parts. He has a superficial
appearance of cleverness that suits well enough in the common run of
society. At the same time he is perfect in the manners of the gentleman,
which has its weight and imposes. He has some little pretensions to a
knowledge in the fine arts, and has a well chosen library, of all the living
languages. It is a pity Mr W. has not learnt in his walk of life to read
characters in their true light. He is easily led by idle persuasion to form a
wrong judgment of individuals, much to their prejudice; what is worse,
when once he has formed that judgment, he is not to be convicted of his
error. But none are perfect, and there would be no great harm, before we
pretend to such strict scrutiny of our neighbour's faults, should we be
honest and ask ourselves one simple question; and if you cannot accuse
yourself of being guilty of the like faults, can you in conscience say that
you have not some of a nature equally to be condemned. But where are
found those that are ready to be self accusers? Altho' we must know our
defects, we are in general very ingenious at finding out the means of hiding
them. Therefore I had best quit this subject, and not turn critic. Let the
World take its course, and if I have more observations to sport to the

Consul's account, it shall be in his favour, for certainly he was respected and liked by those who knew him. He may be called a native of this country, being born in Porto, and had lived here all his life.

He had known none but prosperous days, in this fine climate that was congenial to his nature, and now suited his age. We doubt but it was a severe trial, being forced to quit so many comforts; but all is not lost with Mr W. Altho' he is a sufferer in the change, he must remain with more than sufficient, if vanity will but remain dormant; for he cannot pretend at being the man of consequence in England, as he was in Porto. He may still be a happy man, if he has but philosophy and resignation to the will of Heaven.

Young married men with rising families are really to be pitied, for they are forced from a comfortable establishment, and have no remedy but to resign all future flattering prospects in this country. It is like beginning the world again, but having the interest of their wives and children at heart they will battle with fortune, I do not doubt, and rise again and be prosperous. The richest among those at the Factory seem to me to feel more particularly this blow. Some that are in possession of houses, built with their own good money, altho' of English extraction, have never lived in England. These I do not pity, for they have wherewithal to live in any part of the world.

I must observe that the whole of the Factory have ever been in the habit of abusing this country, the people and everything in it. Now is the time to judge of their real sentiments. The evident consternation, even to weakness, that reigned throughout every family was most striking, when every hope vanished for a possibility for their remaining. This plainly shows how all in general wished not be forced away. This is the way of the World. We seldom present it with our real sentiments, but on the contrary too frequently profess what is least in our thoughts.

In this curious passage of censorious comment, self-doubt and what sounds like personal animus against the Consul William Warre, Harriot was perhaps whistling in the dark to keep up her courage. Against the advice of the whole British colony in Oporto, and probably the strong urging of the Consul, she and the Walshes had decided to stay on in Portugal and risk the dangers of war and invasion. To bolster up her confidence, she needed to condemn the faintheartedness and inadequacy of those who had decided on flight.

18

By mid-October Portugal's danger had become very great. On 20th October the Prince Regent, under pressure from France, declared war on England. Napoleon meanwhile, in the Secret Treaty of Fontainebleau which he made with the Spanish Minister Godoy, had agreed to partition Portugal between France and Spain, and at the end of October a Franco-Spanish army under Marshal Junot crossed the Portuguese border. On 8th November the unhappy Prince Regent, who had continued to hope that he could keep in with both sides, and conciliate the French without taking any real action against the British, was forced to sign a decree ordering the seizure of any British merchants remaining in Portugal, and of British property. He is said to have signed it 'with agonies of remorse, casting his pen from him five times before he could bring himself to use it'. The effect of this decree was soon felt in Oporto, shattering Harriot Slessor's confidence that her position as widow of a general in the Portuguese army would protect her, though not shaking her sturdy refusal to feel fear.

HS   *November 1st, 1807.* The English are gone, and safe at sea; and the Consul too took leave of Portugal, in all probability for good and all, the first of November. Lord William Stewart at anchor off the Bar received him on board his Frigate, and they were soon out of sight.

In what terms can I express my feelings at this, I may call it, most solemn epoch? Should I attempt at describing the various sensations, and so mixed with hopes and fears for future events, fluctuating in my mind, it would be vain; I could not do it. It was truly with a heavy heart we witnessed the departure of the English from our shores. To see the gloom spread over every countenance, and the melancholy quiet in the streets, was sad indeed. We are thought mad for so doing. I hope not quite that either. An unmarried daughter with myself might have gone on this occasion; but then I must have left a married daughter, her husband, and two sweet boys, and the mother in daily expectation of an increase of family, so that without exposing her life, she can hardly venture a voyage so late in the year; besides the circumstance that we must separate, our destination being for England, theirs for Ireland; and my daughter would be alone on board a ship, without a female companion. Her husband would not on any account let her run so great a risk. He has nothing to do with the Factory, no more than myself. He came some years ago to Portugal for his health, and found it, and perhaps more than he could have thought; for he found an amiable and good wife, and since their marriage we have joined families.

I may persuade myself we are safe for the present in this country. The general opinion is that the French will be satisfied, the English being out of Portugal . . . As a General's widow I am entitled to a pension from the Widows Fund, and having lived so many years in the country may be looked upon as a native, and have a right to ask for protection from this Government, altho' with the privilege of a British Subject. Not that I have much confidence in such protection. Such reasons would have had little weight with me. Much stronger than those press on my mind. A mother's feelings for a beloved daughter have more force. There is no leaving her in her present state. Besides the love of a grandmother speaks most forcibly within me; a dear little favourite grandson, that is my delight. These are ties that have fast hold. Surely they are irresistible.

The resolution once taken our minds are much more at ease. We are determined to share each other's fate, for good or will. If for ill, we must manage some way or other, to get away in the Spring, which I trust, should it be necessary, we shall be able to accomplish.

Notwithstanding the departure of the English, the French do not appear satisfied. More condescension is still required of this country. Nothing can be more evident than that the French plans with regard to this poor Portugal, let them be what they will, are to take their course. For lenity, no one in their senses will think of that. The news from Lisbon is, that the French and Spanish Ambassadors have taken leave of this Court, and are gone. To quiet the minds of the people a manifesto is published assuring them that they are to return without delay with full powers to settle all differences, and that there is every reason to expect that a lasting alliance will shortly be settled between the two nations. At the very time that this proclamation made its appearance, it is too obvious to all that great preparations are making, and in all haste, to get a Squadron ready, in case it should be wanted, to take off the Royal Family to the Brazil. But no one is allowed to think it, much less give a hint of the kind.

A very few days after the departure of the English whatever property they have left behind was put under sequester. The great protection that I was led to expect has ended in my being treated after the same manner, as a British Subject. An account is taken of every article in this house, but nothing is touched for the present. I understand that we are also to have sentence of imprisonment passed upon us. I do not feel much alarmed, as I flatter myself it will not be a very heavy one to endure.

While the French, and the pro-French party at the Portuguese Court, were twisting one arm of the Prince Regent, the British Chargé d'Affaires in Lisbon,

Lord Strangford, was grasping the other arm. The British Government had long planned that if the French invaded and occupied Portugal, the Portuguese Royal Family and Government should be persuaded to transfer themselves to Brazil, then a Portuguese colony, their transport being protected by the British Navy. It was for this purpose that Sir Sidney Smith had been ordered from the Mediterranean. In November his squadron was waiting off Lisbon at the mouth of the Tagus. Lord Strangford had to leave Lisbon and embark in HMS *Hibernia*, Sidney Smith's flagship, on 18th November, but he continued to visit and persuade the Prince Regent at his palace of Queluz, near Lisbon, throughout that month of November. Later historians have disagreed as to whether it was Strangford or Sidney Smith who finally induced the Prince Regent to accept the move to Brazil. Sidney Smith, with his fondness for associating with royalty, would certainly have claimed the credit whether it was really his or not; in any case, it was under his escort that the Prince Regent, his crazy mother Queen Maria, the rest of the royal family of Braganza, the Council of State, the Ministers and many of the Portuguese artistocracy finally embarked on 29th November and sailed for Brazil. Next day the French army under Junot, which had met no resistance since crossing the Portuguese frontier, entered an acquiescent Lisbon.

When the news of the occupation of Lisbon reached the assembled British forces under Sir John Moore off Gibraltar, the plan of landing British troops at Lisbon to forestall the French invasion had to be abandoned, and Moore's forces, including John Henry Slessor, sailed on to England, passing Oporto just as Harriot and the Walshes were shut up in their house there waiting imprisonment.

Harriot's diary entry describing the events of the 29th and 30th in Lisbon is dated 28th November, but must have been written some days later, when the news reached Oporto.

HS   *November 28th.* The Royal family residing in the country, altho' not much at their ease, did by no means suspect the extent of their unfortunate situation, when through the means of Sir Sidney Smith they were informed that Junot with his army was at Abrantes, within about 12 leagues of Lisbon; at the same time advising the Prince, without loss of time to remove to Lisbon, and with the utmost expedition get on board a ship as soon as possible. The confusion, alarm and consternation this notice caused throughout the Royal Family may easily be conceived. They hurried to town. A few days' delay might prove fatal. Preparations were made in haste to embark as soon as could be. All got safe on board. The scene of embarcation was moving beyond measure. The Princess Regent on this severe trial showed much firmness and resolution, and would not stir till her whole family had embarked.

The despair of the people, when they discovered that their Prince was going to leave them, was strikingly pathetic. They followed him down to the waterside in crowds, in despair, crying and lamenting that he was forsaking them. The Prince seemed much affected, and did all in his power by kind words to reconcile them to his departure; assured them that he had no choice, but must go; that he was betrayed and sold. The greatest part of the Nobility followed the Prince. Crowds of every description flocked on board the ships ready to sail, with the intention of leaving their country and sharing their Monarch's fate. The greater number were obliged to return on shore for want of room. On this account many hundreds much against their will were obliged to remain behind. The wind proving contrary for some days the fleet could not sail.

The Prince, on hearing of Junot's being at Abrantes, sent to demand what could be his reasons for coming into the country with an army without its being required of him; that such conduct looked like a declaration of hostilities; and being in the faith that peace and a good understanding subsisted between the two nations, extraordinary troops were not demanded. Therefore the Prince requested that the French General would be so good as to return with his army from whence he came. Junot's orders not being comfortable to so reasonable a demand, he gave for answer, that his intentions were not in any way to interfere with His Highness's Government, but that he is come to protect him and his country from the tyranny of the English. The Prince being assured that Junot had not the least idea of quitting Portugal, on the contrary that him and his army were moving on the Capital, he observed 'Then it is time for me and my family to depart'.

On the 28th of November, the wind being in favour for the sailing of the Fleet, to the number of 20 sail, between small and great, all got safely over the Bar, where Sir Sidney Smith hail'd the Royal Family with the usual discharge, and was ready, with any part of his Squadron, to convoy them in security to the Brazil. Arrauge, the first Minister, seems to have played his cards so ill that he has lost the good opinion of both parties. If he had stayed behind he ran a good chance of being demolished by the people; they are so inveterate against him. The 29th of November 1807 must ever remain a memorable day in the Annals of this country. She beholds her good Sovereign (for if he has no other quality to be granted has fallen to his lot, he certainly is possessed of that one) forced to fly from his native shore. He *may meet with* a favourable reception from his new subjects. At any rate it is a sad alternative.

Those that are fated to drudge on in the common walk of life, their feelings are in general suited to their station. Such whose rank in life seems to have placed far above the rubs of fortune, but not the less experience cruel disappointments and griefs far beyond thought. Such persons deserve our commiseration. The Royal Family have my pity most sincerely. Little will it avail in so forlorn a case. We should rejoice that they have got clear from the grasp of him whose ambition makes him lose sight of justice and humanity. There is not the least doubt that Bonaparte's intention was to have got hold of the whole of the Royal Family. His mortification will not be trifling when he is informed that his army did not arrive in Lisbon till after the departure of the fleet, so that this unmerciful project was defeated, to the joy of all good persons. Junot entered Lisbon the day after the Prince etc were safe on the wide Ocean.

It is supposed the enemy's army to be, between French and Spaniards, 18,000 men, that have now entered this country. It appears they were so ill informed that they were perfectly ignorant what the kind of reception might be that they had to expect. The first question raised on the army's entering the country was, if there were troops from England. On being answered in the negative, and with the certainty of being free from so formidable an enemy, they marched on with all confidence. Certainly they might expect to meet with some kind of resistance. On the contrary, Junot with his army was allowed to march through the country perfectly at their ease. Not so with regard to bad weather and execrable roads, which embarrassed the progress of their journey not a little. With many distresses not to be avoided with such an army, they were harassed beyond measure; but as Junot's thoughts were set only on getting to Lisbon, on they must go, full speed, marching through bogs and rivers up to the neck; the General giving the example marching at their head, dashing into rivers that from great rains were not very fordable; he with his drawn sword calling out to his men '*En avant, en avant*'. One poor man lagging a little behind, Junot supposed him inclined to be disobedient to orders, ordered him to be shot instantly.

Pillage and devastation seemed to be the order of the day, for nowhere did they pay for the provisions taken from the inhabitants of the towns and villages. It was all one, from the officers down to the common soldier. The poor people were robbed of their all in many places, and if they attempted to resist, murder ensued. The wretches were not even satisfied with acting in this barbarous manner. It can hardly be credited, but it is too true; what they could not take away with them was destroyed. Wine and oil were set afloat in the streets, and as they marched on, they did all the mischief in their power. Many hundreds of these wretches remained on the highway, either from illness or fatigue, and left to perish one way or another. The Portuguese, wherever they found them, had not the least consideration for these poor miserable starving unprotected fellow creatures. They were murdered in cold blood and put out of pain.

The French army is a composition of all nations, and the best part hardly clothed, without shoes or stockings. On their arrival in Lisbon the men were so perfectly knocked up that they could not carry their arms. The Portuguese did it for them. For many hours after they had entered the city they lay about the streets insensible to every harm that might have happened to them. But the Prince, before his departure, settled a Regency, recommending to those he had appointed strictly to observe his commands, that it was his will, till his return. With regard to his loving subjects, he entreated them to behave peaceably, to receive the French as friends, and help them in every way, as far as lay in their power. The Prince is obeyed, as is seen from what has passed.

Junot, fearing that the Spanish troops destined to take Oporto would not arrive as soon as wished, thought fit to spare a Division from his army, and sent them off for that town. It is confidently asserted that Lasnes, who had formerly been Ambassador in this country, positively refused to accept the command of the army that has now entered it, he giving for reason that he would never come as an enemy into a country whose Government had shown him every attention; not only attention, but it is true, had loaded him and his very pretty saint-like looking wife with the richest presents. If this be a fact, tho' he is a true Bashaw, he shows that he is not entirely void of feeling.

General Junot, the late Ambassador at this Court, is not so delicate on the score of conscience. He had no objection to act as Commander-in-Chief on such a Mission, and is the *Hero that is come to protect the Portuguese Nation.* This General has taken up his quarters at Quintillas, one of the richest individuals in Portugal. He will have a good opportunity of spending his thousands, for certain this *good General* will not contribute a farthing towards his maintenance in all grandeur, with his numerous followers. The dignity and consequence of this great thief must be kept up. In this hostile manner had Napoleon sent his satellites, that in all parts where they passed have left terror and dismay. But they come as friends notwithstanding, and *Junot is an honourable man.*

19

The invaders had not yet appeared in Oporto, which was as well for Sophia Walsh, whose third son was born in the last week of November. Her husband, though liable to arrest as an Englishman since November 8th, had not yet been sought out by the authorities in Oporto, now under orders from the residual Portuguese Government in Lisbon to comply with the French demands for the arrest of British subjects. But early in December the blow fell. The intrepid Harriot describes what followed with a certain ironic amusement at the nimble evasions of 'Senhor Diogo' as she calls her son-in-law James Walsh.

HS *December 1807.* Our expectations are realised. On the 10th of December, a most thundering rap at the House door announced the arrival of these unwelcome visitors. There was no barring our doors against them, so that we had no other remedy but give them free access. The first step was their leaving a guard in sight of the house door, that none of the family should attempt to escape, and two squat, sallow, bad little figures desired an introduction to the family. We had been prepared for their reception by a gentleman that had come just before to say they were soon to be with us. These creatures made their appearance with a great deal of modest assurance, and seemed by their countenance and manner much to enjoy their mission. With a great air of mystery, supposing us to be ignorant of what business they were come to perform, they asked to speak with Mr W——, that they had something particular to say to him, and it must be to himself. That was not so easy a matter, for Senhor Diogo did not feel the least inclination to take up his quarters in a cold prison in the depth of winter. When these wretches came to the door, our gentleman most nimbly stepped out at a window, jumped onto the tiles and got safe into our neighbour's yard, and hid himself in a friend's house. We assured the men that Senhor D. was not at home. They were not inclined to believe us. If he was not at home they must know where to find him. That question was as useless, for of course none of us would give a satisfactory reply. They did not attempt to search the house, but stayed on. At last we assured them that they were losing a great deal of time; that Mr W—h often went to sleep in the country, and most probably had gone there. If they had an inclination to go after him, they might.

Our prison was easily settled, as females are allowed their house for prison, and liberty to go where we pleased, only with a promise that we will not leave the country. These gentlemen, thinking themselves very cunning, gave a hint that if Mr W. would appear only to sign his name it would do, as his imprisonment was to be of the same nature as ours; but it would not do. At last the wretches, seeing that it was of no use to persist in staying, took leave, and went to finish in other families the business in hand with better success, but for the misfortune of those concerned. Several poor individuals, some with wives and many children, were taken from their families that night, and cast into prison. These are poor persons, settled in the country, and have no subsistence in any other. These poor men now confined are deprived of the means of sustaining their despairing wives and children, as they have done till now, by their industry, from one day to another. It is enough that they are English, as well as poor, to be treated in this manner. For certainly the person high in office, that had his orders from Lisbon, could have taken it upon himself to mitigate this order, and suffered such poor insignificant beings to remain in their peaceful homes. Government had more important concerns, that take up their thoughts and time, and may probably never enquire how far such orders have been carried out. Nor do I think it at all unlikely that before long Government itself may be under the necessity of seeking its own safety.

I must return to our fugitive. When the coast was clear, he very quickly returned home. After composing our ruffled spirits we could not but laugh and be amused at the idea how we had baffled these men, that seemed so perfectly void of feeling. Altho' W. had escaped going to prison this time, he was not yet out of the scrape, and the sentence was still in force. Time was not to be lost, to see how he might parry the blow. He was determined not to play more at hide and seek, and our barbarians promised us another visit, and I gave my word that W. should be at home. The order for imprisonment came to the Chancellor of Oporto, an old bed-ridden lump of flesh, a cripple with the gout, and is as big as a porpoise. As for humanity, he had not a grain in his composition. Such is the character we had to manage in this business, and to move to compassion. We feared it would be as easy to move a rock as him. However, at any rate necessity urged W. to make the attempt. Away he posts that very night, and presents himself before the Chancellor, who was not a little surprised at seeing him; for the old gentleman was confident he had by that time the younger one secure. W, told his story in the best manner possible, and that his not being at home at the time was the reason that His Excellency's orders were not put into execution; that he had not a thought for resisting his will; at the same time pleaded his bad state of health as a plea to be allowed his house as a prison. He had a few friends present, who supported him to good purpose, and argued the point very strongly. In particular, the French Consul's son insisted on it that so much severity was not required to be inflicted upon individuals sick or well. As French influence will most likely rule in future, I think the old man more through fear than inclination let himself be persuaded into consent. The Frenchman gained the victory. It was settled the sick well man should make his appearance the next evening with three Physicians at the prison, to attest to the truth of this allegation. This was done, and all was agreed to in the way we wished. The Frenchman in triumph accompanied our gentleman home, to the great joy of us all, and more particularly that of his most anxious wife, who only a fortnight before this event had presented me with a third little grandson.

It certainly will not be an easy matter to efface two such days from remembrance. Our gratitude is due to the Consul, and sincere thanks. It is to him we owe the having settled this matter so easily, and that was of great importance for our peace of mind. There were persons malicious enough to attack the Consul for his assiduity to serve the English. His answer was that, in his opinion, he had only done what a man of honour should do.

Shortly after the above transaction, a publication appeared in the French papers in very strong terms, accusing our poor inoffensive Prince for not having in full force put into execution his promise to the great Napoleon with regard to the English, for which reason he is judged highly criminal; 'that he has forfeited all confidence, and in this consideration can no longer be looked upon as worthy to hold the reins of Government'. 'A country ruled by such a Prince can no longer rank with any nation'. What impudence! Such thundering expressions can only be taken in one sense. The sun of Portugal is setting. Her prosperous days are under a dark cloud: all is gloomy and sad. Her sentence is pronounced, and death warrant signed. Bonaparte tho' will not despise the country, altho' he does the Prince. It is not to be overlook'd, but that he will make a trifling effort to take it under his safeguard, and form it into as fine a nation, as he has done to all those he has already conquered.

Can there be any greater evil inflicted on a nation than to be governed by a weak Prince? This country bears melancholy and strong proofs of this assertion. The leading characters that have for many years ruled in Portugal are so well known that it is useless for me to dwell on the subject. The present Prince is even less capable perhaps than his ancestors to wear a crown. Therefore it cannot be wondered at, if he has not power or abilities to keep it. Nature has, in fact, denied him every requisite to fit him for one. A cloister, his chaplet, and prayer book is what would suit such a nature. Within high convent walls a weak mind, framed as is that of this poor Prince, might be indulged from morn to night in acts of devotion, bigotry and indolence. A character of this description placed on a throne must be exposed at this critical moment to innumerable embarrassments. He may upon trial find the want and advice of those that should be attached to him and his throne. Traitors, I fear, will not be few.

20

Junot's army which invaded Portugal in October 1807 included three auxiliary Spanish corps, one of which, consisting of 6,000 Galicians under the command of General Francisco Taranco, was to march through Vigo to occupy Oporto and the Lower Douro. Taranco and the Galician corps reached Oporto on 13th December, and Harriot's journal gives a full account of their entry to the city and the ensuing occupation. In spite of the heavily ironic bitterness, the opinionated vehemence, with which she writes, she succeeds in giving a vivid picture of life in occupied Oporto in the winter of 1807-8.

She inveighs against the Portuguese failure to put up any resistance to the invaders, and imagines how she would have acted in the Prince Regent's place, but she seems to have been alone in her opinion; everyone else in Oporto thought that resistance against the all-powerful French and their Spanish allies would only have led to massacres, and that quisling collaboration with the invaders was the most prudent policy, as exemplified by Mrs Van Zeller, an Oporto resident whose family was of Dutch origin and whom Harriot describes as making her house available to the second-in-command of the forces occupying Oporto.

HS *On the 13th of December* Spanish troops arrived in Porto, under the command of a Spanish General by name Taranco. On the 18th of the same month an Italian General marched into the town, at the head of more troops, all Spaniards. Between Cavalry and Infantry the total is above 10,000, that are come, I suppose, likewise to defend us from the tyranny of the English. The entry of these troops was a most unwelcome scene for the poor inhabitants of Porto. When the sound of the drums and trumpets announced their near approach, the people ran in great crowds to see so novel a sight, but all was quiet and sad silence. The army suffered great hardships on their march, often having little or nothing to eat, but their conduct on the whole was more humane than that of the French. They passed on the road many French soldiers, some dead, others dying. There appeared none in the smallest degree ready to have compassion on them.

It may be safely said that, from the time the Royal Family were out at sea, the House of Braganca had ceased to reign in Portugal; if ever to return, seems for the present problematical. That good to the country may be expected from the new Government (for a new one we shall have) can hardly be looked for. The fate of other nations is no equivocal warning of the game likely to be played in this. As soon as it was known for certain that French and Spanish troops were to be marched into the country, all the regiments, both Cavalry and Infantry, had orders to quit their usual quarters, and with all speed march to Lisbon. But the enemy was in Portugal before there was time for any of the regiments to effect such orders. They were all on their march when the melancholy intelligence was announced to them of the departure of their Prince, with a counter order not to proceed further on their way; so that where this order found the troops, there they remained, and got quarters as well as they could, until further orders.

There never was an example of so easy a conquest of a country. It cannot be said that it is attained without a groan, altho' without a single blow. I think that if the very stones could have spoken, they would have exclaimed in pathetic moans against such treachery. My romantic ideas may pass the bounds of prudence and perhaps reason, but I firmly believe that had fate placed me on a throne, no Bonaparte should have hurled me from it but with my life. The reply to this observation may be, then you must have resembled some one of the Heroes of ancient times, or even Bonaparte himself; or how could you hope for success? These are not times for kings. Such modern kings, it must be confessed, are made of very poor material. Bonaparte knows the ground he has to go on, and goes secure. Had this country been blessed with anything like a valiant Prince, that had an opinion of his own, it would not have fallen as it did. Even with the present Monarch, had resistance been attempted, and the English sent over a few thousands, the French would not have effected so easy a conquest. There is a great difference in being attacked in your own country or going in search of your enemy in an unknown one, particularly in a country like this, that in many parts is a defence of itself, even without fighting at all. What hardships were there not, that the French had to encounter? Many long nights did they lay with the heavens over their heads, and the rain pouring on them in torrents, without a change of clothes belonging to anyone. These sufferings were as good as an enemy, for they demolished them fast.

When I venture to sport an opinion that resistance should have been attempted, the vote goes against me, and I am asked what would have been the use of it, for suppose the first had been demolished of these savages that entered the country, there were thousands more ready to supply the place of those that were departed, as we all know that Napoleon regards the lives of men no more than the most insignificant atom that crawls on the earth. So that from resistance nothing but scenes of massacre would ensue. 'Tis true, such reflections fill with horror: there is no dwelling on them. But I am rather obstinate to a once adopted opinion. Therefore it cost me to agree to the above judgment, and I cannot think it at all impossible but that a second army might likewise have met with too great opposition to be able to march on without material loss.

There is an appearance of such pusillanimity, such cowardice, and so humiliating it is, to behold an enemy march into your country under the mask of friendship, when you know he comes to conquer you; and not one, no not one, appeared inclined to raise a hand against such false friends. I would have resisted, whether with success or not, even if I had been sure of remaining under her ruins. But the die is cast, and Portugal submits to her fate.

What a change a few fleeting weeks produced in this Metropolis, so lately a flourishing commercial town! Porto is now transformed to Military Government, and nothing is heard but the clink of arms, drums and trumpets. Adieu to English. I must turn to quite a new scene. Melancholy is the prospect. It is well there is no searching into futurity. If we were to know the ills that it is doomed us by fate to endure, our anxious minds would be worn so much before the time allotted for the trial that few natures could have powers of resistance, but sink under it.

The Rua Nova is where the principal English had houses, or their counting houses. The Exchange, Coffee and Factory House are likewise in this street. General Taranco, Commander-in-Chief, both civil and military, on his arrival took up his quarters at the Factory house. His stay there was but a few days. The apartments were too large and comfortless for his mild and humble nature. He has settled himself in a good but smaller house in the same street. This General is a good old Spaniard. Altho' high in rank, of a good family, and much in the estimation of both his King and country, he possesses none of the vain pomposity of the Spanish Nation. His chief care on his arrival was to avoid distressing anyone, and he would not allow the officers to be quartered on private families. The soldiers are disposed of in the barracks and convents, but the Friars are under no obligation to maintain them; they have a good allowance. The empty houses that were inhabited by the English are now full of Spanish officers. Whatever furniture was wanted for the accommodation of these gentlemen, every housekeeper has been called upon to give something towards it. None repined at this tax, being happy to be left in quiet possession of their houses, without intruders. As for me and mine, what we thought cruel usage turn'd a lucky event. We were looked upon as prisoners, and my effects under sequester, so that I am safe from trouble and expense on the present occasion.

Carafa, Second in Command, a cunning Italian, was offered the Factory House, on the General's leaving it, which he refused. He seemed much surprised at such a proposal. 'Could it be supposed that he would for one moment entertain the idea of taking up his quarters in the very house of festivity of the English. That unhappy people deserved every mark of pity. Should he take possession of it, it would look too like triumphing in their fate'. This man of feeling declared that it would be impossible for him to sleep with any comfort in such a habitation. The truth is that nothing will accommodate but a good house with a good lady hostess in the family, and he gave to understand that he expected to be obeyed. In truth he was, beyond expectation. For a rich widow, Mrs V—r, had compassion on him, and received him with a numerous retinue of Aide de Camps, etc etc. This general has good reason to be satisfied with his reception. It may be that he has not often been so well lodged. The mistress of this hospitable habitation has given up her very comfortable apartments. A table is daily prepared for 20 persons, and our gentleman takes upon himself to invite those he thinks proper. Add to this a carriage at command, and society at night when in the humour to enjoy it; and so much good has fallen to his lot, in a strange land, only for thanks.

I may truly observe that the mind must at such time be ever on the alert, wearied with constant hopes and fears, and with anxious expectations for some new event for good or ill. This perfect calm is ominous. It will not, it cannot last. Some nights ago we had a cruel trial. For the first time we joined Mrs V—r's assembly. We were the only English in the room. How sadly impressive was the scene at entering the porch, the first objects that disturbed my sight, and that embarrassed our way to the stairs, were a set of stout surly looking guards (Spaniards) laying at their length, rolled up in their cloaks, and with only their saucy faces peeping out; growling, and looking inclined if they dared to insult us as we passed. On the first flight of stairs is posted a sentinel, and on the second, at the door that leads to the drawing-room, another presents himself to your view. Between Officers, guards and soldiers, that are constantly coming and going, this once nice house presents quite a contrary appearance, and is finely perfumed with the smell of tobacco, it being a rare thing for a Spaniard to be able to pass without smoking.

General Carafa, altho' punctiliously and attentively assiduous to his hostess, does not in the smallest degree overlook the observance due to the parade and attendance attached to General officers. He must have little confidence in this good family, not to lay aside such state, and dispense such guards, after the reception he meets with. Mrs V—r's house faces the Factory. It is a fine extensive building. We have been in the custom of seeing this now solitary mansion gaily illuminated every Monday, the Factory ball night. Mark the change. Now darkness reigns throughout, and glimmering chance lights appear here and there from the lofty windows, as they glide along. While at the General's door all is noise and bustle. Crowds assemble to view the soldiers that attend for orders, with their bands of musick, to amuse the ladies. The drums and trumpets cruelly offend the ear. The bands are excellent, it is true, and the musick good. They fight battles, and express in pathetic moans the agony of the dying, and cries of the wounded. Such music is well suited to the times, but not to my feelings, and I naturally fly from the window where all flock to hear.

The old Spanish General has not been persuaded to go to Mrs V—r's at night. He is no friend of Carafa's. They are quite opposite characters. The Commander-in-Chief takes no state at all on himself. The two extremes are bad. Some state is certainly necessary, but he keeps to the line of conduct which he adopted on his arrival. He will gain little merit in the eyes of the World for so doing. He takes as little as possible from the public for his private expenses, has little or nothing of his own, therefore gives no entertainments, and passes his days in solitude. But there is no one who will not say he is a good old man, and that it will be well for Porto, as long as it remains under so lenient a Government.

Among the Spanish Officers there are some pleasant agreeable men. They are happy to be taken notice of, and take it as a favour to be invited to parties at night. Some of them are noble and thought very good Officers. They cannot disguise the despicable opinion they have of the military of this country. It must be confessed that of late years the army has been neglected. In the last reign it seems to have been the system not to admit any addition of foreign Officers, and as they have not any of their own good for anything, what can be expected? The few remaining General Officers of the time of the Marquis de Pombal have died off, or left Portugal. While the Regiments could boast of being commanded by good English Officers, they made no despicable appearance. The men are hardy, are good soldiers, can bear fatigue, and can live on much less than our English soldiers. As for fighting well, I can venture to say, let them but have confidence and a good opinion of their leaders, that they will do their duty and fight like men. I wish I could flatter myself and think that the time may still come to verify this my opinion. On the arrival of the Spanish troops in Porto, there was a Portuguese Regiment of Infantry from Braganca quartered in the town. They showed a very good inclination to rise against the Spaniards and go to blows. They are a fine set of men, and did not desire better sport. To keep all quiet they were ordered to leave Porto and seek for some other quarters.

As an instance upon what uncertain ground these Generals came with their armies, when Carafa arrived before Coimbra, he was informed that a regiment of Cavalry was in the town. Altho' the Spanish General had a much greater force than the Portuguese Commander, he sent him an order to march out of the town, and to retire to several leagues distance. The Colonel returned for answer, that the troops might march into the town without fear, his Regiment being under good discipline; that he would be responsible for their peaceable conduct. Perhaps the General was not so sure of his own soldiers, not giving up the point, so that the Portuguese had no alternative but to obey. They left the town, and did not return till the Spaniards had quitted it.

Harriot continued to believe in the fighting quality of the rank and file of the Portuguese army, some of whom her husband had commanded. She admitted that the army had deteriorated in recent years, but this was because of bad officers and bad organisation, not for lack of fighting spirit among the common soldiers. Her criticism of Portuguese officers is confirmed by the findings of the English General Beresford who was appointed in February 1809 to command and reorganise the Portuguese army. His verdict was that so many officers had gone to Brazil with the Royal Family, and long peace-time service in small garrison towns had so sapped the energy of the remaining senior Portuguese army officers, that they could not be depended upon for even passable attention to their duties, and there was no hope of making the Portuguese army an efficient fighting force until 'a whole generation of colonels had been cleared away'. The death or departure of John Slessor and his contemporaries, who had joined the Portuguese army in Pombal's time, had left a vacuum of indolence and inefficiency in its higher command which deadened its impetus.

21

While Oporto remained in a state of uneasy calm under the mild control of General Taranco, conditions elsewhere in Portugal were far more unhappy. Junot's army, whose advance force of only 1,500 exhausted men had occupied Lisbon without resistance on 30th November, was now occupying Portugal in strength, with 25,000 Frenchmen and 9,500 Spaniards. There had been faint signs of protest in Lisbon when Junot had the Portuguese flag hauled down and the Tricolour hoisted on all the public buildings, but the protesters were easily dispersed by French cavalry. The officials and military leaders who had remained behind when the Prince Regent and the Government left for Brazil were submissively ready to collaborate with the French. Junot, while issuing proclamations full of fine promises to the Portuguese people, treated them with considerable rigour. The Portuguese army was disbanded, its older soldiers and new recruits being discharged, and the remainder regrouped and shipped off to be used in French operations in the Baltic. On the order of Napoleon an enormous tax was imposed on the Portuguese. The Prince Regent and the 15,000 leading Portuguese citizens who had escaped with him to Brazil had taken with them nearly half the coined money in Portugal; it was now decreed that all property left by the refugees in Portugal was to be confiscated, and fines of 100 million francs to be exacted from Portugal. Some of this was raised by Junot by seizing church plate and royal properties, as well as the properties of English merchants, but the financial burden on the country as a whole was a crushing one, and provoked some local riots which were savagely repressed by the French.

From the precarious security of Oporto Harriot collected reports and anecdotes of French tyranny and cruelty elsewhere in Portugal, and copied into her diary the texts of boastful proclamations and decrees by the occupying authorities, adding sarcastic comments on them.

HS *The 19th of December* produced the novelty of a Proclamation, and for its contents to be well known to every one, printed papers were stuck up in every public street in Porto. The translation is nearly as follows:

'General Taranco, Commander-in-Chief of the Spanish troops and Governor of Porto, calls upon the citizens of this town, to live in peace; likewise entreats the same of the neighbours around, and inhabitants of Dentro, Douro e Minho, e Tras os Montes. Let not your nights be disturbed; rest in quiet, being perfectly confident that the troops which I command will not infringe on your laws, manners and customs. Believe me, you will in every respect meet in them sincere friendship, conformable to the humane disposition and known valour of the Spanish troops. I give you my word, show but confidence in them, and they will correspond with you, in all that you desire. As your General in Chief, with the ardour of justice and clemency, I shall faithfully observe my Sovereign's commands, who is as just as he is beneficent. These commands are directed to but one end, that is to protect you in the deplorable state to which you are reduced by the absence of your Prince, and to deliver you from the dominion of the perfidious English, as well as from her ambitious politics. England in appearance only is your friend. It is for her own ends she makes you believe she feels for you in your present state. But do not you see that notwithstanding she forsakes you. Be assured that every step that is now taken will pave the way for your happiness, and that of your country; the time that it may with truth be said, that you will learn to know the interest of your country, by uniting every effort and goodwill jointly with ours, that we mutually may revenge the ferocious outrages that the treacherous English have committed against all nations in Europe.

We will guard you and secure you from all their cunning and machinations. You shall be blessed and enjoy the protection that my Catholic Monarch, the King of Spain, invites you to accept. And I will, I promise you, most religiously accomplish my word.

> Taranco.
> Porto. December 19th, 1807'

This famous performance was not the composition of the General, nor can I think it to be his sentiments. It is not worth my while to make any comment on it. Every one will see it in its proper light. One thing is most evident, that for the present Porto, Douro, Minho and Tras os Montes are under Spanish Government, and from broad hints from the Spanish Officers, the French have coaxed that Court into the belief that Spain is to take possession of those provinces, as a reward for giving their share of troops to assist in the conquest of Portugal. Bonaparte's future operations will most likely let the King of Spain into a secret, which the weak understanding of His Majesty may not be aware of. Let but a little time pass, for this country to be settled under French government; the Spaniards may then to a certainty look to their own security.

1808. The old General's Government has been but of short duration. January 26th was the last day of his existence. On the 23rd [sic] he was buried with all military pomp. He died as poor as Job, and the public paid the cost of the funeral. This death has cast a damp on all description of persons; on the rich, with the fear that his successor prove the contrary character to that of the deceas'd; on the poor, for they met with a father and protector in him. At the burial ground grief was visible, and particularly so among the troops, who lament this loss to a man.

We must now look up to our new General and Governor, the Italian. The public opinion is not much in his favour. It may be a lucky circumstance his living at Mrs V—'s. Should his nature incline him to tyrannize, out of regard to her, he may put a restraint on his actions. Time will show that soon, if he is capable of such delicacy. How different is our situation, and how much reason so far we have to think how lucky we are not to have seen a French face of those newcomers, while the inhabitants of Lisbon have their houses full of them. There is not a family that has not Officers quartered on them.

Junot has confirmed the Regency, the same as the Prince had settled it on his departure. This is truly farcical, or rather tragical. It is likely an army would march into the country in the hostile manner it did, take possession of the Capital, and all the country besides. To be sure it is his design to resign this easy conquest. Junot will manage better for his Master. A little patience, and we shall see what kind treatment is in store for this devoted country.

Our Prince, when he had resolved on quitting his country, had secured immense sums of his own property on board a ship, besides great treasures of public money. The country was still free when the Royal Family sailed. That being the case, how far this last act was warrantable, some persons might appear to declare against it. But the general opinion was, the Prince did well; for the reason that whatever remained behind would be sacrificed to the rapacity of the French. Therefore the Prince had judged very properly, in taking off all he could, and securing such treasure to himself and new government. Junot on his arrival, being perfectly disappointed in his expectations, not finding where with all to grow rich at once, has hit on the expedient of a loan of no trifling sum, which is to be raised at once.

Lisbon appears a desert in comparison to what it was. A carriage is hardly to be seen in the streets. Not a night passes that murders are not committed, the Portuguese not letting a French soldier escape when he comes in their way. An attempt was made for shutting the Opera House, but Junot did not allow of it. He invited a numerous party to a magnificent entertainment, Ball and Supper. This company, as may be supposed, was composed of a medley of every description of persons. The dancing lasted till daylight. The General told the partners to invite the Ladies to go to the Opera the following night. They did not think proper to refuse. Junot was asked what box he chose. His answer was 'What doubt can there be. *Je connois ma place*. I represent the Emperor, and will have none but the

Prince's.' The House that night was much crowded. The French band played between the acts, and sang a song. The words were *'La victoire est à nous'*. At the same time the French colours were flung into the pit, when every person in it quitted it, and left the house. The boxes likewise were cleared in a few minutes. Let Junot do what he will, it will prove a hard matter for him to reconcile the minds and inclinations of the people to this change. The real sentiment of the nation is repressed, but not subdued. Nor does he go the right way to work to complete this most arduous undertaking. He should employ more lenient measures, which his nature does not seem to comprehend. Nothing but arbitrary ideas are strongly marked in his character.

The first dated entry in Harriot's 1808 diary contains a copy of Junot's latest decree.

HS *January 1st 1808*. To begin the New Year well, and to be known in future times, January is chosen by Junot to publish a decree that is to fix the future happiness of Portugal.

'December 23rd 1807. From our Palace Royal, Milan. Napoleon, Emperor of the French, and King of Italy, Protector of the Confederation of the Rhine.

———————

Le Gouverneur de Paris, Premier Aide de Camp de Sa Majesté L'Empereur et Roi, General en Chief

———————

Inhabitants of Portugal, your interests have drawn the attention of H.M. the Emperor, our August Master. All hesitation must cease. The destiny of Portugal is fixed, and its future happiness is assured, since Napoleon the Great takes it under his all-powerful protection.

The Prince of Brazil, in abandoning Portugal, has forfeited all his rights to the Sovereignty of this Kingdom. The House of Bragança has ceased to reign over Portugal. The Emperor Napoleon wills that this beautiful country should be administered and governed entirely in his name, and by the General in Chief of his army. The task which this mark of goodwill and confidence which my Master and Monarch imposes on me is difficult to fulfil. But I hope to succeed, aided by the cooperation of the wisest and best disposed of the inhabitants of Portugal.'

The decree goes on to promise the construction of new roads and canals, the incorporation of the flower of the Portuguese army in 'one family with the soldiers of Marengo, Austerlitz, Jena and Friedland', the reform of finance and education, the protection of religion, the fair and rapid administration of justice, an efficient police force, the removal of all beggars to workhouses. But the sting was in the tail.

HS　'Inhabitants of the Kingdom of Portugal, be reassured and calm. Reject the promptings of those who want to impel you into revolt, and whose interest it is to see blood shed as long as it is continental blood. Devote yourself with confidence to your work. You will reap the benefit. If you must at the beginning make some sacrifices, it is in order to enable the government to improve your lot. They are moreover indispensable for the upkeep of a great army necessary for the vast projects of the Great Napoleon. His vigilant eye is upon you, and your happiness is assured. But deserve his goodness by your respect and submission to his will.
　　　　　　Junot. Lisbon 1st February 1808.'

Harriot's method of pre-dating her diary entries to the date of the events they record, rather than using the date on which she is making the entry, makes for confusion. Her dry comment on Junot's grandiloquent proclamation was

HS　We are to be well supplied with decrees. They are so many instances against the liberty of this poor country. The present proclamation is full of fine promises, that will none of them be realised, and by way of a good dose a second proclamation was published the same day as the first, that I have just copied. This last has filled all with consternation. It is an order for a contribution to be levied throughout the Kingdom, to the amount, in English money, of four millions, six hundred thousand pounds. This enormous sum is to be given at three different payments. The first is to be collected in the month of February, and the last is to be ready for payment next August. I do not suppose there is so much money in the Kingdom, so that it is difficult to know where and how such money is to be found. Of this nature are the sacrifices imposed on Portugal, as a specimen of the lenity of this new government.

The Spanish Governor of Oporto, the popular Taranco, having died at the end of January, he was briefly succeeded by one of his officers, General Domingo Ballesta, but on 7th February General Carafa took over. Junot resented the independent line, conciliating to the Portuguese, taken by Taranco and Carafa in Oporto, and appointed a French General, Quesnel, to the military command in Northern Portugal, upon which Carafa withdrew from Oporto with his division, leaving the remaining Spanish troops in Oporto under the command of General Ballesta. Through February and March 1808 Oporto was still spared the repression which the French were exercising elsewhere in Portugal, and Harriot's diary for these months is made up of horror stories from less fortunate regions.

22

HS This month, February, a most cruel event took place at the Caldas de Reinha. A soldier of the 2nd Regt of Infantry belonging to Portugal, being in liquor, seeing some French soldiers passing, observed to his companions at the time with him, that he alone would do for seven of them. It seems the French soldiers, understanding something of what was said, took fire and a scuffle ensued. The Portuguese was attacked, but not being equal to so many ran off and got into a house, when the door was fastened within, to prevent the French from entering. They insisted on being admitted into the house, and were about to break open the door, when the alarm was given. Crowds assembled, and a number of the 2nd Regt got together to defend their comrade. But no lives were lost on either side. The French General that had the command of the troops at the Caldas, being informed of this affray, ordered the Regiments to be assembled under arms, and then addressing himself to the 2nd Regt gave them to understand that he was determined to discover those among them that had been so active to promote mischief, and if they were not pointed out to him, no mercy should be shown to the Regiment. Not a single soldier among them all, if he could or not, did appear to betray his fellow soldiers. On the contrary several that were threatened with death if they would not confess what they knew, most resolutely declared that they were ready to submit themselves to be shot. To betray their fellow soldier, it was an act they would never be guilty of. Who is it will say any men with such sentiments would not be ready to defend their country? The fault is not in the soldiers. There did appear an officer, a Lieutenant, that turned accuser. Two Cadets, some soldiers and countrymen, in all seven, were put under arrest. This insignificant event was reported by the Commandant at the Caldas to Junot at Lisbon in a most criminal light. The poor men were tried, and condemned to death, altho' it could not appear that they had committed any excess worthy of death. The first sentence that came from Lisbon, not only the above men were to suffer, but every fifth man was to be shot. This order appeared so very cruel that it was ventured to represent the injustice of it, on which that part of the sentence was not put into execution, but the seven men were executed. A Cadet managed to run away. A Captain of the same regiment with a French officer were sent in search of him, but he was in no danger of being found, his pursuers not having the least intention to perform the business they had in hand. This tragedy concluded with the disbanding of the Regiment, and with an order that neither officer nor soldier belonging to it should appear at the Caldas, no more than in any part of that neighbourhood.

Probably the general wish of both officers and men of the Portuguese regiments will be to resign their commissions. Nor do I believe they would be refused should they ask it. It cannot suit Junot's political system to preserve the national regiments. The militia and artillery have disbanded themselves in some parts of the country. The Colonels of Militia assembled their men, informed them they were no more wanted, and took a very affectionate leave of them, requesting them to go home and take care of their families.

An individual, unluckily for him with a spirit of patriotism too strong to remain quiet, made a vain attempt at raising a party to attack the French. He was betrayed and put in prison. On his trial he was asked how he could think of making an attempt of the kind. His answer was short, that he only regretted his countrymen were cowards; for if they were of his mind, a few thousands, with the like ardour with which he felt himself inspired, the French would soon see the difference, and who they had to deal with. This wretched man was condemned as a traitor, and his family forced to be present at the execution.

The treasure in the Churches has not been overlooked. All that is worth taking has been secured. Between plate and jewels it will amount to an enormous sum. The first payment for the contribution is collecting. The Wine Company gives an enormous sum. Possessors of rich benefices are fined according to their income. Convents of course are included in the same manner. In short every description of person, rich and poor, must give their iota towards this loan.

The French General has been in luck with regard to robbing the Churches. A quantity had been packed up to be put on board a ship, at the time that the Royal Family were preparing for their departure. In the hurry it remained behind. The poor Churches have lost their richest ornaments, their most useless it is certain, but that is not the opinion of the superstitious in this country. I should suppose they imagine a saint to have more virtue, when they behold it covered with rich garb, and ornamented, which many of them were, with jewels of great value. But some profane individuals have appeared that have ventured to break open a Church, and got clear off with the plate in it. It was ready packed to their hands, being ready to be delivered to those employed to receive it.

Another trick was likewise effected with success. An officer of justice, that was employed to collect different sums of money, performed his commission with great punctuality, and then disappeared with it. The gentleman thought the leaving a letter would be quite sufficient for such thieves, and serving them as they deserved. The contents of the letter were, that he had obeyed his orders in collecting the money required, but on reflection he thought he could not make a better use of it than go and distribute it among the unhappy sufferers from the contributions. I much fear this man would not have the conscience to perform what he declared is his intention in his letter, as neither man nor money has been heard of. These are not times for honest dealings.

March 1808. All officers belonging to Portuguese Regiments are permitted to give up their commissions, not wishing to serve; and soldiers that can prove a year's service are at liberty to retire. There are few that will not take advantage of such permission. This is only a prelude of what is likely to follow, with regard to the disposal of the Portuguese regiments. As yet nothing has been determined on. They are dispersed about the country, waiting to know what is to be their fate.

Junot, soon after his arrival in Lisbon, received a letter from a damsel. It was moving and pathetic, asking his protection against a cruel Father, that would not allow her to fling herself away upon a young man not worthy of her. The letter is a masterpiece of adulation and flattery. Her Father is a respectable old man, and one of the best families in Porto. The young lady had the courage one dark night to get out of a window. Love was her guide, so she came to no harm. The object of her affections was ready to receive her, and they absconded together. This transaction had passed before the arrival of the French. The girl's Father and friends procured an order from the Prince Regent to put her into a Convent. Our Heroine's place of abode was soon disturbed by rude intruders. She was forced from her retirement with her lover, and safely lodged in a convent, which to her was a prison. The gentleman was sent to one of Friars. They had been in confinement some time, when Junot's arrival paved the way for their release. The all-merciful Junot's feelings were touched at so moving a tale. His answer to the letter in a very few lines proved most satisfactory to the parties concerned.

> 'Madame
>   it is not in vain that oppressed innocence appeals to the Representative of the Great Napoleon. His power embraces the whole world, and his justice reigns equally over subjects and kings. He ordains that you be set at liberty, and that you should be given a passport for Lisbon. Come here, and from here it will be easy for you to procure the release from the prison of Oporto of the person in whom you are interested, and who like you has been made the victim of the pride of a minister. I will protect you both.

> Madame I have the honour to be your humble
> and obedient servant
> Junot.'

This letter is no bad specimen of the General's boasting style of himself on every the most trifling occasion. If the girl's request had not been attended to, it would probably have turned out better for her. The outlines of her story might serve well enough for the beginning of a romance; the despair and tears of a pretty girl which bad usage forces to jump out of a window and endanger her neck; she is saved by flying into her lover's arms. This is very romantic, but the hero is a wretch not worth notice. They are married. The dream of happiness will, I fear, vanish, and she will experience the misery in store for her. She has nothing, no more than this idol of her affections. Poverty and distress must be her future perspective, from which she will not easily extricate herself. Junot's liberality extended so far as to order a piece of 36 shillings to be given her when she left Porto for Lisbon, to help pay the expenses of the journey.

An order is given for the disbanding the Portuguese regiments, both cavalry and infantry, with the exception of a few chosen thousands. An offer was made to some of the best officers to continue to serve with promotion, but they could not be prevailed on to accept such proposals. One Colonel only has been base enough to remain with his command. He and his regiment are soon to be sent out of the country.

Porto continues to enjoy perfect tranquillity, and there is no reason of complaint against our Italian General. If we did not see the Spanish soldiers walking about the streets, we might suppose none were in the town, and there are above 12,000. They are kept in such good discipline, and at dark are obliged to retire to quarters. The Portuguese and Spaniards were never looked upon as cordial friends, but this change seems to have united them, and they are living together in good faith and friendship. I fear we may look forward for a change taking place in Porto, certainly not to the advantage of all. I believe Junot thinks we are too happy with these Spanish troops. They are being ordered to Lisbon with their Commander-in-Chief, who is preparing to depart. This is a sad stroke, more especially as he is to be replaced by a French General.

Harriot's forebodings of a change in the state of affairs in Oporto was to be justified by events in March elsewhere in the Iberian peninsula which soon had reactions in Oporto, and which were the first tremors of the slow five-year-long landslide that was to propel the French out of the Peninsula.

23

In the spring of 1808 an intense power struggle was going on in the Spanish court and capital between pro-French and anti-French factions. Godoy, Principe de la Paz, the 'Prince of Peace', was the prime mover in the pro-French faction, and he succeeded in persuading King Carlos IV that his son, the Prince of the Asturias, was conspiring against him; the Prince was briefly arrested, but soon released. A popular rising in Madrid then unseated the detested Godoy. But the triumph of the anti-French faction was short-lived, as Napoleon had been pouring French forces into Spain, and on 23rd March Murat arrived in Madrid at the head of a French army. When the report of these events reached Oporto at the end of March 1808, Harriot entered a rather confused but detailed record of them in her diary.

HS *On the 27th of March* accounts arrived from Spain of disturbances in the city of Madrid. The Prince of Peace, it seems, is by his conduct much inclined to disturb the peace. He has been making an attempt to frighten the King, by telling him that Napoleon was soon to pay him a visit in Madrid, and as such a visit could not be supposed to mean good to His Majesty, no more than to the Kingdom, the Prince's advice was immediate flight, and that the Royal Family should seek security out of the country. This advice would likely have been put into execution, the King is of a so weak and insignificant a character, had not the Council discovered what was going on. They happened not to be of the same mind with this treacherous Prince, for certainly he is engaged in French interest. They told His Majesty that the laws of the country did not allow the King to leave his people without the consent of his Council; and that they were unanimous in the opinion that His Majesty must not stir from the Capital. Suppose Bonaparte should take it into his head to pay him a visit. Let him. It could only be of a friendly nature, so that there was nothing to fear. But the minds of the people were on fire, and ready for tumult. The King's Guards and the Prince of Peace's Guards were longing to be at it, and to it they went, with all their might. They fought; the King's Guards were conquerors. The mob on seeing what was passing, became very riotous and ungovernable. They went and attacked the Prince's Palace, burst open the doors, destroyed all they could lay hands on. But the chief aim was to

secure the owner of the mansion, in which they did not succeed, for he had
escaped their vigilance. The Prince is married to the King's niece. It was in
the night that this visit was paid by these unpolished guests. They sent her
word to get up; at the same time assured her that she might be perfectly
easy, that no harm should happen to her; that they respected her as their
King's niece: they would wait till she was ready, and then convey her in
safety to the King's Palace, which they did in her carriage drawn by the
mob. The ungracious wretch that was the cause of this disturbance had
forsaken his first wife to marry into the Royal Family. The populace were
resolved on doing him all the mischief they could. They went to the first
wife's residence and demolished it, as well as other houses that had any
connection with the Prince. He had hid himself in his own house. After
passing two days without food, not to die of hunger he ventured to discover himself to his own guards that were watching in the palace. They
betrayed him and delivered him to the populace. He narrowly escaped, as
they treated him very roughly; but he was rescued by the Prince of Asturias, and put under arrest. The Prince appeared very active in quelling the
mob. It was with difficulty that he succeeded. Nothing would serve them
but the death of the Prince of Peace. He assured them that he was safe in
prison, and that he should meet with the fate that he deserved. This
promise pacified them for the instant, for Madrid was for many days in a
great confusion, many houses suffering from the fury of the populace. But
this is not the beginning of disturbances in Spain. The first was of a very
serious nature, fabricated by the wicked favourite. He had persuaded the
King that the Prince of Asturias had formed a conspiracy against him. The
poor weak King believed this accusation to be true, and the Prince was
confined for some days; but it was managed to undeceive the King, and the
Prince was restored to liberty. Here again we find Bonaparte; he can never
be lost sight of, undermining and intriguing, setting the Father against the
son, to pave the way more surely towards an easy conquest of that unhappy
country.

Meanwhile in Oporto Carafa had been replaced as Military Governor by the
French General Quesnel, who brought with him his staff and thirty French
dragoons. The 6,000 Spanish troops, under General Ballesta, continued to make
up the bulk of the occupying force in Oporto.

HS   Our French General arrived the 7th of April, with his Aide de Camp and a
few French soldiers. He took up his quarters in an excellent house prepared
for his reception. Carafa gave up his command with a heavy heart, and left
Porto on the 9th of the same month. His conduct while among us was mild
and moderate, so that we have great cause to regret his departure. Even
Mrs V—r, who has been at extraordinary expenses for four months that he

was in her house, seemed really sorry to part with him. He alone might have suited her well enough, but such a train that accompanied this noble guest – for he was one of your Italian Princes – if the truth must be told, must have been perfectly uncomfortable in every respect. The Aides de Camp were not the nicest of beings. It is not easy to conceive the state in which the officers have left nice rooms, that had been newly painted and furnished. They are not now habitable. The General on his departure presented Mrs V—r's two sons with a beautiful Spanish horse each. The greater part of the Spanish troops had left Porto before the General, but they had hardly gone when they were ordered back again, with a Spanish General that has no command but of his own troops.

We may now say we are under French government. This new General has none of the liveliness of a Frenchman, and seems sufficiently stupid, but is said to be a good sort of man, and is one of the old Court, and an old officer. Either himself or those about him know very well how to settle pecuniary matters, as the first demand on the public is, that his allowance for his household must be in English money £800 a month, and two carriages every morning at his door, one hired one, and the other belonging to some private family. This latter request is granted. As to the first, the Camara had given for answer, that it is not in their power to provide so large a sum, not having the money. The two principal employments in Porto are given to Frenchmen of known bad characters.

More news was meanwhile reaching Oporto of the rapidly evolving situation in Madrid.

HS Spanish news continues alarming. On the first disturbances the common people had unanimously declared that they would have no other King than the Prince of Asturias. The King has resigned his crown to the Prince, with the declaration that he gives it up to his beloved son, without being influenced by any one, but with his own free will, his health being too bad to bear the fatigue inflicted upon him by governing. Therefore he finds it indispensable for him to retire to peace and quiet to a milder climate. The new King, Fernando 7mo, was presented to the people by the old King, and was received with the greatest demonstrations of joy. This new Monarch is supposed to favour French principles. This may be through fear, thinking he may with greater ease keep his throne by condescending to Bonaparte's commands. He will have enough to do to satisfy all that is required of him. The promised visit is still in reserve. The good and credulous King will hear of it at its proper time. Ferdinand 7th, there is good reason to judge, is not burdened with more sense than his father. Bonaparte is well informed of that, and it suits his plans mighty well. There are a great number of French troops in Spain, and no despicable appearance of Spanish troops in Portugal.

Napoleon was now at Bayonne, wielding ever-increasing control over affairs in both Spain and Portugal. In April he conferred on Junot the title of Duke of Abrantes.

HS   Bonaparte is so well satisfied with Junot's wonderful services in Portugal that he confers a mark of distinction upon him, by a Dukedom. A decree is published that all ranks may be informed that this high rank of distinction is conferred on him. It is worded in the usual bombastic style. I have amused myself by translating it into English.

'His Excellency, General Junot, Commander-in-Chief, is promoted to the high dignity of Duke of Abrantes by His Majesty the Emperor and King. From henceforward this most excellent General is to be known only by that dignified title. The choice of this name is truly historical. It seems that he was destined by fate to possess this ancient name, as a reward for his meritorious services, and likewise to consecrate as a memorial to future ages the accomplishment of a military march the most admirable, the most painful. This Hero with his army effected a journey to Abrantes, notwithstanding embarrassments and difficulties of every description. He braved them all.'

The French have boasted that as soon as the public were informed of Junot's being made Noble, that 'all descriptions of persons flocked together, with an appearance of the most lively joy and satisfaction, and joined the French troops in crowds, and went to Headquarters to felicitate their Commander, on the acquisition of this new dignity'. The French add, that 'from such testimonies of public joy, it may truly be judged how well the city of Lisbon knows to appreciate and show their gratitude, to a Hero whose opportune arrival at Lisbon had saved its inhabitants from anarchy and desolation, that would have been the probable consequences from the departure, or rather flight, of the old Court'.

The most material article that is overlooked in this account is truth. But that is a trifle. One of the ruling systems of the present French rulers is, that wherever they have conquered, they publish to the World what happiness and content they have been the means of procuring to the conquered. If other nations have not more reason to be satisfied than poor Portugal, they have little to boast of. Not the least inclination have our good inhabitants of Porto shown to manifest in any way their joy at Junot's promotion. It would not be very safe to own it, but I am confident that the secret wish of all is to hear that Junot etc etc were safe out of the country.

At the end of April Napoleon received at Bayonne a deputation of Portuguese nobles and clerics, who produced a grovellingly sycophantic report on their reception by Napoleon. Junot gave orders on 12th May that this report was to be printed in French and Portuguese and displayed throughout Portugal as a proc-lamation to the nation, who were expected to show their grateful acceptance of Napoleon's good intentions by continuing to be peaceful and contented. The report expressed a desire to confide the fate of Portugal to the 'Mighty Genius who has restored his country and then reconstituted all Europe . . . If anything could equal his genius, it is the grandeur of his soul, the generosity of his principles'. Napoleon had shown, in his reception of the Portuguese delegation, a profound and sympathetic knowledge of Portugal's problems, and had uttered 'the most touching good wishes for the happiness of her people'. Napoleon had no vindictive feelings against the Portuguese Royal family, and wished only that Portugal should form the last link in the great chain of his Continental System. But Portugal must be rescued from the 'foreign influences which had dominated her for so many years. The Emperor cannot allow an English colony to remain on the Continent'. And so on and so on, in a mixture of flattery, reassurance and threats which was presumably dictated to the wretched Portu-guese signatories – the Marquises of Penalva and Marialva, the Bishop of Coimbra, the Inquisitor General, and ten others – by Napoleon's staff at Bayonne. Harriot copied this shameful document and Junot's covering decree in full into her diary, commenting with heavy irony:

HS By way of securing the few remaining Fidalgos that might shew a feeling for their country, they have been chosen to be sent on an Embassy to Bonaparte. It is proved very clearly that the Portuguese wish to know their fate, and for that reason have entreated Bonaparte to let them know who is to be their King. Bonaparte with a disposition replete with goodness, lenity, and compassion for the abandoned state of Portugal, condescends to grant so just a request to his now loving subjects, of the Kingdom of Portugal.

Listing the signatories to the Bayonne declaration, she comments:

HS Most of these names should never have been seen to witness the approving such a manifesto. The excuse is that they had no choice, and were forced to accept this mission. The truth is, it is nothing but degradation, but I have no pity for such men. They might, and should have followed their King.

Throughout April and May 1808 Portugal was held in an uneasy pause, while Napoleon played cat and mouse with the Spanish Royal Family. Oporto was superficially calm, though both occupiers and occupied knew that their future hung on the turn of events in Spain. In Lisbon Junot was unable to relax and enjoy his new dukedom and the opera. At first it had seemed triumphantly easy to seize control of unresisting Portugal. But the nearest French forces apart from his own were still many hundreds of miles away in Northern Spain. The British Navy, on the other hand, was on his doorstep, all along the Portuguese coast within sight of shore, keeping constant watch and receiving up-to-date information – easily smuggled out to them in spite of draconian regulations – about events in Spain and Portugal. The loyalty of the Spanish troops in Portugal, ostensibly France's allies, could not be absolutely relied on. And though the Portuguese bureaucracy might be mostly cringing collaborators with their French masters, the peasantry and the urban poor were very ready to murder any French soldier whom they found alone.

In an attempt to conciliate Portuguese public opinion, it was announced that Napoleon, as an 'act of clemency', had decreed that the 100 million francs loan should be halved. This still left a crushing burden of taxation which blighted trade and caused the cancellation of traditional Lenten processions. Harriot's diary is caustic and watchful about these developments.

HS The fate of Portugal is so linked with that of Spain that our fears are all alive with expectations of what may be the next news from those parts. The report here is that we may soon expect to see French troops march into the town. This is the last thing we wish for. Junot gives entertainments in Lisbon; has his public nights, and should be a great favourite with the fair sex, as they have been fighting in a fit of jealousy. One was French, the other a Portuguese Countess. Probably the French lady did not approve of partialities that were manifested too evidently, she thought, on the part of her countryman in preference to a stranger.

Our chief Magistrate is a Frenchman. His little insignificant person has chosen a palace of a house for his town residence, and for retirement the Consul's sweet Quinta, where he gives dinners and dancing at night, and each lady is presented with a fine nosegay. He has likewise given an entertainment at his palace in town. To this everybody was invited, and a fine medley there was. Many pretty women shewed off that had never before been seen. W— for political reasons made one in the crowd. As for me I keep firm to my determination of going to no such parties. We have retired to the country, where we are let to enjoy peace and quiet. I must not forget a principal part of the above entertainment, which was marked with an act of clemency from Mr Bonaparte. Printed papers were distributed to every one in the town.

After copying the text of this printed paper, the decree halving the levy to be exacted, Harriot bursts out

HS The thieves! I suspect the French do not feel so much at their ease as they have done till now, and they must know for certain that the Portuguese could not collect such an unconscionable sum. Therefore Bonaparte makes a show of humanity by pardoning the payment of these millions of Cruzados; nor will they be able to pay the remainder. Perhaps it will not be necessary. Some in this town seem to conjecture that it will not be long ere we may expect some new event in the political system. Mischief is brewing. Grant us, heaven, it may turn out to our advantage. We know that our French General is not satisfied with his present situation, and that he had asked for troops from Lisbon. Junot's answer is that he has none to spare. There are a few Spanish troops in the town, and that is all, and if the truth was known, our General has not the least confidence in them. So much the better.

The French General lives very retired; for the present has shewn no very despotic ideas. He talks of giving great entertainments. One is to be at the Factory House. I for one will not go to any of them. The General's Secretary and Aide-de-Camp is a very good man, of Irish extraction. He is in the Spanish service, and came here with the regiments. He is a very loyal subject of the King of Spain, and I believe does not scruple to speak his mind to the General. W— with the rest pay'd his visit to this new General on his arrival. He asked him a few questions, and by his answers, finding that he is a prisoner at large, observed that it is a very easy prison indeed. The General had made a point to return all the first visits, but has excepted Walsh, we conclude because he is an Englishman. I have not seen him yet, nor do I wish it.

Trade is not entirely at a stand. The wine company have leave to ship their wines, to neutral Ports. Likewise individuals have the same privilege. This will prove no bad business to Junot, who receives a gold piece of six and thirty shillings, for every pipe that is shipped. The General here likewise comes in for his douceur, tho' not much. Porto wine will again find its way to England. No time has been lost loading of ships, for fear of a change of orders, and when once over the Bar, let the Captains alone; they will know well enough how to steer their own course north towards the British shores.

Numbers of Portuguese families have emigrated, and altho' it is more difficult since the Spanish Governor's departure, they continue disappearing, and often in the night boats full get over the Bar, and are received by our King's ships, that are on this station, purposely to be informed of what is going on on shore. There are those that are not idle, and venture on giving intelligence, and even sending provisions.

We have not heard from our friends once, since the departure of the English, but we have certainly written more letters than it was prudent to do, as there is a penalty of death on any boatman that takes letters or anything else to convey them on board the Frigates. But a good fee serves well, and all danger is forgot. Even a correspondence is carried on from shore with the Captains off the Bar. So far none have been caught in this business. It is so mortifying to see, as I do see, many a time while writing, the Frigate and Sloop-of-War sailing backwards and forwards, and often close to the Bar, and to know that we have not a chance of seeing any of the officers on shore. How delightful it would be could we but see an English face again.

The Portuguese in Porto have passed a melancholy Lent. There is no money to waste in Processions. The whole six weeks were got through without the people's religious feelings being gratified with a single procession. Perhaps it is the first time in the oldest person's now living remembrance, that six weeks of penitence and fasting should not have had those days that were allotted for these religious ceremonies most sacredly kept. Saints of every description got a good airing on such days, after a year's confinement, and the country people a famous holy day. They flocked into town from the villages round, dressed out in gaudy colours, displaying a profusion of gold chains and long dropped earrings of the same description. A procession day was an amusement for every description of persons. Whatever street it passed through, the windows were ornamented with damask curtains and rich embroidered counterpanes; and every person from whose house it could be seen, invited their friends, so that it was a day of Gala.

My opinion is that it would be well for the country should such shews be entirely abolished. To a reflecting mind there is too much absurdity in such representations. It is long that I have not had the patience to go to any of them. I leave out the procession, and go to the party at night. Let those that can admire bare-footed, half naked penitents, condemning themselves to carry such enormous weights, shocking to behold. Such exhibitions can answer no good purpose in this world. The wretches that walk in this way are often paid for it, and as often hypocritical beings abandoned to vice that think in this way to deceive the world with the appearance of sanctity. The pageantry of these processions is quite the thing to amuse children, till they come to an age of reflection. The numerous little boys, between four and five and six years old, dressed up to represent angels, are part of the ornament of this show. They may be taken for anything as well as angels, for nothing can be more unlike. These little creatures are decked out in gaudy finery, with round stiff petticoats, that looks like hoops, and are all the colours of the rainbow. Their heads are ornamented with a fine powdered wig, with flowers, ribbons and feathers, and their faces are painted and patched. The angels in Heaven certainly do not require so much clothing. The mothers of these children, from religious notions, have a pride in offering them to walk on these days, and do not care about the expense.

24

Harriot stayed away from all parties given by the French, but she kept her ear to the ground, and was able to report in her diary a surprisingly detailed account of the developments in Spain. In May 1808 Napoleon lured the new King Fernando VII of Spain, and his abdicated father Carlos IV, to Bayonne, against the bitter opposition of the people of Madrid. Napoleon then forced Fernando to abdicate in his turn, restored the crown to Carlos IV but then forced him to abdicate too, and virtually imprisoned the whole Spanish Royal Family in France. He then handed the crown of Spain to his brother Joseph Bonaparte. Harriot devoted many pages of her diary to the dramatic events in Spain.

HS Nothing but bad news from Spain. They seem to be going from bad to worse. The country has gained no security from one weak King to another succeeding to the throne. All bears a more melancholy and precarious aspect daily. Bonaparte's demands, let them be what they will, are conceded without hesitation. The release of the Prince of Peace was insisted on, with conditions that he should be delivered up to the French, go to France, and never more return to Spain. That wretch, instead of suffering the punishment he so truly deserved, is set at liberty. He was taken out of prison in the dead of night, for fear of disturbances, and given up to the French. The riches that he has amassed are immense.

   The King and all the Royal Family are preparing to set off to meet Bonaparte, who now declares that he is certainly coming to Madrid, to pay them a friendly visit, and I suppose give them a fraternal hug and Kiss of Peace. It may turn out as false a kiss as that of Judas.

Later in May she added:

HS The important events that have taken place since the beginning of May in Spain are cruel to relate. It too plainly pictures to the World the insignificant character of their Kings. It is not necessary for Bonaparte to fatigue himself with a journey to Spain to gain another kingdom. A few flattering words are sufficient to convince both Father and son. They have no friend in the world to compare to Napoleon, and to prove the truth of this the King with simplicity and credulity believes all the fine promises heaped

153

upon him, and to show how entirely he confides in this deceiver, the whole of the Royal Family have agreed to the proposal of leaving the Capital, to join Bonaparte at Bayonne, with the assurance of settling Spanish affairs for the advantage of the Spanish Nation. The King has appointed his Uncle to govern in his absence. All persuasions are vain to prevent this journey. A confidential wretch belonging to Napoleon is a constant attendant upon the King, and with Argus's eyes will not lose sight of the Royal Family until they are safe at Bayonne. The country in general are exasperated beyond measure at this determination of the King's. He tried on his side to convince the Court that his departure was for the good of all (but none were convinced of that) and that they would certainly return in a few days.

The Royal Family left Madrid, and met with every embarrassment on the road from his good subjects. They entreated, they supplicated him to return to his Capital; that they were ready to defend their King and their country, should it be necessary. He was deaf to the voice of his people. When they found the King resolutely resolved on pursuing his journey, they even repeatedly cut the traces of the mules that drove the carriages. In short the King etc etc got safe to Bayonne. The firm and friendly alliance that already existed between the two countries, and that was to be so durable, was still more firmly settled by Bonaparte's determination to take upon himself the entire protection of Spain, and give her a King chosen by himself. This was a blow never dreamt of by the poor foolish King. After the most natural event to happen he too late saw his folly. Expostulation was of no avail. Justice and humanity are not to be found in Bonaparte's dictionary. The old King lays claim to the Crown in a formal complaint against his son; that it was by compulsion he resigned the Crown; that he had acted a most unnatural part with regard to a Father still on his throne, forgetting the duty he owed him; and that devoid of affection and love, this son had not patience to wait a little longer for the death of a poor old Father; that then he might have taken the Crown as his right, without a crime. Instead of that, no consideration could move him. He took possession, and left his King and Father to spend the remainder of his days in retirement and solitude. Bonaparte, who is most prompt at settling every event his own way – this he would undoubtedly, being principal actor – he did not delay proving to both Father and son that neither of them were capable to govern a Kingdom. Therefore the all-powerful Napoleon proposed to both Father and son the signing a formal renunciation to every pretension or claim to the throne of Spain, both now and hereafter, and that every individual of the family should be equally excluded. The unworthy father and son signed the paper, and all the Royal Family, together with the Prince of Peace, before this are in France, far away from their own country, where they will have full leisure to reproach each other of folly, cowardice and pusillanimity beyond description or belief.

This fatal news soon reached Madrid. General indignation was evident, nor was there a wish to repress it. The people showed an inclination to rise, but without a head what was to be done? So circumstanced, and with resolute French troops to fight against, even so the Spaniards went to it in despair; but the troops and their officers did not join them as they ought to have done. Many Spaniards fell and a few French. After this something like a combat (it was a bloody one for the poor Spaniards) an appearance of peace was restored, and the Duke de Berg remained Governor of Madrid, and Commander-in-Chief in Bonaparte's name. But more mischief is brewing. The cry is, among those unprincipled wretches, '*Le sang a coulé; il faut le venger*'. Spain is in for it. Blood will flow. Certainly there will be a struggle for liberty.

What sad times these are; so replete with horror that the mind sickens at the very idea, wondering when it is to be at rest; and how unaccountable it is that this Sycophant of fortune should be still allowed the power of tyrannising over the world. It must, it cannot be called a crime, should every advocate of human nature pray to him that directs all to grant the prayer of thousands and thunder his judgment and vengeance upon the head of an individual to whom fortune had been so blindly prodigal. But how niggardly has virtue figured in all his actions. The flowery path has plained the way, and invited him to go boldly on to combat, and to soar above the most mighty on earth. Every stride he makes leads him on most rapidly to grandeur, and success till now has gratified to the full his unbounded rage for power and glory. Ambition is Napoleon's God. He knows no other.

The situation looked black indeed for both Spain and Portugal, but the next news to reach Oporto was to prove a turning-point in the history of the Peninsular War and of Napoleon's domination of Europe.

25

The Spanish Royal Family's abject desertion of their country aroused the indignation of the Spanish people against France. The people of Madrid rose on the historic Dos de Mayo, the second of May, and although the revolt was bloodily crushed by the French army in Madrid under Murat, the fiery spark of the Dos de Mayo caught the kindling of unrest throughout Spain and resistance began to smoulder all over the kingdom. During May some reports of this reached Harriot in Oporto.

HS   The news from Spain is, that the Spaniards continue to show a great spirit of resistance against the arbitrary encroachments of the French. There has been more fighting in Madrid. The Spaniards did not remain so ill treated as in the first attack. The whole country have declared vengeance against the French, and are arming in all parts of the Kingdom. The men will fight, for they are brave and hardy, but they have no commanders of any note to lead them on to conquest, and in whom they might have confidence, so that final success is very doubtful.

    A Junta is formed in the King's name, for them to act and consult what is to be done for the defence of the Kingdom. A formal declaration has been declared against Napoleon. May success attend a people in so just a cause. If they do but prove persevering in consistency and courage in this glorious resolution much may be hoped for. The first thing to be done should be to request some good officers of the English Government. Then should I have confidence in the contest. All Europe now looks on; must take a lively interest in what is passing in that poor betrayed country. Our spirits are elevated somewhat beyond the moderate pitch, with the idea of the good that may be in reserve for Portugal. How easily we mortals catch at every trifling hope that may give a little variation in the progress of this disposer of Nations. Hopes and fears are alternately at war with one another, and we are doubly anxious, having the fate of Spain at heart, as well as that of Portugal. Spain will now sue for peace with England. It would have been well for her had she known how to distinguish between true or false friends; but wiser heads have been deceived too often by false advisers. The Prince of Peace has been long working his country's ruin.

Tho' he may have succeeded, yet his views have been frustrated, and his plans end in banishment and disappointment.

By the end of May there had been risings against the French in the Asturias, Galicia, Andalusia, Murcia, Valencia, Aragon and Catalonia. Juntas had been appointed to organise the insurgents, and regiments of the regular Spanish army were joining them. The setting-up of the Galician Junta at Corunna was to have an immediate effect on the situation in Oporto, as orders were sent from the Junta that Ballesta and his Galician troops who were occupying Oporto should leave the city and withdraw to Spain to join the insurgents there. Ballesta seized the French General Quesnel and his small escort of dragoons, and marched off with them to Spain, to join the Galician insurgents under General Blake. Before he left, he advised the leading officials of Oporto to hoist the Portuguese flag and establish a junta to organise resistance against the French forces under Junot who still occupied Central and Southern Portugal. After Ballesta's departure there were no French or Spanish troops left in the northern Portuguese provinces of Tras os Montes and Entre Douros.

Up till now, Harriot's diary of 1807-8 had been a good deal made up of second-hand accounts of events in Lisbon and in Spain, and of the texts of French proclamations and decrees. From 5th June 1808 she had an eye-witness story to tell of the dramatic changes of fortune in Oporto and her account of what happened there in June and July 1808 is vivid, detailed, sharply observant.

HS *June 1808.* This month will be a month to be remembered in the Annals of Portugal. On the 5th of the month were assembled at our house in the country a set of Spanish officers to spend the evening, with various other persons. The French Consul's son made one among them. He was particularly lively that night; sang his Italian and French song, which he does with great taste, and then play'd Country dances for the company to dance. One of the Spanish officers gave his partner to understand – he was quite a boy – that he had a secret which he dared not venture to divulge, tho' it seemed a painful distress to him to keep it. At the same time, he said, it delighted him beyond measure that it would be known the next day. True enough; the next day, the 6th, this interesting secret was made public. It was nothing less than an order that had arrived from Spain to the Spanish General to put the French General under arrest, with his Aide de Camps, and every Frenchman to be found in the town; this done, to march without loss of time with the Spanish troops and the prisoners away to Spain. The order was put into execution at night. It was vain for the General to think of resistance. He was taken by surprise. The troops were under arms. He had not a Frenchman to defend him. Guards were posted in different parts of the town, to prevent anyone from leaving it that night, and at 8 o'clock next morning all these good people were on their way for Spain.

The news of this extraordinary event reached us in our retirement nearly as soon as the departure of the French. The surprise was great indeed. When I joined the family at breakfast, I was wished joy. Every countenance was full of wonder and delight. What wonderful news have I to be informed of, was my first question. Nothing less, was the answer, than Porto is free. The Spaniards are gone off to Spain, with the French as prisoners, and if you wish to see the Portuguese colours, you have but to look out of the window, and you will be gratified by seeing them flying at the Castle at St John's. W—h lost no time, but posts off to town, to be informed how such a wonderful event had happened in so few hours. He found Porto in the greatest confusion. Crowds had followed the Spaniards out of town, with no little abuse of the French.

The General's Aide de Camp that I mentioned being of Irish extraction, and in the service of Spain, it was not in his option to refuse the appointment of Secretary and Aide de Camp to the French General. But altho' this was forced on him, they could not rob him of the sentiments of a good and loyal subject to his King. He very honestly declared that no motive in the world could tempt him to raise a hand against his country; but on this occasion, altho' he already looked upon the French as the enemy of his nation, fearing for the life of the General from the rage of the populace, he accompanied his litter, and guarded him from insult.

The first impulse of the people was to assemble in immense crowds, and as the news spread like wildfire the country people flocked in from all the villages round. Every hour brings us fresh intelligence of what is passing. Porto is at this minute a scene of wild disorder, the people running about the streets wild with joy at the idea the French are gone. The bells ring without ceasing, and the cry unanimous is 'Viva Portugal, Viva Englaterra, e Viva Espana'.

W—h is returned, and this first day that may be called of renewed liberty has passed off free of mischief of any description. It is lucky, as the whole day nothing was heard but noise and firing of guns. The French had never ventured to display their national colours, and the Portuguese had not been allowed to hoist theirs. An English Brig, sailing off the Bar at St John's, soon perceived the Portuguese colours flying at the Castle, and the same Castle fired away as signal of good news. It was well understood by our countrymen. It was a fine day. No time was lost. The boat prepared, and an officer was sent ashore to be informed of what was passing. On the departure of the French a Portuguese officer residing here with his family, with the rank of Brigadier, took upon him the command of the town. The English officer was presented to him, and met with a very cool reception. He was told that tho' the French were out of Porto, it was still under French government, and that he could not act contrary to the present system. The officer, hearing this, and fearing lest he might be put under arrest, not feeling comfortable on shore in this predicament, made his bow to his gentleman and returned to his ship.

A Junta was duly proclaimed in Oporto on 6th June, but not much was done for the next ten days to break free from the French rulers in Lisbon. Some of the Oporto officials in fact sent secret offers of submission to Junot, and Luis de Oliveira da Costa, who had taken over as military commandant after the departure of Ballesta, was pro-French and would not allow the Portuguese flag to be kept flying over the citadel of San João da Foz. But out in the country the people of Tras os Montes had risen and taken command of their districts, appointing their own military commanders.

Harriot took a poor view of Luis de Oliveira and was impatient for more effective resistance against the French.

HS Conjectures are various what to think and hope from this sudden change and departure of the Spanish troops. It looks as if Spain was not losing ground against the French. We are all impatience for news from these parts. Porto is by no means restored to quiet. Very little encouragement would be sufficient for the inhabitants to rise against this new set up Governor. The public voice is, that he favours the French, therefore he is an enemy to his country. The people are much enraged against him; they even threaten vengeance on his head. This officer, by name Luiz d'Oliveira, is a man of large property, and had he been wise might and should have kept quiet at his Quinta with his family, where they were before the arrival of the French in Portugal. For the first time he settles them in Porto, and there they remained, making a most insignificant figure, no one taking notice of him, while he presented himself in all the parties, paying his court in a most servile disgusting manner to the new Commanders-in-Chief. Those neglected and despised him. I fear by this conduct he may have worked much mischief to himself and his family, who are really amiable and much to be pitied. He is a silly insignificant character, and more through fear than real inclination to be false to his country he wished to make his party good on the strongest side, and by that means secure himself and family from harm. He would not want for advisers that would point to his weak mind the certain ruin of his country. At any rate he can never serve as a useful member in any party, having no power of action but from the impulse of others, who lead him astray; and every step he now takes leads him to ruin.

June. A Spanish officer with the command of two hundred 50 men sent to ask leave of Luiz d'Oliveira to allow him to march through Porto on his way to Spain. The request was not granted, but it was all one to the officer. He waited till the dead of night and all was quiet in bed, then marched into the town in all leisure, finding none to oppose him. There are a few

Artillery men in Porto, the only military to guard us. An order has been given to the officers to be on the alert, and not let the Spaniards enter the town. So far from preventing them, it is pretty clear that, if it had been necessary, there were numbers ready to help these troops on their way to Spain.

26

After the removal of the French General from Oporto, connections with Lisbon became uncertain, but some news – and another of the inevitable proclamations from Junot – did get through. Junot was now cut off from Spain, but he still held Lisbon and the south with a force of 26,500 French troops, and was prepared to hold on with a mixture of bravado in speech and genuine cool courage in action.

HS *June 13th 1808*. All is quiet at Lisbon. Bonaparte has granted this country a King. Beauharnais is the man; Madame Bonaparte's son, with a beautiful Princess. These are the mortals supposed to be destined to fix the happiness of this country. Napoleon declares that, having freed Portugal from slavery, he is determined to give them a King of equal greatness of mind with his own, and that all the grievances without delay shall be redressed.

As soon as the news reached Lisbon of the Spaniards having left Porto, taking with them the French General etc etc, Junot thought it advisable to give the public a little good advice on the occasion of this event.

Junot's proclamation to the people of Portugal, which Harriot quotes in full, warns the Portuguese that the period of six months of 'security and perfect tranquillity' which they had enjoyed since the French entered Portugal was now likely to end, because of the treachery and desertion of the Spaniards; he particularly attacked the Spanish General Ballesta for his cowardly treatment of the French General Quesnel, whom he had failed to protect from insult as well as capture. Junot describes his disarming of the disaffected Spanish troops round Lisbon, and ends with a flamboyant appeal for Portuguese loyalty.

HS 'Portuguese, your conduct so far meets with my approbation. I am satisfied. You have known how to appreciate the good that must result to you from the all-powerful protection of Napoleon the Great. Confide in me, and pursue the same conduct. Keep steady in it. I will save you from invasion, from dismemberment. If the English, who only seek to foment discord, should pretend to attack you, they will find us ready to defend you. Your Battalions of Militia, your regiments commanded by our brave officers in Lisbon, with a part of the French troops, will assist in the

161

defence of your frontiers. Let them appear, we shall soon drive them away. A Frenchman knows not fear. We will teach them the art of war. And my happiness will be to put in practice with you, the lessons I have learnt of my mighty Master, Napoleon. I will lead you to glory. I will teach you to conquer.

> *Vive l'Empereur.*
> Duque de Abrantes'

This same Duque de Abrantes it seems is coaxing the Portuguese to keep quiet. We may judge so from the way he addresses them in the above performance. But it will not do with the inhabitants of Porto. They are ready for a struggle at shaking off French power. The number of French troops in Lisbon is by no means formidable. Of Spanish troops there are at least 5000, quartered in the neighbourhood of Lisbon, under the command of the Italian General, Carafa, that lately left Porto. These troops show a very good inclination to be troublesome, but none have been put under arrest. Carafa made his complaint to Junot, and asked him to tell him how he was to manage them. The answer was, to do the best he could with them. I believe the objection would not be great for their deserting and going off to Spain.

The Commander-in-Chief, I suspect, does not feel quite comfortable in his present situation, and would be more satisfied could he see troops arrive from France.

On 16th June the customary religious processions of the Corpo de Dios were held in both Oporto and Lisbon. Harriot describes both.

HS To gratify the public, it was determined that the Corpo de Dios should be allowed to walk. The 16th of June is the fixed day for this annual procession. The regiments on that day all attend, and line the streets. The few that are in the town were ordered under arms, and most imprudently the Governor, Luiz d'Oliveira, ordered the display of French colours, instead of Portuguese. This the French had not even ventured to do. This open attack on national customs, as it was supposed to be, drew forth the indignation of all to a high degree, and without hesitation the order was not obeyed. Invectives against the Governor was unanimous, all vowing vengeance against this Traitor to his country, as they called him. The day, that ever was here, as well as in Lisbon, a most famous day in the year, passed off in discontent and disgust.

We hear that the Corpo de Dios did not pass off in Lisbon no more than here without confusion. While the procession was walking, a great tumult arose. The troops that accompanied the procession, instead of trying to disperse the mob, ran away. Much mischief was done, as the crowd was excessive. Legs and arms were broken. Poor ladies, in all their finery, with their clothes half torn off their backs, were screaming for help; others fainting. This work lasted for some time, and no one could guess at the cause of so great disorder. When the fury of the populace had exhausted itself, they dispersed, and the procession, that had been perfectly at a stand, was at liberty to move on. Junot with all his officers etc favoured this religious ceremony by walking in the procession. What an occasion lost! The troops had not returned to their post. Junot was perfectly unguarded. Hundreds might have fallen upon him, and every Frenchman, and demolished them without mercy. Lisbon that day might have been free. Junot knows the nature of the cowardly people, and did not fear for his person. Much is still to be done, before liberty can be restored to this country.

Harriot's account is unfair to Junot, who showed great coolness and courage on this occasion. The Lisbon mob, frantic with fear and excitement because of rumours of earthquake and of the landing of a British force, broke through the cordon of French troops lining the route of the procession, and the French gunners were just about to fire on the mob when Junot, who was marching in the procession, threw himself in front of the crowd and got them to disperse without bloodshed. In this passage, as in many others in her diary, Harriot's unrelenting francophobia makes her a not wholly reliable recorder.

She admits that it was now difficult to know just what was happening in Lisbon. This gave the remaining supporters of France in Oporto the chance to circulate alarming rumours of a French advance on the city. The French Consul in Oporto strolled about the streets, on the day of the Corpo de Dios procession, with triumphant boasts that his compatriots were coming.

HS We have no news from Spain, nor do we know what is passing in Lisbon. No one ventures to write, as all letters are opened; and probably from henceforward all communication will be put a stop to between this and Lisbon.

The French Consul is still in Porto. I do not understand why the Spaniards did not take him and his son off to Spain, when they departed with the French as their prisoners. On the 16th June, the old gentleman appeared parading the streets in Porto, and in particular the most public one, the Via Nova, publishing in most triumphant high spirits, to those that thought proper to listen to him, that the next day 900 French troops would dine in Porto. It is natural to suppose it is what he wished, but that alone was not sufficient to bring them. The next day passed as usual, and not a Frenchman appeared. The foolish old Consul and his son were obliged to hide themselves, and cannot with safety appear any more in public.

The false report of an approaching French army precipitated a new overturn in Oporto.

HS　*From the 16th to the 18th* little inclination appeared for tranquillity in the minds of the people. And the 18th of June 1808 may be pronounced a day to be remembered by the inhabitants of Porto. For on that day they shewed their real sentiments, and anxious wish to be free of French despotism.

The populace only wanted some one to appear that would invite them to rise in defiance of the present Government. Such were found, and a cry of *'Viva, O Principe'* spread like wildfire. Hundreds assembled in great confusion and fury. The torrent directed their steps towards the depots. Lock and key were no embarrassment. The doors were made to fly open, and all that thought proper supplied themselves with arms, of which there were plenty. The town, as may be supposed, continued in a state of the greatest fermentation; the bells incessantly ringing; and resounded from all quarters *'Viva, O Principe Regente; Viva Englaterra, Viva Espanha; e more os Franceses'*. The town was soon crowded with thousands. All ages left their home from the neighbouring villages, and came and offered their services in defence of their country.

The town is still in a most unsettled state, the bells night and day ringing, and guns firing. The country people passing our door are innumerable; numbers of old men with long poles, with their idea of helping their countrymen to exterminate the French and free the country, seem to have quite forgot that old age may prove an embarrassment to their fighting to any purpose, but at any rate such ardour is good. What is really extraordinary is that no accident has happened during these days of tumult and confusion. It was most natural to fear that some evil-disposed persons might have taken advantage of such times, and satisfied private resentment with murder. Such events happen too often in quiet times, but the present rage is all directed to one end, the preventing the French returning to Porto. And likewise let those be on their guard that are inclined to favour any one of that nation. Their lives can by no means be secure.

Our Bishop of Porto is a most respectable good old man. The general voice has appointed him Governor. He is to act in the name of the Prince Regent. For the present appearances are that the town will be restored to quiet; but we must expect to hear of Junot. He will without doubt pronounce us in the act of rebellion, and as rebels we must be punished; but this time they will not come to attack us without opposition. Tras os Montes is arming, and seems resolved on fighting. The public in Porto amuse themselves saying that Junot's last manifesto to the people was his farewell dying speech. It was no sooner stuck up in the principal streets of the town, than it was torn down, with indignation. The former ones had been treated in the same manner. The Friars had for a long time been exerting all their powers of elocution in their sermons to animate the populace against the French. Long before the 18th of June inflammatory papers had been handed about, so that many who were observing in silence what was passing were prepared for a change in some way or other.

The Portuguese flag was again hoisted, and a more effective Junta established, headed by Dom Antonio de Castro, the elderly Bishop of Oporto. Harriot's admiration of the bishop was warm; some British historians have seen him in a very different light. William Napier, the historian of the Peninsular War, who resented the Bishop's later protest against the Convention of Cintra because it reflected on Napier's hero Wellington, called the Bishop a 'meddling ambitious priest' who hoped to become leader of the whole Portuguese insurrection and to see the seat of government transferred from Lisbon to Oporto. But Harriot's picture of a well-meaning old man whose sudden popularity rather went to his head is a convincing one.

27

When the Spanish forces withdrew from Oporto and the Portuguese flag was at first hoisted over the citadel, a naval officer from the British Fleet which was stationed off Oporto landed in the town to see what was happening, but was coolly received by Luiz d'Oliveira. Now that Oliveira had fallen from power and was a fugitive, and the return of fine weather enabled the British ships to come closer in to the Portuguese coast, British naval officers landed again to reconnoitre. The possibility of British military intervention began to be discussed, and the Bishop appealed to London for help.

HS   The weather had been so bad that for some weeks no ship had been able to approach the Bar. On the 19th of June, the day after the joyful event of the rising of the people, the day turned fine and serene. The *Talbot*, Captain Jones, appeared in sight, and what was his surprise when he beheld the Portuguese colours flying. He fired, he was answered by a friendly salute from the Castle, and invited to come ashore, which he did fast enough. Walsh was in town; they soon met. The first step was to present this welcome guest to the Bishop, who received Captain Jones most cordially. The next step was to introduce him to his family in the country. W—h anticipated the pleasure and surprise such a visit would give us. So off they posted, in the middle of the day, in a broiling hot sun, on foot, to walk a long league. We knew nothing of Captain Jones being on shore, when wonderful to tell an Englishman stood before us; so unexpected, so little thought of, that our excess of joy was certainly ridiculous. He was an entire stranger to us, but no matter for that. The occasion would admit of no less. We received this Navy gentleman in the true style of an old friend. He seemed as happy as we were, and returned our kindness with perfect good will. The truth is he was as much pleased to get on shore as we were to receive him. It was many months that he had been condemned to beat about on the wide ocean, and battle with the boisterous waves, without ever once leaving his ship. He made but a short visit, being obliged to return to the *Talbot* at night.

This day was passed in great content on both sides, and the next produced another Navy gentleman. Captain Jones was so pleased with his first visit, that he returned with Captain Creyke of the *Eclipse*. He is the

Commandant on this station. The evening of this day turned out so bad that our gentlemen could not venture on board. No ships of any size can come over this Bar at any time, so that Frigates and Line-of-Battle ships have no remedy but laying at anchor within sight of the Bar, and often cannot do that, as in bad weather it is not by any means safe to keep your station too near this enemy, where many a ship has been lost. We could not set our gentlemen adrift, after receiving them so cordially, to look for beds where they could find them. The matter was soon settled. We had house room in plenty, and no want of beds; so that instead of their being rocked asleep in the usual manner on board a ship, they passed the night in calm composure, and in the morning waked to see from the windows the beautiful orange tree full of flower and casting its perfume around; the tall Acacia likewise, waving its elegant branches with white clusters of flowers in the wind. Nor must I omit the display of geraniums and myrtles intermixed that clothe the walls. This scene appeared something like enchantment to our Tars, that have been banished from all that is pleasing to the sight, as well as from the comforts of society, for such a length of time. It appears more particularly delightful to Captain Jones, as the first day he came he declared he could fancy himself in a little Paradise.

Captain Creyke, of the Brig *Eclipse*, has had a conference with the Bishop. He was attended to the Palace by crowds, with shouts and huzzas resounding from all quarters. W—h is turned interpreter, and figures as a person of no trifling consequence. It is settled that Captain Creyke is to send a party of his Sailors, to mount the guns of a large Brazil ship, the command of which is to be given to an Englishman, and destined as a floating battery to defend the Bridge, in case the French should come to attack on that side, and attempt the passing the Bridge. This bridge is formed of boats, that in a very few hours can be taken up. I should think this would be the surest way to embarrass the French in their attempt at crossing the river; but there seems to exist great confidence in the mind of every one that we are in no danger of any attack of the kind.

Since the 18th June Luiz d'Oliveira thought proper to abscond, and for a few days wandered about in disguise. He tried to obtain protection in different families, but in vain. His enemies were determined that he should not escape. One very respectable family from compassion took him in. He was soon traced, and the house without the least ceremony was beset with armed men. But while they were searching one part of the house it was managed to hide him in the other, so that he escaped, for this time. From this house he did us the favour to knock at our door, which he did for some time, as it was two in the morning, and all was abed and asleep. At last a watchful old maidservant, that has lived with me between thirty and forty years, heard the knocking and went to see who could come at such an hour. Before she would agree to open the gate, she thought proper to desire to be informed of the visitor's name, and what he wanted at so unseasonable an hour. This request was not complied with, but rather with threats the gentleman answered, that she had best let him in, or she might have reason to repent. This did not move her in the least. Seeing he could gain nothing of her but by telling the truth, he told his name, which she knew as well as he did himself, and that he wished to speak with a Portuguese officer in the house. She gave the message, and with reluctance he was admitted. He wished and begged hard to remain in the house. But that could not be. We could not betray the confidence the public had in us, no more than forfeit their good opinion, as certainly he could not be safe with us no more than elsewhere. We prevailed with difficulty on a poor family in the village to take him in for the night. The next day we sent him his breakfast, but could hardly prevail with any of the family to take it to him. As for the poor man's dinner, when it went, he had been locked up for some hours, the owner of the house's fears being so great that when he went out in the morning he secured him under lock and key, so that he got nothing to eat from breakfast to night.

It was soon known that this fugitive had come our way, so that the village in the evening was visited by armed men. They were even told that he was hid in a mine in our grounds. They did not fail running over every part of the Quinta. It was dusk. During this transaction Luiz d'Oliveira appears under our window beseeching us to take him in, and hide him in the house. We could not comply, but told him his danger, gave him one of our labourers to see him safe out of the village and some way on into the country, when he left him at a farmer's house. He remained but a few hours there, being from his appearance, and the way he was left, looked on as a suspected person. He was turned out of doors, helpless, not knowing which way to turn. In short he informed his family of his situation, and as the less evil, being in constant danger of his life, they advised him to give himself up to Government, which he did, and he is safely lodged in prison, with many other suspected persons.

The French Consul with his son acted over the same part, with so little success, and in the same manner resigned themselves to their fate, and are prisoners. The Intendente of the Police, that had been appointed to that office on the arrival of the French General, managed to hide himself when the Spaniards left Porto. He is a French thief, and for the short time that he enjoyed this place he pillaged the public beyond the bounds of prudence. His venturing to appear in the town was the cause of something like a disturbance, the mob surrounding him, and would soon have done for him, if his good luck had not at the time introduced the two Navy Captains and W—sh, who were passing. They could not suffer the wretch to be murdered, and they looking on, altho' his crimes do not deserve compassion. Captain Jones, who is a tall stout man, claimed him as his prisoner, got him by the collar, and dragged him clear of the rage of the people. He assured them that they should see no more of him, for that he would send him immediately on board his ship, which he did. This act was accomplished with some difficulty. It was only the unbounded opinion and respect the Portuguese have for the English that kept them within bounds on this occasion, and made them relinquish the act of no less than murder they were determined on.

Our present situation I look upon as much more precarious than last year, when the English left Portugal. Now is the time for England to assist this country, and perhaps save it, but it must be without loss of time. She must send troops, and able Generals. The Bishop is well convinced of the necessity of this measure, and demands it of the English Government. He had not officially announced the departure of the French, and his appointment as Representative for the Regent. It was time to do it, and the following lines inform the ministry in England of this happy change.

'The Bishop of Porto cannot longer delay to inform the English Government that with the unanimous voice of the people and of the different Provinces, he has been appointed on the departure of the French, President of the Junta, and of the supreme Government established by the Prince Regent when forced to quit the Kingdom. It is not sufficient that French government is abolished in Porto, and the Regency again established. The French are still in Portugal, and are Masters in the Capital. Fresh dangers threaten. The Bishop, full of loyalty in such a cause, and ardour for his Prince, can have but one object in view, that of serving his country. But as the will unfortunately for defence appears in greater magnitude than the means, and the enemy within a few leagues of Porto, the actual emergency requires a speedy remedy. The saving this country must undoubtedly prove of importance to Europe. Our ancient and faithful Ally can hardly look on and not assist us in this glorious struggle for liberty. In this persuasion the Junta in all confidence depends on the good will and power of the British Admiral, Sir Charles Cotton stationed off the Bar at Lisbon, and requests that he will, without loss of time, attend to the demand for a considerable body of infantry, artillery and ammunition, with military Commanders, and whatever more succour may be in the power of the Admiral to give. Porto June 20th 1808. Bispo Regenti Governador'

It is understood Sir Charles Cotton has power to act for the good of this country, as occasion may offer. Captain Jones is the Ambassador for the Bishop to the Admiral. He sets sail as soon as possible, and we are full of hopes that whatever can be granted for present defence will, till a greater supply can arrive from England, as Sir Charles has troops on board transports in his fleet.

All is military now. Our good Bishop's guard is composed of Priests. The Dean of Porto, with the rank of Colonel, is Commander-in-Chief of this new-fashioned Corps. They parade every day under the Palace windows. It must be a most curious scene, as none can possibly know what they are about, no more than the Colonel at their head. Nor do they even know how to manage their arms, and when the word of command is given to turn to the right they are sure to turn to the left. But all ends in good humour. The Bishop is pleased, and amuses himself giving his blessings to all present. These kind of laughable scenes pass off, as long as there is no enemy to fight. Serious measures must be put in execution for the defence of the country. In the North they keep firm in the determination to resist the French, and are collecting the troops.

28

Rumours that a French force was advancing to attack Oporto continued to circulate, and defence measures were worked out between the Bishop and the British Naval officers.

HS The news of today is, that 3000 French troops are marching for Porto, and that they are within a few leagues of it. This report is alarming, altho' we can hardly believe the truth of the report. Our servants are very valiant in words. They each have their gun, and declare they are ready to attack the French. How far valiant some of them would be in deeds I much doubt, or how they would acquit themselves. They have never seen firing, and do not even know how to manage their guns.

On the 24th June we got a little alarm. When we were going to bed, the bells in the neighbouring villages began ringing at a great rate. We have in the house what we call the tower, that is high enough to overlook the surrounding mountains. In an instant we all assembled in this tower, to see if we could guess how near danger threatened. Our fears rather increased on viewing the mountains, and on seeing lights moving on, in appearance in different bodies, at distance from each other, we really began to dread it might be the French coming to Porto. It had been for some days passed so strongly reported that they were marching towards it, and that way from which we traced the lights is the direct road from Penafiel, 6 leagues from Porto. The bells did not cease from ringing, and the country people in numbers passed our door, on their way to Porto, with their guns and long poles. This lasted till morning, but as we could get no information till next day, we went to bed, but not to sleep. I certainly did not close my eyes, being too anxious about W—h's situation, he having remained in town that night. However, we were quits for some hours' uneasiness, as this alarm prove to be nothing at all but the restlessness of the people, who from some trifling occurrence imagined the enemy near at hand, so set the bells ringing in the village where this idea originated. The others around followed the example. While we were fearing for the safety of our good friends in Porto, they were passing the night in quiet sleep, for they were perfectly ignorant of apprehensions or danger of any description. The Bishop was obliged to give an order that no bells in future, on pain of

punishment, should be set a ringing. Supposing there to be any real cause
of alarm, he promises that the bells at the Cay shall be run, to give notice;
and likewise that no guns could be allowed firing any more. The Bishop
recommends to the people to keep their powder for real danger. This order
was most necessary, for ever since the 18th of June the public have been in
constant alarm with this kind of work.

For the present of Navy gentlemen we have only Captain Creyke. His
little vessel is laying in the river, by desire of the Bishop. He is a great
favourite, but has it not in his power to serve his Reverendissimo in the
way he has required, that is, he wants ammunition and men. Capt C— has
spared 30 barrels of powder out of his stock. He praises the Bishop much,
and is surprised to see the composure with which he gives his orders, and
with what judgment all his measures are taken. It is the more to be
wondered at, as his life has been one of retirement, and the best part of it
has been in solitude passed in a convent of Friars, that being his order. He
has in his old age entered into a very busy scene. He may find it a difficult
task in these wild times. There is one great thing in his favour, that the
public have the greatest opinion of him. The Navy gentlemen are lodged
and boarded at the public expense. They have a very good time of it. Our
two first friends upon further acquaintance did not in the least go off in our
estimation, and have proved very pleasant company to us in our retirement; and certainly not unpleasantly for them, to have a family to go to in
the country, where they were sure they would be welcome guests.

The French Consul, his son, and some other individuals, in all about
thirty, were about this time shipped off prisoners for England. A contribution is required to be raised from our little government, and I think it is
well judged. No limited sum is fixed. It is left in the option of everyone to
give according to their means. On such an occasion all will most willingly
come forward, and put in their mite, for the general good.

The 29th of June Capt Jones returned to Porto, with a most satisfactory
answer from Sir Charles Cotton. He promises a supply of troops, and that
England is ready to assist Portugal in every possible manner in her power.
The Admiral has written a very flattering letter to the Bishop, compli-
menting him in the handsomest terms, for his patriotic conduct, as well as
praising the courageous spirit and determined resolution that those under
his government seem to exert for the resistance of French subordination.

On 28th June definite news arrived at last that a French force was on its way to
attack Oporto. It was led by the much-hated French general, Loison, known as
'Maneta' (One-hand) and a notorious ogre in Portuguese memories for many
years for his ferocity in sacking and burning towns and villages. His base was at
Almeida where, in mid-June, he heard of the insurrection in Oporto and Tras os
Montes, and marched north-west towards Oporto with two battalions, crossing

the Douro at the ferry of Pezo de Ragoa on 21st June and making for Amarante. The fiasco that followed is vividly described in Harriot's diary entry for 29th June.

HS Yesterday's news was not so grateful. A messenger arrived with intelligence that between 2 and 3000 French troops had arrived at Pezo de Ragoa. So far they had marched on without opposition, and had crossed the river, Loison at their head, the one-arm cruel Loison. Notwithstanding much boasting, not the least exertions have been made in those parts for anything like resistance. On the contrary some towns had actually shewn a backwardness in coming forward in defence of their country.

On our side of the river, that Loison had crossed, there was nothing like an army to resist him, but there was a little band of forty that had collected, with a little Captain their Commandant much the size of Tom Thumb. He called a council to be informed what was the opinion of his brave companions. They all agreed they had not the least inclination to run away. During this debate a set of boys, that had their guns, by way of amusement were trying their skill, and discharging them in the air. That part of the country is very mountainous, and the roads, windings and turnings shockingly bad. Our French Hero, with the one arm, was perfectly unacquainted with this part of the country. Hearing the firing he was panic struck, and feared to advance, with the idea that the Portuguese were laying in ambush in great force to demolish them, as they marched on. Let this account be true or not, it is almost certain that the General, fearing a plot, in all haste took a flight with his army over the same river he had passed some hours before. In their hurry they left two pieces of artillery. The Portuguese neglected taking them off. They were not so lucky with their baggage, which the Portuguese took possession of. It contained clothing, arms and money. The General little knew how entirely he had been deceived, for if he had but sent to reconnoitre, he would have known what sure ground he had to go on, and the brave forty must have taken to their heels for safety. It is very fortunate, for if Loison had pursued his plan he would have met with no resistance, and might have satisfied his rage for plunder in every village through which he and his army, as merciless as himself, would have to pass.

The destination of this army was Porto, and Loison, it was said, was coming with full powers to lay great contributions, and that many individuals were marked out for destruction, in particular among the Friars and Clergy, for having been so busy persuading the people to rise to rebellion. It is well for Porto that this visit did not take place, for till we are better prepared 'tis better to hear of these armed men at a distance. For the present we have no regular troops. What good can be expected from a wild mob, without even one more reasonable than themselves to direct them?

With such description of persons, when danger appears at a distance,
boasting to perform great deeds is very easy; but on trial it is not to be
imagined they could resist or defend themselves against a regular army,
and such desperate men as compose the French army, in the least. At any
rate the occurrence of the Pezo may prove of use, and animate the public to
act with greater energy.

This alarm prompted a Captain of infantry to collect about 180 men with
the idea of going to wait for the French. They took up their quarters on the
bank of the river. Some of our servants asked leave to be of the party, and
walked off in great spirits, with their guns on their shoulders. They had no
other weapons of defence, and I am perfectly sure they will do no mischief, as not even a sparrow has ever been in danger of death from the
hands of those that went from hence.

Harriot looked at the keen but disorderly amateur Portuguese troops with the
eye of a professional soldier's wife, and was apt to think that – whether they
were Portuguese ex-Militia men or Spanish guerillas – such volunteers could
only be made into effective fighting forces by being commanded by British
officers. Her perfect conviction that the British were always the destined arbi-
ters of mankind reads oddly now, but was then shared by most of her compatriots, and the events of the next few years in the Peninsula did much to justify
the belief.

A more organised resistance was beginning to build up in Oporto, though
surges of popular anti-French violence within the city were still apt to test the
Bishop's control. The peasants armed with pikes and scythes who poured into
the city, to the number of 12,000 to 15,000, were in fact the old Militia which
had now been called up, and the officers and men of the regular army which had
been disbanded by the French in the winter of 1807-8 were now reassembling,
including the 2nd Infantry Regiment, seven of whose men had been executed
after a scuffle with French soldiers. This reassembled force of regulars finally
amounted to about 5,000 infantry and cavalry, with a few guns. British naval
officers, and a special envoy, Colonel Browne, with a roving commission to
report on the state of affairs in Northern Portugal and to help organise the
growing but chaotic Portuguese regular army and militia contingents, were now
frequently coming and going in Oporto, and hopes grew that the British Government, to whom the Oporto Junta had appealed, was really going to send
effective help.

HS Many of the officers and soldiers of the 2nd Regiment of Infantry belong-
    ing to Porto are coming in daily. This is the same regiment that was treated
    so cruelly at the Caldas de Reinha. It will soon be formed again. The
    general voice among them is to be led to fight the French, that they may
    revenge the death of their comrades. The device of the regiment, by

unanimous consent, is '*Viva O Principe Regente e Vincanza*'. These words are printed on a ribbon which both officers and men wear in their hats.

Our servants are returned, after an absence of some days. No enemy appearing, as they had little food, and no beds, they gave up their first campaign, and I suspect are not a little pleased to find themselves in a comfortable home again.

The communication between Porto and Lisbon is at an end by land. By sea the information is very uncertain, and little to be depended on, with regard to what is passing in Lisbon. Spain has made peace with England; so that England, Spain and Portugal may, and will, unite to chastise the French. Spanish troops are arrived in Porto.

Our good Bishop finds it a hard task to manage the populace. They are inclined to govern as well as him, and have marked out a few individuals that are in prison for execution, pronouncing them guilty, and are very clamorous, insisting that death must be their fate. Immense crowds assembled yesterday at the Palace crying for the blood of the guilty. The Bishop, whose nature is full of clemency, is determined that these prisoners shall have a fair trial; resists the mob with great firmness; at the same time he assures them that the guilty shall be punished. This promise has quieted them. Many persons are in prison with certain proofs of giving information to Junot of all that is passing in Porto. Such persons are well deserving of death. Compassion to them is weakness. What depravity exists in human nature, that there should still appear wretches, and not a few, that for a little gain are ready to betray their country. And to whom? To a nation that in every part of the world, where they have introduced themselves, have left traces of devastation, rapine and murder. The scenes already witnessed in this country, since the French entered it, speak for themselves. And they came as friends! Now that they are declared enemies, what can be expected? A repetition of the same sad tale over again.

The *Blossom* Frigate, Capt Pigot, came to anchor off our Bar July 2nd, and on the next day the *Antelope*, Capt Galway. The latter takes command of this station.

On the 8th of the same month, the *Peacock* Brig, Mr Peak, arrived from England, in five days, an extraordinary short passage. Colonel Browne and Mr Windham came passengers. Colonel Browne is sent by the Duke of York, to be informed of the real state of Portugal. It seems when they left England, it was a doubt if we were or not still under French government, and they were very well pleased at finding our port again open to the English. With other officers they were presented to the Bishop, who seemed most gratified with this visit. The next day they all dined with the Bishop, and it was settled that next day, the 10th of July, that the Bishop, with Colonel Browne etc, should ride out into the country and point out the proper situations most eligible to annoy the enemy in case of a visit. As appointed, a very numerous assemblage of persons met early in the morning on the 10th at the Palace, to accompany the Bishop. The party made a formidable appearance, the Bishop at their head, between officers, clergy, and gentry. They were out the whole day, and the old gentleman seemed not the least amused of the party, without an appearance of fatigue. His affability and good humour gain the hearts of all. That very evening Colonel Browne went on board the *Peacock*, and set sail to join Sir Charles Cotton off Lisbon. His intention is to return to Porto in a few days. This looks well, and as if some good was in meditation of importance for this country.

Junot is again at the old story, publishing manifestos, in all quarters of the Kingdom, and representing to the poor deluded people of Portugal the danger they ran if they do not immediately return to the humane and all-powerful government of the invincible Napoleon. He might as well preach to the winds, for none our way will regard him; so that his eloquence is flung away upon the ungrateful.

Some of the prisoners have had their trials. One officer in particular has had sentence of death passed on him. The memorable 18th of June, he appeared the chief of those that declared against future obedience to the French, and with great ardour and spirit animated the people to constancy and resolution in this glorious contest. But it seems that his ambition, or rather folly, has since carried him too far, having ventured to sport an idea that he might be as capable to rule as the Bishop. This disposition in him was by no means approved of, therefore checked by imprisonment. The laws of Portugal allow of pardon to the first criminal that is condemned to death on a change of government. The officer had not conspired against his country. He could hardly be called guilty of death. At any rate the Bishop was determined to save him, and to avoid disturbances managed to have the officer taken out of prison during the night, and sent him over the Bar to the Frigate. The next day it was soon public what had passed. The mob assembled in crowds, and went to the Palace in a most tumultuous manner, demanding the prisoner and showing great inclination to rise against the Bishop. He without shewing the least fear at this outrage, with the greatest composure ordered his carriage, and drove away to the prison, to see that all was quiet there; after which he alighted and in procession walked thro' the streets, and in terms most suitable he persuaded the people to return to their duty. He told them that, being convinced all his actions since his appointment to govern them had only been with a view for their welfare and the public good, therefore his conscience being perfectly at ease, he could not fear death. Nor could he suppose they would be so unreasonable and so unjust as to venture at disturbing the public peace at so critical a time, when all parties should unite with ardour in the common cause, and direct their anger where it was due, and where they had vowed vengeance.

The Bishop's reverend figure commands respect. This good old man with a most interesting countenance moved his hearers. All admired and venerated him. Peace was restored, and the minds of the most unruly were pacified.

Our thoughts are now most anxiously turned towards England in expectation of the arrival of troops.

July 21st. Colonel Browne is returned. He brings the best possible news, which is, an assurance that a supply of troops may be daily expected from England. The 21st of this month was a gay day for us, and my daughter's birthday. Colonel Browne, Mr Windham, and about half a dozen Navy Captains dined with us. At night we had a large party and dancing. What a difference between this party and that of a few weeks. The change is great indeed. May it last. The present prospect is a fair one.

29

HS Colonel Browne's intelligence has proved true. On the 24th of July Sir
Arthur Wellesley arrived in Porto from England. Him and his officers, etc,
etc were without loss of time presented to the Bishop. Sir A. Wellesley
informed him that they had left off Cape Finisterre 70 sail of transports,
with 10,000 troops, so that they might be hourly expected. The next
morning early the whole fleet was in sight off the Bar, and really a most
delightful one for every individual to behold. It consisted of about 80 sail.
The same day the General embarked, and set sail with the fleet for
Figueira, where the troops are to be landed. 5000 more are shortly expected from England.

It is now that the Portuguese have confidence in this contest proving
successful. They could not persuade themselves the troops could come
from England. On the conviction of their arrival the joy is excessive. They
have such faith in the English that now they have no doubt but that victory
will be the reward of this effort for liberty.

The British Government had been at last convinced, by the news of the Spanish
rising and the arrival of deputations from Spain and Portugal to ask for help
against the French, that it would be worth while to send an army to the Iberian
Peninsula. Sir Arthur Wellesley with 9,000 men under his command were to be
sent from Cork; he was to be joined by 5,000 men under General Spencer who
were already at sea off Spain. Wellesley sailed in HMS *Crocodile*, and called
first at Corunna, to concert plans with the Junta there for measures against the
French. Then on 24th July he arrived at Oporto to confer with the Bishop and
the Supreme Junta there. By now the Junta had succeeded in arming a local
force of 5,000 infantry, and 300 cavalry, under the command of the Portuguese
General Bernardo Freire; there was also an enthusiastic but disorderly force of
about 12,000 peasant volunteers armed with pikes. Wellesley agreed with the
Bishop that the latter force, for which Wellesley would try to provide more
effective arms, should be left to guard the Douro frontier, while Freire's 5,000
men were to march south to rendezvous with the British. The Bishop also
agreed to collect horses for Wellesley's cavalry and pack-mules and oxen for
his artillery and transport.

Next day the British fleet with Wellesley's army on board was seen sailing past Oporto, and Wellesley took ship southwards to confer with the British Naval commander, Admiral Cotton, who was stationed off Lisbon.

The risings in Oporto and Northern Portugal produced yet another reproachful manifesto from Junot, and vicious retaliatory action by Loison and his troops against the Portuguese population further south.

HS For the last and farewell of Junot's manifestos, I will insert the following, and hope most sincerely this country will be soon free of him and them.

'The most excellent and illustrious Duke of Abrantes, etc, etc. This address is to the inhabitants of such parts of the Provinces of Douro, Minho and Algarve, that are so blind as to have forsaken their allegiance to the Magnanimous Napoleon.

Portuguese, what delirium is this! What an abysm of evils are you preparing for yourselves! For your destruction you listen to perfidious counsels, and are in rebellion, without having calculated the impossibility of a durable success, or security for so irrational at attempt. It can only tend to your inevitable ruin. Seven months have been passed in perfect tranquillity. What can your reasons be, that you now run to arms, and against whom do you turn them? Against a Protector, against an army, that would secure to you every comfort, and your independence; that would maintain the integrity of your country, without which you will finally cease to be ranked among the Nations. Who is it that can have had the power to induce you to betray your interests? Do you then wish that the ancient Lusitania should become a Province of Spain! What have you to expect against a numerous army of men trained to arms, of warriors used to conquer and of course full of confidence and valour, before whom you will in an instant be dispersed like the sands of the desert, that are blown away by the tumultuous winds of Mid-day. Cannot you see that those who give you this advice have not your interest at heart, but have only in view to satisfy their rage. They care not for the shedding of blood, can they but succeed in keeping the Continent in confusion. Should those insolent Islanders invade your coasts, leave it to me to fight them. It is the duty imposed on my troops to defend you. Yours consists in remaining in the bosom of your families, and cultivating your lands for their maintenance. Yet if you remain deaf to my voice, *tremble*, for your punishment will be *terrible*.

The Emperor, thinking he had reason from the accounts he had received to be satisfied with the appearance of loyalty and public spirit throughout this Kingdom, in his great clemency had revoked the half of the contribution (what goodness!) and at that very time that he was conforming himself to your every wish, and everything that you could desire, you have shown yourselves ungrateful to a degree, by listening to false advisers and

deceivers. You have yourselves asked a king, and with ardour you requested one. The Great Napoleon has granted you what you wished. This
King might, with the All-Powerful Monarch's assistance, procure once
more to your disgraced country order and happiness, which is your due.
Your new King on his arrival (for he is coming) will expect to find faithful
subjects. I hoped to have given him a pacific Kingdom, and a flourishing
city.

If on the contrary he meets on his arrival with nothing but dismay, will
he be pleased? Certainly not. He does not expect to reign over a country
lost to all sense of honour, and that is exposing itself to the sad alternative
of seeing ruin and devastation in every quarter. Your laws have been
preserved to you; your customs, all have been reverenced. It is you that
have broken the laws. But you are still in time. Follow the example of the
Capital. You have happiness in view; you are flinging it far from you, and
without even a hope of being your own masters, for you will remain slaves.

Portuguese, while you may, implore Napoleon to have compassion on
you. Do it. You have no time to lose. His troops are on the point to enter
Portugal, from different parts of Spain. Should you hesitate, your destruction is inevitable. Lay down your arms. If you do not, every town in
rebellion, with its inhabitants, is doomed for destruction. Fire and Sword
will rage with all their fury against you. Your wives and children, all will
perish. You must not deceive yourselves. You know your fate, and if you
persist in your error, you have none but yourselves to blame.'

The above proclamation had no better effect than the former. France
must fight and conquer to keep Portugal. Loison, the General that took
fright some weeks ago, and crossed the river in such a hurry at the Pezo,
has met with no success. He has had his encounters with the Nationals, but
with loss, between 2 and 300 French troops have been sent to Porto, and
Capt Jones has gone off with them to the fleet. We daily hear of the
barbarity of the French troops, wherever they appear. When they first came
into the country, they were bad enough in acts of cruelty; now they exceed
all bounds. They neither spare youth, nor infirm old age. Women and
children, poor little innocent children, all fall before these savages. They
have mutilated persons in a manner too shocking to relate. One village has
been perfectly demolished, and every person in it that had not the luck to
escape in time perished by the sword. This account may appear exagger-
ated, but is perfect fact. Bonaparte has entirely mistaken his politics with
regard to the management of this Kingdom. He probably concluded he
might be able to keep it with as much ease as it had been taken possession
of. Had the fair and flattering promises held out to the people on Junot's
arrival in the country, and which he assured them it was his intention to
perform, been fulfilled, there is the greatest possibility that the best part of

the Nation would have submitted to the change with little or no resistance, or even reluctance. This country, from its weak government, was an easy prey to any power that might think proper to seize on it. The late event has proved the truth of this assertion. The great, as well as all ranks, were dissatisfied. They were oppressed, they were poor; and the greater number wished for a change with the vain hope of better times. But since they have experienced that change, their eyes are opened, they find, contrary to expectation, that they have in every respect been treated like a conquered nation. At the period of such a disappointment what would every individual have given to have recalled a few weeks; to see the country such as it was, tho' governed by a weak Prince, in preference to the fearful and melancholy bodings that were then presented to the imagination?

But now a gleam of hope again reanimates this desponding Nation. Courage, that seemed dead, within them is roused. The spirit of revenge calls for vengeance on these intruders. But the Portuguese must have an army, which they have not, and if they had they must learn to fight and stand the charge of French discipline. For the present they trust all to the English. Their confidence in safety depends on these faithful allies.

Encouraging accounts continued to reach Oporto of successful action against the French by the Spanish insurgents, including the news of the brilliant victory of Baylen in Andalusia, at which on 23rd July the Spanish General Castanos surrounded and captured a French army of 18,000.

HS   The news from Spain is good. They have been fighting and gaining some advantage over the French. That Government have declared to the English Ministry that they are not in want of troops, but demand of them arms and ammunition. They should likewise ask for good officers, otherwise it may go ill with them. In that respect they are as ill off as we are. Spain is famous for her manifestos. Many are published by the Junta, supposing that such fine expressions will keep up the spirit of the people. But they will not gain battles.

On the 27th of July arrived an official account of the total defeat of the French in Andalusia. Those of the French troops that escaped death surrendered themselves prisoners, with their Generals, their Artillery, and their baggage. It may be concluded from this account that Andalusia is at this moment free of the French. But the Duc de Berg is still in possession of Madrid, and as long as that is the case, the great work remains unfinished.

I am tempted to translate one of the best Spanish manifestos, it being short, and, I think, very impressive, that the Junta have produced. If they could conquer in this way, they certainly would, as there is no end to these publications.

'Spanish Manifesto. July 1808.

Far, far from us be dissensions, love of interest, the love of gain, honour, or command. The love of our country demands still greater sacrifices. Silent be those great and vain disclaimers on patriotism, who have no other object but to satisfy their own ambition. Silent be the writers of so many insipid papers; and silent be the malevolent, who endeavour to enfeeble the energy of the people. The enemy is still in Spain, and new legions of Vandals threaten to inundate us. The first duty of the supreme Junta is to organize and maintain the armies; and the obligation of good Spaniards is to serve their country in whatever station or office they may be called upon to fill. Let us then sacrifice our passions, and if required give our fortunes, expose our lives and all that is most dear to us for the safety of our country. We will give to the world a proof that whatever glory we may claim from conquering our enemies, we claim a still greater from subduing ourselves. But should there appear individuals base enough to consider and regard their private interest as distinct from that of the whole nation, and shall dare to foment discord or disobedience, and directly or indirectly oppose the unanimous voice of Spain for conquest or death, let him be brought to judgment without delay. Let him die an ignominious death, and his ashes be deemed unworthy of Spanish soil.'

To finance the newly-formed Portuguese regiments under Freire, the Supreme Junta in Oporto had to call for donations and raise a large loan, but according to Harriot the public willingly contributed this.

HS   Great contributions have been collected in Porto. The regiments that were disbanded are forming again, but have no clothing. This contribution is to help towards fitting the soldiers out. Great donations have been given. The Wine Company have given 4000 pairs of shoes (200 are made in a day) and many thousand shirts, etc, etc. In short whole regiments will be completely clothed. Very large sums have been presented to the Treasury by rich citizens of Porto. On such an occasion there are not even the poorest individuals that have not come forward with their mite. This kind of work puts one in mind of English patriotism.

On the 29th July the Junta of Portugal gave notice that they had determined on raising a loan of two millions of Cruzados. This step is taken much against their will. It is necessity that forces them to this measure, to enable government to discharge the enormous expense incurred in the payment of the new-raised regiments. The Regency secures 5 per cent interest for the money given.

Harriot's son-in-law James Walsh was now in the thick of negotiations and transactions between the Portuguese authorities and the British military ones.

He had already been employed as an interpreter between the Bishop and British naval officers; now he took on the job of army contractor, was hand in glove with Colonel Browne, the British roving emissary in Northern Portugal, and at the beginning of August left Oporto for the south with Browne to join the British army when it landed. Freire's cavalry rode south from Oporto on the same day to rendezvous with Wellesley.

HS The first of August Colonel Browne took leave of Oporto, in company of his brother, Mr Windham and W—h. They are gone to join the army at Figueira. The same day marched out of Porto a Squadron of Portuguese Cavalry entirely new dressed. They made a very handsome appearance. My good son-in-law thinks less of going to England than ever. His active mind has cut out business that will give him full employment. He is engaged in the contract for the providing the troops, so that now he is attached to the army, and seems mighty well pleased. He may prove a useful person to the military gentlemen, having a knowledge as well of the country, and since his arrival in it he has made his various excursions, and has given a pretty good guess at the general character of the people.

It was also on August 1st that Wellesley's army landed at Montego Bay, near Figueira da Foz, halfway between Oporto and Lisbon. Walsh seems to have shuttled to and fro between the British army and Oporto; he was in Oporto on 7th August, but by the 16th he was back with the army. He sent detailed reports of the French and British moves, and of the three days of battles which followed when the two armies met, back to his family in Oporto, and Harriot copied them into her diary, adding her reflections, still partly pessimistic ('I am something of a croaker,' she admits) on the outcome of the struggle for the Peninsula.

HS *August the 7th.* W—h is returned from the Camp. He praises Sir A. Wellesley, and the news is that 5,000 troops are arrived from England. This is very good news and keeps up our spirits.

  Last week a convoy of Merchant Ships sailed from hence for England, and one is expected from that part of the world here. A very little time has brought about a wonderful change in Porto. We now see nothing but content in every countenance, and those that are willing to work may have full employment. It is right ever to look on the bright side, and when all is animation and in good faith that we are safe out of the scrape, it may not be proper in me to despond. But I am something of a croaker, and cannot exult too quickly. May this transition prove solid. All know Bonaparte's unbounded ambition. He will now move heaven and earth for the final conquest of Spain. The fate of Portugal depends on events in that now unhappy country, either to fall or rise with it. We are so much in the custom of hearing from all quarters of the success of that disturber of the peace of all nations, that it is difficult to think that this country is acting on secure ground, and that every step now taken may bring new dangers in future. But such reflections may be fabrications of disturbed imagination. Whatever may be my reflections, it signifies little for the good or bad of the cause. It is now in a good train; every effort must be exerted for final success. W—h stayed a few days with us, and then returned to the scene of action.

On the 17th of August we were regaled with the sight of near 200 sail of transports. They bring 20,000 troops and money for the Regency. Both are most acceptable. Two Generals arrived (Germans) in this fleet. They are to remain here. The fleet sailed the next day for Figueira, where they are to land. There are now in Portugal, for to fight our battles, 30,000 infantry and 8000 cavalry. The French army is supposed to amount to 20 thousand. They have some thousand Portuguese among them. Junot has not as yet ventured out of Lisbon. There must be some good fighting before the English can clear their way for the attack of that city. To spirit up the Portuguese in the French service they have an increase of pay. The English army, commanded by Sir A.Wellesley, are encamped in the neighbourhood of the Caldas de Reinha, and the French not far distant. Their Generals are Thomières and Laborde.

That cruel-minded Loison, with his as cruel officers and troops, continue their ravages, and fill the poor inhabitants of every village with horror, as nothing but murder and devastation is displayed to their view. They go into houses, and in cold blood kill the helpless sick in bed. Some soldiers dragged a beautiful girl away from her distracted parents. She on her knees begged her life, but it was in vain. The savages, the worse than wild beasts, were deaf to her moving, heart-breaking entreaties. One of the wretches with his sword cut off her head, and holding it up on the point of the sword that had performed this ferocious act presented it to view, saying that it was a pity he had killed her, for she was very handsome. Such cruelty strikes the imagination. We read of wars having been waged in ancient times with great barbarity, and do not wonder at it, conforming our ideas to unpolished rustic manners. But what has the world gained, it may be asked, by civilization and refinement? We behold a nation famed for polished manners and all the arts, and that all other nations were proud to mimic. This very nation, which acts of cruelty have they not been guilty of? Surely if they have not exceeded, they have certainly equalled the barbarity of the Ancients. It is a reflection on humanity. The present wars are carried on by rapine, injustice and every species of cruelty. All circumstances taken together, the French Revolution may be looked upon as the most extraordinary that has hitherto taken place in the world. Wonderful events have been brought about in many instances by means the most contemptible. The beginning of confusion in France, when quite in infancy, appeared feeble. Those of the best judgment could not foresee its rapid progress growing by moments into a strength that seemed to wage war with heaven itself. On the reflection of scenes so jumbled with crimes of every description, minds of the least sensibility must necessarily alternately experience sensations of horror and indignation. And out of the rapid progress of such events has arisen the unbounded, gigantic power of Napoleon! By some means or other, success has crowned all his most arduous and adventurous undertakings. Bribery, great resolution, great cunning and deceit, will often have stood his friends when he might fear arms would not. The more the difficulty, the greater resolution and perseverance he seems to have shown for conquest, and to gain the end proposed, and on more than one occasion with little or no fighting. Bonaparte may certainly boast, besides his conquests, that he had the art to create traitors and cowards to their King and country, wherever his mind was set on so doing. We have now to see if our General will not find the means to turn the scale somewhat against this powerful man, and prove that his arms are vulnerable.

Harriot's stories of the cruelties of Loison's troops were not just the usual atrocity rumours; just before the British army landed at Figueira, Loison and his men had massacred all the men of the resistance force in Evora, with all their women and children. The historian William Napier – no friend to guerrilla insurrection as opposed to 'manly warfare' – considers that the harsh French treatment of the Portuguese insurgents was justified by the 'custom of war', the right – by inflicting terrible retribution – to protect the French army against the anarchic attacks of insurgents not held by the 'bounds of civilised warfare'. But even he concedes that the virulent Portuguese hatred of Loison must have been provoked by heinous acts of cruelty.

30

On 16th August the first encounter between the British and French forces took place. Wellesley's army, reinforced by the arrival of General Spencer with 5,000 men at Mondego Bay on 5th August, had advanced through Leiria, Batalha and Alcobaça, and was now approaching Obidos. A small French force was posted at the windmill of Brilos; they were driven out by a detachment of the 95th Rifles, who rashly pursued the retreating French till they came up with the main French force. The British detachment would have been annihilated if General Spencer had not advanced with his brigade and rescued them. Two British Officers and twenty-seven men were killed. Rifleman Harris, of the 95th, gives a vivid account of the skirmish in his *Recollections*, describing the heavy French fire which mowed down his comrades all round him; how he fired back with his rifle resting on the body of a friend who had just been killed, and how they withdrew to a hillock where they stayed all night till they could rejoin the main British army. The report of this skirmish which James Walsh sent back to Harriot probably came from Colonel Browne who was with General Spencer on his rescue advance.

HS *August 18th*. We have just received letters from W—h, Caldas de Reinha, with the following account. The evening before an alarm was given by a firing at the outposts. 'About 400 English attacked a body of French, and beat them out of a place about a league from Caldas, and then were obliged to retreat, as the whole of the French army came to attack them. The English lost about 30 men and an officer. The loss of the enemy is supposed to be between 60 and 70 men. The only advantage they have over the English is the knowledge of the country, and that is a great one. General Spencer and Colonel Browne narrowly escaped being killed.'

The day after the encounter at the windmill of Brilos, August 17th, was the day of the Battle of Rolica, the first full-scale Franco-British battle of the Peninsular War. The French General Laborde with an army of 4,000 men was drawn up in front of the village of Rolica, with a horseshoe of mountains behind and on his flanks. Wellesley's attack eventually drove the French over the crest of the hill behind, and forced them to withdraw, but only after a day of ferocious to-and-fro fighting among rocky ravines and tangled woods, in which some senior

British officers were killed during rashly gallant onslaughts. James Walsh's description of the battle has not quite the grim immediacy which Rifleman Harris, who was in the thick of the fighting, gives to his brilliant account of the struggle on the steep slopes: his leaps to run for cover behind another rock and to fire again, the white smoke of the rifles which hid all but the immediate surroundings, the triumphant shouts that went up when cannon fire mowed a lane through the French ranks, the wretched figures of the women camp-followers searching for their husbands' bodies when the battle was over. But James Walsh's account is sufficiently detailed to suggest that he was a fairly close spectator of the battle. His estimate of the numbers engaged, and of the casualties, is however not accurate. Wellesley had 13,500 men (though only about 4,000 of these were actively engaged), Laborde only 4,000; British casualties were nearly 500, French ones about 600. Laborde himself was badly wounded, and won Wellesley's admiration for his cool-headed skill and re-source in the desperate day of withdrawing, re-forming, fighting back.

HS *August 17th.* 'Yesterday's skirmish was nothing, as only 30 men fell. This day did not finish without the loss of many a brave Englishman. The French had their outposts for nearly a league from their camp. The English army came up to the enemy. They had the advantage, and such a position never was better for defence. The engagement began early in the morning, and lasted till nearly five in the evening. The mad D—s, for so they might properly be called on this occasion, marched up a precipice that seemed impossible to attempt. Only very few of them were engaged, and yet they forced the English from their entrenchments back through pine woods and groves, whose branches they had cut for the advantage of firing, and continued a sort of running fight, but so cunningly that the English could never get near them, and they always keeping the advantageous places, to which they retired and galled our troops from them all; till the English came to a more even extensive country, on the top of a hill where the regiments could get up and act, which they did to good purpose. For then there was as sharp fighting as could be, and such banging and cracking of great and small guns that astonished many present that had never seen the like before. This work lasted about two hours, and then the French re-treated, but in good order as could be collected about a mile and a half from the English army. 1500 is supposed to have been the number of the French army. They were at least 4000 under Laborde and Thomières. The French displayed their usual skill, and the soldiers their accustomed valour and discipline. Words cannot describe the valour of the brave English on this occasion. Unluckily they wanted guides. The Portuguese refused to give them information, either from stupidity, or through fear of the French. If Sir A. Wellesley had known the country, his right and left wing might have circumvented the enemy's army, and their position might have been the cause of the defeat or surrender of the French. They may have lost between scattered and slain about 200. The loss of the English in proportion has been more severe on the officers than on the privates. Many are badly wounded. The English that were engaged were chiefly riflemen and light companies, among whom were the Portuguese light infantry, who behaved very well, and some few are wounded and slain. Laborde lost a leg. The English in dead wounded and missing have lost 450 and some valuable officers. 30 of the wounded officers are at Torres Vedro, well taken care of by the Portuguese.

It is melancholy to say with what unconcern the dead were seen scattered all over the country, as far as Villa Verde, above a league of country, every inch fought with desperation, till the French retreated beyond reach. The dead were soon bereft of clothing, as the survivors' business seemed to be which could secure the most of what was but a few hours before the property of their poor comrades, now laying lifeless before them. Soldiers' wives appeared in plenty on this sad scene, some looking for their husbands, many others to plunder. It must be understood that altho' in the beginning of this engagement the French were only 1500 strong, that on the contest growing warmer Laborde came forward with his whole force, and it appears they have suffered considerably. The English army engaged might be about six thousand.'

After the Battle of Rolica on 17th August, the French withdrew into the mountains near Torres Vedras. There they were joined by Junot and Loison, whose forces combined with Laborde's made up an army of between 13,000 and 14,000. In the next three days Wellesley's army of nearly 14,000 also received reinforcements; 4,000 men from England were landed at the mouth of the River Maceira near Vimeiro, and with them on the 20th arrived Sir Henry Burnard, who had been sent out to take over the command from Wellesley, and who rejected Wellesley's well-thought-out plans for advancing on Lisbon. But next day, 21st August, Junot's forces advanced from Torres Vedras to attack the British positions round Vimeiro. In two hours of fierce fighting the French forces, whose advancing ranks Rifleman Harris had seen flashing in the early morning sunlight, were broken by deadly fire and bayonet charges and were fleeting back towards Torres Vedras. General Brennier and several hundred other Frenchmen were taken prisoner, and there were more than 2,000 French casualties. It was a brilliant victory for Wellesley, but Burnard did not allow him to follow it up, though Wellesley told him that they could be in Lisbon within three days if he were given a free hand to advance.

James Walsh's account of the Battle of Vimeiro is comparatively tame, and was probably sent from well behind the lines, out of sight of the brutal aftermath of the battle that Rifleman Harris described: the stripping and looting of the dead, the screams of wounded men having their legs amputated in an open-air field hospital in a churchyard, the shivering soldiers cutting branches from the trees to cover them as they lay out on the cold hillside the night after the battle. Walsh's commonplaces about 'a very proper drubbing' and 'our brave fellows' read rather glibly in face of the bloody realities of Vimeiro.

HS   *'The 19th of August*, the army was at Laurinham, near Peniche, where it is waiting a junction of 4000 men (Guards) from England. Then the intention is to proceed to Lisbon, where the enemy, with part of the army joined Loison, and retired in confusion.

     On the 21st of August another engagement took place, when the French got a very proper drubbing. The battle for the space of four hours was as desperate as it could be. The enemy, in retaliation for the English storming their entrenchments at Calumbaura, thought to force the English from their encampment, which they found no easy matter; for certainly there never was a more desperate undertaking, without success. To see the style in which 1500 of our brave fellows stood it, till they forced the French to face about and run for safety, exceeds belief. The English and Portuguese cavalry dashed in amongst them and played the D—l; but our brave men were dreadfully cut up, and lost about half their number. General Brennier and Charlot were taken prisoner, with 300 men, who are sent on board the fleet. Their loss is supposed to be 2000 men, and that of the English, between dead and wounded and missing, 730.'

After entering Walsh's reports in her diary, Harriot commented with some prescience on the probable sequel of fiasco and missed opportunity.

HS   This action took place at Vimeiro, where the army still was when the above account left the place. The English and French Generals, the express says, were in close conference, and had been so for above six hours. The general opinion is, that the French General will never be able to assemble half their forces, so that the English may have advantage of defeating them in parcels; that is, if it be thought advisable to follow up the advantage gained by our brave General. But I much fear this long conference will not end comfortable to our most ardent wishes, and that the French Generals, with their usual slyness, are working out a termination to this campaign to their own advantage. The first news from Lisbon will put it out of doubt one way or another. It is a great pity the brave Sir A. Wellesley should not be allowed to act according to his own judgment. There then would be little doubt how the contest would end.

31

The day after the Battle of Vimeiro, General Sir Hew Dalrymple arrived to take over from Burnard the command which Burnard had taken over from Wellesley two days earlier. Dalrymple sided with Burnard in the cautious decision not to allow Wellesley to follow up his victory by an immediate advance on Lisbon, at least until Sir John Moore, who had been sent from England with reinforcements, had reached Maceira, which he did during the following week.

Any possible advance by the British was forestalled by Junot, who on 22nd August sent General Kellerman to negotiate terms for an armistice, and nine days later this was ratified by the Convention of Cintra between Dalrymple and Junot. The Convention of Cintra was bitterly vilified at the time by the British and Portuguese press and public opinion, including Wordsworth and Byron. Later judgments have concluded that it gave some solid advantages to the victorious British: it freed Portugal of all French troops, ensured that Lisbon and all the Portuguese fortresses were yielded undestroyed and without further loss of life. Wellesley, though he disagreed with its detailed terms, approved it in principle.

There were, however, two disastrous flaws in the Convention; it was negotiated without any proper consultation with the Portuguese, and it allowed the French army to take all their arms and personal property with them when they were evacuated. The French put the freest possible interpretation on 'personal property', and bore away astonishing quantities of looted Portuguese treasures – Church plate, pictures, medieval manuscripts and botanical specimens from museums, carriages, household linen, great sums of money extorted from private Portuguese citizens and even from public funds.

When the Portuguese heard the terms of the Convention of Cintra, they were bitterly indignant. The advantages to Portugal of getting rid in this peaceful fashion of Junot's still powerful army, which could well have devastated the country by fighting its way back to join the French armies in Spain, were not at first apparent; the insult to Portuguese dignity and the loss of Portuguese treasures were much more obvious. The Bishop of Oporto, who received early information of the terms of the armistice, sent a copy of it to the Portuguese Legation in London, accompanied by a strong protest. Owing to Dalrymple's dilatoriness in reporting home, the Bishop's news was the first to reach London, and it caused such a furore that Dalrymple, Burnard and Wellesley were all recalled and had later to face a Court of Inquiry. According to William Napier, the Bishop's action was part of a deep-laid plot to make himself ruler of Portugal, but it seems likely that it was the natural and justifiable reaction of wounded Portuguese pride and sense of property.

Harriot Slessor had no doubt that it was the latter; her diary for late August and September severely criticizes the terms of the French capitulation.

HS   *On the 21st of August* transports arrived from the army with the wounded. 2 French Generals come, badly wounded. General Dicken has received despatches from the Commander-in-Chief, of the 25th of August, to inform him that the armistice had been granted to the French. When the despatches left Vimeiro nothing more had transpired from this tedious meeting; nor can good be hoped from it.

The news from private letters are not of a pleasant nature; that a capitulation was on the point of being signed. Let the French alone. I will answer for them, they will manage in the best manner possible for their own advantage, and if obliged to quit the country, they will do it with much too reasonable terms.

September. All is settled, and the capitulation signed. This intelligence is sent to our good Bishop, merely informing him of its being signed, and not a single hint is given him, with regard to the manner in which all is settled. Tho' the Bishop is not informed of this shameful transaction, it cannot long be kept a secret from him. We hear more than we wish to know. The French General, Kellerman, has had the art and cunning to outwit our Commanders. The French are to leave the country, and are allow'd to remain with their arms, ammunition, artillery, and whatever they think fit to denominate their private property. Both officers and men were known to have come into the country with no other property than what they brought on their backs. They will depart, there is little doubt, in very different plight.

Are these terms for a conquered army? The French leave the country with every article granted that was insisted on by the expert French Generals. It may be truly said that those Heroes take their departure as the conquerors, not the conquer'd. We had hoped for a brilliant end to this campaign. Our flattering hopes end in disappointment. The public minds were in unison with ours. Our confidence was such in Sir A. Wellesley, that nothing less was expected from his valour but the submission of the enemy's army to whatever terms he thought proper. We had good reason to think so. It seems that Sir A. Wellesley, on the success of the battle on the 21st of August, was not for allowing the French to collect in any force, being confident that he had every reason to believe and flatter himself, had he been allowed to follow up the very great advantage already gained, and even pledged his honour, that attacking the enemy without loss of time, would have proved the annihilation of the French army, or forcing them to surrender at discretion. Unfortunately Sir Henry Burnand and Sir Hew Dalrymple arrived on the morning of the 21st of August. They being of superior rank to Sir A. Wellesley, of course his right to command was at an end. The battle of that day was still undecided. The General offered to resign his command, but Sir H. Burnard declined the acceptance, saying it was but just that Sir Arthur should have the honour of the day. He had a good right to it, and would have gained complete laurels, had he been allowed his request. Pursuit was absolutely refused him. The reasons that were given him were, that it appeared an undertaking too hazardous, and that the English truly on this occasion had shewn what they could do, and had sufficiently distinguished themselves. This was a most mortifying denial to our favourite General, and most unlucky was it that the two Generals had not been detained only four and 20 hours longer. The reason they did not make their appearance sooner was that they were delayed by contrary winds on their passage from England.

It is of no use to repine at what is past. The mischief is done, and the consequences of letting the enemy go out of the country, with their General, in the way they are going may in future prove of much harm to this Nation. The honour of the British troops does not seem to have been properly understood on this occasion, no more than the welfare of this country. Wiser heads than mine may settle this point; I leave it, and wish I could forget the disappointment. The impression it has made on the public is extraordinary. They shew a good inclination to reflect on the conduct of our English Generals, which I think they have little right to do. At any rate what a state this country would have been in but for the English; perfectly in the power of the French. If our Generals are to blame, it is not for the Portuguese to complain. What has been done to liberate them has been without their assistance.

James Walsh accompanied the British army when it entered Lisbon on 15th September, and he and one of Harriot's Naval friends supplied an account of the British arrival, the French evacuation, the fury of the Lisbon mob against the French, and the situation of the Russian squadron under Admiral Siniavin which was anchored in the Tagus, claiming neutral status and holding aloof from both French and British. Under the terms of the Convention the Russian ships were sent to England while the officers and crews were allowed to return to the Baltic.

HS   *On the 15th of September* the English entered Lisbon. The troops marched into the city in triumph, and were most joyfully received by the inhabitants. The French standard was instantly hauled down at the Citadel, and the Prince Regent's flag hoisted everywhere, with a Royal salute. At night the city was brilliantly illuminated, and every demonstration of joy was conspicuous on the occasion. The first Division of the French was on board before the grand army made their entry into Lisbon, and on the 16th the last Division quitted the city for the same purpose. On the signing the Capitulation a General officer was sent off with troops in order to preserve the peace in Lisbon. It was very necessary, for the French soldiers were much inclined to be unruly. A French General, thinking he might still impose on a Portuguese, in whose house he had been quartered ever since the entry of the French, made a last attempt to exact money from him, knowing him to be very rich. The gentleman ordered the Portuguese to provide him without loss of time a sum of money to a most unreasonable amount. Times were changed, and instead of such a demand being complied with, he went and informed the English General of this transaction. The General ordered him a guard in his house, that when the money should be required the proper answer might be given, instead of money. This little occurrence gave cause for the French to say, that the Nationals were already become insolent and violent, now that the English rogues had got among them.

Our Navy friend writes word that the confusion was very great on the embarkation of the French troops. A party of French passing through the streets were attacked with stones, and might have been badly treated, had they not got into the dockyard. While the embarkation lasted, it was hardly possible to pass in the streets. The English, the Portuguese, and French troops were mingled together at every turn. It was impossible to keep order. A greater scene of confusion could hardly be presented, when baggage, artillery, waggons and guns were driving through the city at full speed, to escape the fury of the enraged mob, who murmured discontent and hatred against the French. They will not be persuaded but that they go off with immense property, stolen from individuals. I fear it is too true, and deserves no other appellation. The riches the French have amassed the few months they have resided in this country were most certainly not voluntary gifts. They were obtained by extortion, and no other way. The Navy officer adds that it was amusing to see how regularly accoutred all the French troops and officers were to go on board a ship, as if they were going to battle; and so exceedingly courteous and civil, wherever they met an English officer, they paid them the military compliments, presenting their arms. Perhaps they thought they could do no less than pay them this little attention, as thanks for being allowed to depart so much more handsomely than they could have expected.

The French Generals are each to be sent off in their separate Frigates. Junot has thought fit to be terribly offended at not being honoured by being allowed to go in a line-of-Battle ship.

Walsh entered Lisbon at the same time with the British troops. He says that nothing can exceed the magnificence of the Tagus. It is beautiful, that fine river, so ornamented as it is at this present crisis with every description of vessel; the Russian fleet, laying at anchor with their majestic ships, waiting with impatience to be sent to England.

Sir C. Cotton has appointed our Navy friend to the command of a Portuguese Frigate. It proves most difficult to keep the peace between the French and Portuguese, during their stay in the river. The English are bound to do it by the late Convention. The French get on shore at night, and commit every kind of excess. The Nationals are not behindhand with them. Wherever they meet a French man unguarded, murder ensues, so that hardly a night passes that dead bodies are not found in the morning. There are not wanting persons that would rejoice to see a serious fight if it could give a just pretence for breaking the treaty. There is no great danger of that. It is too well settled for anything of the kind to happen.

Junot, fearing the loyalty of the Spanish troops, had taken the precaution to have confined in the hulks no less than 5000 Spanish troops. They are now liberated. Illuminations continue in Lisbon. There is no end of vain show in that city.

Conditions in Oporto were meanwhile comparatively peaceful, as Harriot reported with gratitude for present prosperity, but with misgivings for the future.

HS The Hospital in Porto is full of French prisoners, and are attended to with great care and humanity. The Bishop has visited them, and distributed money amongst them. Our Navy friend of the *Eclipse*, that had the command of this station, is going to leave us. He will be a loss, having proved a pleasant addition to our family party, in our retirement in the country.

We are living in great quiet and content in Porto under the government of our good Bishop, and have not an idea to wish for a change. The Regency is reinstated. Some of the members, that were appointed by the Prince Regent on his leaving the country, have been dismissed, and others supposed to be more true and loyal to the cause are appointed. Little can be expected from such a Government. Good men may be found among them, but if new measures are not adopted the old despotism will again reign over a subjugated people, irresisting and helpless. I am sorry to say how low the Portuguese are in the estimation of the English, and their officers seem to be conscious of their demerit. Yet my opinion remains firm, that could we have an English army in the country for any time, much might be effected. The men would make good soldiers with English officers and English discipline. The Portuguese soldier is submissive and capable to bear more hardships than the British. He does not require such substantial food, and with confidence in their commanders they would, I can hardly doubt, fight with ardour. I will not be quite positive with regard to the Lisboits. They are, I fear, degenerated to a state of effeminacy and of cowardly indolence, not even having the least inclination to resist the overbearing power of the French at a time when they might have attempted it, perhaps with success. It is far different with the inhabitants of the North of Portugal. They are loyal and brave, with good inclination to fight for the liberty of their country.

But what hopes can be entertained for the future welfare of this country? The English troops are ordered home, and Portugal will again be left destitute. At last the Spaniards have demanded troops from the English Government. It would have been wise in them had they accepted the offer in the beginning of the contest. They are a vain, proud nation, with hardly a good officer among them, and the greatest part of the country seems not even inclined to fight for their country. In this case the chance is much against them for the freeing the country from so inveterate a foe.

Porto has been very gay for days past, with the arrival of English Generals and their Suites. They are now on their way to Spain. Some patriotic families have feasted them with great magnificence, and dancing at night. The news from Lisbon is, that Sir A. Wellesley is recalled on a very short notice. Mere jealousy is supposed to have been the cause of his having been left at a lonely place, and another sent to take possession of Lisbon, which Sir A. Wellesley had wrested from the French. There never was more savage conduct. But no one can deprive him of his fair fame. Sir Arthur is much beloved by the army, and has the good opinion of his officers. There exists much discontent among them for such proceedings, and Sir Hew Dalrymple is the talk of all, not much to his advantage.

The following diary entry is dated 8th August, but this should presumably have been 8th September, after the French capitulation at the end of August. The French garrison at Almeida surrendered the fortress there and marched to Oporto for embarkation. Harriot's account of what befell them in Oporto mentions Sir Robert Wilson, who had been sent by the British Government to raise and organise a regiment of Portuguese soldiers, the Lusitanian Legion, who were to be sent to Spain to support the Spanish insurgents against the French.

HS *On the 8th of August* the remainder of French troops arriv'd in Porto from Almeida, to embark for their own country. They came guarded by some English soldiers. They had been allowed to remain with their arms, and did not show the least inclination to be riotous. On their arrival they were sent on board the transports. The populace in unruly tumult marked their dissatisfaction, declaring that the French should not have been allowed to keep their arms; that they were taking off Portuguese property and must be searched before their departure. They were not content with such clamour, but in crowds went on board the Transports laying in the river; forced every French soldier to come on shore, and then pillaged without mercy, and took every description of thing they could lay hands on, so that they cleared the Transports of every article of provisions laid on board for the voyage, and then returned on shore with their booty, meeting with no resistance. On the contrary, the coast was perfectly clear for them to do just what they pleased. The Commanders of the Transports, not much to their credit, on the appearance of the Portuguese rabble, took to their boats in all haste, and got on shore. The mob, much elated by such success, shew'd no inclination to disperse, and much inclination to abuse the English, with the pretence that they protected the French.

Sir Robert Wilson, who is lately come from England, with permission from Government to raise a Regiment, thought proper to interfere with these disturbers of the public peace. He got among them, and told them, that if they were not satisfied with the mischief they had already committed, and disperse and go quietly home, that there were troops enough in town that he would soon assemble, and he, at their head, would soon teach them their duty. This advice was taken in good part, and the rabble thought proper to retire without further mischief.

The French are to remain on shore till the Transports are ready to sail, and the officers are received in private families. The English are all gone for England, and the Russian fleet is off likewise. They were allowed their own officers to command on board, and sailed off with colours flying. Sir C. Cotton is recalled. The Captain that he had appointed to a fine Portuguese Frigate has been obliged to give up his command, and returns again to his old friend the *Eclipse*. He is to sail for England with the Fleet.

32

All French troops had now left Portugal, and a large British army was established there. The summer of 1808 had seen some striking successes by the Spanish insurgents against the French. Joseph Bonaparte, named as King of Spain by his brother, had entered Madrid on 20th July, but had to withdraw only eleven days later when news arrived of the defeat and capitulation of the French forces in Andalusia at the Battle of Baylen. In September the Galician and Asturian insurgents under General Blake captured Burgos and Bilbao. Spanish forces under Castanos and Palafox were massed along the Ebro. Hopes began to dawn that the French might be kept out of the Iberian Peninsula, but the realistic Harriot had no such confidence, and her diary for the last months of 1808 recorded her misgivings and her dread of Napoleon's merciless intentions.

Her fears were justified. Napoleon was freeing his hands to be able to concentrate on Spain. In September he met the Tsar Alexander of Russia at Erfurt, and signed a treaty which, combined with some conciliatory moves by Austria, secured him from threats to his rear while he dealt with Spain. In October and early November French forces defeated Blake at the Battles of Zanoza and Espinosa, and his fleeing troops were further depleted by the hardships of retreat through the mountains; Burgos was recaptured and sacked by the French, Santander fell. On 23rd November Castanos was defeated by the French at the Battle of Tudela. On 3rd December the Junta of Madrid capitulated, and Napoleon, who had arrived in Spain in November to take overall command, entered Madrid on 4th December. Although he did not allow his troops to loot the city, much monastic and official property was seized.

Meanwhile Sir John Moore, now Commander-in-Chief of the British army in Portugal, had marched from Lisbon on 18th October to join forces with the Spanish insurgents and with General Baird who had landed at Corunna with a cavalry contingent. Moore's invasion of Spain was hindered by shortage of transport and misinformation about routes, and it was not till 20th December that he and Baird and all their horses and guns were assembled at Salamanca. The promised cooperation with the Spanish forces failed to work. All English observers at this time, including Harriot Slessor, felt a mixture of admiration for the courage of the Spanish insurgents and exasperation at their inefficiency and unreliability. The British army in Spain was eager to confront the advanc-

ing French – Napoleon had left Madrid on 21st December with a huge army –
and was cheered by a dashing cavalry victory by Lord Paget over the French at
Sahagun on 20th December. But Sir John Moore decided that retreat was
inevitable.

News of what was happening in Spain reached Harriot Slessor in Oporto in a
series of letters to herself and to others which she copied into her diary, and
from British officers passing through Oporto. She became more and more fearful that the French would again invade Portugal, and that the attempts being
made to arm and defend the country were pitifully inadequate. Surveying the
past year since she and the Walshes had made their decision to stay on in
Portugal, she felt that they had been surprisingly lucky so far – her son-in-law
had even profited by his employment as interpreter and contractor to the British
army – but she felt no confidence that this luck could last much longer.

HS   Sir John Moore has left Portugal with his army for Spain. It is late in the
     autumn. Should the rains set in his troops may be involv'd in great diffi-
     culties, besides the great disadvantage of the country not being known to
     either General or officers. Likewise it is well known that the military in
     Spain are by no means cordial towards English Commanders, so that I
     much fear that Sir John Moore may have cut out a difficult part to act, and
     I hope he will not with his brave army fall a sacrifice to intrigue, as well as
     want of support from the Spanish troops. They have promised an army to
     join Sir John Moore. Time will show how far they will be as good as their
     word.
        Spain for the present holds out against the French. Joseph Bonaparte has
     been obliged to quit Madrid. This will be a most insignificant event for
     Bonaparte. His mind is employed on important political plans. All is well
     settled between him and his dear *friends* the Russians, as well as the Aus-
     trians. His cunning has cajoled them to agree to whatever terms he has
     thought proper, having them secure for as long as it suits him for quiet and
     servile forbearance. Most likely he will turn his unmerciful thoughts our
     way, and with his great army attempt the entire conquest of Spain and
     Portugal. He has prepared us for what is to happen, by a proclamation that
     his intentions are to go in person to Spain, to settle his brother Joseph more
     firmly on his throne. It is true enough, it has till now proved an unsteady
     one. Nor do I believe that Joseph has much ambition to be so highly
     elevated.
     November 1808. Another year has flown and we are still in Portugal. The
     first of November 1807 was a memorable day for me and mine. The Consul
     was the last of the English still in Porto. On the first of November he sailed
     for England. What a day that was for us. It was an awful crisis, and still
     impressed strongly on my mind. We could not but feel most poignantly the
     critical situation we had voluntarily placed ourselves in. I have not a doubt

that if any one of us had on the occasion had honesty enough to confess our secret thoughts, we should have shown but forlorn hopes for future satisfaction. This country has suffered much within the year from an inveterate foe. Nor can it be said that the winding up of the campaign has secured us from future evils. For this time we have weathered the storm, and may say, not without some wonder, without danger or loss in any way. On the contrary one person in the family has no reason of complaint, having been employed to good advantage. But should the French pay us a second visit, Adieu to Portugal; it will no longer be the country for us.

The French have now the road clear from Spain to Portugal. They will take advantage of it. Portugal is again left in a situation incapable of defence, without troops. Should they be able to raise them, the difficulty will not be trifling, where to find officers capable to command those troops. When the French enter'd this country last year, their professions were for friendship and protection. It is true, their conduct and actions soon show'd the kind of friends we had to deal with; yet none attempted to resist such unwarrantable entrance into the country. The French took quiet possession of it. The case is now changed. Napoleon has pronounced Porto and the Northern Provinces in a perfect state of rebellion. Porto has had the courage to rise against the Usurper, and has everything to fear in its defenceless state. For it is so unquestionably, with only a few Auxiliaries to boast of.

Sir Robert Wilson is indefatigable in forming his Legion. He is a most active officer; is up early and late. It is an arduous undertaking. The great difficulty is the finding officers, and a great many, too many, are boys that compose the companies.

The month of November, except the departure of the English Army and Fleet, – this month has passed off both in Lisbon and Porto without any event to mark it. Spain cannot boast the same. The news from that country is not favourable. Despatches of the 20th November give an account of the defeat of General Blake's army, and that the French were marching into Spain in great force.

On the 28th General Mackenzie with several British officers arriv'd in Porto from Corunna. The accounts these officers give are by no means of a nature to set our minds at ease. On the contrary, all reports are dark and dismal. Many of General Blake's officers have behaved shamefully, as well as his men. Upon the whole it seems to have been a runaway business. Some of the officers have been shot. I hope this may have a good effect, and make the others fight, not to share the same fate.

Sir Robert Wilson has shipped off some hundreds of soldiers' wives for England, with their infants. It seems very injudicious to allow such numbers of women to leave their homes to come on such expeditions. The Legion begins to make a figure. Sir R. succeeds beyond his expectations.

The men have not all their clothing or arms. They are expected from England. His nature is for constant employment, and having now little to do, he has determined to set off for Spain, to offer his services to that Government.

On the 13th of December 700 of the Legion, with the Colonel (Mayne), left Porto for Lamego, on their way to Spain. We were present to see them march out of town. Nothing pleases our good Bishop so much as the military. The Legion assembled for him to see them before their departure. The Bishop walked along the ranks, and with reason praised their handsome appearance. The men are all Portuguese, with some foreign officers. He gave them his blessing. The Brigadier, Sir R. Wilson, then made a short speech, assuring his men he did not doubt the ardour with which every officer and soldier present must be inspired to fight for their country. He warned them that they might look upon themselves as in equal danger with their neighbours the Spaniards, and that altho' he was their Commanding Officer, from henceforward he should look upon himself as their comrade, would share the hardships they may have to encounter, and be the first to show the example, not to fear the enemy, to face every danger with courage and resolution. Sir Robert particularly recommended to the soldiers obedience to their officers, regularity of conduct and unanimity among themselves. Then telling them he should soon join them, he wished them a good journey; and with three cheers, and '*Viva, O Principe*', with drums beating and colours flying, they marched out of the town, all appearing, officers as well as men, in high spirits.

On the 15th of the same month Sir R. Wilson left Porto. The remainder of the Legion are to follow when complete, and the clothing arrives from England. When Sir R. took leave of us, he wished us a good voyage to England, saying we should be there before him. I do not doubt it. According to appearances, we shall not be long before we think seriously on the subject of departure.

I fear the Bishop does not manage to get information of what is transacting in Spain. It is of the utmost importance for Portugal. Too many Frenchmen were allowed to remain in Lisbon. Most of them are mere spies, and it is little doubted that there are now a few in Porto. Many evilminded persons amuse themselves fabricating news to deceive the public, and of a nature to make the Bishop flatter himself that he has every reason to believe the Spaniards are gaining ground on the French. It is not very easy from public report to know what to believe.

Harriot then quotes a hopeful letter from General Anstruther (who had led a division at the Battle of Vimeiro, was now in Salamanca with Moore, and was to die of dysentery at Corunna a month later), following it up with a copy of a letter from a staff officer in Salamanca to one of the Warre family (who had apparently remained in Oporto when Consul William Warre left in 1807) which gave a gloomy account of the situation of Moore's forces and the apathy of their Spanish allies, led by General Romana. All Harriot's forebodings were confirmed by this letter, and another from an English friend in Vigo, and she added a censorious commentary on the Spanish insurgents in general, and on Blake – whom she had met in Oporto the previous winter – in particular.

HS General Anstruther, that is in Spain with Sir John Moore, has sent the following account to our Bishop.

'December 10th, 1808. The Spaniards are holding out at Madrid, as their forefathers did at Saguntum, and I hope with better success. The whole of South Spain has risen en masse, and all the great towns have sworn to follow the noble example of the Capital, and there is every reason to hope the glorious flame, tho' obscured for a moment will burst out with redoubled lustre. Say to His Ex'cy the Bishop, all shall be well yet, but that he must infuse a portion of his spirit into his colleagues of the Regency, and rouse the nation to exertion. He will soon hear of the movement of the troops. I trust they will be successful. If otherwise, he will at least hear they have done their duty like brave soldiers.'

This good and respectable General expresses what he ardently wishes, success to the cause. But a very few days after the receipt of this account, the Bishop got certain intelligence that Madrid had capitulated, and that the French were in possession of it. It seems the nationals did not make the defence that was expected of them, and so much hoped for. On the contrary they hardly attempted any resistance, which they might and should have done. No sooner was the Capitulation signed, and the French in possession of the town, than the usual sport was exhibited of plunder. No regard was given to the conditions of the Capitulation. The Churches were plundered of their riches, no trifling booty. The Grandees' houses did not escape pillage, and those among them that are suspected of loyalty to their King and Country are sent to France. The treasure taken out of the Churches etc is travelling the same way in carts and waggons.

How can it be expected other parts of Spain will do their duty, when the Capital has behaved so shamefully. If the Spaniards should attempt, the chances are much against their success. A fine regiment, a part of the troops that were last winter in Porto, have been cut up to a man, the Colonel, a noble man, at their head. They fought like Lions. Poor fellows, they bravely fell. Their Colonel, after being badly wounded, still persisted to fight on his knees, till he fell to rise no more. If there were more to be found of that description, Spain might soon be free of Frenchmen. The country has lost some good officers in this desperate fight, which they can by no means spare.

We have seen a private letter in town, which gives a sad account of the present state of Spain. I have a copy of the letter. It is from an Aide de Camp of General Berringer's, and is as follows.

'Castanos's defeat was complete; his army dispersed over the country, in the greatest confusion. The battle was lost by bad generalship. Their position, I am told, was quite absurd. The men seem to have fought with bravery for three hours. There was a great deal of useless firing on both sides at a most laughable distance. The French themselves did not shine in point of bravery, and gained the battle by the perfect ignorance of their opponents, and their cowardice. The chief loss of the Spaniards was caused by their complete confused retreat, likewise from their extreme weakness, as many of them had not tasted bread for several days, and only arrived in this state the morning of the action. Blake's army also made no fight. Their loss might amount to 2000, and they actually ran as fast as the French approached. The men blame the Generals, and I believe with reason. My opinion is frankly that the state of this country is desperate. The people, I think, were they properly led on, would fight; and well enough, for the defence of their independence, and have affection for the cause. But they have nobody to lead them, or excite them. I have not, since I am in this country, seen the smallest appearance of alacrity or energy. They talk a great deal of what might be done. They are four leagues only from the enemy, and I see no activity, not a drill or a levy, or an appearance of defence, except at Zamora. The 17th Dragoons (French) rode paramount thro' these places before our arrival, and ordered contributions of meat, etc, and everything to be sent to Placencia, and were obey'd. Even at Toro, with four companies of Invalids, they robbed with impunity the Post Office. We are advancing to form a junction with Sir D. Baird, and what is to be done then God only knows. What is certain is that all we can do will avail little with people who will not act for themselves. They want subordination, inclination, discipline and heads to direct them. We can place no confidence on troops with scarce any officers, except a few of the worst description, and were we three times our number, it would be folly to think of defending Spain by ourselves. Our men are in high spirits, and pretty healthy, considering the severe frost and cold we have suffered. They wish for nothing more than to meet the enemy. Nor, should we be nearly matched, can I doubt the event.

Portugal, as dependent on Spain, is a most critical situation. I fear much for the conclusion of the contest. All the victories of the French are real; those of the Spaniards only in the English newspapers. Most infamously has our General been misinformed on the real state of things; far, very far, from the light in which they were represented. Enthusiasm, Patriotism, are fine words to an Englishman. I wish I could see glow the least symptom of anything of the kind on this country. But really the apathy and inactivity forebodes no success to the enterprise. Unless some unexpected change occurs, the prospect of success at any rate may be looked upon as far distant.

The 18th Inf. D'ns have been tolerably successful at the outposts. They have taken away 70 carts loaded with cotton, belonging to Junot, besides 50 prisoners, horses, mules, etc. The whole booty worth £30,000. They took also two nights back a French Colonel of 24th Chasseurs. A hundred men have been taken in all. December 18th, 1808.'

The above is a melancholy picture of the present state of Spain. The truth of it may be depended on. A letter I have just received, the contents by no means mend the matter. My letter is from the British Consul's wife, Mrs Hunter. He is the only Englishman in Spain at the present time, acting in a public character. Mrs Hunter's letter is dated from Vigo, Janry 3rd 1809. This letter informs us that Barcelona has surrendered, and also on the 20th of last month Lord Paget with 400 cavalry attacked 900 French and defeated them. He made 260 prisoners. 30 were killed and a great many wounded. The account officially published by the Junta mentions that not an Englishman was killed, and only 18 wounded. Castanos has been arrested, and sent to Andalusia for trial. The force of the French movable army is supposed to be 90,000 strong.

The British suppose a junction of Sir John Moore, Baird's and Romana's army may exceed 70,000 men; but it may be feared the Spaniards will not join the English forces. They have not as yet taken any steps towards it. On the contrary, they evidently on all occasions show their dislike to serve under English officers. It is all jealousy on the part of the officers. They do not like strangers should take the command from them. They are so obstinate in self conceit that it will not be easy to convince them of their ignorance in Tactique. The only chance the Spaniards have for conquest is to allow English officers among them to organize them and teach the soldiers somewhat of English discipline. The worst is that from this sad inaction Sir John Moore's situation becomes more critical daily.

As for General Blake, not the least confidence can be placed in him and his troops. He appears very plausible with pen, ink, and paper. The general voice pronounce him a very good officer. But since the French first entered the country, almost on the first onset his officers have proved panic struck, and found safety in their heels. The soldiers of course would follow the example of their leaders, and leave the field of battle with equal swiftness. What could the poor General do, being left alone, but run too, or let himself be taken? I think it is the best thing he could do, and join his friends in France. This General is of Irish extraction; was born and bred in Spain, and never visited Ireland, and does not talk a word of English. He was last winter in Porto with the Spanish troops. He had with him a very lively little Spanish wife, and well educated daughters. General Blake is rather forbidding in his appearance; has a stern, severe, reserved countenance; has a decided dislike for the English, and certainly not the so essential art of gaining the love and confidence of his officers and men. He passed a very melancholy winter in Porto, excluding himself and family entirely from society.

Harriot's relentless denigration of every nationality but her own makes her unjust to the courage of Blake and his starving troops, exhausted by retreat through the wintry mountains, and to all the Spanish population, who might be lacking in energy and efficiency, but were strong in courage, love of country and hatred for the French. It was easy enough, from the safety of Oporto, to reproach the Spaniards for not resisting – without adequate arms or supplies – the huge and superbly organised French army; to gloat over the shooting of deserters and mock the soldiers who ran away. But she was now well aware that if the British, without effective Spanish support, could not hold the French advance in Spain, Portugal's turn would come next.

33

Early in January 1809 news began to reach Oporto of the terrible retreat of Moore's army across icy mountain ranges to Corunna, pursued by the French under Marshal Soult. Harriot and the Walshes realised that there was no hope of their remaining safely in Oporto, once the British army had withdrawn from Spain, and Portugal was left defenceless against the inevitable and vengeful French advance. It was all the more urgent for the family to get away as Sophia Walsh was again pregnant. When she had been in the same condition in the autumn of 1807, it had been considered too dangerous for her to risk a winter voyage to England, and this had been the cause of the family's remaining in Oporto when all the other English families left. But now a worse danger than a winter voyage threatened, and the family made up their minds to go.

As they prepared to leave the country which had been Harriot's home for thirty-six years, she continued to record in her diary the letters and rumours, and finally official accounts, of the disasters of the retreat and the final battle, and to make dogmatic pronouncements as to how the British Government ought to have organised the expedition.

HS I have another letter from my Spanish correspondent, from the same place, Vigo, January 9th. It is likely to be the last. The game seems nearly up in that country. Mrs Hunter says 'You may have heard of the retreat of the English, and all that you heard is perfectly true. An officer of Engineers arrived here on Saturday to say that the First Division would probably be here today. But yesterday another arrived, who gave out in Town, before he went on board the Admiral, that their retreating was only to deceive the enemy, and that they were now going to meet them. However, Mr Hunter soon received confidential information to say, they were still retreating, only that instead of embarking here, they would embark in the Bay of Betanzos. All the Fleet and Transports go round there to receive them, and we are going on board to sail this day if possible. At all events we embark at one o'clock on board the *Ville de Paris*, in which vessel we are to have the Admiral's accommodation, there being only a Captain in her. The after destination no one here has the smallest idea of. I shall write you when we know, or when we arrive at our destination; for as our quarters on board will be so commodious we shall probably on no account think of going

ashore all the time of the embarking. There will be such confusion. The
retreat was not on account of any battle. The day before Sir John Moore
intended to attack the enemy, he discover'd that Bonaparte was coming
with an immense force upon him on the other side.'

Such gloomy news from Spain naturally revives in full force our fears
for the safety of Portugal. Besides, from too good authority we are assured
we have no good to hope for, and every evil to fear. Therefore our thoughts
must now be turned towards England, and yesterday all was settled for our
departure, with the Captain of a Merchant ship. He gives the whole cabin
for 70 guineas, and we provide provisions. Between young and old and
servants we are ten in family. Now that we have set our minds on departure, every anxious wish must tend to the effecting of that purpose. The
month of December set in with storm and rain, and has continued in the
like manner ever since. Many weeks have passed and not a vessel has been
able to come in over the Bar, no more than possibility for any ship to put
out to sea.

A person is arrived from Spain. He gives himself out as head servant to
Sir John Moore; is a Frenchman, married to a Portuguese and is natural-
ised. This man's report is a sad tale if true. He says that on the 16th of
January the English and French had fought most furiously before Corunna,
that many were killed on both sides. The action lasted a few hours, and
ended in the retreat of the English, who got into Corunna. Sir John Moore
was mortally wounded, and another General officer; but he could not tell
his name. Sir John was carried off the field of battle in a blanket. On
finding himself dying, he declared to the officers that surrounded him, that
he did not in the least regret life, being confident that he had done his duty,
and served his country to the height of his power. He desired his Secretary,
Major Cockburn, to get his keys from his servant, for him to take charge of
his papers for England. He seemed perfectly composed, and lasted about
three quarters of an hour, after he had expressed his wishes. And on his
death the officers each took a lock of his hair, and embraced the body. The
same person adds, that the troops that escaped the slaughter of that day,
full of woe, got safe on board a ship that night, the 16th, and sailed; that
the French fired on the ships from the shore, and owing to the firing and
bad weather, some of the ships got on the rocks, and were lost. The next
day the town was summoned to surrender. They were allowed three days,
at the end of which the French took possession of the town.

The servant asked permission to return to Portugal after his master's
death, but was refused it by Maréchal Soult, the Commander-in-Chief. He
said he should be absent for some days, and on his return to the army
would see. Soult asked many questions about Sir John Moore, praised him
much, and seemed to lament his death. He said he had known him in
Friesland. Laborde took the command in Soult's absence. The servant

made a second attempt with him, for leave to go and see his wife and children, but without success. He told him to wait a little; that there would soon be a French army in *Portugal*, and that he might make one among them. But not being inclined to travel in such good company, he managed to escape alone.

It seems that Sir John Moore's army was not much more than 15,000, Bonaparte's double that number. Our English gentlemen have questioned the man most particularly, and in no way can get him to contradict himself. He insists upon it that he has reported nothing but the truth, and that it will soon be known to be a fact.

All communication has been at an end for many weeks between this country and Corunna. Yet our good Bishop is still confident that there is no danger of a visit from the enemy. I fear he will soon have reason to think otherwise. I have heard no more from my Spanish Correspondent, which is no good sign. If she had any good news to communicate, she would have managed to have written.

27th January. The weather bearing a more favourable appearance, we went on board our ship to settle our separate berths, which we did as comfortably as a small cabin will allow of. The Captain seemed to think there was some chance for the Ship getting to sea the next day; therefore pressed us to send our provisions etc. Most willingly we consented, and all was safe on board by night. But Alas! the next day our flattering hopes were disappointed. The weather proved as bad as ever. The wind blew, the storm ranged, and the sea appeared mountains high, dashing its unmerciful waves on the rocks, as if to spite us poor mortals and teach us more patience and resignation. I have seen the like scenes at a distance from my windows for many weeks past, and now still more do I view it with the painful thought that to a certainty our situation becomes more critical daily. The few remaining English here do not in the least diminish our fears. On the contrary, they are in and out all day long, with various reports, forever saying that the French are within a few leagues of Porto. Luckily such reports till now have proved without foundation.

The servant's account of Sir John Moore's death proves but too true. The official account is arrived, and nearly the same. The English must have fought like Lions, not to have been all demolished, their numbers being so inferior to the French. It is cruel to reflect how many brave men have lost their lives in this last affair. It seems as if a fatality had attended Sir John Moore's army from the time they enter'd Spain. They had to encounter every difficulty; bad weather, with days of constant rain, and of course the roads in many parts almost impassable; want of provisions, as well as a proper supply of money. It may be conjectured that Sir John was not expert enough at getting good information. Neither him nor his officers were in the least acquainted with the country, with a handful of men in comparison with the French. This little army stood alone to fight, in vain inviting the Spaniards to join the English army. Their Generals, with some frivolous pretence or other, kept aloof. Assurances and promises were not wanting for speedy assistance, but nothing more. Sir John Moore, well convinced how critical his situation was, knew too well that he and his brave army had nothing for it but to retreat; to effect which they were obliged to fight every step of their way; and it is a marvel how few fell in the flight. More particulars of this truly tragical tale will soon reach England. The French are said to have suffered a greater loss of men than the English. But what then? Bonaparte has an immense army in Spain. He cares not for the loss of thousands of his troops, if he does but gain his ends, which he has completely effected in this conquest. He triumphs perhaps beyond what he could have expected. He sees every English man leave the country. He has seen them flying from those shores, where so many brave officers and men have met their graves. If report tell truth, the English have sustained great loss, in Artillery, ammunition and baggage, likewise in horses, great numbers having been shot rather than that they should fall into the hands of the French.

It would be well could such events be buried in oblivion. The impression they make on the mind cannot be effaced. I must indulge myself in a few reflections on the failure of this expedition to Spain. Had different measures been adopted at home, the sacrifice of so brave an army could not so easily have been effected, and Sir J. Moore might still have existed, to fight more battles for his country, and his family not have had to mourn his loss. It is not sufficient for Ministers to send troops off to foreign countries. Much more is required. Many more material particulars to a certainty should not be lost sight of. It is natural to conclude that the Generals sent on such important expeditions have the confidence and good opinion of those that appoint them. Therefore they should be laid under no restrictions, and allowed full power to act according to circumstances, which was not the case. Sir John laboured under every difficulty; want of a sufficient number of troops, want of money, to provide for every necessary, even for so small an army. Can it be wondered at that such a disaster should have taken place? Rather might it be wondered at had it not. We must, in spite of our good wishes to see an end to such tyranny, own Bonaparte to be no common enemy. England I truly believe is the only power he fears, and even stands in awe of. But for England to keep such an enemy within the limits of moderation, every exertion, every effort, can hardly suffice. Bonaparte deserves the appellation of an usurper. It is likewise too true, it signifies little by what means; for the misfortune of Europe success attends him in every attempt he plans. Extraordinary events require extraordinary exertions. Not only courage is necessary but judgment, great activity and diligence, to cope with so formidable a foe, whose rapid movements can hardly be equalled.

Spain is perfectly bare of English troops, so is Portugal. So that the French have nothing to prevent their entering again into this country. The little resistance the Spaniards may attempt will avail them little. Palafox has been performing wonders, fighting the French and killing great numbers. La Romana is a fugitive in Portugal. So is Blake. Romana came with his military chest and no trifling sum of money. He is at Villa Pouca, in Tras os Montes, guarded by Spaniards. There are likewise at the same place many Spanish officers, with their wives and children. This is the way those good people fight for their country.

We may soon get a summons to go on board, as the weather seems inclined to be more favourable.

From 27th January to 16th February Harriot and her party had to remain in Oporto while the weather prevented their boarding their escape ship. Weeks of violent gales made Oporto a sealed port; nothing could enter or leave the harbour. Meanwhile the news of the French advance on Portugal became ever more threatening. The town of Corunna had surrendered to Soult, and French troops were massing on the Portuguese border. The remaining British troops in Portugal were concentrated round Lisbon, ready for evacuation, and the Portuguese Council of Regency was attempting to raise a militia force, but had no arms for them except pikes and a few muskets. In Lisbon and in Oporto riotous mobs assembled, calling for vengeance on anyone believed to be pro-French, and even insulting the British for abandoning them. Relations between the British and the Portuguese in the first half of 1809 were not happy. The Portuguese felt betrayed by the British plans to withdraw, and offended by the arrogance and distaste shown by British officers stationed in Portugal, and the bad behaviour of some of the British soldiery.

Harriot's prediction as to the probable fate of Luiz d'Oliveira, whom she had already seen as a fugitive from mob violence the previous summer, and who was now in prison, was to be fulfilled; he was assassinated by a mob a month after she left Oporto. Her admiration for the Bishop of Oporto was beginning to wane, and she had no confidence that the amateurish attempts to raise local troops and build defences would be any protection against French regular troops. The men of the Lusitanian Legion, raised and trained by Sir Robert Wilson, 3,000 recruits of excellent quality, would have been some protection to Oporto, but more than half of them had been moved to Villa Real in December.

HS *February 16th.* The Bishop has received an official account that the French are in numbers no less than 10,000 troops on the opposite Spanish shore, between Caminha and Valenca. They had seized all the boats they could lay hands on, and even had got many conveyed on carts from Galicia, and filling them with troops made an attempt at crossing the river that separates the two countries, to see if they could effect a landing on our side, to take possession of a small fort on the banks of the river. That done they would soon have succeeded in getting over their troops; but for the first time they met with proper resistance. The country people were too alert for these invaders. The alarm was given, and crowds assembled on the shore to prevent the enemy from landing, which they did most effectually; took many of the boats, dispersed others, and sent two to the bottom, with a General and officers, for food for fish. I flatter myself we shall be sailing away for England before a second attempt is made, for certainly this meditated invasion will not easily be given up.

February 18th. The last news from Lisbon I can hardly think deserves credit, that France and Austria are going to war. It would be a lucky event for Spain. There has been a most desperate fight between the French and Spaniards at Saragossa. That part of the country were ever famous for being brave and loyal to their King. They fought on this occasion desperately, were terribly cut up, but had the glory to remain conquerors. Even the women join'd in the battle, and after all was over 180 women were found slain on the field of battle.

La Romana is returned to Spain, and has collected 13,000 men to try his luck again. He can have no great confidence in his Galegos. They fight just as the fancy takes them, and seldom stand the brunt of a battle, and think it no shame to turn their back on an enemy, when they are tired of fighting, and run away. If convenient, they carry off their arms, sell them, and return to their families, and when tired of rest, begin again the like work.

Sir Robert Wilson is still at Ciudad Rodrigo. He is so great a favourite with the Spaniards that they will not part with him, and have given him the command of troops to organize. There are near a thousand of the Legion still in Porto, under the command of the Lieut-Colonel, Baron Eden. Sir R. Wilson wished them all to join him, but the Bishop will not consent to part with them. The case is that he is beginning to fear for the fate of his town. He allows the clergy to quit their retirement and priest's habit, and put on a uniform to fight. Should Porto be attacked, the Reverend Gentleman declares he will be ready to put himself at their head, and meet the enemy. He little knows what he says. Flight I fear will be his only security. Could we but see a very few thousand good English troops among us at this crisis, some hopes might be entertained for the redemption of Porto. But no reasonable expectation can be entertained of the kind. Just now I do not suppose that England has a thought on the subject.

It appears extraordinary to see how still the inhabitants of this town, as well as the country people, persist in their confidence that there is not the least danger of the French coming again so soon. They even say, should they venture, they are confident that Porto is in a fine state of defence, as well as the resolution of the country people to attack the French on their way from Spain. One very material reflection has not occurred to these good people, that is, of what description are those who have come forward for their defence. Troops there are none. The good Bishop with his motley attendance, most likely, on a day of confusion and attack, will be making the best of his way to Lisbon, or wherever he may be most secure, not to be kidnap'd by the French. The country people declare that they will fight. It is true they flock together in great numbers. Thousands I have not a doubt will assemble, and very few among the number that have been taught the use of arms. They are willing to think, and I believe do think, that as long as an enemy does not appear, that they are capable of performing wonders. But let a formidable French army present itself, well disciplined, full of ardour for conquest and rapine, – how soon will confusion, dismay and distraction be mingled in the probable annihilation of thousands. One terrible sentence has been pronounced by a set of Portuguese in Porto, that should this town fall into the hands of the French, marked victims are to be sacrificed. The Brigadier Luiz d'Oliveira, that is still in prison, and had shown too marked an inclination to favour the French, he is one; and some other officers equally suspected of not being loyal to their country. I fear they run a sad chance for their lives. The rage of a mob in general are regardless of reason. When worked up to fury, it surpasses all bounds. Many wretches, with minds prone to cruelty and revenge, have vowed that the above shall not exist to meet protection from the French.

Engineers are hard at work to put the town into a proper state of defence. It appears that they cannot be very knowing, as some persons, that seem to have a little judgment of what is going on, have ventured to observe, that there is not an appearance of common sense in all that is doing. The Bishop attends at the works every day. It is certainly out of his way; so that let them be what they will, all appears well done to this respectable Reverend character.

It was not till 21st February that Harriot Slessor, James and Sophia Walsh and their three little boys, Harriot Amelia Slessor and three servants were at last able to board their escape ship. It was none too soon. Soult began the invasion of Portugal on 9th March, and on the 29th he captured and sacked Oporto, and massacred so many of the inhabitants that their heaped-up bodies, flung into the Douro, rose above the surface of that deep river.

34

Safely on board ship at last, Harriot had leisure, and relief from anxiety, in which to write a flowery farewell to Portugal, and a more natural and endearing account of family events.

HS   *February 21st.* At length we were summoned to go and sleep that night on board a ship. We obey'd with alacrity, and late in the evening set forward with our train to the waterside, to take boat. We were followed by a set of melancholy servants, that we were forced to leave behind, drown'd in tears. I believe their sincerity when they declared that, in losing our family they lost their only friends and protectors. We were safe over the Bar the next morning by ten o'clock, but did not sail till the 23rd February. We have been at sea a fortnight, but have had such contrary winds that we have made little or no progress on our voyage. The weather is fine, and the ship with very little motion. And as I am neither sick, or much sorry, I will while the calm lasts, indulge in retrospect of the late interesting event of our final departure from Portugal, an event, and what has passed in that country, the last year we were residing in it, cannot be forgotten; which remembrance will long be preserved to us.

    Many, many months before we left Portugal our life was a mixture of fear and anxiety, dreading what the morrow might produce. I was determined to pass the last Christmas day, to all appearance, in Portugal, with something like cheerfulness, and invited to dine with us every Englishman of our acquaintance. A turkey of an extraordinary size, a native of Ireland, was executed on the occasion, in honour of our guests. This turkey had for a long time tyrannised with despotic sway, and reigned paramount in the back yard. Not even those of his own kind were secure from death. He was Sultan all powerful of the feathered tribe. Destruction attended his steps, wherever he appeared. My young grandchildren had an idea that whatever came under the denomination of cruel must resemble Bonaparte; therefore had given it that name, and for his crime had condemned him to death, for the many murders he had committed in cold blood. The sentence was confirmed by upright judges, and when the cruel tyrant was not suspecting any harm, strutting in great glory, and displaying his sleek and shining plumage in the bright sun, the wretch was seized and his head struck off

212

with as little mercy as he had shown to others. The joy at this death was as great as if Bonaparte had fallen. The gentleman was suspended for many days, in hopes that he might prove better in the eating than in deeds. Even in that point we met with our disappointment. The old rogue promised fair, outward appearances were flattering. In the dish he looked plump and tempting, but on trial proved so hard and tough that our good company would have been badly off had there been nothing else for dinner.

This convoy has cleared Porto of every English person; and likewise some Dutch families have followed our example, as well as Portuguese, a French Bishop and Abbés. The day that marked our departure was very fine and mild. The fleet was between 30 and 40 sail. Every passenger on board the different ships appeared on deck, anxious to view the picturesque and moving scene, that attracted hundreds of the natives, who lined the shore. Many a sorrowful one among them would have come to take a last sight of those ships that were carrying off some good friend. The sight was lively and interesting, to see the vessels when preparing to take up their anchor, sure signal for departure. On the ships beginning to be in motion, hurry, bustle and noise was predominant on board every ship, each at their best exertions to be foremost in getting safe over the Bar. The same Bar, that a very few days before had raged so furiously, was at this crisis so perfectly serene that it seemed to invite for departure. We had just sufficient wind, with the tide, to clear the Bar, and with so little motion that we could hardly perceive when on it. Another description of moving scene was noticed on board our ship, that even in the bustle did not pass unnoticed, the melancholy parting of lovers. On our departure being finally settled, a disconsolate swain, prostrate at our feet, in humble supplication and tears entreated that we would have compassion on him, and grant his suit, which was, to admit his future bride as a fellow passenger among us; that the favour would be the more to be valued, every ship in the fleet being full of passengers. Our cabin was already perfectly crowded, and the lady to be admitted is rather on the Amazonian scale. Compassion for such moving distress prevail'd. The lady hereupon refused to depart, saying that she could not forsake the object of her affections, and insisted that she must remain and share equal dangers with him. This was not to be allowed, but go she must. Between persuasion and force we got the Dame safe on board, but no further than the hatchway, where she plumped herself down, and fell to writing. It was natural to suppose that leaving her friends in a hurry, she was taking leave of them. No such thing. They were least in her thoughts. A nobler passion engrossed her entirely, altho' the sole object of her affections was alongside of her, heaving deep sighs. Most interesting was the subject of the lines that flowed from her pen. They were the effusions of a mind that wished to express sweet sentences, in a strain most likely to comfort her lover, and for him not to resign himself entirely to despair. The next day, when the parting scene took place, the precious lines were given him, and when the last Adieu was pronounced, to solace him in the many lonely hours that must pass before the happy time arrives that he can join her in England.

Then once more Adieu to these well known shores. It is truly pitiable that so fine a country should be laid waste by an unmerciful enemy. No stranger can sail along that fine river without being struck by the beauty of the scene that opens up on the sight. The town of Porto appears to advantage from the river and the country on the opposite shore displays varieties of mountains that out-top each other, some of a dark hue, others ornamented with plenty of the tall pine. The lower grounds on the banks of the river are richly beautified with verdure and wood intermixed with country houses, with their gardens and vines, that luxuriously flourish in conscious pride. But above all, the eye and attention must be attracted by the Convents. They are sure to be placed in the most healthy fine situation. One particular Convent towers above the rest, from the height it stands on, and the fine grounds that belong to it, full of shade from beautiful, ancient trees, under which the rich, lazy Friars repose like drones, careless of all the ills that are passing in the World. The Friars of this Convent have always been famous for entertaining visitors magnificently, and producing great choice of fine wines, etc. They may well suppose themselves the lords of the creation, and look down upon this ample theatre with disdain. I would wish them not to be too confident. The time may be very near at hand that rude intruders may prove unwelcome guests. They may not in peace enjoy the moving scenes, ever before them which they behold on the river. I own I have less compassion for persons of such description, that serve for no purpose in the world. This country is over-run with Convents of both sexes, full of useless beings, and that it is known in some parts only serve to impoverish the country.

This retrospect of the past has carried me so far that it seems as if I had quite forgot that we are sailing away in the middle of the wide Ocean. Not sailing very fast certainly, as the Captain is quite out of patience at the very little advancement we have made on our passage. The weather continues fine, the wind seldom favourable; and when a breeze of favourable wind now and then arises, hardly any advantage is taken of it. Some ships in the Fleet are leaky, others bad sailing vessels, and as they must be protected, we are for ever laying to, that they may come up to join us. The first days we were out at sea, we had in company a Frigate, Capt Mackenly, to guard us, but since he has taken leave of us, all we have to boast of to defend us is a little insignificant King's ship, it is true, but nothing like the size of the ship we are in. It is well the enemy's Privateers are not on the look out. One of them well armed might take the best part of the ships. We have had one alarm, which lasted some hours. A sail appeared at a good distance, apparently under full sail to come up to us. Our Captain, with all the help of his Glass, could only conjecture we were to have an enemy to deal with, seeing no friendly colours flying. As our Captain boasts that he is the best sailing ship of the whole convoy, he declared he would not be taken, could he help it, therefore had settled that, danger of capture being certain, or flight, all sails were to be hoisted, and away we were to go. It was best not to be put to the trial. We were quits for the fright, as on the near approach of the vessel it proved to be an English one. Could we have been allowed to sail without convoy, probably we should have been in England by this time. There hardly passes a day that ships of different description do not appear, all friendly, which so far may have secured us from an enemy. We must hope the same good will attend to the end.

The weather still continues fine, which has tempted some of our floating neighbours to be sociable and come and spend the day with us. On such grand days, to receive the company with proper decorum, the cabin is laid into a parlour. Our Captain is a very good cook, and has presided at the roasting of the turkey, and then joins the party at dinner, in the best good humour. We have spent several pleasant days in this manner, that have made a little variety and taken off the attention of watching the wind and waves in slow succession dashing on the sides of the ship. No ladies with the gentlemen have ventured to favour us with their company.

I begin to have my fears, from appearances, that a little being may very shortly intrude upon us. When the English last year left Porto, I determined to remain on account of this same daughter of mine. She has us now secure, to take care of her. She can have no doubt but that we shall do it, with all love and affection. Yet my mind can be little at east till all is well over.

My suspicions have soon been realised. On the evening of the 17th of March we were all inclined to be particularly cheerful. The Captain never favoured with his company at supper. He is most watchful on deck, and generally remains up till a very late hour. For once we tempted him to join one party at supper, and drink our health in a glass of Punch. Sophia as usual supped and drank her glass. We none of us suspected in the least the event that was to take place before morning. At the usual hour of eleven we retired to our different berths; but I was not allowed to remain long in my warm bed. I had hardly settled to sleep when a gentle push roused me, and informed me that my presence was required to attend to the birth of a little grandchild. Poor gentle Sophia, when she found how matters were, she sat up in her bed and wept. This same scene moved our trusty servant, that had always attended her on the like occasions, and almost damped her courage and composure, of which she has a large share. She asked Sophia why she was in tears. Her answer was that 'I fear not for myself, being confident I shall do well, but do not reconcile myself to the idea of giving you and my mother so much trouble'. This sensibility struck me most forcibly. My heart, I must confess, sunk within me; but I had nothing for it but to pluck up my appearance of courage, and with a face of smiles made quite a joke of her fears. Had I allowed a thought of danger to intrude in so critical a situation, we were in for it, and nothing but fortitude would serve. In the middle of the wide Ocean, without assistance in case of all not turning out according to our most ardent wishes, – had I reflected at all, I fear all power of action might have forsaken me. We were rewarded by the speedy and happy birth of a little boy. Excess of joy or grief have been known for the instant to have nearly equal effects. On this occasion the joy was excessive. It had no bad effects on my spirits. They were soon restored to serenity, in the certainty that my dear daughter was safe in bed. No one on deck had the least suspicion that a little stranger had made his appearance, till a fire was kindled in the cabin. The Captain, seeing the smoke, roared out in a great fright, fearing the cabin was on fire, it being quite a new thing our kindling a fire in the dead of the night. This same smoke was near being fatal to poor Sophia, as the cabin in an instant got so full of smoke that she was alarmingly affected. The windows were instantly thrown open, which had the desired effect and brought her to herself. The Captain appear'd much surprised to hear what had happened, and really seemed quite pleased. The birth of a child on board ship is looked upon, I believe, as a lucky event.

As soon as possible in the morning we heard our Captain with his trumpet proclaiming to our friends the safe arrival of the little stranger. This event produced a few visits, in the course of the day. It is likely we shall have no more visits, as the weather seems to foretell a change, with the prospect of a fair wind. It is time, that we may see an end to this tedious voyage. We are very lucky in our Captain, he being a famous seaman, and a good creature. Everything on deck goes on without noise, and with great good will. Altho' we have plenty of provisions, he does not spare his own, and often gives unasked.

My dear daughter is as well as possible, and we are making progress towards the wished for port. The number of ships in our fleet diminish as we get nearer England, to go into different ports, to shorten the voyage. On account of the sick lady, we must keep quiet on board our own ship. We see the ships sail away, with some little impatience, I must own.

Yesterday evening, the 25th of March, we came to an anchor off Portsmouth. The wind being contrary, the next morning the Captain went on shore for fresh provisions. The last fowl had been killed the night before. Our mutual desire being to get out of such close confinement, the Captain was to find us a lodging. But after he had been on shore some hours, he returned in a hurry. The wind turning fair, we set sail without delay, so that now we shall think no more of going on shore till we cast anchor in the river. It may be lucky we had not the choice of leaving the ship at Portsmouth, it being very early for Sophia to be moved. Besides the demand for only landing our luggage was out of all reason. I shall write no more till we are settled in London.

35

The next diary entry was written in the London lodgings to which the family repaired when they landed from the Thames.

HS Gloster Place, Camden Town. Between London and Hampstead. On the 28th of March we came to anchor in the river Thames. By choice I would certainly have gone on shore sooner, with the fear of some days longer delay on board. As it turned out, I was perfectly reconcil'd that we remained, the weather proving very mild and fine, and the wind fair, so that we were on deck the whole day. My attention was fully engrossed with the lively beautiful scene before me; the innumerable, as well as variety of, shipping that presented themselves in majestic array, as we smoothly sailed along. For so appeared the line of Battle ships, that seemed to command respect, as well as the fine East Indiamen. We likewise beheld the melancholy looking Russian ships, all dismasted. The view along the shore is very pleasing. Greenwich Hospital appears to great advantage, and must be admired as a fine building.

It was late in the evening when we came to an anchor, so that no going on shore that night could be thought of. The next morning Walsh went on shore to seek for lodgings. He returned at night with the pleasing news that he had succeeded to his satisfaction. Five weeks confinement on board ship had completely tired us, and our impatience was great to quit the ship, which we did the day after, on the 30th of March, 1809. Good luck attended us to the end. We had a fine mild day for Sophia to get on shore. The Captain took care of us on his own boat, and would not leave us till he had placed us safe in the carriage, when we parted the best friends in the world; and I think I may say, mutually satisfied with each other. We certainly had every reason to be so.

Walsh may boast of his good luck in meeting civil and obliging persons at the Custom House, so that he got our baggage clear without the least examination, and all was safe at home almost as soon as ourselves. It was very amusing to see the numbers that had assembled on our landing, and with what impatient curiosity, to see the poor sick lady, with the baby of 15 days old. Of course they would think that she must have suffered much at sea. In an hour from the waterside, we were safe in our new habitation, perfectly satisfied at its appearance. If it had been a hut, it is probable we should have had ingenuity to have discovered some comfort in it, after so long confinement, and at sea, the most unpleasant of all lives. We really had some reason to be pleased with Walsh's choice. It is a perfectly pretty box, nice and very neatly furnished, the situation what we could wish, airy and with a view of fine green fields, within a ride or walk of London.

A fortnight after our arrival, the infant died, that was born at sea.

With that sad little note, the mood of Harriot's diary, so spirited during her voyage and first arrival in London, changed to concern over the news from Oporto and to apprehension about her future in England, without means of her own, and dependent on the support of her rich relations who, she touchily expected without much justification, might patronise her in her new poverty. Her regular diary for 1807-9 here ends in mournful remembrance of a happier past.

HS The first news from Portugal was no less than what was expected. The French entered Portugal the 29th of March. For many successive days every horror was committed that can be imagined. Our servants had the good luck to escape with their lives. One young man, that had married a servant in the family, had set up his shop, and was living happy and contented. In a few hours, what a change! A hasty flight, with a very old mother, a wife and set of young children, was the chance they had for safety, and happy they were to escape with only the clothes they had on their backs. All they possessed remained for the merciless savages, who pillaged the shop and house of everything. The Portuguese during those days of horror were not idle, and took all they could lay their hands on.

Those that had promised revenge on a few individuals, kept their word. As soon as it was certain the French could not be prevented from entering the town, a cruel band of them went and forced the prison, and dragged out of it the Brigadier Luiz d'Oliveira and murdered his body in the most inhuman manner possible. His amiable wife and daughters remain to lament his death, a death so truly marked with blood that time can never efface from the memory of those unhappy days such an act of barbarity. The like wild act was on the point of being repeated on the old helpless Chancellor. But the Bishop in good time rescued him. Some other officers were not forgot in this day's work. Two brothers, young men, were cruelly butchered for no other reason but prejudice against them. A Major-General was at the time in Porto, was pursued in his flight with two Aides-de-Camp, and cut to pieces without mercy. The Aides-de-Camps were deserving of a better fate, being very loyal, and would not have taken arms but in defence of their country. I will not venture to say so much of the General. I fear he was not a true man, certainly not a brave one. Cowards in general, to save themselves, turn to the strong side, let it be right or wrong. He has fallen with little regret from anyone.

The good Bishop did not attempt to put himself at the head of his people. It would have been useless had he done it. On the near approach of danger and all hopes of safety for him at an end, he made the best of his way to Lisbon, and was received there, as his respectable character had a right to expect, with love, honour and respect from all ranks, for his exemplary government during his residence in Porto.

Here ends this matter of fact relation. That I have taken a last farewell of Portugal I may safely say to be the case. Let its fate be what it may in future, mine is likely to be fixed far distant from those well-known shores. I am arrived at an age to roam no more. Eight times have I crossed the wide Ocean, and but once did I remember to have been in imminent danger. This last voyage, though a tedious one of five whole weeks, our good Captain declared that the many years he had been a seafaring man, he did not recollect ever having made a voyage with such constant fine weather.

When all was peace in Portugal, my fixed determination was to end my days in that country, where I had passed above thirty years of my life. It is certain my family wished it, and used their influence over me to remain. Sophia and Husband, with my little grandchildren, had no thoughts of going to live in England. This was a great inducement. Where could I go better than with those most dear to me? I cannot say the arguments used to persuade me not to think of England had any weight with me. It was alleged that it was too late in life for me to be changing from a warm climate, and leaving the congenial sun of Portugal for the fogs and cold of England. I have not so bad an opinion of the English climate as to think I may not enjoy good health in defiance of fogs and cold. It is my native country, and I have ever retained an ardent love for it, and have with constancy been warm in its praises, when occasions have been offered for me to put in a word in its praise. Nor do I in the least feel distressed to find myself on English ground again.

I am well aware that I have difficulties to encounter, and most likely mortifications. For the present all future plans are in embryo. I must enter on new scenes, new plans, and what is worst of all, new friends and new acquaintances, that will neither care for me nor I for them. Perhaps in a little time hence I may be able to relate in what manner I have managed to extricate myself from various embarrassments. I believe I had best go and ask advice from some of my rich relations. It is true, I never was much famed for a philosophic turn. A small share of it might be of use to me in my present situation, in the new world I now enter upon. Which way shall I turn? All future plans must be directed towards one point, that of economy. This is new to me. What if it is? It is good to persuade that the insolence of wealth is a wretched thing, and will creep out in some shape or other to vex and mortify others. In truth it is too often the case. The best of my days have flown away without having been much troubled with such description of persons, who seem to value their consequence according to the thousands they can boast of. I care little for characters of that nature.

When I reflect on the various occurrences of my life, so mingled with pleasure and more pain, now all is passed, and I have outlived too many most dear to me, I could almost fancy the chief of what is gone by as a dream. At any rate the waking part is to come. What more remains to wind up the closing scenes of my existence, may it be near or not, as the Power above decrees. That death alarms me, I cannot say it does. May I be prepared is my wish, when I cease to exist.

Time waits for no-one. 'Hours, days life flies: Virtue only remains'. *Hora, dies et vita fugit. Manet unica Virtus.*

PART IV

Campaigns in the Adriatic, Italy and France 1808–1816

36

While John Henry Slessor's mother and sisters were living through these stirring events in Portugal in 1807-9, he himself has been left waiting on the quay at Portsmouth where he and his regiment landed on 1st January 1808, sent home by Sir John Moore when the forces sent from Sicily to intervene in Portugal arrived too late to land and avert the French invasion. John Henry was not allowed to stay long in England.

JHS *1808. On the first of January* I found myself on shore at Portsmouth. Next morning at daybreak began our route to Kent; but judge of our surprise, when the Regt arrived at Croydon, A General Officer made his appearance, and a draft of 300 men was ordered back to Portsmouth, there to embark for the Mediterranean, and join the 1st Battn. Government are alarmed about Sicily, which is threatened by Murat. I happened to be the first Captain for duty and immediately marched to the right about, having only two non-commissioned Officers to assist me. On reaching Portsmouth we were quickly crossed over to a large military depot on the Isle of Wight; but I had little or no time to see this beautiful island. Wished much to go up to London, but not an hour's leave of absence could I get. Obey was the word, and early in February a convoy was under weigh.

Other Officers had joined us, and we made the best of a bad bargain. Here is my third trip through the Straits. Nothing very particular happened on the voyage. One brig transport foundered: I shall never forget our anxiety about her. It blew during the night a gale of wind. Our ship was ordered to keep close beside her, but the sea ran mountains high, and a boat could not be lowered. As long as guns were fired there was hope, and most fortunately in the morning the storm abated. We took all hands out, women and children; some were so exhausted, the men by the fatigue of pumping, the women from fear, that with difficulty they got up the side of the ship. They lost all their baggage. She was a store ship, and had but few people on board. Half an hour afterwards she went down bodily.

29th March. Got into the harbour of Messina.

John Henry's transfer to the 1st Battalion of the 35th caused him to miss the expedition to the Scheldt in July 1809 in which the 2nd Battalion took part, but he was returning to plenty of action in the Mediterranean. 'Government are alarmed about Sicily, which is threatened by Murat,' was his laconic summary of the situation which had caused him to be so rapidly sent back to Sicily in a force commanded by General Spencer, which encountered such fierce gales in the Channel that it was forced back to Falmouth and did not finally sail till 21st February. While John Henry was still in Egypt in the summer of 1807, the Treaty of Tilsit between France and Russia had obliged the Russians to surrender their bases in the Adriatic. French forces took over the Ionian Islands and the whole Adriatic coastlands. Joseph Bonaparte in Naples was ordered to recapture Scilla and Reggio from their Sicilian garrisons, which he did in February 1808, and to prepare for the invasion of Sicily. By the time John Henry landed again in Messina in March 1808, the Kingdom of Sicily and the British forces there were under increasing threat from the French in Calabria, and in face of this an Anglo-Sicilian treaty was signed, the day after John Henry landed, under which England undertook to maintain at least 10,000 troops in the island, and to pay an annual subsidy of £300,000.

When John Henry arrived, the army in Sicily was under the command of General Sherbrooke, who had succeeded Sir John Moore, but in April he was replaced by the much-disliked Sir John Stuart, the victor of the Battle of Maida. The effect on the army in Sicily was dismal. 'Our army, though increased in numbers, was in the summer of 1808 declining in what is nowadays called the morale,' wrote Bunbury. 'There was no longer the hearty good-will and energy of which it bore the stamp under Moore and Sherbrooke; and even the officers of high rank were anxious to leave us . . . There grew up grumblings and scoffs amongst our officers; duties were neglected.' Moreoever it was an unusually sickly season, and at one time nearly 3,000 British soldiers were in hospital.

John Henry was promoted to Major on 25th April 1808. His account of his activities during 1808 and 1809, during which Capri was recaptured by the French from its British garrison, and Procida and Ischia were briefly taken by the British, does not confirm Bunbury's picture of lackadaisical army morale.

JHS *March 30th.* Landed and joined the 1st Battn at Contessa, my old quarter. The whole World appears to be involved in war. French power and influence prevail. In this quarter of the Globe, altho' on a small scale, we are not idle. In the Bay of Naples, along the coast of Calabria, we are constantly at work. At one time we were masters of the islands of Capri, Ischia and Procida; the castle of Scilla was taken and retaken. I was once sent with the command of 300 men, in a transport, gun-boat and galley, to make a diversion in the Bay of St Euphemia, with orders about sunset to put the troops in the boats and pull along the coast as if intending to land, but on night coming on to get on board again. Reconnoitring one morning, I followed a fishing boat close in, with the idea of gaining some information about the enemy. On approaching the shore, about thirty Frenchmen jumped up from some brushwood and opened a fire of musquetry. Had they allowed us to get a little closer, we must have been made prisoners, as not perceiving any troops I should have landed to endeavour to speak to the fishermen. Our boat was struck, but fortunately no-one hurt. We returned on board, thankful to Providence for having escaped. Another time I was over at Scilla and Reggio. But all these little excursions, tho' often fraught with danger, were desultory and merely kept us and the enemy on the alert.

I once went on an expedition to Lower Calabria with the Navy, the *Warrior* Line of Battle ship, the *Spartan* Frigate, Gun, Mortar and Rocket boats, 500 picked men. I was second in command of the troops. We anchored before the town of Gallipoli, where we hoped to find ships, stores, etc. The French Commandant was summoned to surrender; he refused; so towards evening the boats commenced firing shells and Rockets, and the troops ordered to land an hour before daylight. But to our surprise and disappointment at the moment we were ready to get into the boats, counter orders came, and at day light we weighed and stood off. The gallant Captain Brenton and all hands were indeed annoyed. After sending in a flag of truce, threatening and battering, 'twas humiliating. The French commandant's name afterwards appeared in the foreign papers, rewarded for his gallantry, with a pompous account of having beat off an English fleet. We returned to Messina without glory or prize money.

When not engaged on attempted raids on the Calabrian coast, John Henry enjoyed the first half of 1809 in Messina.

JHS In *1809* the 35th were quartered in Messina. Our time passed pleasantly enough, mind and body always on the *qui vive*. I had a beautiful Egyptian mare, on which I one morning rode to Milazzo, a distance of 25 miles, and back again, a tremendous hill to go up, called Corkscrew Hill, in four hours and 35 minutes. I had five hours to do it in: won 200 dollars: much money won and lost; the Garrison and a great concourse of people out to see me: hard work, much fagged.

This summer quartered in the Citadel. Every Packet that arrives from England is interesting: brings accounts of battles, expeditions etc. The Peninsula seems likely to become the scene of active warfare. Here we have various reports of Murat's intentions against Sicily.

John Henry may, though there is almost no hint of it in his diary, have carried out another exploit that summer besides his ride to Milazzo. It is possible that he had a liaison with a Sicilian woman who bore him a daughter. A few years ago a cutting from an Australian newspaper was sent to John Henry's great-great-grandson. It contained an obituary of a 98-year-old lady who died on 19th

May 1910; she was described as being born in Sicily and as 'an only daughter of Major-General Slessor who was wounded in the Battle of Waterloo in 1815'.

Apart from the fact that John Henry was not wounded at Waterloo (though he was present in the reserve at the battle, and did eventually become a Major General), this remarkable old lady – whose Christian names were Maria Natalizia, and who emigrated to Australia by sailing-ship with her husband and ten children in 1852 – cannot have been either John Henry Slessor's only, or his legitimate, daughter. He did not marry till 1820, eleven years after he left Sicily, and there were three daughters of that marriage. If, as Maria Natalizia's death certificate states, she was 98 when she died on 19th May 1910, she cannot have been John Henry's daughter, as she would have to have been born, at earliest, in June 1811, and John Henry left Sicily in September 1809 (noting in his diary that the 35th, when they left for the Ionian Islands, 'left the women and heavy baggage in Sicily'; could Maria Natalizia's mother have been one of 'the women', that is, a camp-follower?). But after a lifetime of nearly a century, Maria Natalizia's memory may well have been a bit vague about her date of birth. 'Natalizia', her second name, means 'born on Christmas Day'; if she was born on 25th December 1809, she could have been John Henry's daughter, though she would then have been 100, not 98, when she died. She seems somehow to have acquired, and passed on to her descendants, a rather garbled account of John Henry's later military career, although she was apparently unaware of the existence of his legitimate family, or she would not have claimed to be his only daughter.

While John Henry was enjoying life in Messina in 1808-9, the threat to the British position in the Mediterranean, and to the route to India, was growing. In September 1808 Marshal Murat arrived to succeed Joseph Bonaparte as King of Naples, commissioned by Napoleon to drive the British out of Capri and eventually out of Sicily. In July 1809 Napoleon's defeat of Austria at the Battle of Wagram increased the threat in the Eastern Mediterranean, where France now occupied all the former Russian and Austrian territories in Dalmatia and the Adriatic. While the French had the Ionian Islands as naval bases, they could secure the passage of their supply ships entering the Adriatic to reach their armies in Northern Italy and Dalmatia, and could put pressure on Albania, the Morea and the whole Eastern Mediterranean. Ten years earlier, Napoleon had said, 'The islands of Corfu, Zante and Cephalonia are more important to us than the whole of Italy.' If the British were not to lose all access to the Adriatic, and were to have any chance of protecting the route to India, something had to be done. In October 1809 Admiral Collingwood, the Naval Commander-in-Chief in the Mediterranean, suggested to Sir John Stuart that the Ionian Islands should be seized from the French, and Stuart reluctantly agreed to provide troops for this purpose. This opened to John Henry a new phase in his military career, perhaps the one he most enjoyed.

37

On 23rd September 1809 a force of 1,800 men, commanded by Brigadier Oswald and including 35 officers and 919 men of the 35th First Battalion, embarked at Messina with an escort of the 74-gun HMS *Warrior* and two sloops, and sailed for Zante, which was held by the French. On 1st October Oswald's forces anchored in a bay four miles from the town of Zante, and next day 600 men, including four companies of the 35th and commanded by Colonel Hudson Lowe, landed on the island in two columns, one of which turned the defences of the town while the other surrounded the castle. The garrison of the castle, mostly Italians with some Albanian auxiliaries, soon surrendered. John Henry's account of his part in this operation makes it clear that he was in command of the first landing party.

JHS *The latter end of September* the 35th with some other troops under General Oswald embarked on an expedition against the Greek islands. We anchored off Zante on the 30th, previous to which we were ignorant of our destination, having left the women and heavy baggage in Sicily.

On the 1st October at daybreak, the necessary arrangements being made for landing, we got into the boats, and soon after pulled to the shore, with three cheers. I had the command of the advance. We quickly landed on the beach: my party soon formed and in position; but the French retired into the Castle. In about an hour the troops had landed, and the whole ready to move forward. We quickly invested the Castle. Flags of truce passed soon after a few shots having been fired. The enemy were too weak in numbers to make any effective resistance: altho' they at first refused to surrender the next day surrendered. We had only two men wounded. The Garrison marched out prisoners of war; about 400 French and Italians, and 300 Albanians laid down their arms on the glacis: the former were sent off to Malta, the latter detained at Zante. The great majority of the Zantiotes were attached to us, and indeed offered to assist us in expelling the French. They had been long looking out for us, and Mr Foresti, our principal and guide on the occasion, had no doubt been in secret correspondence with Admiral Collingwood and Sir John Stuart. Perfect order was kept, and the inhabitants greeted us as friends everywhere.

Spiridion Foresti was British Consul, and later Resident Minister, in Zante, and was described by a Scottish visitor in 1810 as 'attentive and zealous' but not sufficiently 'austere' in his political notions, which I take to be a polite way of hinting that he took bribes. His daughter, described by the same visitor as 'a woman of considerable personal beauty, though a little too political in her conversation' was married to Prince Comuto, a Senator of Venice who had been head of the short-lived Septinsular Republic and who now lived in Zante. John Henry dined with him on the very day the British forces captured Zante. The Zantiotes, though they had done nothing actually to assist the British forces when they landed, welcomed their arrival; as Bunbury put it: 'We found warm friends among the islanders, a people hating the French.'

The people of Zante were used to welcoming, or at least tolerating, one foreign occupying force after another. Franks, Turks, Venetians, Russians, French had all taken over Zante. The four-century rule of the Venetian Republic ended in 1797 when the Treaty of Campo-Fornio gave the Ionian Islands to France. In 1799 they were reclaimed by Turco-Russian forces, and in 1800 they were established as the Septinsular Republic, tributary to the Ottoman Empire. In 1802 they became a Russian Protectorate, in 1807 the Treaty of Tilsit returned them to France. Now it was the turn of the British.

This constant change of rulers had not prevented Zante from being, in the early nineteenth century, a little paradise of cultural and natural fertility. The poets Ugo Foscolo and Solomos (author of the Greek national anthem) were born there. The capital, Zakynthos, was adorned with elegant Venetian churches, palaces and arcades (almost all destroyed in the terrible earthquake of 1953, but still in perfection in John Henry's day). The countryside was rich in orchards and olive groves, and prospered from its romantic-sounding exports of currants, olive oil, soap, silk, oranges, lemons and flowers, and the pitch which bubbled up through the water in the Bay of Keri, and was used for caulking boats. 'Zante, *fior di Levante*,' the Venetians called it, but its frequent earthquakes made its beauty rather menacing. Its inhabitants, however, were famed for their longevity and their light complexions, a sturdy industrious well-fed people.

This was the Eden where John Henry was to spend his happiest and most successful years. His affairs prospered from the moment of arrival. In the next ten days Oswald's main force moved on from Zante to occupy the other Ionian Islands of Cephalonia, Ithaca and Cerigo, which capitulated with hardly any resistance. Oswald then set about appointing commandants and stationary garrisons in the islands, and encouraging the islanders to raise a local militia and fly their own flag of the Septinsular Republic. He established his own headquarters on Zante, but he made John Henry Slessor the Civil Governor of Zante and Commandant of the Island Militia, at first only as a temporary measure, but later the appointment was confirmed. John Henry's diary reports his gratification at this promotion.

JHS *2nd Oct 1809*. Dined with Prince Comuto. Some of the French Officers were present, and as merry as if nothing had happened. Gen Oswald put me in orders to take the command of Zante during his absence, and to consult with Count Comuto on any civil or police affairs. A few troops were left with me. The General and the remainder re-embarked this evening, and the next morning were out of sight. The Islands of Cephalonia, Ithaca and Cerigo were easy conquests, and in a fortnight Gen Oswald returned and established his headquarters at Zante. During his absence everything went on very smoothly. I received the following note:

Zante October 14th 1809

My dear Sir

As from the custom of the service you are likely soon to be superseded in the command of this Island, I cannot let slip the occasion without thanking you for the judicious, conciliating and firm measures you have pursued, all in perfect conformity to my hopes and wishes. The inhabitants are loud in their approbation of your conduct, and in acknowledging the benefits which have arisen therefrom. I shall at all times have great pleasure in testifying my approbation, and beg of you to accept of the assurance of the esteem with which I ever am,

My dear Sir,

Your very faithful and obedient servant

J. Oswald Brigdr Genl

To Major Slessor 35th Regt'

The above note was very flattering, and somehow or other, altho' there were several officers senior to myself in the Regt, I was confirmed in my appointment, and my name appeared in General orders as Head of the Civil Government of Zante, and Commandant of the Island Militia, amounting to near 2000 men, a kind of volunteer force, armed at their own expense.

I received in addition to my army pay and allowances, four Dollars per day from the revenues of the Island, a tolerably well furnished house, private Secretary, and an English Officer as my Adjutant. No time was lost in establishing a Provisional Government. Four respectable Zantiotes and myself formed the Presidency with a Secretary. These were my counsellors in all civil affairs. Competent tribunals and other Magistrates were named, as also an administrative body composed of forty Members; commercial, financial, police, military Regulations adopted; a little Kingdom in miniature. The novelty was pleasing and everybody seemed satisfied. One of our first works was to improve the roads, and put the Fortress in respectable state. A code of laws were drawn up, as supposed to be best calculated for governing these people. The revenues were spent in the Island, whereas the French sent the greater part to Corfu. In December the heavy baggage arrived from Sicily.

There is independent testimony of the good administration of Zante under the Control of Brigadier Oswald and John Henry Slessor. The Scottish novelist John Galt visited Zante in February 1810, and in his *Letters from the Levant* he gives a very favourable account of what had been achieved by the British in Zante. 'A Provisional Government has . . . been formed, which consists of four native counsellors, with a British officer as president for the executive, and a senate of forty members, which may be considered as the legislature and controlling part of the Constitution.' The new administration had abided by the old Venetian code of laws and 'As far as I am capable of judging, the whole proceedings in Zante since the arrival of the British have been eminently judicious . . . A militia of four thousand men has been raised in Zante, and the public revenue is placed on a better, and more productive footing . . . The tax on snuff is appropriated for making the public roads, and keeping them in repair.' The revenues of the monasteries, confiscated under the French régime, were to be restored to enable the monastery schools, the only ones in the island, to open again. 'It is so seldom,' reflected Galt, 'that one hears of our military country-men bestowing their attention on objects of this kind, that I felt no small degree of satisfaction on receiving this information.'

The militia raised locally included the Greek Light Infantry, a regiment of 800 men who wore Albanian dress. Galt dined at the officers' mess, and heard the militia-men singing Albanian songs in Greek, which he likened to Highland pibrochs. John Henry, as Commandant of the Island Militia, was presumably present at this festive occasion, though Galt does not mention him.

38

JHS While we are living in peace and quiet, I may say, active operations are
   going on in other quarters. In Portugal we are making a good fight under
   the great General, Wellington. Sicily has been attacked, without success;
   Murat will not so easily conquer it. 'Tis said he has 40,000 men in
   Calabria, and we know that he has a large flotilla.

The 'great General Wellington' had driven Marshal Soult out of Portugal, and
advanced into Spain to win the Battle of Talavera, in 1809, and in 1810, though
he had to retreat to Portugal, he was to defeat Massena at Busaco and to
construct and hold the Lines of Torres Vedras. During the summer of 1810
Murat had assembled 500 transports, with 100 gunboats to protect them, along
the Calabrian shore, and on 17th September the order was given to cross the
Straits and invade Sicily. But only one division of the French forces actually
got across, and they were soon driven back by the British troops stationed
round Messina.

   Although Zante itself remained a haven of peace, there was action close at
hand in 1810, as well as in the Peninsula and Sicily. In March 1810 Brigadier
Oswald sailed from Zante with 2,500 men, including 602 men of the 35th, and
on 16th April he captured the strategic island of Santa Maura, or Levkas, off the
Albanian coast north of Cephalonia. Corfu, further north again, remained in
French hands until 1814; throughout 1810 the British commanders in the Mediterranean had hoped to capture Corfu too, but by the end of 1810, that hope had
been abandoned. John Henry did not take part with his regiment in the capture
of Santa Maura, and he records it only briefly in his diary.

JHS General Oswald this year took the island of Santa Maura, not without some
   trouble and loss. Major Clarke of the 35th was among the killed, and
   several Officers and men were wounded. We are now in possession of five
   of the Greek Islands. The Albanians in our service behaved badly, the
   rascals.

He has much more to say about the character and progress of his own little
kingdom of Zante. He does not seem to have been impressed by its handsome
Venetian buildings, he is sceptical about archaeological remains, and he

describes the Zantiotes and their customs with a cool observant eye, but he clearly loved his small realm, its climate, its food, its landscapes, its smiling prosperity.

JHS *1810*. The trade of the Island flourishes. Packets are established between us and Sicily: and the best understanding between us and the neighbouring continents of the Morea, Albania, etc. General Oswald is forming a Regiment of Albanians, principally from the fellows we took prisoners, to be commanded by an English Officer.

The Island of Zante (the ancient Zacynthus) is about 70 miles in circumference, 20 in length, 18 in breadth. No vestiges of antiquity are to be met with. The tomb of M.T. Cicero is pointed out to you; imagine it to have been so or not. The climate is mild, and generally healthy. Principal branches of commerce are the currants, or Uva di Corinto, a most delicious grape, oil, wine, cotton and salt. The public revenues of course vary, according to the seasons: at present they may be estimated at 140,000 dollars. Fish is not very abundant: meat and poultry good and plentiful: vegetables good: a hare now and then, woodcocks, quails and doves in abundance, on their passage, fat and delicate. Corn grown only for about four months' consumption: every year hundreds of the natives go to the Morea in harvest time, and bring back sufficient for their families. The Moreottes, Albanians etc supply the island with every kind of provision. The nearest part of the Continent is about 17 miles across. The population exceeds 30,000, nearly half of which are in the City, which is in general well built, and the houses secured against Earthquake by bars of iron. We have experienced several shocks already. There are about 300 Jews, who have a part of the City allotted to them, walled in, and the gates shut every night. A small proportion are Catholics, the remainder Greeks. The modern Greek language is very corrupt: the better class generally speak Italian. Public documents, papers, proceedings and minutes of the Government, Tribunals etc are kept in Italian. The Greek churches are neat, and the services performed with decorum: their tutelar Saint, Dionizio, an embalmed human frame, or rather disgusting remains, is carried about in a glass case once a year in procession, with all due solemnity, is said to have been a most exemplary character and performed miracles. The sick and deformed frequently prostrate themselves in the middle of the street that he may pass over them and effect a cure. Excepting the poorer sort of people, the inhabitants partake of many Turkish customs. Whenever you pay a visit, coffee is immediately offered in china cups. Women until married seldom appear out of doors, and the parents generally make up a match by contract for their children. The bridegroom is introduced three days before the nuptials. It is for better for worse indeed.

The consequence from such a system is that the women have little or no education: move awkwardly, without manners or address: dress without taste: frequently make use of both red and white paint: and perfumes they are very fond of. The men, Masters of the creation, are certainly not remarkable for morality, I should say the contrary. A shrewd and intelligent race of people, easily excited, jealous and revengeful. Under the Venetian Government I have been told that three hundred murders have been known to have been committed in one year: that for a dollar or two you could easily find an assassin. Of late years the crime has greatly decreased. The French used to send troops to live at free quarters when a murder was committed, until the culprit was made known.

The Greek priests are permitted to marry. The pitch wells are curious; the bitumen is used for caulking boats, and has been taken medicinally as a diuretic. The valley where the vine is cultivated that produces the currants, as we call them, is beautiful, and it is very interesting to see the process of drying them, etc. It is altogether a delightful island.

A number of English travellers are beginning to make their appearance among us; go from hence to Greece, on to Constantinople, Egypt etc: a national mania, and the astonishment of Foreigners.

John Henry's mocking comment on the 'national mania' which was bringing so many British travellers to Greece reflects the upsurge of such tourism in 1809-10. 'The Napoleonic Wars had been the making of Greece as a tourist country, since the occupation of so much of Europe by the French had diverted the Grand tour towards the Eastern Mediterranean,' writes C.M. Woodhouse in *Byron and the First Hellenic Tourists*. In 1809-10 Athens was full of British travellers: Byron and John Cam Hobhouse, arriving there in December 1809 after visiting Ali Pasha in Janninna; the archaeologist C.R. Cockerell; Thomas Gordon, historian of the Greek War of Independence; Frederick North, son of a former British Prime Minister; the novelist John Galt after his visit to Zante. But the most spectacular British traveller, and the one who probably provoked John Henry's ridicule, was Lady Hester Stanhope. She arrived in Zante in August 1810 in the frigate *Belle Poule* (as the niece and grand-daughter of two Prime Ministers, she expected Royal Navy ships to be provided to transport her about the Mediterranean). With her were her lover Michael Bruce, her personal physician Dr Meryon and her maid Mrs Fry. Lady Hester was now a woman of thirty-four, still darkly handsome but often irritable and always capricious, taking it for granted that she would always be the centre of attention but with moods of icy *hauteur* towards those around her. She stayed in Zante for a fortnight, after which Brigadier Oswald, probably glad enough to get rid of her, supplied her with transport in a Government *felucca* to Patras. The way in which the English, travelling for pleasure – like Coleridge to Malta in 1804, for instance – blithely set sail in the Atlantic and Mediterranean throughout the

Napoleonic Wars, when the British and French fleets were constantly chasing and grappling each other in the same waters, is one of the most surprising aspects of the Wars.

39

For the last four years, John Henry's diary had not mentioned his family. He presumably knew that his mother, his sister Harriot Amelia and the Walshes had stayed in Oporto during the first French occupation. He may have heard, before he left Sicily in October 1809, that they had got away to England in February of that year, just in time before the French under Soult sacked Oporto, killing ten thousand of its inhabitants. If any anxiety about his family troubled his complacent satisfaction with his situation and achievements in Zante, it did not get recorded in his diary.

But news of a family tragedy did get through to him in 1810, to cast a shadow over his paradise. His diary bleakly records

JHS The melancholy news of my dear brother William's untimely death in the East Indies now reached me. He was out shooting, with a double barrel gun; incautiously blew into a barrel the pan of which hung fire; the other, being cocked, went off, God knows how. Poor fellow, he died on the spot; cruel sacrifice; had he been killed in action, his loss might have been reconcilable. I will not dwell on the painful subject; thus am I the only male left.

Of all the Slessor family, William is the saddest and remotest character, all but lost from sight in the mist of distance and separation. As a child he had, his father thought, 'a trick of behaving sometimes in a sulky manner'; he was later praised for having succeeded in 'leaving off that foolish custom', but well-meant paternal exhortations to him to be as affectionate and good-humoured as his elder brother probably did not help his diffident character. As children John Henry and William were closer to each other than to the rest of the family. Exiled to England from the happy home at San Pedro when they were eleven and nine, the brothers endured together the horrors of Dr Thompson's school, and enjoyed together the pleasant regime of their later education at Sunbury and Peterborough, and the happy reunion with their father when he came to England in 1792-3. When John Henry got his commission in 1794 and left Peterborough, he 'affectionately embraced my dear Brother, little thinking that William I should never see again'.

William was the godson of General Edward Smith, the old friend of William's father, and influential patron in finding openings for the Slessor boys. It was probably he who secured a cadetship for William in the East India Company's Service. This was already being talked of in General Slessor's letter in March 1795, and later that year William was definitely appointed, 'called upon to act his part upon the stage of the wide world' as John Henry rather grandly put it. William's appointment was regarded by his parents as a piece of good fortune, providing for his future, 'though it will be some time before he can hope to attain your rank,' wrote General Slessor to his eldest son, already a Captain-Lieutenant. William embarked for India in 1796, but it was not till 1797 that his family received his letters announcing his arrival in Calcutta. 'We hear he is doing well, but the intervals of notice from him must be long,' his father wrote. In May 1799 John Henry's diary noted briefly that 'My brother William is doing well in the East,' but he was so far away, and his letters took so long to arrive, that his image seemed to be fading from the family consciousness, though his eldest sister Louisa seems to have written to him fairly regularly.

Only once, in the fourteen years which William spent in India without ever coming home or seeing his family again, does he become vividly present again in the diaries. In 1800, when General Slessor died, Louisa took on the task of writing to William in India to break the news. Harriot treasured William's long letter in reply – written nearly a year later, so long had the news taken to reach him – and copied it in full into her diary.

WS My dear Sister

Little is it in the power of words, at least of my poor ability, to describe to you the dreadful melancholy, and totally unexpected shock inflicted upon me by the receipt of your letter. I will truly say, the very first one, my dear Sister, received from you, that did not give real and heart-felt satisfaction. The date of yours is September 23rd. You must know that your first letter, of June 21st, which you so kindly intended as a preparation for an event which you saw was then so soon about to happen, did not come to hand till after the other, Heaven knows by what mischance. You have performed to me the part of a kind and affectionate Sister in the execution of a task so painful to be performed as distressing. The sickness and last struggle in this world of the best of parents Heaven ever blessed children with. One year has very nearly passed away since that unhappy day, and the best part of another certainly will, before this reaches you. I must not therefore, at such a distance of time and place, by attempting to paint my feelings on such an awful subject, aggravate your sorrow and unavailing regret, instead of offering that consolation which my dearest Mother and Sisters must so much have stood in need of. Time and our own good sense, as you tell me yourself, are the best remedies. But this rest assur'd of, my dear Sister, that from your own letters to me, tho' the messengers of fatal intelligence, I do derive more real consolation than I could have done from the feeble resources of my own mind. Time may now have deadened that keen anguish occasioned by witnessing the death of our dear parent; but we must ever venerate his memory and lament his loss. Some months indeed of misery and suspense were given you to prepare for that event that you must have inevitably seen was advancing with such rapid strides. To me never arrived intelligence so cruel, and particularly from being entirely unexpected. Still has it been known to me but a few days, and to think of the happy ignorance I have so many months been slumbering in, while you were plunged in sorrow, is not a source of comfort to me. Much indeed the reverse, tho' impossible to have been prevented. You will, I am sure, and my dearest Mother, give me every credit for those sentiments of deep regret you have at so great a cost yourselves been taught to feel. Excuse therefore my dwelling on the painful subject; for where an immediate antidote to evil fails, patience and resignation are our last refuge.

That our revered Father lived in the World loved and respected, and went out of it so regretted as you have so feelingly described, is what I was ever convinced could not but have been the case. All that you have said, and that possibly could have been said on that head, will barely be doing justice to his many virtues, and most excellent character, which I am sure no-one could have been acquainted with at all without sincerely admiring. To you all his various good qualities must have been more familiarly known; but the last time of my meeting him, little indeed did I dream, it would be the last. His parental kindness, and affectionate concern for his sons, made an impression on my heart that cannot be effaced, and which will ever be cherished in my bosom with reverence and gratitude. Nor was I then so young, but that I could observe that he commanded the respect and esteem of all who saw him, and were happy enough to be acquainted with him. It has been my particular misfortune to have been, almost from childhood, a total stranger to those most dear to me. The few fleeting months of my poor Father's residence in England in the year 1792, when our dear Henry came with him, to be put to School, were the happiest, I may say, that I have ever known. The days of our infancy at St Pedro I will not mention. I had not then known what it was to be torn from a parent's arms, and after a separation of a few years again to find myself pressed in their embraces; and of everything we must judge by comparison.

I will proceed to that part of your letter in which you desire me to give my opinion and vote as to the disposal of property left, and it's a subject which shall not fill a large space in this sheet. Our Father, you must well know, was liberal to a degree in the education of his sons, and laid out a great deal of money on that account. He moreover provided for them all in such a manner as ought to absolve his estate from any further demands on their part. It is therefore my final and unalterable determination, from which I must insist you will not endeavour to make me deviate, never to take any share whatever. Whatever may fall to me, I make over and fully give without restriction to my three dear sisters, and earnestly entreat you will all without scruple take it, and put it to the best use, and have only to hope that it may be considerable enough to be of benefit to you.

You will naturally suppose I am waiting with the greatest impatience for fuller accounts from and regarding you. I cannot keep my mind at ease until I hear that you have all been left, most of all my dear Mother, so as to be able to support yourselves at least in a state of comfort and independence. These are now become points on which I cannot but feel myself so deeply and so warmly interested, that my present state of suspense and uncertainty is far, very far from pleasant. I have just heard of the arrival of some India ships in Calcutta, and many letters have come, but Alas not a line for me; not a single letter for your anxious and impatient brother. Would to God I could see one, before I close this. But these are times of trouble, and very unfavourable to regular correspondence, and indeed to everything else.

Promotion has been as rapid as I could have expected. But the essential here to a soldier as it is everywhere else has been much reduced by Government, and I now find myself obliged to practise all the little economy of a Subaltern in England, which is a thing not calculated for a country like this. I still, however, continue to make myself as easy and happy as I well can be under such existing circumstances; but have not yet, and am certain I shall never be able to reconcile myself to the idea of wedding myself for ever to this country, as many have done before me, notwithstanding the pressing entreaties of all their friends at home, and having ample means. Fortunes are not to be acquired here now, as formerly used to be, money having become just as scarce as it is in other parts of the World. My uncle may perhaps – and has almost promised to do something for me, having good interest, and this is my only chance almost of getting on. But time is flying quick, and I should be much better pleased with him were he to make haste, and set about it immediately. I hear not a syllable of my Uncle's leaving this country. Is not that an unaccountable thing, that a man with such an immense fortune, a Wife and family, and many other connections pressing his return, should not wish to enjoy what years he may have to live among them, instead of staying on here, as he does, daily adding to his immense store of wealth. People say it's his love for money that keeps him, but I will not pretend to determine with what justice.

As to John Neave, he is very well, and like all the rest of that family, has been a very good friend to me. But he has been exceedingly unfortunate in losing a large part of his fortune, which will keep him much longer in this country than he had intended.

Your ever loving Brother

Puttyghar 15th August 1801

The opening pages of William's letter, with their conventional rhetoric of filial grief, are not very moving, but when he speaks of his 'particular misfortune' in having been a stranger since childhood to those most dear to him, and recalls the months he spent with his father in 1792 as the happiest he has ever known, a pang of real feeling vibrates. To be sent alone to India at the age of seventeen, never to see any of his family again, to depend on their long-delayed letters for the 'real consolations' which he could not summon up from the 'feeble resources' of his own mind, was a common enough fate for younger sons at that time, but reads piteously all the same.

His renunciation, in favour of his sisters, of any share in his father's estate, was generous, especially as he was not finding it easy to live on a subaltern's pay, and his expectations that his Neave relations would use their influence on his behalf seem not to have been realised. His uncle was Sir Richard Neave, later Governor of the Bank of England, who had married Harriot's sister Frances, and his cousin John Neave, second son of Sir Richard, was Chief Judge in Benares.

Harriot's comment on this letter, though admiring, is hardly a vivid pen-portrait of the son she had not seen for so long.

HS This letter is a true picture of a good nature, most affectionate and disinterested. Tho' quite a youth when he parted from his Father, he was truly sensible of the many good qualities that formed his respectable character, and knew how to value the kind love and interest his father ever showed for the welfare of his dear children. William returned this love, with gratitude and good conduct.

No more is heard of William, in either Harriot's or John Henry's diaries, till the grim description of how he died which John Henry recorded in his Zante diary. William's tragedy is obscured by his remoteness; it is impossible to see far into the personality of this lonely young man, trying to face the future in which he saw no prospect of escape from India but was unable to reconcile himself to the idea of spending his life there.

40

The peace and good order of the Ionian Islands in 1811 made it possible for John Henry to make some interesting excursions in that year. He deliberately renounced the attempt to describe any Ancient Greek remains seen on his travels, well aware how many English travellers were in Greece at this time, eagerly taking notes for their subsequent publications; but he cast a professional eye on all military and administrative arrangements, and his description of a visit to Ali Pasha, if not to be compared with Byron's letters from Janina two years earlier, is lively and sharp-edged. Ali Pasha at this time was being keenly wooed by both the French and the British. Colonel Leake, the British agent in Albania, was pouring promises and blandishments from the British Government into Ali Pasha's ear, and at the same time was writing topographical reports on Albania for the benefit of any British force which might be landed there to forestall the French.

JHS I have been making a little tour myself. Visited Santa Maura, Cephalonia, Ithaca; went over to Prevesa, passed a day among the ruins of Nicopolis; but shall leave the task of describing Ulysses' Castle, Arethusa's Fountain, Temples, Pillars, Catacombs etc to a more able and classical traveller. My object chiefly was to make a comparative sketch of the improvements, regulations etc adopted by the Officers Commanding in other islands with my own.

Later in the year, when General Airey had taken over from Brigadier Oswald as Commander-in-Chief in the Ionian Islands, John Henry accompanied Airey's wife and a party of friends on a trip to Janina.

JHS I have been on an excursion to Albania. Our party consisted of Mrs General Airey, Mrs Col McCombe, three Officers, besides myself. Mr Foresti, whom I before mentioned, and who has acted as British Consul, had previously made every arrangement for us. We met at Santa Maura; from thence proceeded in a Scampavia [an armed fast boat] up the gulph of Arta; landed at Salagora, where we found a guard of Albanians, horses etc ready for us; slept here, and with the assistance of our canteen got tolerably well off. Started early the next morning; the ladies brought their side-saddles. We traversed a very fine country, but the hand of the despot was everywhere remarkable. Our Dragoman ensured us respect and attention, which probably without him would not have been the case. Every fellow you meet, is armed either with a gun, pistol or dagger, sometimes with all three. On the road we halted at the Pasha's Palaces, one a noble building, beautifully situated in a wood by a mountain side; the furniture quite Turkish, no tables, chairs or beds. On our approaching Janina the view appeared most interesting. The town is situated close to a fine lake on a high plain, and neighbourhood of lofty mountains. About three miles from the city, we were met by a cavalcade of horses, richly caparisoned, also a carriage for the ladies. We felt much flattered by this attention, soon dismounted our hack horses, and entered the capital of Albania in due form and style about six in the evening. Alighted at the house of a Greek, where orders had been given to provide us with every comfort and accommodation free of expense. The horses, carriages and attendants were dismissed, with a few dollars. We were shewn our apartments, and previous to dinner, or rather supper, coffee and sweetmeats were offered. The whole family joined without ceremony, and we formed a merry party. Immediately after our repast the Pasha's Secretary came to enquire after our healths, and hoped we were properly treated, with a message at the same time to say that at 9 o'clock the next morning His Highness would be glad to see us at the Palace, would send a carriage for the ladies and horses for the officers. The moment the Secretary was known to be at the Hall door, our landlord's eldest daughter, a beautiful young woman, darted out of the room, fearful of the Seraglio. We also received a visit from the Physician, by name Velara, a Greek, in high favour with the Pasha, reported to be clever, and apparently a man of great adroitness. He conversed with us for some time, when we gladly retired to comfortable beds.

The next morning, after a good breakfast, we proceeded, at the hour appointed, and were ushered into the presence of the mighty monarch. There was a strong guard of cut-throat-looking fellows, both horse and foot, in a spacious courtyard; sometimes a victim's head is to be seen over the gateway. Ali Pasha received us very graciously: coffee and pipes were handed, and thro' the medium of an interpreter he paid the English some compliments, asking many questions. On Mrs Airey and Mrs McCombe being invited to visit the Seraglio, a well dressed middle-aged woman appeared in order to conduct them. I shall not easily forget the terror that was depicted on her countenance; the summons probably was sudden and unexpected. The common manner of putting a woman to death, is by tying her up in a sack, going out into the lake, and then throwing her overboard.

We soon took our leave, were shewn some spacious apartments, the Armoury, etc; nothing very magnificent. The ladies remained away so long a time, that we became rather alarmed for them; but about five o'clock they joined us, quite tired, having been obliged to dine. They gave us a very interesting account of the women, amounting in numbers to about 300, very few of them handsome. Our cavalcade returned in the same order.

This city covers a great deal of ground, for besides the Mosques and cemeteries, all the better houses have spacious areas and courtyards, trees and flowers. Many wealthy Greeks are settled here, and the trade is very considerable. The Police is authoritative and strictly enforced. Ali Pasha is sole Governor of Albania; Veli his son rules the Morea; and so powerful are the two united, that they obey the Porte or not, just as they find it convenient. Ali professes much attachment to the English nation. He is a dignified looking man, about 60 years of age, of considerable talent and information. I longed much for a diamond mounted dagger he wore. He has accredited agents or consuls at his court from England, France and Russia; can command probably 40 or 50,000 troops; but withal he combines the barbarism of the Turk. Some years ago, in order to punish some revolt against his government, or disobedience of his firman, he put to death without distinction of age or sex, the inhabitants of a village called Gardiki, by confining them within a walled enclosure, and deliberately shooting them, with the exception of the leader, whose eyes were put out, and sent to an island on the lake, where there is a prison. The population of Janina is said to be about 40,000. We could with difficulty make our way thro' the streets forming the Bazaars, particularly when the ladies were with us; then we found our Albanian soldiers absolutely necessary. Mr Foresti unfortunately was absent.

On the 5th day we took our departure, pleased with the reception we had met with, still glad to get away from such barbarians. The ladies as well as ourselves were somewhat disappointed at not having received any present; we brought none, 'tis true. We returned by another route, performing our journey without any inconvenience, embarked at Prevesa, from thence to Santa Maura, where I remained a couple of days with my friend Col McCombe, from thence in a gun-boat to Zante.

41

News of events in other theatres of the war was slow in reaching Zante. In his 1811 diary John Henry was still commenting on Sir John Moore's retreat to Corunna in January 1809, and on the disastrous Walcheren expedition of July 1809, in which a British force of 40,000 men (including the 2nd Battalion of the 35th, in which John Henry had served till 1808) was sent to the Island of Walcheren in the mouth of the Scheldt, with the object of capturing Antwerp as a base for attacking the French fleet; but almost half the British troops died of fever in the Walcheren marshes, and the expedition returned ignominiously to England. Since then Wellington had been keeping the French out of Portugal, besieging Almeida and winning the Battle of Fuentes d'Oro against Massena, while in Calabria Murat had abandoned the attempt to crack the British defence of Sicily.

JHS More glorious news from the Duke of Wellington, and Murat's army has fallen back on Naples. Notwithstanding Sir John Moore's retreat, he by his judgment saved the greater part of the army, who covered themselves with glory in the hour of trial, at the expense of a gallant General. The French did justice to his remains; his country and the Army lamented his fall. The Walcheren Expedition has proved a complete failure; lavish and useless expenditure of lives and money. How England continues to show a front to Bonaparte's gigantic power is almost incredible. In these Islands everything goes on quietly; we are indefatigable in improving them.

The indefatigability of the British officers in improving the condition of the Ionian Islands which they now controlled was resoundingly celebrated in the divisional orders issued by General Oswald when, in February 1811, he handed over his command to General Smith. John Henry gives the full text of this order in his diary.

JHS General Smith is now our Commander-in-Chief. General Oswald, previous to leaving us, issued the following orders.

'DIVISION ORDERS. Headquarters Zante. 18th February 1811.
Brigadier-General Oswald cannot resign this honourable charge without

forcibly expressing to those he has the honour to direct, of every rank and station, how much he feels indebted to their uniform good conduct for the credit and satisfaction he has derived from this command. Every individual of this part of the Army may exult in the reflection of his conduct having contributed to raise the reputation of the English forces, in a quarter where it forms so striking a contrast to the military body who preceded it. The high expectations which the inhabitants of these Islands formed of the advantages to be derived from the protection of His Majesty's troops have indeed been largely surpassed, and they have beheld, with sentiments of mingled admiration and gratitude, a brave and disciplined Army, beneficent and generous to their friends in proportion as they are formidable to their foes. To Lieut-Colonel Lowe, who has so ably seconded the General in every operation connected with these Islands – To the Commanding Officers who have guided and cherished the good disposition of their Corps – To the Heads of Departments who have so judiciously exerted themselves in the discharge of their respective functions, the General offers his warmest acknowledgments; and he recurs with the utmost satisfaction to the able manner in which Lieut-Colonel Lowe, Majors Slessor and De Bosset, Captains McAlister and Gentera, have aided him in administering the internal affairs of the Islands. In their diligent, equitable and judicious discharge of these novel duties, they have offered to the communities they have presided over the most laudable examples for imitation. The General would be unfeeling if any motives could call him from such a command and such associates without experiencing the most lively regret. This sentiment is moderated alone by the conviction of the command devolving into the able hands of an Officer under whose directions he is persuaded they will merit fresh marks of their Sovereign's gracious consideration, and enhance their claims to the gratitude of the British Nation, and the communities they are appointed to defend. To convey these impressions and feelings to His Excellency the Commander of the Forces is a duty Brig-Genl Oswald will discharge with equal pride and satisfaction, and he is convinced they will call for renewed testimonies of His Excellency's approbation and regard for the Division of the Forces in the Ionian Islands'.

The commanders of both French and British occupying forces in the war issued general orders and proclamations asserting how happy the inhabitants of the occupied countries were to have them there. Oswald's divisional order is less grandiloquent than Marshal Junot's proclamations about how blessed the Portuguese were to be ruled by the French, which so much aroused Harriot Slessor's scorn, but Oswald was just as sure that the people of the Ionian Islands preferred British rule to the preceding French one, as Junot was that the Portuguese were grateful to be delivered from perfidious English influence. Such orders and proclamations are inevitably propaganda, whichever side they come from, but it does seem as if John Henry and his fellow Governors in the Ionian Islands did deserve congratulation for just and efficient administration. Oswald, who was succeeded by General Smith, and then after a few months by General Airey, left with marks of honour from the grateful Zantiotes, and in the Adriatic, if not in the other theatres of war, things altogether were going well for the British in 1811.

JHS Affairs in general appear to go on prosperously both by sea and land. In the Adriatic there has been a gallant naval action. Sir John Stuart has paid us a visit, and was received by the inhabitants with great rejoicings. The civil Government, also the Military, gave him sumptuous entertainments. General Oswald has been presented by the Zantiotes with a sword of honour, gold mounted.

John Henry's own affairs were not all happy in this second year of his appointment as Governor of Zante. He heard of his brother William's death in India, he had eye trouble and fever, he foresaw that his cherished period of duty in Zante must soon come to an end and was worried about what his next appointment would be, and his hopes of being transferred to serve under Wellington in Spain were dashed.

JHS I suffered severely this summer from the ophthalmia, being confined to a dark room for six weeks. In the Autumn I was also attacked by a fever which brought me to death's door. Some of our soldiers died, while I was so unwell, as also some officers and men in the other islands.

My period is expired, for my appointment by General Oswald was only for two years. I regret much that the 35th Regt is not ordered to Spain, for there is the field for honour and promotion. However, I have this consolation, that I made application, both here and in England thro' my friends, to serve in the Peninsula. It is at the same time never desirable that troops should serve long in one quarter.

1812. I now made preparations for resigning my post, having held it two years and eight months. At the last assembly of the administrative body, I took my leave with the following address of farewell.

John Henry made this diary entry in June 1812, and he copied into his diary the proceedings of the farewell session of the Administrative Council over which he had presided. He quotes the speeches made on this occasion in Italian, presumably from the printed record of the Council's proceedings, but as he himself could not speak much Italian, he probably made his own speech in English and it was translated by an interpreter. His speech, the reply of a member of the Council, and a resolution proposing that he should be given a sword of honour, are here given in English translation.

JHS 'Zante. 5th June 1812. As the Constitutional Authority of this island is about to be changed, and as I myself am to be replaced, this may well be the last occasion on which I shall have the honour to preside over an assembly of the illustrious Administrative Council. To my great satisfaction in the course of the almost three years of my Presidency, I have admired your zeal and concern for the good of your Country, and your gratitude and attachment to the British Nation. I should be failing in my duty on taking leave of you, if I did not express publicly my very high esteem towards each and every one of you, Illustrious Gentlemen, for that very high quality which I have recognised in you in all circumstances, and with which you are so conspicuously endowed. I shall always be proud of having occupied for so long a post so honourable, for which I cannot claim any merit, since I am only the humble instrument of the orders of my superiors. I wish I could speak Italian so that I could express more forcefully the feelings of my heart, and the lively interest which I cherish in the happiness of the inhabitants of Zante. I can assure you that even when I am far away it will be a comfort and consolation to me to feel that the good fortune and prosperity of this beloved Island are always increasing; and I shall be still more pleased if circumstances offer me the opportunity to contribute by any means in my power to the general well-being of the island. I ask that these remarks should be noted in the official record of this session.

Answer by a member, Signor Nadal Voltera.
The beneficence of your great Monarch and of your illustrious Nation towards this Country of mine is boundless. This is known to all my fellow citizens, who pay the tribute of gratitude due. It is engraved in all our minds, it engages all our hearts, it is incessantly repeated by us all. I am sure that the Illustrious Deputy Signor Foscardi had communicated to the august Sovereign of the Three Kingdoms that gratitude which we all so strongly feel. I must now add that among the benefits which we have received must be numbered that of having had you as Governor, from the first day on which this Island was occupied by the glorious British Army, to this moment in which a new regime is about to begin. The rectitude of your heart, the purity of your judgment, the mildness of your character are the distinguishing features of your personality, which have made you beloved by us, and which, as we see your term of office coming to an end, and the imminent disappearance of your valued presence, make us suffer much from the loss of you which we are about to endure. To you, with the consent of all of us, I present the homage which is due to your many virtues, and the gratitude which is evoked by the many labours on our behalf which have occupied you. Accept this simple tribute, and permit that it should be recorded in the proceedings of the Administrative Coun-

cil, over which you have presided for this last time, that you have by your generous observations consummated our gratitude. It will be the mission of the Illustrious Presidency to mark by a lasting tribute, to be preserved for posterity, the general sense of gratitude towards our noble Governor, Major Slessor.

A motion was then proposed on behalf of the Illustrious Presidency: The Illustrious Presidency, pleased with the Illustrious Function performed by His Excellency the Governor, Major Giovanni Slessor, both on account of his praiseworthy conduct, and by the nobility of the sentiments manifested by him, and approving the reply which the Administrator Signor Nadal made to him, recommend that the well-deserving President of the Council should be presented with a lasting token to represent our common gratitude to him, and it is therefore proposed that our Illustrious Council should, in the name of the Country, present to the aforesaid Major Slessor a gold-mounted sabre in testimony of the general satisfaction with the merits of his Governorship.

No sooner had the above motion been read, than it was carried by acclamation amid the applause of the whole Council.'

Presenting swords of honour was something of a national custom in Zante. General Oswald got one when he left in 1811, and so did the Venetian Admiral Angelo Emo in 1785 for protecting Zante from the Barbary pirates. But the presentation to John Henry does seem to have marked his real popularity with the Zantiotes. There is a note almost of surprise in the tributes to his rectitude, praiseworthy conduct, purity of judgment; an incorruptible official was something of a new experience to the Zantiotes. John Henry himself, though he acknowledges his gratification at the tributes, explains them as partly due to his being their first experience of British ideas of justice.

JHS Vanity is the weak side of most people. There are a thousand ways of administering flattery, and I must say on this occasion I was highly gratified with so public a mark of my conduct on the part of the Zantiotes. I was in fact the first English officer they had known, consequently more intimately acquainted with them, and am persuaded that the greater part regretted parting with me.

He treasured the gold-mounted sword for the rest of his life, and bequeathed it to his descendants, who have it still.

42

JHS Having now made every arrangement for my departure, and given over the
reins of Government to Lieut-Colonel Moore, 35th Regt, I bade adieu to
Zante, and embarked for Sicily, determined to try to get to Spain, or else
obtain leave of absence for England.

It was not surprising that John Henry wanted to get to Spain; every keen soldier
in the British Army anywhere in the world must have been longing to be on
what he described as 'the field for honour and promotion' in Spain in those
years. In January 1811 Wellington had stormed Ciudad Rodrigo, in March he
had captured Badajoz with terrible slaughter, and at the moment when John
Henry was leaving Zante, Wellington was in Central Spain, about to smash
Marmont's army at the Battle of Salamanca.

That month of June 1812 was a kaleidoscope of shifting events, for and
against Napoleon, in the progress of the war. In his favour was the American
declaration of war against Britain on 18th June. The British Government's
enforcement of the blockade of Europe by using the right of search on neutral
ships had long been resented by America, particularly since the British insisted
on their right to seize all seamen on American vessels who were believed to be
deserters from the British Navy. A good many of them were in fact deserters;
the crews of British warships, many of whom had been forced into the service
by press-gangs, knew that they would be welcomed on board American naval
vessels and would receive higher pay and better food (though no rum) in the
American service. But since it was not easy to distinguish between the two
nationalities who shared a language, many genuine American seamen were
seized and impressed to serve in the British Fleet, a point not understood by
John Henry in his patriotically indignant lament for 'poor dear little England',
now threatened from across the Atlantic as well as from Europe.

But in this same month of June Napoleon's vast ambition led him into the
fatal mistake which was to bring about his downfall. A week after the American
declaration of war on England, Napoleon led his Grand Army of 680,000 men
to invade Russia. John Henry's diary here shows clearly how he sometimes
made later insertions of hindsight to add to his contemporary comments on war-
time events. What he wrote about the Peninsular and American Wars and
Napoleon's Russian campaign is simply entered in his diary under the year

1812, when Wellington briefly ceased to 'carry everything before him' in Spain and had to retire from Madrid to Portugal. But in October 1812 Napoleon was still in Moscow, and it was not for another two months that he was to desert the last of his decimated army as it struggled through the snow on its way back to the Russian border. John Henry in the far-off Adriatic could not have heard of the Retreat from Moscow, which only ended on the last day of the year, in time to record it in his 1812 diary.

JHS I am sorry to say that war is declared with America. Poor dear little England, what will become of you at last! In one or two naval conflicts we have come off second best, a novel circumstance indeed, but easily accounted for. The Yankees carry heavier metal, larger vessels, altho' rated the same as ours, prime seamen, and to our shame be it said, many among their crew are Englishmen.

In Spain Lord Wellington carries everything before him, thrashes the French Marshals one after another. Bonaparte has declared war against Russia; put himself at the head of an overwhelming army: invades that country. History I believe affords no instance of so fine an army being annihilated in the manner this one was. The Russians having burnt Moscow, was the Emperor's deathblow. Here again he deserted his brave followers, and returned to Paris, leaving thousands to perish by the inclemency of a Northern climate in the depth of winter.

If he was not to be given the chance of serving in Spain, John Henry hoped for some home leave. It was four and a half years since he had set foot in England, and that had only been for the very brief turn-around between getting back from Egypt and being sent out to Sicily again, in 1808. It was nine years since he had last seen his mother, his sisters and his brother Henry when they all met in Bath in the winter of 1802-3. Now that Harriot, the Walshes and Harriot Amelia were back in Ireland from Portugal, he had an additional reason to wish for home leave. But when he arrived in Sicily, he found that neither of his hopes were to be realised.

JHS Four days brought me to Messina, and after performing quarantine, I immediately called upon the Adjutant-General, who in rather a peremptory manner informed me that my destination was the Island of Lissa in the Adriatic, whither some English troops had already preceded; that I would be second in command; patience! Capt Tritton, with whom I was already acquainted, was on the point of sailing for that station, and gave me a passage.

I landed at Lissa early in July: rocky island, producing nothing but wine: we trust entirely to smugglers for fresh provisions, and altho' beset on all sides by the enemy are abundantly supplied. There is a fine harbour, and we have always a Man-of-War here.

Here we pass our time quietly enough, principally in erecting a fort and strengthening our position. The Navy carry on a desultory warfare, and make many prizes. This climate is uncommonly healthy, for we scarcely ever have a man in hospital. Admiral Freemantle commands the Navy, Col Robertson the Army, but I regret to say they do not pull together, a circumstance much to be lamented, and at the same time very injurious to the service. Bonaparte's disastrous campaign in Russia, and his reverses in Spain, have totally changed the aspect of public affairs, and we may naturally soon expect a general peace.

The stony island of Lissa, or Vis, and a subordinate post under a quarrelling superior officer, were a dismal exchange for the fertile paradise of Zante where John Henry had reigned supreme over congenial subjects. But it did enable him to see some exciting small-scale action. The island of Lissa, halfway up the Adriatic off the coast a little south of Spalato, had been garrisoned by the British as a base for raids against the crumbling French control of the Northern Adriatic. Lissa had been occupied in January 1812 by a British force sent by Lord William Bentinck, who was now Commander-in-Chief in Sicily and Minister to the Court of the Two Sicilies. Two months before John Henry landed in Lissa, Turkey had signed a treaty with Russia, abandoning her alliance with France, and French control of the head of the Adriatic was correspondingly weakened. This was a chance – while Napoleon had drained his forces in Southern Europe as well as in Spain for his grand assault on Russia – to organise a series of small combined operations between the British Army and Navy in the Adriatic to mop up outlying French garrisons there. The 'general peace' which John Henry had foretold at the end of his 1812 diary drew nearer throughout 1813, but that spring Napoleon had assembled another vast army to replace the one lost in Russia, and was confronting the Prussian and Russian armies. The major British war effort was still in Spain; in the Adriatic it was a question of picking off small targets one by one, and John Henry records in his 1813 diary his share in these actions, the successful occupation of the islands of Korzula and Lagosta, and an unsuccessful reconnaissance of the port of Rogoznica on the Dalmatian mainland.

JHS In this quarter we have not been idle; have taken the islands of Korzula and Lagosta, both of which harboured Privateers and annoyed us often. I shared on this occasion 700 dollars as prize money. This conquest completely intercepts the enemy's convoys, going to Ragusa, Cattaro etc along the coast of Dalmatia. I am happy to say that our two chiefs agree better together. For my own part, I have always found the Navy a most gentlemanly, liberal, gallant set of fellows, and we spent many a pleasant day together, both on duty and in social intercourse.

Ragusa, in Istria, Dalmatia the inhabitants only wait for assistance to shake off the yoke of the common enemy.

In the month of August I was sent by Col Robertson to reconnoitre a large convoy of boats in the harbour of Rogoznica (it being in agitation to attack them with the *Weazel*, brig of War). I started in a Scampavia with a gunboat; just as the sun rose I landed on a small island at the mouth of the harbour; was quietly planning the best mode of attack, when I was discovered. I quickly re-embarked; it was calm, and we pulled like devils. Ten large boats, armed, colours flying, cheering etc, came out after us, full of sailors and soldiers. They gained on us fast, and came even within shot, fired several rounds, but fortunately without effect. A light breeze now got up, and the fools gave up the chase. Half an hour later, and we should all have been either killed or taken prisoners. The fact was, they suspected we wanted to entice them out to sea, as the *Weazel* Brig of War, my friend Capt Black, hove in sight. I thanked my stars that we returned safe to Lissa; nothing more was done.

For his share in the capture of Korzula and Lagosta, John Henry was mentioned in despatches by Colonel Robertson, and his name appeared in the Gazette.

JHS 1813. This year has commenced with signal advantage to the general cause. Bonaparte has shewn most unparalleled power and energy in organising another army: appoints Maria Louisa regent, and heads his troops on the Rhine. The King of Prussia and Emperor of Russia unite; in fact Mr Pitt's grand coalition, as if by magic, is now brought to maturity and about to take effect.

This note in John Henry's diary was probably written about June 1813. In January the Russians and Prussians had aligned themselves against France in the Treaty of Kalisch, and the French forces occupying Prussia had been pushed back to the Elbe. But Napoleon, in an astonishing rally from the disaster of the Retreat from Moscow, had raised another army of 200,000 men and had marched against the Russians and Prussians, defeating them at the Battles of Lutzen and Bantzen. Austria had remained neutral, and in June an armistice was concluded between France and the Russians and Prussians. But meanwhile in May Wellington had again advanced from Portugal into Spain, and his rout of Jourdain at the Battle of Vittoria in June drove the defeated French flying back over the Pyrenees. The other French forces still in Spain were now in an untenable position, Madrid was abandoned and the Peninsula was all but free.

The effect of this on Austria was immediate; on 27th June she allied herself with the Russians and Prussians. Napoleon had been going through the motions of negotiating with them to turn the armistice into a peace, but nothing came of this, and when the armistice ended, the three powers were aligned with Britain against France, and on 12th August the Emperor Francis of Austria formally declared war on France. Austria sent an army of 70,000 men under General von

Hillar to attack the French forces in Northern Italy and Illyria. The Austrian army entered Illyria in August; aided by a rising of the Dalmatians against the French, the Austrians captured Trieste and the whole of Illyria by October, and advanced across the head of the Adriatic to confront the French forces under Prince Eugène de Beauharnais, Napoleon's stepson and viceroy in Italy, which were occupying the Veneto and Lombardy.

It was at this point that the sporadic British raids and captures in the Adriatic began to be integrated with the Austrian advance and the main Allied strategy against Napoleon, and the actions from Lissa in which John Henry was involved in August, September and October were combined operations in which his own small contingent of the 35th cooperated with the British Navy and the Austrian land forces. The first of these operations was an abortive attempt in August to capture Fiume.

JHS The Navy had a short time before this landed and made themselves masters of Fiume. I went to see the place. Admiral Freemantle was acting in concert with a General Nugent, who commanded the Austrian troops. I had not been on shore two days, when the General was attacked by a very superior force, and compelled to retreat into Istria. The Archduke Maximilian had arrived the day before. The inhabitants shewed the best disposition, and asked for him to defend their properties. It was at first so arranged that we should defend the town. The Admiral landed the Marines, and honoured me with the command of them. The night was passed in giving out arms and ammunition, and the Priests actually headed their parishioners; when to our astonishment and disappointment the Admiral and the Duke changed their plans, and at daybreak we re-embarked. Many of the inhabitants, who had been the most active, came off with their families. We saw the French march in. Probably the measure was prudent, and saved a useless and temporary loss of lives, plunder, etc; for the enemy occupied Fiume only two days, and behaved with unusual moderation. Still it was grating to our feelings. We weighed anchor, and sailed to Pola, where General Nugent came on board for a short time to communicate with the Admiral. At Pola you see the ruins of a superb amphitheatre. Returned to Lissa.

Soon after this he succeeded to the command of the small residual garrison of Lissa, and in the following months he and the Navy cooperated in the capture of the port of Spalato on the Dalmatian coast and the island of Lesina, or Lussin, from the French. They were then handed over to the Austrians.

JHS Col Robertson has embarked from Lissa with the greater part of our little garrison, and left me in command. He is gone to join General Nugent at the siege of Trieste. Capt Hoste and myself had been at a place called Spalato, which surrendered on our summons. We gave it up to the Austrians, and on our return to Lissa, planned an attack on the island of Lesina. I knew that the Croatian troops and inhabitants were favourable to us; had also information that the officers slept in the town, the men in the fort. A *coup-de-main* was our object. Lesina is about 14 miles across. I procured as our guide a trusty native. 'Twas a beautiful moonlight night, when we embarked in the boats with 150 men, and stood across with a light breeze. The greatest order and silence was maintained. Landed a mile and a half from the town, about three in the morning, my faithful guide close to me. Capt Hoste with some Marines took a road which lay between the Fort Napoleon and the town: I marched direct to the town: reversed the men's arms, turned the shining plates of their caps to the backs of their heads. Not a whisper heard, and as we approached, the moon still shining, the French sentries distinctly called out 'All's well', and strange to say we reached unperceived the gates of the town, where was their mainguard. The wicket was half open; I rushed in with some of the 35th; the sentinel was instantly bayoneted; the rest of the Guard quickly shut the Guardhouse door, but on my promising to spare them, surrendered. The guide now pointed out the officers' quarters, and in less than an hour I secured the officers, tho' not without some resistance; for at one house I was compelled to fire several shots. Apprehending that the firing and noise might bring down the enemy from the fort, whereby we might be much annoyed, I hurried away with my prisoners to where we landed. The day began to break just as we reached the boats. To see the group was very entertaining, at least to us. The French Commandant had lost his hat; another had only one boot on, a third in his dressing gown, and so on. Two or three wives cried and begged to be allowed to follow their husbands.

So far nothing could have succeeded better. The Frigate had just come to an anchor, and the prisoners all safe on board. A flag of truce was sent into the town for their effects. They were very vociferous afterwards among themselves as to who was to blame, and 'twas singular, the very day before they had held a council of war, and decided that every officer was to sleep in the Forts. One French Officer alone, of the Engineers, escaped. We summoned him and his garrison to surrender, but without effect. Capt Hoste and myself were of opinion the main object of our enterprise was accomplished, so all hands returned to Lissa, and he soon after set sail for his station off Ragusa. We very luckily did not lose a man.

Two days after a flag of truce came over from Lesina, with proposals of capitulation. The garrison consisted of Croats, French and Italians; they lost all discipline, quarrelled and threatened to murder the Engineer Officer. I quickly went over with a few English soldiers, and established order. The Frenchmen and Italians I sent to Ancona; the latter swore they would never serve Napoleon again; the Croatians to Dalmatia: brought away some gunpowder etc, and gave the island over to the Austrians. The tide is running strong against Napoleon; a general peace must ere long be the result.

The French are driven back over the Pyrenees, and after many a bloody battle the British Army under Wellington is established in France. Where are now the forebodings of the Opposition and fears of timid croakers!

The tide was indeed running strongly against Napoleon. On 16th-19th October at the great Battle of Leipzig, the Allied armies of 300,000 men utterly defeated Napoleon's 170,000, inflicting huge casualties. Still Napoleon refused to accept the Allied offer that France should withdraw inside her 'natural frontier', the Rhine, the Alps and the Pyrenees.

JHS Bonaparte refuses to make peace. Austria, Holland, in fact all Europe, tired of the horrors of war, are all against him.

John Henry from his outpost in Lissa could see the approaching end of the horrors of war in which all his adult life had been spent. There was now no need for the 35th garrison to remain in the little island which had become, more than ever, on the periphery of the main action, and late in November 1813 he was recalled to join the battalion which was now established on the Italian coast north of Ravenna, as part of the Austrian advance in Northern Italy. Two Royal Navy ships carried him and his little detachment to Trieste and then on to Italy; by December 5th he was once more with Colonel Robertson and his battalion.

JHS *Nov 27th.* I embarked with a detachment of 70 men on board HMS the *Elizabeth*, Capt Gower.

Nov 30th. Anchored at Trieste, after a stormy passage. This city, once flourishing and rich, now presents magnificent buildings, both private and public, neglected and deserted; a number of ships dismantled. A short time, however, will alter the aspect of affairs. At the siege we lost several killed and wounded. The Navy and troops underwent great fatigue; the weather was very unfavourable. There was a singular instance of a Midshipman who was wounded, and when carried off by two sailors, a shot from the castle killed one and wounded the other; the youngster crept away and recovered.

Dec 3rd. Embarked on board the *Tremendous*: sailed and on the 4th landed at Magna Vacca.

43

British participation in one late section of the Napoleonic Wars, the North Italian campaign of 1813-4, does not often get a mention in the history books, and when it does, the focus is chiefly on the vagaries of Lord William Bentinck, or the self-congratulating reports of that false prophet Sir Robert Wilson. Bentinck was Commander-in-Chief of the British forces in the Mediterranean; Wilson was British Military Resident with the Austrian Army in Italy, and was involved in the tangled negotiations between the Austrians, the King of Naples Joachim Murat – who deserted his brother-in-law Napoleon to join the Allies – and Bentinck. John Henry Slessor, who was with a British contingent attached to the flanking section of the Austrian Army under General Nugent, took part in the confused advances and retreats resulting from Murat's and Bentinck's devious intrigues and calculated delays, and observed them with a puzzled and critical eye.

The French Kingdom of Italy which Napoleon's Viceroy Beauharnais was defending consisted, at its zenith, of Lombardy, Modena, the Papal territories, the Veneto, Dalmatia and the South Tyrol. Beauharnais, son of Napoleon's first wife Josephine by a previous marriage, had been appointed Viceroy of the Kingdom of Italy in 1805, when he was only twenty-three, but already a seasoned soldier. He was brave, cultivated, amusing, a hard worker and on the whole a capable administrator, and he was unshakably loyal, resisting all the attempts of the Allies, and of the turncoat Murat, to get him to desert Napoleon's cause. Murat was a very different type, a brilliant soldier, a dashing and apparently genial and warm-hearted character whose only real loyalty was to his own interests. His actions were aimed at ensuring that, whoever won the war, he would be able to keep his Neapolitan kingdom; he hoped also to see his rival Beauharnais humiliated, and perhaps to secure for himself the Kingdom of all Italy, and with this in view he got in touch with Italian liberals in the north, posing as the champion of Italian independence.

The chief British actors on the scene were Bentinck and Wilson. Lord William Bentinck had been appointed Commander-in-Chief of the British forces in the Mediterranean, and Minister to the Court of the Two Sicilies, in 1811. He, too, though with more conviction and less self-interest than Murat, supported Italian aspirations to independence and unification, supplying money to finance the activities of the Italian liberals, and making contact with secret societies

such as the Carbonari. He was a proud and wilful man, apt to use his own
initiative rather than follow his instructions from the British Government.

Sir Robert Wilson, who has appeared earlier in this book as the organiser in
Oporto of the Loyal Lusitanian Legion, was a very brave and resourceful officer
who had a distinguished record in the Peninsular War, had been sent on mis-
sions to Turkey and Russia, was popular with the Emperors of Russia and
Austria, and who in December 1813 was appointed British Military Resident
with the Austrian Army in Italy. He was also cocksure, intolerant, given to
confident prognostications which generally turned out to be wide of the mark,
and apt to see his role as negotiator as being more important and decisive than it
actually was. He was much disliked by the Prince Regent and was frequently in
hot water with Castlereagh and the British Government. His lengthily-titled
*Private Diary of Travels, Personal Services and Public Events During Mission
with the European Armies in the Campaigns of 1812, 1813, 1814* gives the
fullest account from the British point of view of the war in Northern Italy, but
presents almost everyone except himself in an unflattering light.

These, together with the Austrian commanders-in-chief, were the central
figures in the five-month war in Northern Italy in 1813-4. At the beginning of
November 1813, the Austrian C-in-C General Hillar advanced from Trieste,
forcing Beauharnais to withdraw westward from Udine; on 4th November
Hillar's troops entered Verona. Venice was still in French hands, and remained
so until the end of the war, but the Austrians occupied Mestre and, with the aid
of British Naval detachments, imposed a blockade on Venice. On 9th December
an Austrian force under General Stahremberg occupied Rovigo, and Venice
was encircled. By mid-December most of the Veneto was under Austrian
control, and another Austrian force had crossed the Alps and was advancing
down the River Adige to threaten Beauharnais from the north. General Hillar,
who was considered to have been too hesitant in pressing on with his advance
after invading Italy, was replaced as Austrian Commander-in-Chief by General
Bellegarde on 15th December. Comte Henri de Bellegarde was a Savoyard who
had distinguished himself as both soldier and diplomat.

This was the situation when John Henry Slessor and his seventy men landed
near Commacchio on 3rd December and marched south to rejoin the 35th, who
were now under the orders of the Austrian General Laval Nugent. They spent
the last few weeks of 1813 in or near Ravenna, where they heard premature
reports that Murat and his Neapolitan forces had joined the Allies and were
marching north. The weather was appalling; it was Italy's worst winter within
living memory, with frequent snowstorms and, in between, downpours of rain
which produced such quagmires of mud that the troops could hardly march, and
even the lightest carriage needed twenty draught oxen to draw it.

JHS *Dec 5th.* Marched to Commacchio four miles, most part of the way above
    our ankles in mud. This post a few days before had been gallantly de-

fended by a party of Marines and sailors against a superior French force. Called on General Nugent, who gave me an account of his retreat from Ferrara. He spoke in high terms of Col Robertson and his detachment. He had advanced to that fine town, but after a smart brush with the French obliged to retire. Commacchio from its isolated situation is strong, a Venice in miniature. The quantity of eels caught here is almost incredible; 'tis said that 100,000 pounds might be taken in a day. This forms the chief branch of commerce, and in a very severe winter, they tell you that many thousands of ducks have been shot in a day. There are some extensive salt works here. The numerous examples of leprosy among the inhabitants are most disgusting.

Dec 8th. Col Robertson, who had been at an outpost, came in, and we are now obliged to act on the offensive, as General Nugent's force does not exceed 5000 men. Report says that Murat is advancing with large columns, one from the side of Ancona, the other from Florence. Venice is closely blockaded.

Dec 10th. Every day brings accounts of the decline of the French cause. Our quarters here are tolerably good, and according to the Austrian system we are found in everything free of expense.

Dec 26th. An order to advance: part of our little force moved on to Ravenna; slept at Primaro, at the mouth of the Po.

Dec 27th. Entered the ancient city of Ravenna amidst the acclamations of the inhabitants. The English were cried up as their deliverers. The Austrians had taken possession without opposition a few days previously. Excellent quarters, living gratis. At first we wished to pay for everything, but General Nugent said No, saying that it would breed jealousy. All these burdens were borne with patience, and repaid by contributions on the community at large, of course subject to much fraud and imposition. The Austrians are not only lodged and fed, but clothed. I have seen an Austrian Officer go into a shop, order a great coat, pantaloons, etc, then give a *bon*, or receipt, and leave the shopkeeper to settle the bill with the municipality. The Churches are numerous, but had been stripped by the French of any valuables. Convents, Nunneries, etc converted into barracks, magazines and storehouses. The Cathedral and St Vitali are well worth visiting. The marble pillars at Classe, three miles from the town, are splendid. The present Telegraph is erected where once stood the Light-house, in the centre of the town; and remnants of the Roman Dockyards, Arsenal etc; for the sea has receded to the extent of three miles. Large rings are shewn you in the old walls, to which the galleys were made fast in ancient times. The Rotunda built by King Theodore, the tomb of the Empress Galla Placida are worthy of notice; also the Library, Museum with a few paintings. A work published by Francisco Biltrami gives the best account of the rise and fall of Ravenna. It is walled, has five gates, but weak at all points.

Dec 29th. The Neapolitans have halted: it is evident some negotiations are going on. Either Murat is playing a deep game with the Viceroy, or else endeavouring to remain neutral. What General Bellegarde, the Commander-in-Chief, is about I know not. He appears to be very dilatory, altho' said to have 70,000 men, and Beauharnais cannot have near that number. Verona is occupied by the French on one side, by the Austrians on the other. More good news from the Allies. They have issued a proclamation, or address to Bonaparte and the French nation, which augurs well. Napoleon returned to Paris, *au désespoir*. Lord Wellington follows up his success. Wherever I have been, in Dalmatia, Istria, Italy etc, the French are as much deprecated as the English are extolled. It is quite astonishing what excesses, what cruelties the Agents of the French Government have everywhere committed; what artifices and deceit they had recourse to, by proclamations, public rejoicings, Te Deums, etc, to blindfold the inhabitants, to degrade the English character, as cruel, reserved, haughty; some more credulous were even led to believe that we eat our prisoners.

Dec 30th. Rode over to Forli. This was once a populous town, about three miles in circumference. A courier from Murat rode thro'. 'Tis reported that he is at Ancona. The Austrians occupy Forli, and have their advanced posts at Rimini, close to the Neapolitans. Dined with Gen Nugent, Austrian generals etc. I admire much the Hungarian Cavalry: they understand their business, have a soldier-like appearance, active and brave, took good care of their horses, which tho' small are hardy and strong. The Austrian Infantry I cannot speak of in such high terms. Returned to Ravenna: the weather very cold: snow and frost. I am happy to say we have received a reinforcement.

January 1st 1814. The English have made a descent near Leghorn; taken some batteries. Denmark and Switzerland joined the Allies. Good God! what a joyful decree of Providence. In the same number of weeks I may say, has Bonaparte provoked Europe to declare and unite against him, as he took years to enslave it. He now stands alone, and rejects an honourable peace, with the Rhine as the boundary of France. Spain and Russia signed his death-warrant. His boundless ambition was his bitterest enemy. England, proud England, – with reason I say it, and your children's children will ever repeat it, – to your firmness, courage, perseverance must mainly be attributed the approaching general peace. Thro' your policy the effusion of blood will be stopped; quiet, peace, commerce, domestic happiness will be restored to Europe, and the World in general. The Almighty has favoured your cause, the cause of liberty, justice and humanity.

Pausing only to start a new paragraph, John Henry proceeded straight from this burst of resounding patriotism, which opens his 1814 diary, to a lively picture of the habits of the women of Ravenna. Like his mother, he was apt occasionally to clamber onto a high horse, but he was more entertaining when he jumped down from it. He enjoyed Ravenna. After his lonely year in barren Lissa, it was good to be back with his regiment, to dine with Austrian generals, to drive to the theatre in a fine carriage, to visit the splendid Byzantine churches and ride about the richly fertile countryside.

JHS The women here carry about with them earthen jars, called *scaldinos*, with hot ashes, in the house; they cover them over with their petticoats, between their feet. They are lively and agreeable. To Signor Pompeo Raisi (with whom I was quartered) I feel particularly obliged for his kindness and attention; and indeed with few exceptions we have been received as friends. There are many good equipages, and I frequently went to the theatre in that of my landlord. The town is lively, considering the pressure of the times. The people anxious for the restoration of the Pope. Country about is pretty, abundant and fertile. The drain for the army of young men has been very great: women work in the fields, as well as indoors.

44

The pleasant interlude in Ravenna came to an end in mid-January, with a dramatic change in the balance of power in Italy. On January 11th Joachim Murat deserted Napoleon's cause and signed a treaty with the Austrians, on condition that he could remain King of Naples. Sir Robert Wilson, who had arrived at the Austrian headquarters in Vicenza on the day after Murat's defection, commented drily, 'However useful the treason, what must be thought of the traitor?' Professional soldiers like Wilson and John Henry Slessor could not help contrasting the turncoat Murat, advantageous as his change of sides was to the British cause, with the steadfast refusal of Beauharnais to listen to any solicitations by the Austrians to abandon Napoleon. They admired the constancy of Beauharnais, enemy though he was. The Allies had twice offered him the crown of Northern Italy, of which he had so long been Viceroy and which he had hoped that Napoleon would bequeath to him and his son, if he would change sides, but he had said No; he had shared in Napoleon's glories and would not desert him as they faded.

The news of Murat's change of sides soon reached John Henry in Ravenna.

JHS *Jan 12th*. The mask is at length removed. Murat has declared for the Allies, most unwillingly, I believe, but he sits on a tottering throne. Beauharnais, brave and high in principle, will listen to no terms, but will stand or fall with Napoleon. A great many deserters come daily over to us, principally Poles and Germans. Col Robertson has permission to form them into a separate Corps. Active, fine fellows they are, and shew much animosity towards their late rulers.

Murat rapidly advanced north from Naples with his army; he occupied Rome on January 16th, Florence on the 31st. On 3rd February he signed an armistice with Lord William Bentinck, Commander-in-Chief of the British forces in Sicily, and in February his troops occupied Ancona and all Tuscany. But he was wary of moving further north to support the Austrians in a decisive joint attack on Beauharnais until he had secured his position *vis-à-vis* Bentinck, who looked with a critical eye on the Neapolitan occupation of so much of Central Italy. Beauharnais meanwhile had abandoned Verona and the line of the River Adige and had withdrawn to a defensive position behind the River Mincio.

262

Bellegarde, the Austrian Commander, entered Verona on 4th February, and four days later he attempted to cross the Mincio and dislodge Beauharnais; he was unsuccessful in this, and had to withdraw his main forces to Verona, leaving advanced posts to keep watch on the Mincio; but the French had suffered heavy casualties in this Battle of Valeggio, in which Wilson distinguished himself and was nearly captured by the French. For some weeks after this indecisive action, in which neither side gained any real advantage, Bellegarde remained inactive while he waited for Murat and Bentinck to resolve their quarrels and to move forward in support of the Austrians.

The section of the Austrian army under Count Nugent, an Austrian general of Irish origin, in which John Henry and the 35th had been incorporated, was not involved in the action on the Mincio. Nugent's force, mostly of Corsicans and Calabrians apart from the British contingent, was on the left flank of the main Austrian army, and early in February they began an advance from Ravenna which was to carry them north-west across the whole length of Emilia, and then a withdrawal halfway back again, in a confused manoeuvre caused by the delays and intrigues of the Allied leaders in Italy. Their advance took place in weather still atrocious: cold so intense that whole orchards of mulberry trees were killed by the frost and had to be cut down. The sun rarely shone, never for long enough to melt the ice which coated the roads. Even indoors, water in bottles froze into solid ice. It was 'cold enough for bears to go to sleep in,' said Wilson and cruelly more than cold enough for human beings – no fewer than 28,000 of the Austrian army had gone sick.

John Henry's detailed diary of the movement across Emilia of Nugent's force frequently mentions the snow and bitter cold. He also gives some vivid pictures of encounters with Murat and some of his army, as they moved uncertainly from Ancona up the left flank of Nugent's force; now overtaking them to get to Modena first, now hanging back so that Nugent's little force was dangerously exposed.

JHS *Feb 3rd.* Orders to move forward; the ground covered with snow. Took leave of Signor Raisi and his family; both Officers and men were sorry to leave Ravenna.

Feb 4th. At 5 o'clock this morning marched off, on our way to Forli. Got a billet in a noble mansion, beautiful glasses, satin linings, sofas, etc but withal a great deal of splendid poverty. The style of building and architecture in Italy is magnificent, but I am not surprised that the inhabitants become effeminate and vitiated; their mode of living, education, religion, climate, combine to make them naturally so.

King Joachim passed thro' from Ancona on his route to Bologna: he has sent troops in advance. Curious times we live in; yesterday sworn enemies, today in alliance. Lord Wellington at Bayonne: Prince Schwartzenberg at Langres. Went to see a guillotine. 'Tis true one reflects with horror at the thousands that were executed, when it was invented, but it is an effica-cious, merciful mode of execution.

Feb 7th. Moved on to Faenza, by the ancient and famous Via Emilia, a road commenced before the Christian era. No time to see this town.

Feb 8th. Breakfasted at Imola: on to St Pietro, where we slept; cold work. We were cheered by the people, tho' in truth but a motley sample of British troops: 150 only of the 35th, the rest composed of detachments from De Rolls, Corsicans, Italians, Calabrians and deserters from the enemy, altogether amounting to under 1000 men.

Feb 9th. On to Bologna. Regretted I could not see this once populous fine city. About 10,000 Neapolitan troops are here. They are stout young men, well cloathed and appointed, and certainly if you judge from appearance fit for any service, but whether their hearts are in the right place, I will not pretend to say. Loud complaints against them: great marauders, even murderers: nor do their Officers take much pains to restrain them, probably even set them the example. The shops are shut, and after nightfall scarcely an inhabitant ventures out of his house. How different would be the behaviour and discipline of an English army.

Feb 10th. A long and fatiguing march to Modena. Murat passed us on the road, and as we entered the town was reviewing about 5000 of his troops. His Garde-de-Corps, all French, are a fine body of men, capitally mounted, and well appointed. A Mameluke is his constant orderly. Here the murmurs of the inhabitants are loud against the Pope. This beautiful and rich country has in all ages been the envy of monarchs, and consequently ever subject to the horrors of war.

Feb 11th. The Arch-Duke Francis has by proclamation been restored to the Dukedom of Modena. General Bellegarde has crossed the Adige. His Headquarters are between Mantua and Verona; yet Beauharnais has all the strongholds. Modena is a pleasant place. The Duke's house is a splendid palace. A carriage may be driven round the ramparts. Saw the Botanic garden: it is not in the best order. Here is a fine pillar erected by Bonaparte, with a golden spread eagle on a globe. At Ferrara there was a statue of himself, holding the World in one hand, and a sword in the other. In most places is to be seen some memento of his grandeur. The Austrians on our right have had an action, but no advantage gained.

Feb 13th. Advanced to Reggio: dined with a Neapolitan General. He had lost by the cold in the Russian campaign the first joints of his left-hand fingers. His description of the sufferings and privations of the French army in that expedition is most horrible.

Feb 14th. To Parma. The French had evacuated this town six days previous to our entering it. We are now on French territory; or rather this part of Italy forms part of the French Empire.

Feb 18th. Obliged to flog a Calabrian Sergeant for mutiny, he having claimed a right to the discharge of the detachment, and to return home; but we soon brought the gentlemen to their senses. Two Austrian soldiers were shot at sunrise this morning for robbery, and according to their rules of war, the corpses are left exposed and uncovered till sunset. Orders to march with three days' provisions: some Neapolitan troops arrived.

Feb 17th. Our advance posts crossed the Taro, and moved on Piacenza.

Feb 18th. A false alarm this evening from the side of Mantua. It originated in a French officer, with a flag of truce, crossing the Po, and reporting that the Allies had lost an action in France. We remained under arms all night, bitter cold work in the snow. The painting of St Girolamo, reckoned very valuable, was taken away from this town by the French, and sent to Paris. Parma is rather a handsome town, walled round: has a citadel, in bad repair. Flat country, but fertile, and most abundant: scarce a stone to be seen. Met some gentlemen of Irish extraction: dined repeatedly with Mr McGawley, who is at the head of the local Government. We are tolerably comfortable: of course always on the alert. Piacenza is not yet attacked. The Neapolitans are very slow in their movements. Gen Nugent is gone off post haste to see Murat at Reggio. He has in our rear about 25,000 men. I hope he is not playing a double part.

Feb 19th. Orders to serve at the shortest notice.

Feb 22nd. Our situation rather critical, between the enemy and the doubtful Neapolitans, with so small a force. Rode out to the village of Colorno, three miles on this side of the Po. On the other side, at Castel Maggiore, are the French. Visited a beautiful Palace belonging to the late Duke of Parma. The furniture, paintings, pleasure grounds, etc, singular to relate, remain in perfect order. On my return the garrison had marched out, but returned in the evening. The Ballestero, Museum and celebrated ancient theatre at Parma are worthy of notice.

Feb 25th. Murat made his appearance this morning, but made a short stay.

Feb 27th. Our outposts from Piacenza driven in and the enemy advanced as far as the Taro, five miles from us. All hands under arms.

Feb 29th. Bivouacked all day and night outside the town in the snow. The King of Naples rode to the outposts. The enemy fired some cannon shots at him across the river. He returned to Reggio in the evening. His conduct appears mysterious, and until his army comes up, we cannot advance. He is a soldier-like-looking man on horseback: rides well, courts popularity, affable in his manners to the English. He frequently addressed me by '*Monsieur le Major*'. Tho' I was pleased at his politeness, yet I reluctantly answered with '*Mon Roi*'.

Mar 1st. Rode out to the pickets on the Taro. The sentries looking at and abusing each other.

Mar 2nd. The Viceroy crossed the river in three columns, and attacked at about 8 o'clock in the morning. Some of the Austrians were surprised and made prisoners. My servant with baggage horse nearly captured. We retreated on Reggio, keeping up a brisk and regular fire, in good order. Rain and wind all day. The ground was well contested, but numbers prevailed. The rascally Neapolitans never came into action. The enemy were reported to be 20,000: our force a little more than half that number.

Mar 3rd. At daybreak, as firing had ceased, altho' we had been up all night under arms, fell back again on Modena. Sent the sick and wounded, with heavy baggage, to Ferrara. Murat joined us.

Mar 4th. The enemy pushed on their pickets to within five miles of Modena, but nothing more. They think us rather formidable now, I suppose, with the macaroni gentlemen at our back. A courier has arrived from the Grand Army, stating that Murat has signed a treaty of Alliance, and acknowledged King of Naples, guaranteed by England. The Allies are everywhere victorious. The Austrian system is abominable, and the Generals I think are rather jealous of our Commander, Gen Count Nugent, and the hearty cooperation he has all along received from the British Navy. Had he been at the head of a larger force, I have no doubt that he would have performed most essential services; but he was obliged to carry on a desultory, harassing service of posts, advancing and retreating, no staff of any kind. Ever active in mind and body, brave and cool in the field, mild and gentlemanly in manners. His medical department cruelly bad. I believe after a poor fellow is wounded, little more is thought about him, unless he can crawl away to a hospital. As I said before, heavy contributions are called for and exacted for provisions of all kinds; meat, bread, wine, spirits, tobacco, oats, hay, straw, iron for all purposes, cloathing, shoes, etc; and nothing but receipts given. To satisfy the public rests with the Municipality, and it is indeed wonderful with what patience the community bear these burdens.

John Henry's surmise that other generals were jealous of Nugent is borne out by the harsh strictures on his action in Emilia which Wilson recorded in his diary. He claims that after the Battle of Valeggio he sent a message to Nugent, warning him to be prudent and not to advance in aid with his force of 10,000. Nugent took no notice of this, or of Murat's advice, but advanced to a perilous position on the Taro beyond Parma, from which he was forced back by a French sally from Piacenza. On 4th March, contrary to express orders to avoid all serious action until it was certain that the Neapolitans would support it, he chose the moment when the Neapolitans had temporarily withdrawn to engage with the French on the Taro. In the ensuing action, at which the Viceroy Beauharnais led the French attack, Nugent was reported to have lost a park of artillery and 3500 prisoners. Nugent was full of self-important ambition,

Wilson maintained; his action on the Taro was 'most unjustifiable, ill-conducted and disastrous. His excuse is that he wished to preserve some detachments. To save a few companies, he lost battalions. Certainly there are not less than three thousand men hors de combat' and his remaining 6000 men were 'so divided that they may be dispersed in an hour'. The utmost that Wilson would concede was that Nugent had been 'placed in very difficult circumstances, which scarcely admitted of his harmless extrication'.

John Henry, who was actually present at the action on the Taro, not sixty miles away in Verona as Wilson was, would not have agreed that Nugent's force could have been 'dispersed in an hour' after the battle. Nugent's force, fighting a French army twice its size, had 'well contested' the ground, though without the Neapolitan support they had expected, and when forced to withdraw, had done so in good order and keeping up a regular fire.

Three days later there was a new development in the Allies' favour. Bentinck landed on 7th March at Leghorn with 9,000 British and Sicilian troops, and a week later he was in Reggio, claiming that Murat ought to hand over Tuscany to him, as a base for an attack on Genoa. This suggestion naturally did not appeal to Murat, and much of March was spent in negotiations between Bentinck and Murat (who was also still secretly in touch with Napoleon and Beauharnais about possibly changing sides again; he was afraid that the Allies intended to restore the Bourbons to the throne of Naples). Wilson took part in the negotiations with Murat, and agreement was finally reached. While these negotiations were going on, Nugent's force was again advancing from Modena; Murat and his elusive Neapolitan forces were now cooperating again, and they and Nugent's army together took Reggio from the French, and advanced to Parma.

JHS *Mar 6th*. Troops in motion. Austrians and Neapolitans advanced: some prisoners made this evening.

Mar 7th. The Army marched at 3 o'clock in the morning to attack: heavy rain: at 8 the firing commenced. By 1.0 the enemy were driven into Reggio. Murat came up at full gallop soon after. He had a beautiful train of artillery. As he passed, his troops cheered him. A French General saw him from the town, and calling out to his men, '*Allons, mes enfants, nous irons prendre le Roi*' [Come, my boys, let's go and capture the King] gallantly made a sortie. But this brave little party were driven back, and we heard afterwards that a cannon ball had taken off the General's leg. Our artillery began to play on the town, when a flag of truce came out. All firing ceased, and the enemy were allowed to retire at the moment when we had nearly invested the town, and might have made the garrison prisoners. The Neapolitans showed every inclination to fight, and lost a few Officers and men. Our total loss on this night and the 2nd might amount to 1800, killed, wounded and prisoners.

Mar 8th. The advance re-entered Parma.

Mar 9th. Resumed our old quarters; welcomed by the inhabitants. The enemy recrossed the Taro.

Mar 10th. An alarm: under arms all night.

Mar 11th. Lord William Bentinck has landed at Leghorn with about 9000 men from Sicily. The Austrian General, Bellegarde, is still before Mantua, and guarding the strongholds; but I think Lord William will cause a fine diversion on our left.

Mar 12th. Under arms all night: heavy rain. A Regiment of Neapolitans marched in, by no means welcome visitors. We are fortifying the Citadel, and oblige the country people to work.

Mar 13th. All quiet. Many deserters come over, principally Italians. The game is nearly up. Lord W. Bentinck arrived at Reggio; confers with Murat and Bellegarde. A heavy cannonade heard in the direction of the Po.

Mar 18th. Col Robertson has seen Lord William. We are to join the British army in Tuscany, but I now hope to avail myself of the leave of absence which I had obtained four months ago, which I declined accepting, so long as any service was going on.

Mar 19th. Lord William came to Parma, reviewed our detachment, appeared satisfied, and much pleased with the report made by General Nugent of our conduct while under his command. My leave was granted, and Col Robertson and party ordered to cross the Apennines immediately.

Mar 21st. Report of a general peace.

The evolution of the Italian side-show was being overtaken by events in Northern Europe. On 30th March the Allied Armies, which had crossed the Rhine three months earlier and overwhelmed Napoleon's desperate resistance, entered Paris, and on 11th April Napoleon abdicated. Beauharnais fought on for a little against the now combined forces of the Austrians and the Neapolitans, but on 16th April he capitulated and signed the Treaty of Schiarino-Rizzino with Bellegarde. By the end of April Beauharnais's army was withdrawing across the Alps, and the whole Napoleonic 'Kingdom of Italy', including Milan, Mantua and Venice, was in the hands of the Allies.

John Henry had not waited for the formal end of hostilities. It was clear that the great war which had lasted for the whole of his adult life was at last ending; the 35th were not going to see any more active service for the time being; at last he could claim his overdue leave, and go home.

45

JHS *Mar 22nd*. Bid adieu to my brother soldiers. Eight years on active service, and a long separation from those dearest to me, whom I had not seen since the death of my two brothers, and an almost certainty of peace, were strong inducements to get home.

'Parma. 21st March 1814. I do hereby certify that Major Slessor of the 35th Regt volunteered to remain with the detachment under my orders until this time, in consequence of our being on active service, and I am under many obligations to him for his zeal and exertions on the occasion.
J.D. Robertson Lieut Col, Commdg'

John Henry could not set out directly towards England, as he had to get back to Lissa first, to settle his affairs there and arrange for the despatch of his heavy baggage. At this stage, before the Allied entry into Paris and Napoleon's abdication, he still planned to return home by sea from the Adriatic.

JHS *Mar 24th*. After retracing the old road as far as Forli, I struck off to the right. My route and passport, according to the general system, authorised me to press a carriage and horses at every stage, free of expense, and now entering a country under the Neapolitan Government, I took care to get my papers backed by the competent authorities. I took my German, Tomasi, with me. Went to Cesena and Rimini, crossed the Pisatello, ancient Rubicon. Having alighted to walk up a hill, I was accosted by a countryman, who asked to kiss my hand. On my enquiring the reason, he answered *'Perche vedo che siete un Inglese'* [Because I see that you are an Englishman.]. The roads are everywhere good, the country fertile, and cultivated with great neatness and regularity.
Mar 28th. Continued my journey to Ancona; stopped to breakfast at Pesaro: but it being a Festa, the crowd about my carriage was so great, excited by the curiosity at seeing an English Officer, that I had much trouble in getting by. At Semiaglia I was received with every mark of civility: high encomiums on the British Nation, how rich, how brave, how powerful by sea. This last idea is prevalent everywhere; our Army are thought little of; they say the English by water, the French on land. However, on this subject their ignorance will soon be removed.

On my arriving here, the Mayor sent word that he wished to pay his respects to me, but I declined the honour, as I was anxious to proceed. At 6 o'clock this evening I arrived at Ancona. Dined the next day with the Neapolitan General, who gave a public dinner in honour of the birthday of the Queen of Naples, a sister of Bonaparte. In the evening went to the theatre. The town was illuminated. It is really ridiculous to see the Neapolitan Officers wearing crosses, ribands, etc. One half at least are decorated with some badge. I heard of an Officer, to whom Murat had promised an order, reminding the King, who said, 'Yes, you shall have it, for you deserve this mark of distinction'. On which the Officer took a cross and ribbon out of his pocket. His Majesty answered, 'Very well, wear it'.

Ancona has a good harbour, and well fortified. Our Navy well know this coast. From hence were fitted out privateers, and vessels of all sorts sent out with troops, stores etc, for Corfu and Ragusa. The General was civil, and having received a letter to give me a passage to Lissa, ordered one of his Scampavias to be ready.

Mar 26th. Set sail in the evening, with a fair breeze. Nothing particular occurred. We naturally conversed much on the sudden change of affairs, privateers, prizes, etc. The sailors complained much of bad pay and ill usage.

Mar 29th. Arrived at Lissa at 9 o'clock at night.

Mar 30th. Despatched the Neapolitan back.

Apr 1st. The Continent being now open, I decided on going home overland, so soon arranged my affairs, disposed of all my heavy baggage. Adieu to the Adriatic.

Apr 6th. At 7 o'clock this evening was out of the harbour on a Gun boat. I took two Officers with me as companions. They wished to make a little excursion. Sailing among the islands is beautiful. Landed at Lucine etc: sometimes spread our repast on a rock. If the wind proved contrary, put into some creek or town: amused ourselves shooting or fishing. At Zara, the Capital of Dalmatia, we were well received by the Austrian General, Tomasic. This Officer had got honours and promotion, made Governor of Dalmatia, owing to the zeal and courage of the English, who had liberated the whole country, from Trieste to Cattaro; whereas the Austrians themselves did comparatively nothing in the general cause. Their system is bad, no energy. The General at the head of 5000 men, had sent to me at Lissa, asking for two guns and gunpowder. Zara is strong, and mounts at least 200 pieces of Brass guns, and ought to have been ours as prizes, when the place surrendered to Capt Cadogan R.N. Count Bartolozzi paid us every attention, and shewed us the lions. The Dalmatians appear to me the largest race of people I ever saw.

Apr 10th. Set sail for Fiume. Fine weather.

The universal admiration of Britain, the striking civilities shown to him personally, rather went to John Henry's head, and he began to feel that the British alone were responsible for the Allied triumph in the Mediterranean, with little help from the Austrians and none from the Neapolitans, whose medal-laden breasts provoked his ridicule.

It was the news of the Allied advance into France which decided him to return home by land across Europe. When he landed in Fiume on 12th April, his triumphalist mood was sobered by the news of the desperate stand by Napoleon in the north and Soult in the south of France, the sanguinary Battle of Toulouse, and the disastrous failure by a British corps, sent to Holland under Sir Thomas Graham, to capture Antwerp or Bergen-op-Zoom.

JHS *Apr 12th.* Landed at 9 o'clock at night. We here heard of our disasters at Bergen-op-Zoom; melancholy work, by way of a finale; and 'tis said that the sacrifice of life was most wanton at Toulouse, as the Prefet and Soult both knew that an armistice had taken place, but Soult thought to beat Wellington.

Apr 13th. Dined with the Austrian General. According to the Hungarian custom, when dinner is announced, a glass of rum, or a liqueur is handed round. Much attention is paid us by Mr Adamitch, the British Consul. He has a very pretty place near the town. Parted with my brother Officers, who returned to Lissa.

Apr 14th. Went by land to Trieste. The change and bustle of business is almost incredible in so short a time. Baron Lederer assured me that the population had increased by 12,000, since the month of November last.

Apr 18th. The joyful news arrived of the Allies having entered Paris. The National Guards turned against Napoleon, who has abdicated. What a pity that an English Army had not been amongst the number. The Duke of Wellington at Toulouse. Capitulations, treaties, etc signed.

Apr 19th. Great rejoicings: a ball at the Governor's house. Convention signed with Beauharnais.

Apr 20th. Louis the XVIII has entered Paris. Field Marshals and Army in general hoisted the White Cockade, and taken the oath of allegiance. Bonaparte retires to the Island of Elba.

At Trieste, news of the Austrian occupation of Venice caused John Henry again to change his route home.

JHS I have met with Mr Kerr, a Scotch gentleman; agreed to travel to Paris together, and settled to go by Vienna; but Venice falling, changed our route.

Apr 21st. Set sail this morning in a country boat, but towards evening, weather bad, put into Groa, a poor place: passed the night.

Apr 22nd. We started again: arrived at Venice at 6-0 in the evening. On approaching the harbour, we were fired at by a Man-of-War boat. Went on board, then landed. The entrance very beautiful. Heavy rain and storm, after we reached our Auberge.

Apr 23rd. There is nothing but noise and bustle. A *mélange* of troops and all kinds of flags flying, on shore and afloat. Ports, batteries, etc given over to the Austrians. Outside is Sir J. Gore with a proud British fleet, but he refuses to come on shore. Walked about, 'tis a wonderful place. Crowds followed us, the women calling out, as we passed '*Benedetto di Dio*' [Blessed of God].

To describe Venice would fill a volume: the houses as it were built in the water: 2000 gondolas rowing about with a single oar from house to house. Every family of any respectability have one of these boats. The black awning or canopy looks dismal; they move with great skill and velocity. The Piazza of St Mark is splendid. From hence were removed the famous horses by Bonaparte. The celebrated Rialto is a single arch over the Grand Canal, bold and striking from its elevation, great extension and solidity. The population about 150,000, but the spirit that once animated these people is now dormant, and they have paid dear for the treachery that delivered them into the hands of the French. Weak and imbecile, yet gay and lively: gamblers, naturally musical, effeminate. During the blockade they suffered much, but now supplies and provisions are abundant. We are well accommodated at the Locanda Britannica, and I would recommend my countrymen always to bargain at so much a head for board and lodging. Good shops: the gold chains beautifully worked. There are here now four French Line of Battle ships, Frigates, Brigs and about 200 gun boats, besides several vessels on the stocks. Venice so strong and singularly situated, I should say, cannot be taken but by treachery or starvation.

Apr 24th. Went six miles off to Malamocca, a fine sheet of water. The number of islands, forts, batteries, render the scene most interesting. It is at this place they transport Men of War over shallow water, fully equipped, and ready for sea, by affixing to their sides a machinery called camels, curious and clever contrivance. Had the English taken Venice, what prize money they would have shared! I this day dined on board the Flagship, with Sir J. Gore. Met an old shipmate of my dear brother Henry.

Apr 25th. Visited the Arsenal in company with Capt Black R.N. who here joined us to complete the trio. We saw the greatest profusion of Naval stores, above 20 vessels on the stocks: order and neatness thro' out the whole establishment. The Austrians will take possession tomorrow: also a common foundry, powder mills etc. Here is a naval school. We saw 400 boys: were told that they were generally chosen from the poorest classes, taught navigation etc. This was one of Napoleon's grand projects. Today is the Festa of St Mark, but until the French move out there will be little rejoicing. Genoa has surrendered to Lord Wm Bentinck. The Duke of Wellington appointed Ambassador at Paris.

Apr 27th. Got our passports: left Venice at 1-0 o'clock in a gondola for Mestre: then took chaise for Padova. The country and road as far as the Viceroy's residence is beautiful, a continuous succession of Villas, casinos, etc on each bank of the river. Asking the postilion if Prince Eugene had bought that place, he answered, '*Si, Signor, l'a comprato, ma non pagato*' [Yes, sir, he bought it but he didn't pay for it]. Arrived at a comfortable Inn: good supper and beds.

The postilion's anecdote about Eugène Beauharnais and the Villa Pisani, Strà, is unfair. It was Napoleon who had bought this palace on the Brenta, built for a Venetian Doge, in 1807 and had given it to his Viceroy. Prince Eugène and his wife, Princess Augusta Amelia of Bavaria, had never liked it as well as their other palace of Monza. Augusta Amelia said that it was damp and the rooms were awkwardly arranged, and that it was 'too big for a private residence but not large enough for a court', the professional comment of a born princess on this splendid palace with its long water and groves and labyrinth, its statue-adorned stables and its immense white and gold ballroom with a ceiling painted by Tiepolo with hurtling deities amid rosy clouds.

JHS *Apr 28th.* Rose early, and visited the Botanic garden, which we found in high order, the Church of St Antonio, town hall, etc. Few cities can boast of an origin so ancient or so honourable as Padua. The Abbey of St Giustina, the Library, spacious Piazza of Prato della Valle, the Cathedral, the University, famed all over Europe, attracted our notice. The wool here is esteemed the finest in Italy. After a breakfast a *l'Inglese*, started for Vicenza, a town ornamented with numerous Palaces, splendid and beautiful. The celebrated architect Palladio was born here. On to Verona, which we reached rather late. Made all snug for the night.

Apr 29th. Called on Sir R. Wilson, who asked us to dinner. In the evening introduced to Marshal Bellegarde. This town is finely situated on the Adige, which sweeps thro' it. The Amphitheatre is a noble monument of Roman magnificence, repaired by order of Napoleon, at an expense of 50,000 francs. Forty-five ranges of seats rise from the arena to the top of the second storey of outward arches, entire with their respective staircases and galleries of communication. A bull bait was exhibited here in honour of the Emperor Joseph. Another time the Pope, at the request of the Magistrates, poured forth his benediction on the prostrate multitude. The French had frequent farces and pantomimes acted for the amusement of the Army. Singular contrasts. There are several very ancient gates. The chapels of St Bernardino and Zeno are worth seeing, but as usual, every article of value had been removed by the marauding French. Verona gave birth to many men of genius. Monte Bolca and Calle Ronca, fifteen miles distant, are picturesque and produce curious minerals. Beauharnais is here. Such changes on the grand theatre of politics appear like a dream. We found Verona pleasant during the short time we stayed. One evening went to the café, where *conversaziones* are held: the ladies quite at home: ices, etc, etc. We now decided on buying a new carriage, which cost 80 Louis d'or.

If John Henry had enjoyed the provincial pleasures of Ravenna, he was still more excited by Venice and Verona, and his diary is full of gondolas, arsenals, churches, botanic gardens, libraries, Palladian villas, and ladies eating ices in cafés. His observations have no striking originality, they are much what other English travellers in Italy recorded in their diaries, but there is a sprightly air of enjoyment about his journal entries for this month in Northern Italy. He was now a man of thirty-seven, who had seen a lot of fighting and garrison life in a good many countries, but had never before experienced the sophisticated pleasures of peace-time life in the most beautiful cities of Europe, and he was exhilarated by this belated Grand Tour.

46

At the end of April John Henry set off from Verona with his companions Captain Black and Mr Kerr, to travel across North Italy, Austria, Germany and Switzerland to Paris. It was a heart-stirring moment for such a journey. Fragments of the gigantic clouds which had hung over Europe for the last twenty years still chequered the weak sunshine now falling on a continent of shattered institutions, disputed frontiers, economies ruined by blockades and rapacious armies. Napoleon was on his way from France to Elba when John Henry was travelling in the opposite direction, but everywhere on the route men were still talking of Napoleon, of his ambition, of his Russian campaign, of his two wives, of the followers who had betrayed him and the ones who had remained loyal to the last. Of these, Beauharnais seems to have specially interested John Henry, who admired his courage and fidelity, and collected stories about him. Now he was to encounter him on the road to the Tyrol.

Beauharnais was still only thirty-two, but he had campaigned in Egypt and Syria, had taken part – like Henry Slessor – in the siege of St Jean d'Acre, had distinguished himself at the Battles of Marengo, Wagram and Borodino, and had played a heroic part in the retreat from Moscow. He had also ruled the Kingdom of Italy for nine years, capably and leniently on the whole. Now, since his capitulation of 16th April, he was no longer Viceroy and had no hope of maintaining any position in Italy. On 13th April his wife had given birth to a daughter, Theodolinde, in the old Ducal Palace of the Gonzagas at Mantua, but as soon as she and the new-born child could travel, the family had to set out for Munich to take refuge with the Vicereine's father, the King of Bavaria. There was a rumour that Beauharnais had to travel disguised in an Austrian uniform, because the people of Tyrol, through which he had to travel, were bent on assassinating him in revenge for the execution in 1810 of their hero Hofer, the champion of Tyrolese independence. The rumour was in fact untrue; the Beauharnais family travelled quite openly, with an escort of an Austrian officer and twelve men provided in their honour by General Bellegarde. They moved by easy stages from Mantua to Verona and on to Rovereto, where John Henry and his party overtook them. He heard and believed the rumours against Beauharnais, but felt sympathy at such a downfall.

JHS *Apr 30th.* Having made all our arrangements, we started this morning for Dijon, Sir Robert Wilson recommending us not to go by Milan and Turin. Our Postilion, the first stage, was completely German, extremely sulky and uncivil. We travelled all night. At Rovereto overtook Beauharnais. He was sleeping at a miserable Inn, with about a dozen sentries in and about the house. There are ugly reports that he will not be allowed to pass unmolested thro' the Tyrol. His wife, daughter of the King of Bavaria, is with him, as also an infant child. 'Tis said, that had he remained much longer at Mantua, he would have been assassinated. As it was he was burnt in effigy, and now travels in the uniform of an Austrian officer, attended by an Austrian General. How precarious is human grandeur! We had some difficulty in procuring horses, and were told that we should certainly be stopped on the road. However, we started.

May 1st. Met with no impediment. Passed thro' Trento at 6 o'clock in the morning. This town is situated in a small but very beautiful valley, renowned for the Treaty of Trent many years ago. The country all the way from Verona must be very fine. The road leads along the Adige, between two chains of mountains and hanging cliffs. We this day very nearly lost our carriage, for the postilion dismounting on going down a declivity, the reins left carelessly loose, the horses set off. I immediately jumped out: so did Black and Tomasi my servant. We escaped unhurt, but poor Kerr, a large heavy man, sprained his wrist, and was otherwise bruised: lay sprawling in the dust. The horses ran for at least a mile, and were stopped by the leader (for we had three horses) getting entangled in the harness. The postilion kept crossing himself and saying his prayers. We ran after the chaise, and strange to say nothing was injured, and overjoyed we were, for we fully expected that our 80 Louis' worth would have been dashed to pieces. At 7-0 in the evening arrived at Botzem. Had a little dispute with the Landlord, for I at first suspected that his was not the head Inn, and went out to look for another, when on my return he sulkily gave us supper and beds.

May 2nd. Got off at 8-0 in the morning, still with the Adige in view; on to Brixon and Steinach, where we slept, and were well accommodated. The post boys put one quite out of patience, and the post regulations are abominable. If you arrive with four horses, you are obliged to take the same number on; at all events, take them or not, you pay for them. Met processions of countrymen, who at this season of the year come many miles to do penance. Our Saviour on the Crucifix is put up in numberless places. We are now in Bavaria.

May 3rd. Took our coffee, and paid our bill, which appeared rather exorbitant. Got under weigh by 6 o'clock. A fine morning. Reached the source of the Adige, fifteen miles from Innsbruck. 'Twas a beautiful waterfall, issuing as it were from the mountainside. Arrived at Innsbruck about 5-0 in the evening. Here the post-master insisted on our taking three horses, tho' we had contrived to come the last stage with only two. Shewed us his tariff, and told us sullenly, if we did not like it, we might remain where we were, which was in the middle of the street. I applied to the Austrian Military Commandant, but without effect. This was rather provoking, for our next stage was a short one and a level road.

The only way we took to annoy them was by chance meeting another carriage half way exactly, the same number of horses, which the postilions wanted to change, but we positively refused. Crossed the river Inn: stopped to a late dinner at Zierl. The landlord was extremely civil: took some fresh trout out of a reservoir, which he quickly cooked. These with a couple of black-cock afforded a good repast. He told me that the late Bishop of Derry, Lord Bristol, had been in his house some years ago.

The people in their manners and dress resemble the Dutch, and even this village had felt the generosity of the English. For when the French ravaged and laid waste the country, a subscription was made up in England for its inhabitants. There are extensive forests here, and great quantities of timber are seen floating down the river. Mineral salt works on the side of a mountain. The Alps look truly majestic, topped with snow. These inhabitants appear much attached to Austria.

Travelled all night: fine clear moonlight: immense overhanging cliffs. The postilion now and then sounding his horn, gave scope to romantic ideas. The road excellent, but we met with no Marmontel's *bergère*. I regretted much we had not passed in the daytime.

May 4th. This morning got pretty clear of the mountains, and the break of day expanded to our view scenery we contemplated with delight. All the valleys appear to be well cultivated, and thickly inhabited. At 5-0 in the evening reached Kempten. The town in a complete uproar, expecting the arrival of Marie Louise, late Empress of France, on her return to Vienna. The people behaved very civilly to us, and particularly inquisitive on the subject of politics. We are now in Swabia. Went as far as Lutchisch, where we slept. Indifferently treated and overcharged: two circumstances, which apparently contradictory, often occur. The country between Nesselwang and this place is pretty.

May 5th. We have been particularly fortunate in the weather. Started at 9-0 o'clock this morning: passed thro' Morsberg, electorate of Baden. The country and evirons are beautiful: the Palace situated on the banks of Lake Constance, which separates this country from Switzerland. What a delightful retired spot. Quantity of fruit trees dispersed all about, in full blossom, looked luxuriant. We travelled all this night, and reached Schaffhausen on the bank of the Rhine at 9 o'clock in the morning.

The 6th. The waterfall and rapidity of the river is well known. We remained on the bridge for some time looking with admiration. Were told of some Englishmen, who were rash enough to attempt the passage in a boat, but paid the forfeit of their lives. Here met part of the suite of Marie Louise, with a large retinue, and no doubt great wealth. She had gone this morning to Zurich, so that we lost the opportunity of seeing her and her son, Napoleon the 2nd, King of the Romans, who may some day make an noise in the World. We were anxious to reach Paris, so proceeded and crossed the Rhine (the King of rivers) at Lausenberg, a strong pass. We were now on Swiss ground. Stopped to a late dinner at a village, beautifully situated: Black forest on our right. The rate of posting much increased. I hope our finances will last out. It came on to rain, so we halted for the night.

May 7th. Started a little before 7-0: recrossed the Rhine: again crossed at Basel, a fine large town. Had our passports renewed and signed by the Austrian General, previous to entering the French territory. Got a good breakfast *à-la-fourchette*. Continued our route to Trois Maisons. Here broke French ground. Went on to Belfort, where we dined. Our postilion from here was very entertaining. He had been a soldier, and wounded: talked with all the nonchalance possible of the eventful times: '*Ma foi! la fortune de guerre*': was going to look after two horses the Austrians had pressed from him. We met some columns of the Allied troop evacuating France, savage looking Cossacks, Russians, etc. The White Cockade is displayed everywhere, but from what I can observe, altho' the people rejoice at a change, and the comforts of peace, still as a Nation they feel their humiliation. The Army most decidedly lament the fall of Napoleon. We travelled all this night.

May 8th. *Déjeuner* at Vezoul. Price of posting much reduced. The devastation of an invading army everywhere conspicuous. Stopped to supper at Langres. Here the Emperor and King of Prussia had established their Headquarters for fifteen days on their approach to Paris.

May 9th. At Chaumont: on to Troyes. All this line of country had been the scene of warfare; many dead horses lying on the high road. Bonaparte made an ill-judged movement, by attempting to get in the rear of the Allied Armies, by which his communication with Paris was cut off. To our great mortification our carriage broke down in a village, where was raging a contagious fever. We slept in clean straw in a stable. Luckily got our *voiture* repaired. Next day passed by a Palace belonging to the mother of Napoleon. The walls alone remained, it having been destroyed by the Russians. Villages entirely burnt down, and the inhabitants begging *en masse*.

May 11th. Passed the Seine at Granges. All the way to Paris for at least 50 miles is a paved road. We entered the capital of France at 8 o'clock this evening, and took up our abode at a hotel in the Rue de Richelieu. Indeed with great satisfaction did we contemplate the journey we had just performed, and only lamented having traversed such interesting countries so rapidly as we did; yet had good reason to be thankful for getting safe and sound thus far.

The three men might well feel satisfaction that they had crossed the heart of Europe, immediately after the end of twenty years of devastating war, with no worse adventures than a slight carriage accident and some overcharging on inn bills. They had rattled comfortably in their chaise through a succession of superb landscapes, which had given John Henry 'scope to romantic ideas'. His description of travelling all night in brilliant moonlight between overhanging Alpine cliffs, which re-echoed the postilion's horn, is quite a fine Mrs-Radcliffe-style piece of Romanticism, though the literary allusion which the scene evoked in him was to a work in a pre-Romantic pastoral tradition, Jean François Marmontel's libretto for Joseph Kohaut's opera, *La Bergère des Alpes*. Perhaps he had recently heard it on one of his Italian opera-going nights.

47

Ten days in Paris, among the hectic excitement of the coming and going of the Allied sovereigns and leaders, followed. John Henry and his companions managed to get into the great thanksgiving service in Notre Dame, and actually to sit next to Marshals Ney and Soult, which must have felt strange for two British officers who had been fighting the French till a month earlier. Most of the time was spent in energetic and enthralled sight-seeing.

JHS *May 12th.* Breakfast over, we sallied forth, having hired a Swiss *valet-de-chambre.* Called on Lord Aberdeen, but did not see him. The three Monarchs of Russia, Austria and Prussia are at Paris. Lord Cathcart, Castlereagh, Sir C. Stewart and Duke of Wellington were here for a few days, and gone again. We walked ourselves nearly off our legs, greatly interested and amused with all we saw. Streets generally filthy: no footpath: so that you must be always on the look out, for fear of being run over. The principal beauty of Paris seems to me to consist in the Tuileries, Louvre, the immediate environs, such as the Place Louis XV etc, The Faubourgs appear thinly inhabited.

May 13th. The Parisians are all life and gaiety: anything for a change. Foreigners of all nations and descriptions pouring in daily, particularly English. The terms granted to France have been too lenient. It is disgusting to see Talleyrand, Fouché, and a set of double-faced fellows, vehement in their oaths and declamations in favour of a dynasty they had so lately sworn to annihilate. Visited the Louvre. How beautiful, how splendid! What paintings, what statues! Divest your mind of the feeling that this magnificent collection is the work of plunder, and you are struck with delight and admiration, even allowing that France is not deficient in Artists. The regulations at Paris, with regard to National Exhibitions, are very liberal. You are admitted gratis. Guards always in attendance, and little apprehension of any mischief. Any artist may go into any gallery at stated hours, and copy. On the triumphal Arch leading to the Palace of the Tuileries are the four celebrated bronze horses taken from the Piazza di San Marco, at Venice. This evening went to the Opera, which, as well as five or six other theatres that are every night open, was full: good music, dancing, etc. I was surprised to see every Restaurateur, café, etc constantly

280

crowded. People's minds alienated and corrupted by so many years of military despotism, deeds of blood and rapine; and altho' the French appear generally to be polite, lively and frivolous, still there is still a degree of ferocity and brusquerie, which peace and time alone can do away with.

May 14th. Attended a grand religious ceremony at Notre Dame: oration, masses, for the soul of Louis XVI; the best musical performers in Paris. All the Bourbons present: the Allied Monarchs, Ambassadors, Marshals, etc. 'Twas a grand sight, and I wished much that the Duke of Wellington had been present. Capt Black and myself sat next to Ney and Soult. The religious ceremony was awful: the assemblage, dresses etc splendid. We were very glad to get back to our hotel, and put on plain cloaths, as an English Officer in Uniform was stared at as we walked the streets. We sold our carriage at a loss of only ten napoleons: very well off. Kerr went off to England. The Column in the Place Vendôme is a noble monument, erected by Napoleon. It is covered and ornamented with figures and trophies, of the feats and victories of the French Army. The Palais Royal is a handsome Square: a sink of gambling, dissipation of every description.

May 15th. Left our names at Lord Castlereagh's. Walked about in the Champs Elysées, which are shady and pleasant. This entrance to Paris by the bridge of Neuilly is a handsome approach. At 2 o'clock attended a concert of the students in music: Emperor of Austria and Prince Schwartzenberg present: several premiums awarded. In the evening Black and I generally visited a theatre.

May 16th. Took a cabriolet: went out to Malmaison. On our being announced to Josephine, she received us very cordially, tho' apparently assuming a degree of consequence, not to say Majesty, but Gracious. Three or four attendants, dressed in silk stockings, swords by their sides, etc. Black brought a letter from Prince Eugène, which Sir R. Wilson had given him at Verona; a good introduction, of which we availed ourselves. She conversed with us for a short time on the extraordinary times, praised her son, whose honour was unstained, said the Duke of Wellington was a great General; and as she knew the English were great admirers of paintings etc, showed us her galleries, where she desired we might remain as long as we liked, and wished us good morning. The house is not worth mentioning: the grounds and garden are laid out with much taste: saw a couple of black swans. It must be a delightful summer residence. Returned to Paris, making a detour thro' the Bois de Boulogne.

May 17th. Visited the Hôtel Royal des Invalides, a noble edifice with a gilt dome, and the interior admirably painted. Saw a number of aged, crippled Officers sit down to a comfortable dinner: a fine national establishment this. Walked about in the Luxembourg, a handsome quarter of Paris. We were much amused at the Restaurateurs, meeting so many well dressed and

fascinating women, with their high bonnets, calling for the *garçon*, looking over the bill of fare, ordering dinner, etc. At Grignon's we sometimes
saw twenty, some of whom had their private carriages in waiting. I always
observed the great decorum: no *grossiereté*, such as whistling, a drunken
person, keeping your hat on, etc. There are so many lures and temptations
thrown out, so much to be seen, so many amusements on cheap terms, – in
fact the French study the enjoyment and *passe-temps* of the present moment – that Paris I should think must be as dangerous a Capital to live in
as any in the World; and to see all worthy of notice in the city and environs
would require at least a month.

May 18th. Passed an hour in the King's library, where they say are 300,000
volumes. You are permitted to read any book gratis. Paid another visit to
the Venus and Apollo in the Louvre, an inexhaustible source of gratification. Had Napoleon reigned longer, he would still further have embellished
Paris, but he lost his opportunity of making peace, and remaining a great
and powerful monarch. 'Tis said the Allied Powers offered him the Rhine
as a boundary: his pride and ambition ruined him.

May 19th. Went to Versailles. The grounds, gardens, water-works etc in
good order: not so the Palace, and outhouses. The once gay theatre of
Madame de Pompadour quite in a state of dilapidation. Returned by St
Cloud: did not enter the Palace. Stopped at Sèvres, to see the famous
porcelain manufactory.

May 20th. Walked up to Montmartre. The Allies took it by storm. In a
military point of view it is of much importance. We afterwards took
carriage and went to the Castle of Vincennes. In one of the ditches was
murdered the Duc d'Enghien. Neglecting to have an order from the
Ministère de Guerre, we could not gain admission. I now thought of
wending my way towards England. I avoided the society of my countrymen, and mixed with the crowd: knew only one French family. As to the
great people they were so taken up with politics there was no coming over
them. The Musée, Jardin des Plantes, birds, beasts, etc afforded us ample
amusement for a whole day. Five couple of monkeys dancing quadrilles, a
rabbit firing off a gun, a man with one arm playing the violin, a Charlatan
giving lectures on natural philosophy, at a sou a head, attracted notice. The
police is uncommonly well regulated, and you rarely hear of a robbery.
Streets badly lighted: water publicly sold.

The only outstanding part of this ingenuous account of Paris and its character
and notable sights is the visit to Malmaison. That two obscure British officers
should have been so graciously received by the Empress Josephine at this
particular moment is astonishing. It is true that Captain Black was the bearer of
a letter from Josephine's son Eugène Beauharnais, but Prince Eugène himself
was at Malmaison by now, having come on there on 9th May after leaving his

family in Munich. He, his mother and his sister Hortense, the ex-Queen of Holland, were in deep anxiety about what position the Allied sovereigns were going to offer him. During those days of mid-May, a stream of royal visitors called at Malmaison; the Tsar of Russia was there on the 14th, and he was followed by the King of Prussia and his sons, Crown Prince Ludwig of Bavaria, and two young Russian Grand Dukes. Moreover, Josephine was increasingly ill, so much so that she could not show her royal guests round her property. On the last day of May, she died. How was it that she could find time and energy, two days after the Tsar's visit, to talk to two unknown British officers and show them round her galleries?

48

On 21st May John Henry, having parted with his companion Captain Black, and sold their shared chaise, set off by public coach, the Diligence, on his way to England. He did not take by any means the shortest way; he wanted to see as much of Europe as possible, and he wanted to visit his old friends in the 2nd Battalion of the 35th, the 'old orange facings' (the scarlet uniform of the 35th was distinguished by silver lace and orange collars and cuffs). The 2nd battalion was now stationed at Antwerp, and John Henry spent a few days there with them, and parted with his German servant Tomasi, whom he had taken on in Italy from Nugent's motley Corsican Regiment, who had been with him on his travels since then, and who had nimbly jumped out of the runaway chaise above the Adige with John Henry and Captain Black. As Tomasi was a German, it is not surprising that he deserted when left behind in Antwerp with the 35th. Presumably, like so many thousands of soldiers of every European nationality who had been conscripted and were now plodding home across Europe, he meant to make his own way back to his German home, now that he was within reach of it once more.

JHS *May 21st.* Having procured a passport, took leave of my friend, Capt Black, and started in the Diligence for Antwerp, where I expect to find our 2nd Battn. Adieu, Paris. I cannot think you will be long quiet. Your Army will soon get tired of peace, and Napoleon's party, more particularly the Military, will not easily forget their leader. As long as the Allied troops remain in France, their bayonets may enforce quiet; but when once over the frontiers, let the Bourbons look well to themselves. We were much crowded in the Diligence, 9 inside passengers, 3 in the cabriolet, and 5 on the top, besides a mountain of baggage. An unwieldy machine drawn by five horses, 2 wheelers and 3 leaders abreast. One postilion on the near wheeler drives. The horses are trained, and get on very well. Travelled all night.

May 22nd. Breakfasted at Peronne, a fortified town with extensive outworks, but in bad repair. Passed the Cambrai: no time to visit the Citadel, etc (one of Vauban's). Rained the whole day. My fellow passengers civil, but dull. Arrived at Valenciennes at 9-0 at night. Had an excellent supper, wine etc, for 4 francs. Amused by the loquacity of two

284

French Officers, who abused the Bourbons, and attributed the fall of Paris to treachery, and not to a fair trial of arms. These gentry have a rare and happy manner of reconciling and accounting for defeats, reverses, etc, ever inventing some reason, which they start with a great deal of plausibility. You hear of Marengo, Austerlitz, Lodi etc etc advanced in their arguments, but Spain, Egypt, Russia are sore subjects. Bundled into our *voiture: en route* all night: incessant rain.

May 23rd. Now got into the country of canals and dykes. Stopped at a very neat clean cabaret to breakfast. At 3 o'clock entered Brussels. General Graham and a British army were here: I was delighted at the sight of a red-coat again: stayed too short a time to see much of this fine city and its environs.

May 24th. At 3 o'clock in the morning set off to Antwerp, where I arrived at 11-0, and found the old Orange Facings. They were not at the affair of Bergen-op-Zoom.

May 25th. Traversed the town and citadel, which mounts above 900 pieces of ordnance: visited the Docks, Arsenal, etc. This was another grand depot of Napoleon's. At one time there were above 30 ships of war, an infinity of Prams, Gun-boats, etc. Here the fleet practised in the Zuyder Zee. What a beautiful river is the Scheldt: last winter was everywhere particularly severe. An English soldier was found frozen to death upright in his sentry box with his firelock in his hand. In the Duke of York's campaign (1794) a soldier's wife was frozen to death with her infant at the breast, on the roadside. My presence not being required with the 2nd Battn I stayed but a few days with my old friends. Left my servant Tomasi, who two days after deserted. He belongs to the Corsican Regt.

May 27th. At 5 o'clock p.m. started in a Diligence for Amsterdam. Arrived at Breda at 9-0; slept at a dirty Inn.

May 28th. Rose at 4 o'clock. Met with a very gentlemanlike man, a Dutch Colonel, who had been taken prisoner by the English in Batavia. An indifferent carriage, only two horses. Shortly after we started, the iron hoop came off one of the wheels, which detained us above an hour. At 10-0 o'clock reached Workum, where we crossed the water to Gorkum. This last place had been besieged and suffered much: nothing but Orange flags and cockades to be seen. Got some refreshment, then proceeded on our journey in a much better vehicle. Excellent road, paved with brick. Beautiful and extensive plains of pasturage, which with thousands of cows grazing clearly told us what a butter and cheese country we traversed. Numerous canals, so that you frequently see boats sailing along, without having a view of the water, which has a pretty effect. The neat and cleanly look of the houses is a proof of the industry of the inhabitants. At 4 o'clock reached Utrecht, where the Colonel left me. He was a pleasant companion, and was then within a short distance of his wife and family, from whom he had been separated 7 years: spoke with great feeling about his anxious meeting.

Utrecht is a nice town, and the road for about 12 miles on to Amsterdam is a continuation of woods, shrubs, water, country seats, arbours and tea-houses, so that you entirely forget you are on the high road; and the evening being particularly fine, numbers were out enjoying themselves, and on the canal was a band of music. In Brabant and here the lower class generally wear wooden shoes. Entered Amsterdam at 10 o'clock at night: eat my cutlet, smoked my pipe: rather fagged.

May 29th. Sunday morning. What a difference between this capital and Paris, where the shops are all open on the Sabbath day, as well as theatres etc. Here just the reverse. Inhabitants neatly and plainly dressed, devoutly attended their houses of worship: very few carriages to be seen, and several drawn by one horse with a kind of sledge underneath instead of wheels. The streets are well paved and clean, look more countrylike than citylike. Fine canals, with rows of trees on each side. The ladies take great delight in having reflecting glasses at the window sides, where they sit and see, themselves unseen, the passing throng. I visited the Arsenal; several Line-of-Battle ships building here also: from hence are taken to the Helder, and fitted out for sea. Being totally unacquainted, my curiosity was soon gratified. The Dutch have a peculiar boorish manner and ungracious physiognomy. I dined every day at an excellent table d'hôte, where I met the Mynheer. In the evening to a public garden.

May 30th. I was struck with the thin structure of the houses, and the great number of windows, in this fine city. Very uncomfortable with an attack of ague, which I attributed to not wearing flannel, sleeping on a ground floor, and drinking water; so I soon changed my system in every respect and soon shook it off.

May 31st. Determined to proceed on my journey, so took the packet boat to Rotterdam. Fortunately met with a pleasant companion; eat our dried salmon, smoked a pipe, and lay down in our great-coats. The Dutch sullen and sulky: cannot bear to be found fault with. We did not land at Rotter-dam before 2-0 o'clock the next day.

June 1st. Saw little or nothing of this city; crowds of English vessels in the river.

June 2nd. Started for Helvort in a packet boat with my fellow traveller. Landed some miles from it, then travelled in a covered cart or waggon: got confoundedly shaken, but arrived in good time. Bad entrance into Helvort sluice. Poor place; people not above civil. Embarked this evening in the Packet for Harwich, full of passengers: could not get a berth. Had a stormy passage, but thank God the next evening at four o'clock found myself on *terra firma*. Quickly passed my light luggage at the Custom House, and on going to the Inn, met with two brother-Officers on their way to Antwerp to join. We passed a pleasant evening. Happy was I, after the many countries I had seen, the various duties performed, the vicissitudes, risks, dangers I had experienced, long absence, to find myself in old England once more.

He had been away from England for more than six years, ever since the brief month at the beginning of 1808 when he had landed at Portsmouth from Sicily and been sent almost straight back there. Since he last saw England he had been in action in Calabria, Egypt, the Ionian Islands, the North Adriatic and Italy. He had travelled through Austria, Germany, Switzerland, France, Belgium and Holland. He had encountered Austrian generals and French marshals, Italian peasants and Swiss postilions. For more than two years he had been ruler of an island larger than the one over which Napoleon was now reduced to reign. Now he had come back to his own country, to find it superficially *en fête* over Napoleon's downfall, but reduced by the long and costly war, by over-rapid industrialisation, high prices and low wages, to conditions of starving misery for the working class, who had responded by Luddite riots. John Henry noticed little of this when he first landed, though he was to comment on it later. His chief concern was to rejoin his family as soon as possible. The strong feeling of the Dutch colonel whom he had met in Breda about his forthcoming 'anxious meeting' with the family he had not seen for so long was a mirror of John Henry's own concern. He scarcely paused in the glittering London scene of June 1814, when all the Allied leaders had arrived from Paris. He stayed in London only long enough to hear that he had been promoted, on the day of the King's Birthday, to Lieutenant-Colonel.

JHS *June 4th*. King's birthday. Started this morning in the mail for London. Here all was bustle and gaiety. The Emperor of Russia, King of Prussia seen everywhere: old Blücher in the throng, with various other public characters. Men, women and children left their homes to see the show. Proud Nation are we, who kept in motion the grand machine, until all united against the common enemy, and brought about a general peace. The Emperor of Austria did not come over, probably from political feeling, as Father to the Empress of France. I remained but a few days in the Metropolis, my dear Mother and sisters being in Ireland. Soon made my arrangements and started for Bath, where I spent a couple of days with my good Aunt Girardot and the Andrés: then proceeded by the way of Birmingham to Holyhead.

June 21st. At break of day landed at the Pigeon House, Dublin. As soon after as I could, I took a post-chaise and drove off to Stedalt, the seat of Mr Walsh, my brother-in-law and husband to my sister Sophy. Having refreshed myself at the Man-of-War Inn, about 18 miles from Dublin, I was not long in going a few miles further, and descended from my chaise at the bottom of the hill leading to the cottage of Stedalt. My heart beat as I took them all by surprise, and great indeed was our reciprocal joy and happiness at meeting after a separation of twelve years nearly. Sophy was now the mother of six children. So long a lapse of time had naturally made visible alterations in us all. My dear Mother was astonishingly well. Almost her first words were 'Thank God, I have one son left'.

49

Since March 1809, when Harriot Slessor, Harriot Amelia and the Walshes landed in London after their escape from Oporto, they had all been living in a cottage on the Walsh family estate at Stedalt, in County Meath near Balbriggan and just over twenty miles from Dublin. Harriot had helped to beguile those five more years of separation from John Henry, whom she had not seen since 1803, by editing her diary of the last troublous years in Portugal. She decided to frame it in the form of a letter to John Henry, and to incorporate a description of the family's early days at St Pedro, copies of letters from William and Henry, and an account of Henry's life and death. This task seems to have been performed, or at any rate completed, in 1813. The compilation was too long to trust to the uncertain overseas post, even if Harriot knew exactly where John Henry was in 1813, but she mentioned the project in her letters to him, and he replied that he would much like to see it. In 1813 Harriot therefore composed an explanatory address to him as a prologue to the compilation, explaining how she came to write the diary in the first place.

HS My dear Son

At any rate this is addressed to you, not as a letter, for I suspect it may turn out too long a story for that, nor as a dedication, most certainly not; as you might with no little surprise suppose me to have lost the little understanding at the best I was ever possessed of, and taken it into my head to turn Author. Do not fear; such an idea never came across me.

I must explain myself before I go further. The forlorn state in which we were placed the last year of our residence in Portugal, ours being the only English family that had the courage to remain in Porto. After the English were banish'd the country, many months passed without the possibility of our being able to hear from our friends, or our writing to them. It was a melancholy crisis, and the future prospect not less so. Time seemed to linger. By way of diversion, it seemed to me no bad idea to write something like a journal, in that way in some measure to help on the heavy hours. There was full subject for such an occupation. The pity is that an abler hand did not undertake the task.

I do not doubt, when we were safe in England, that you will have a recollection of my having mentioned in some one of my letters, that I had taken a sketch of the changes and remarkable events that had passed in that memorable year for Portugal, and not a little so for me, certainly not. The next year terminated our stay in Portugal. We only did what our countrymen performed the year before, fly the country. When I informed you of this performance, I told you that no person had seen it, nor should see it. Too well I know its defects and its insignificance. To me it is interesting: to you it may be too. I wrote you word you might peruse it, if you wished it. Your answer was, that you would like it much. But when is the time to come that we are to meet. I had flattered myself that long before this you would have been restored to the company of your dear Mother and Sisters. It is above four years that we arrived in England, and near ten years that you left us on the Packet at Falmouth. It was a melancholy parting, and never more have we met.

I began this by observing that I would not call it a letter, it being likely to be of too great a length to come under that denomination. To say the truth, I had it in my mind at the time, that I could hardly resist the inclination I have to take a review of past times, and that so far back as when you were all happy children at St Pedro. According as it turns out when finished it shall or shall not be committed to the flames.

She inserted here and there into the diary further maternal longings over her eldest son, as when she recorded William's death in India and added

HS You, my dear John, are the only son left me. I will hope you may be saved for future comfort to your affectionate mother and sister, the only companion left me.

She concluded with an epilogue which once again expressed her yearning to see John Henry again.

HS The extraordinary events of that Autumn which fixed the fate of the English in all appearance for future good prospects in Portugal, are related in my matter-of-fact account, should you think it worth the loss of time in perusing. It answered the end I proposed. In those times of anxiety and alarm, I found great relief, as well as amusement, in writing a kind of journal of events as they passed on; and likewise, with the reflection, that should we again be restored to peace and comfort either in Portugal or England, I may have it in my power to read over again, in an idle hour, the little, to me interesting account of dangers passed. Though some parts of it must revive melancholy and painful feelings, of trials indeed, the loss of those most dear to me, as well as all of you, yet I should remember many happy days, and be thankful.

We must now look forward and hope that a happy meeting is not far distant, and that you will soon be restored to an affectionate Mother and Sister. And may the heavens protect you in all risks you may be exposed to, of loss of existence, or not to return with a leg or arm less, is the constant prayer of your affectionate parent.

Now, a year later, in June 1814, they were all at last reunited – John Henry, Harriot, Harriot Amelia, Sophia and James Walsh and their six surviving children, William, John, Henry George, Harriot Jane, Jane Wilhelmina and Sophia Louisa, none of whom John Henry had ever seen. (It is quite a surprise, among the endlessly repetitive Christian names which the Slessors gave to their children, generation after generation, to come across a Wilhelmina, even as a second name and as the female version of the name of that far-off brother in India who had died so tragically three years before this niece's birth. This Jane Wilhelmina was to grow up into a 'ravishing blonde', tender-hearted, unintellectual but a good musician, and to marry Thomas Dobrée, the richest man in Nantes.) The reunited family only had three months together. John Henry's diary explains what happened.

JHS Contrary to my hopes and expectations, our social and domestic life was quickly broken in upon. My brother-in-law became involved by the failure of a commercial house in Dublin, and his health so alarmingly decayed, that the Physician decidedly declared that remaining in Ireland would be his death. This was a trying moment to us all, but necessity has no law. A vessel was quickly hired in Dublin to convey the family to the South of France. The establishment was as speedily broken up, and I witnessed the distressing scene of parting with my dear sister and her nice children, and waving our handkerchiefs as long as the little barque was to be seen.

My mother and Sister Harriot remained but a short time in Ireland, which I rather regretted, wishing to pay visits to some of my old friends.

John Henry, his mother and Harriot Amelia spent the winter of 1814-5 in a pleasant round of sight-seeing, theatres and visits to friends and relations. Their London base was with Harriot's sister Catherine, widow of General Fraser, in Edward Street, but another and dearer aunt, Louisa Girardot, was claiming them to make their home in Bath with her and the André sisters, and there they all arrived on New Year's Day 1815. Their Bath gaieties did not altogether blind John Henry's eyes to the unsettled state of the country, but all war, including the war with America, had now ceased, the Congress of Vienna was settling the new map of Europe, and the horizon ahead looked bright.

JHS *Sep 21st.* Embarked at Dublin, on board a Liverpool packet. Had a prosperous voyage, fine weather and pleasant companions. Two musicians occasionally played beautiful Irish melodies. The distant views of the Welsh mountains were very grand, altho' not to be compared to those of the Wicklow mountains on entering the Bay of Dublin. It was on a Sunday morning we sailed into Liverpool, and all hands were delighted with the splendid and rich variety of the entrance into one of the most enterprising cities in the World. With the kind assistance of an Oporto friend, Mr Van Zeller, who was expecting us, we quickly passed our luggage at the Custom House, and established ourselves at a good Inn. We stayed three days, and visited everything worth seeing. The Institution for the Blind was extremely curious and well conducted. By easy stages we traversed highly cultivated counties, Leicester, Northampton, etc, and on our arrival at the Capital, occupied good Aunt Fraser's house in Edward Street, Portman Square. We now commenced a round of visits, the first to old Oporto friends, Mrs Nash's family in Richmond, Mr and Mrs Weston at Cobham in Surrey. My sister and I took a trip to Brighton, one of the Royal residences. Frequently we went to Drury Lane and Covent Garden. Kean and Miss O'Neill were great attractions. Mornings and evenings were passed in pleasuring. Mr Beeston Long at Croydon, Lady Neave at Dagenham, Sir Thomas Neave at Hampstead, all received us most cordially, and the variety was charming. In December we meditated our journey to Bath, as Aunt Girardot expressed uneasiness at our absence.

30th Dec. Quitted the Capital.

31st Dec. Obliged to sleep at Devizes, owing to a heavy fall of snow.

Jan 1st 1815. Drove up in good style with four horses to Marlboro' Buildings, Bath. The good old lady seemed delighted to see us. Gaieties of all kinds going on, and invitations without end: old and young carried away in the general vortex. Peace with America. Sad riots in London, caused by the Corn Bill. There is an old adage, war abroad, peace at home, now reversed. Sad work after 25 years of suffering and taxation; but we live in an age replete with wonderful events.

50

JHS *Mar 1st.* The political horizon was clearing, when all at once, as if by magic, Napoleon escapes from the Island of Elba, with a few chosen and faithful followers: lands at Fréjus, advances to Lyons, is joined by the very troops who marched to oppose him, and who had recently sworn allegiance to Louis XVIII. Enters Paris without the shedding of blood, the Bourbons having fled. How well did he concert his plans, and how devoted must the Army have been to their old leader. Now will the Allies lament their mistaken lenity, their magnanimous treatment to a treacherous people. 'Twill prove a dearly bought lesson, and should Fortune again put Paris in the possession of her enemies, I trust they will make her smart. In vain have torrents of blood been shed: in vain have treaties been made, England lavished millions, sacrificed her sons in all quarters of the Globe, loaded her subjects with taxes. Still I trust the day of retribution is not far distant, and that all hands will cordially join with heart and soul, so as to ensure a permanent and general peace. The English are returning from France, with all speed, fearful of another sojourn at Verdun. All Officers ordered to join; so Adieu, dear Mother and Sister. May we meet again.
March 1815. How uncertain and inscrutable are human events, how restless the inhabitants of this world. At the moment when everybody thought a general peace was established on a solid basis, the ambitious and bloodthirsty Bonaparte again opens the temple of Janus, and lucky for Europe that he did return at this period; for a few months later, and the Allied Armies would have been too far removed to act in concert with that energy and promptitude which the awful crisis required. But most probably Bonaparte apprehended a discovery of his plans, so thought delay dangerous, and his case desperate. Capt Usher R.N. and Sir Neil Campbell were supposed to have a lookout.

These diary entries, though dated March 1815, sound as if they had been retrospectively adjusted by John Henry in a later and more pontifical mood. The first entry is dated 1st March – the date on which Napoleon landed at Golfe Juan after his escape from Elba – but covers his triumphal entry into Paris on 26th March. When the news of Napoleon's escape reached the Allied leaders at the Congress of Vienna on 8th March, and then they heard of his welcome at

Grenoble and Lyon, his rapturous reception in Paris and the flight of the newly restored Louis XVIII, they began at once to recall their armies and raise a million men to mass on the Rhine. England produced a subsidy of £11 million and 40,000 troops from England, with another 40,000 raised from Belgium and Hanover, the whole 80,000 to be based in Flanders under the command of Wellington. Throughout April British reinforcements gradually assembled and crossed the Channel. Among the recalled officers was John Henry, who rejoined the 35th 2nd battalion at Ostend. The battalion had landed in Holland in December 1813 with Sir Thomas Graham's force, and had remained there (though not taking part in the disastrous operation against Bergen-op-Zoom) till hostilities ended with Napoleon's abdication in March 1814. John Henry had visited them in Antwerp in May 1814 on his way home on leave. They had moved to Ostend, and were waiting to be sent home and disbanded, when Napoleon's escape from Elba gave them a chance of action and honour instead of disbandment and half-pay.

JHS I lost no time in setting off to rejoin my regiment. In London the public mind was indeed in a feverish state, particularly when it had been officially made known that Bonaparte had quickly kicked out the Bourbons, and again settled himself on the throne of France, a grand event in the pages of history. I proceeded to Ramsgate, where I took the Packet for Ostend. A few hours wafted us to our destination.

Mar 29th. The Regiment had marched to this place on its return towards England, previous to being disbanded. How unexpected a change! All now looked forward with anxious hope to active service, promotion and honours. Bustle and activity prevail in every department: more troops arrive daily from England. I saw the ill-fated Louis XVIII get into his carriage with a very humble retinue indeed. His first intention was to have taken refuge in our favoured isle, but he now went to Ghent. He exclaimed to the Guard of Honour, and the numerous Officers who were present, 'I am happy to surround you all' (meaning to be surrounded by us all), 'happy and envied Nation'.

Our Engineers have some thousand men at work on the fortifications, which will soon be in a respectable state. Fort Napoleon is a beautiful French work. Every house is thronged with Military. The harbour's entrance is narrow and dangerous, coast bad, sandy and ugly. The Mynheers and Vrouws are civil, but in a melancholy state; naturally enough; trade is at a standstill, their future fate doubtful.

Apr 8th. Orders to be in readiness to march at a moment's notice.

Apr 10th. This evening embarked in canal boats for Bruges, leaving women and heavy baggage behind. I had no time to see this city, but heard a favourable report of it. The regiment having been quartered here, no soldier allowed to go on shore. Arrived at Ghent next night. Early on the morning of the 13th landed, and immediately marched to Oudenarde; consequently had no opportunity of exploring this fine populous city, well worth the traveller's notice. At Ghent the last treaty of peace with America was ratified. The country now wears a beautiful appearance, highly cultivated and fertile. The Duke of Marlboro' fought over this ground. Here again the Engineers are at work. I have a most comfortable billet in the Hospital Convent. Mrs Long, the Lady Abbess, is an Englishwoman. I shall ever remember her kindness. She was educated at Brussels, but early in life changed her religion, and for many years has dedicated her time to the service and comfort of her fellow-creatures. In most towns in this country there are similar Institutions, which are obliged to maintain the poor; but in the late wars and revolutions, they were also forced to receive sick and wounded soldiers. The French appointed Committees to watch over the revenue and expenditure, of which great complaints were made, for no doubt the French Agents lined their pockets pretty handsomely.

John Henry and the 35th spent a few days in Oudenarde, where he was comfortably established in the 15th century Hôpital Notre-Dame, a convent of the Bernardines Order. Oudenarde was the headquarters of a division commanded by General Colville, elements of which were to be deployed along a front stretching from Nieuport on the Channel to Courtrai. On 16th April the 35th were moved from Oudenarde to Courtrai, where they remained for the next two months, flanked on the left by Wellington's main line between Ath and Nivelles, with Blücher's Prussians beyond them, while Napoleon with his newly raised army of 250,000 men moved up to the Sambre.

John Henry, who generally managed to get himself quartered in pleasant lodgings and to be on good terms with his hosts, had a particularly congenial landlord in Courtrai, with whom he talked, walked and drank. He quoted with satisfaction what was presumably his landlord's contrasting description of the alert readiness of the British troops and the dead-alive sloth of the average *'bonne compagnie'* who 'linger idly in bed till the sun has moved half across the sky, who can't either sleep or get out of bed, who lose so many precious hours in this half-way house between life and death, and yet who complain that life is too short'.

During these weeks of inactivity, John Henry managed to ride about much of the country round Courtrai, and even as far as Ostend, and to turn an observant eye on the Belgian way of life. He also, as he saw Wellington, Colville and Blücher reviewing the troops, meditated on the realities of war and army life, the crushing responsibilities of military commanders, so little understood by the public at home.

JHS *April 16th*. Sudden march to Courtrai. I with regret parted from the old
  ladies. This is without exception the highest cultivated country I ever saw;

universal verdure and vegetation. The neatness and cleanliness with which every spot is kept quite astonished me. Corn, flax, rape, clover, etc is truly luxuriant. These are poor people, but no wretchedness: the country thickly inhabited: the houses and cottages neat and clean: people orderly and industrious. This town is not fortified. The Duke of Wellington and Lord Hill are appointed to the army. Our Brigade now consists of the 54th, 59th, 91st, 2nd Battn 35th. I found the natives very civil, and am a member of a Société Littéraire, where I see all newspapers. Everything portends hot work. Fulsome addresses to Bonaparte, professing the enthusiasm of the troops, attachment of the French Nation, etc, and much stress is laid on the wish that England is averse to war, that a good understanding exists between France and Austria; but at the same time feels it his duty to make unavoidable preparations, lest the territory of the Grande Nation should be violated. Many French Royalist deserters, Officers and men, cross the frontier and join Louis at Ghent. Should we gain anything like a general action in the onset, another Revolution may be as rapid as the last, altho' of a very different nature. At all events the preponderating and imposing Mass of Allies must ultimately succeed, and I should not be at all surprised if we enter France by the King's birthday. The Prussians are strong on our left, and the Army under Wellington will soon be formidable. The French are equally active along the frontier and in the interior.

Apr 19th. Rode to Menin. Our Sentries and French within musket shot.

Apr 20th. Went over to Ostend (crowded with troops) thro' Roeselare and Torhout; returned the next day to quarters. 'Tis melancholy this fine country should be devastated by war; still they have ever been subject to its horrors, and 'twould fill volumes to describe the different actions and sieges. At Courtrai indeed the inhabitants appear quite indifferent about the matter. The Belgians, I am told, are indefatigable in cultivating their land after it has been laid waste by contending Armies, and will immediately set to work to repair damages. Labourers' wages I should suppose are low. I often see 50 or 60 men and women weeding a field, merry and happy, singing: generally say that it is their interest to belong to France, but abuse Bonaparte.

May 1st. Not a shot fired yet. Our time passes pleasantly enough: very good friends with the inhabitants, who in general speak French. They have neither the heavy, reserved manner and air of the Dutch, nor the versatility of the French.

May 10th. Rode to Ypres. The Cathedral is worth seeing. Roads all paved, thro' long avenues of trees, extremely tedious. I also visited Tournai: a citadel built by Vauban is under repair. The town looked wretched and poor. In one respect a fortunate epoch for the King of Holland. Our presence and our money will repair his fortresses and organize his Army.

May 28th. Wellington and Blücher have reviewed the British Cavalry and Artillery: a splendid turn out. Blücher said he had only one complaint to make, and that was that such fine troops did not belong to himself. All communication is now cut off with France. The tug of war commences. We are under arms every morning at daylight, and always on the *'qui vive'*. *'Pas comme la bonne compagnie qui languit dans un lit oiseux Jusqu'à le soleil ait fait la moitié de son tour, qui ne peut ni dormir ni se lever, qui perd tant d'heures precieuses dans cet état moyen entre la vie et le mort, et qui se plaint que la vie est trop courte.'*
May 31st. In La Vendée the Royalists begin to shew themselves, but the public are assured that the rebels will speedily be crushed by an army already marching against them. In the Department du Nord the people are said to be generally averse to Napoleon, but from the Capital and many provinces he receives support. As usual in his addresses to the Army, at public Fêtes etc, he fixes upon the anniversary of such battles as Marengo, Austerlitz. etc.

Good news for the Allies from Italy provoked a robust comment from John Henry. Murat, King of Naples, had – in spite of his desertion of Napoleon to join the Allies in 1814 – kept in touch with him on Elba, and when he escaped, Murat decided to change sides again, and led his Neapolitan army to attack the Austrians, but was soundly defeated on 3rd May at the Battle of Tolentino. He was now a fugitive with a price on his head, and five months later he was to be captured after a desperate hand-to-hand fight, court-martialled and shot. John Henry, who remembered the dashing figure of Murat on horseback outside Parma, could not help thinking that, misguided as he might be, he had made a better King of Naples that the Bourbon Ferdinand who would now be restored.

JHS *June 1st*. The die is cast, the fate of Napoleon decided. Naples to begin with is in the possession of the Austrians. Seldom have the Austrians shewn so much energy and promptitude, or a kingdom in so short a time been completely upset. My friend Count Nugent gained deserved laurels. Murat, blockhead as he was, had he remained faithful to the Allies, might have continued King probably. He had done more for the Neapolitans than ever a Bourbon had head to accomplish, a Re-de-Macaroni. They will now return to priesthood, corruption and imbecility, such as in the time of Lady Hamilton. A grand mistake to suppose that the same old dynasty is good policy, under the existing Revolutions of Kings and States.
June 4th. Celebrated our good old King's Birthday with much conviviality, as the whole garrison dined together. A speedy sight of the enemy was drunk in bumpers of champagne. My prognostic of being at Paris on this day was premature.

June 8th. The Duke of Wellington, and Sir G. Colville have reviewed us: the latter commands our Division, Major General Johnson our Brigade. The greatest energy prevails in all ranks. The enemy are concentrating at Laon.

June 12th. We, however, amuse ourselves as usual. All articles of living are most abundant and reasonable. My landlord, Mons. Durgs, shews me the greatest attention. Walking with him one evening, in a beautiful garden, I copied the following, from a figure of Cupid, with his finger to his mouth, as if imposing silence

> *Sous ce feuillage, Cupidon*
> *Semble prescrire le silence.*
> *Mais fuyez le petit fripon:*
> *C'est à vous, peut-être, qu'il pense.*

[Beneath these boughs, Cupid seems to enjoin silence, but flee from the little rogue, perhaps it is you that he has in mind.]

Archery is a favourite amusement in this country: at the cross-bow they are very expert. A large ballot of recruits is going on in Belgium, and as soon as drawn, are marched off towards Holland, and the Dutch troops brought forward. This looks rather suspicious. We may find men here who served in the French army in Spain.

June 14th. Fine weather for campaigning. Little do our friends in England know the sufferings and privations of a military life on active service; the wounded, the sick, the arrangements necessary for the transport of ammunition: often want of cloathing, shoes, irregular issue of provisions, difficulty of cooking, forage, etc, etc: movements of large bodies of men, nature of ground for attack and defence, knowledge of the enemy's force: strength of fortified towns, forts or batteries: roads, rivers, storming, medical department: often want of water, strictest attention to discipline, etc. For such, with many other incidental circumstances, is the Commander-in-Chief responsible to his country. The people in England read in the papers of a battle, killed and wounded, with as much sang froid as they do of a ball or rout, little thinking what a head it requires for a Commander-in-Chief to sacrifice with judgment the lives of thousands of his fellow creatures.

June 15th. News of the French appearing on the Sambre, My landlord thinks Bonaparte will first attack the Prussians, and mastering them, that the British will be an easy conquest. May he be disappointed in both instances. Bonaparte has taken the field; but we have the greatest confidence in Wellington, being personally opposed to Napoleon (what he has long wished for) will rouse the energies and military talents of the two great rivals to their zenith.

51

On 16th June came the great moment for which the Allied Armies had been waiting. The French advanced from Charleroi towards Fleurus, scene of many historic battles. Napoleon fell on the Prussians under Blücher at Ligny and drove them back towards Wavre with heavy losses. Ney attacked Wellington at Quatre-Bras, in a ferocious engagement in which Ney failed to break the British infantry line, but Wellington had to withdraw as his left flank was now exposed by the Prussian retreat to Wavre. He fell back on Waterloo, only twelve miles from Brussels.

The 35th were still at Courtrai, on the right flank of the British forces, on the 16th, but on that morning they received orders to move. John Henry's rather wild shots at Belgian place-names make their route difficult to determine. He says they marched to Oudenarde, Grammont and Mons, finishing up in Tubize. Mons is many miles to the south of their possible route, which was probably through Oudenarde, Grammont, and Halle or Enghien to Tubize.

JHS *June 16th*. This morning at 9 o'clock received orders to march. At 11-0 we were clear out of the town, accompanied by crowds of the inhabitants, wishing us success. Much conjecture on this sudden move: some thought we were retreating, and fearful that they might be left a prey to a merciless enemy: others that we were going out to battle. I shook hands with my landlord: took a parting glass of curaçao. He was a clever man: passionate admirer of Voltaire. This day was extremely warm. Passed through Oudenarde: eat a hurried dinner with Mrs Long. Heavy rain at night, and the men much fagged.

June 17th. Waited for a few hours at a small village; heard of yesterday's disasters on the well known plains of Fleurus: a bad beginning, bloody work indeed. The general idea was that Bony would have awaited the attack of the Allies; but he came on with his usual confidence and impetuosity, probably rather unexpectedly on our part. Brussels in great consternation. This successful onset greatly raised the spirits of the enemy, and animated their partizans in Belgium. Bonaparte felt naturally elated: immediately crossed the Sambre, and is said to have exclaimed '*Je tiens donc ces Anglais*' [So I've got these English in my hands]. We were now pretty well aware of the hard blows awaiting us, and ready and determined

to return them with interest. Our Division marched on thro' Grammont and
Mons.

Early on the morning of the 18th took up a position at the village of
Tubize, on the extreme right of the Army. Remained under arms the whole
of the day and night: heard firing at intervals, but ignorant of what was
going on.

Throughout the fateful day of 18th June, Colville's 4th Division, which included the 35th, was kept waiting at Halle and Tubize, with orders to defend
Halle. During the night of the 17th/18th General Colville had sent Colonel
Woodford to Wellington to ask for further orders, but the reply came back that
it was now too late for the Division at Halle to move up to join the main force at
Waterloo. Military historians have expressed surprise that Wellington left a
force of 16,000 men idle at Halle, instead of calling them up over the short
distance to Waterloo during the desperate to-and-fro struggle on the 18th. John
Henry attributed Wellington's decision to his expectation that Napoleon would
try to turn the right flank of his line, and cut him off from Brussels. But it was a
crushing disappointment to the 4th Division to have been kept idly waiting at
Halle and Tubize while the great battle was going on a few miles away.

JHS At daybreak on the 19th moved to some heights, and at the moment we
were relieving a Dutch Battalion, Sir Charles Colville rode up and ordered
us to give three cheers. We had heard cheering a few minutes before, and
thought the enemy were coming on. Judge of our surprise, our chagrin,
when he told us of yesterday's battle, that Bonaparte was beaten, totally
routed, had lost 200 pieces of cannon, and the English Army covered itself
with glory and honour. We gave three cheers, 'tis true, but cursed our
unlucky stars at not having been under fire. Had we not halted at Tubize,
where it was evident that the Duke expected that the enemy would attempt
to turn his right, we should have been in the thick of the action about 4
o'clock. Saving broken heads is a poor recompense for not sharing in the
laurels of such a glorious day. We immediately moved on to Nivelles, and
here joined the main body of the Army. As Regiments met or passed each
other, you yet observed the bloody enthusiasm, the military ardour glowing in the soldier's countenance, proud of his country, his regiment, and
himself, tho' deeply lamenting the fall of many a gallant comrade, and
anxiously enquiring for a friend or relation. When did so decisive or hard
fought a battle take place? The French Cavalry behaved nobly, but were as
nobly repulsed by our infantry. Our heavy Dragoons distinguished themselves, but naturally our loss has been very severe. The great Captain was
indefatigable, and 'tis said that Napoleon made great personal exertions;
but when he saw the day turning against him, he harangued his Garde
Imperiale, entreated, cursed, cried, and at last, fearful of being taken

prisoner, exlaimed: – 'It is time to save ourselves. *Sauve qui peut'*. After which he was no more seen. The Elite of the French Army, his faithful adherents, in complete deroute and dismay. The day of retribution is at hand. We shall be Masters of Paris, and the French Nation will awake from their dream.

That the Army under Wellington had beat off the enemy before the Prussians came, there is no doubt; but that we could have followed up our success, or even kept our ground, I think is quite uncertain. Therefore the timely appearance of Marshal Blücher decided the business. Never was a battle contested by such a mass of men in so small a space of ground. To describe the field on the morning of the 19th would extract tears and sympathy from a heart of stone. Many a Frenchman in the agonies of death uttered with his last breath *'Vive l'Empereur'*.

As John Henry was unable to give an eye-witness account of the great battle he had missed, he later padded out his diary with what purported to be a blow-by-blow account by someone who had been at Napoleon's side throughout. He quotes several pages of the colourful story of a Flemish eye-witness whom he refers to as Lacoste. This is clearly the notorious Jean Decoster, the peasant who claimed to have been forced to act as Napoleon's guide throughout the Battle of Waterloo. Decoster seems to have been variously known to his contemporaries as Da Costa, d'Accoste or Lacoste. Walter Scott, who visited the field of Waterloo in 1815, two months after the battle, and talked to Decoster, called him Da Costa in his earliest account of the conversation, Lacoste in his *Life of Napoleon Bonaparte*, and Decoster in later editions of *Paul's Letters to His Kinsfolk*. This last, published in 1816, contains a detailed account, 'Relation of what was done and said by Napoleon Bonaparte in the course of the 18th of June 1815; during and after the Battle of Waterloo:- Drawn up from the Deposition of Jean Baptiste Da Coster' which was clearly the source that John Henry quoted; he reproduces it almost word for word, though with some omissions. It is odd that John Henry did not reveal his sources, simply introducing the narrative into his diary with the preliminary sentence: 'The following narrative is said to be correct.'

In fact it was anything but correct. Decoster, whom Scott described as a 'shrewd simple man', was more shrewd than simple; he made up the whole story. He was soon afterwards proved to have been safely in hiding, miles away, during the whole battle, and never to have been near Napoleon; but this did not stop him from earning his living for the rest of his days as a guide to the battlefield, and telling his anecdotes over and over again to whomsoever would listen. He became the Ancient Mariner of the Field of Waterloo, stopping visitors by holding them with his glittering eye so that he could teach his tale. His descriptions of what Napoleon did and said on that day are so vivid that it is a great pity they are not true. I have not included this fictional narrative as quoted by John Henry, as the original is well known from Walter Scott's use of it.

Though the 35th had no share in the glories of Waterloo, they joined the main body of the Army at Nivelles next day, and with them advanced into France, took part in the storming of Cambrai, and forged ahead to Chantilly and St Denis. John Henry's diary quotes the texts of Wellington's proclamation to the French people as he crossed the frontier, and of Napoleon's address to the Assembly in Paris eleven days before Waterloo, promising constitutional monarchy, financial reform and the defeat of the Allied kings who were jealous of French independence and wished to humiliate France. John Henry was contemptuous of this effusion.

JHS All rational people must see the duplicity and unsatisfactory tenor of this address, but Napoleon well knew the character of the French Nation; no one had studied it with better effect, and knew better how to humour their caprices.

On the 21st we broke French ground, with three cheers, on passing the line of demarcation. The Duke of Wellington rode thro' the Army, and was repeatedly cheered. A lively demonstration of joy and pride was displayed thro'out all ranks, along a line of march extending many miles. We trust the French will once more give us battle, which will be their dying speech, their last effort. Some people are sanguine enough to believe that no more blood will be spilt, as the Allies are entering France at all points with an overwhelming force.

23rd. Entered Coteau, and were well received by the inhabitants. A great number of French soldiers remained in this town. Loud complaints of the conduct of Napoleon's Army, who in their retreat committed every excess, thereby even more dreadful to their own country than an invading army.

From Coteau our Division proceeded towards Cambrai. Here the tri-coloured flag was still flying, nor would Monsieur le Commandant listen to terms. On the morning of the 24th the Duke of Wellington came to reconnoitre, and without hesitation ordered the place to be taken by storm. Every arrangement and preparation being made, the different columns moved forward to the assault, preceded by the forlorn hope with scaling ladders etc. We soon succeeded in getting into the town, and drove the French into the Citadel, (lost one officer and 28 men) on which they capitulated to Louis the XVIIIth, who entered the town the day following. After the Battle of Waterloo this unfortunate Monarch kept in the rear of the British Army, guarded by his Maison, or Household troops, and a few Volunteers. Our grand object was to follow up the blow of the 18th, and not lose time in besieging strongholds, but march on Paris without delay. On entering Cambrai it was singular to see many soldiers of the 91st shaking hands with the inhabitants. Some of this fine regiment had been a long time prisoners there.

We now experienced very warm weather, from which the troops suffered much. Many men were left behind. Nothing could restrain them from drinking water, even muddy and stagnated, so powerfully does thirst act upon the human frame. The Cavalry and Artillery passing quickly by the Infantry almost suffocated them. The few natives we saw gazed at us as we passed along, little expecting so sudden a change, and rarely did they vociferate '*Vive le Roi*' tho' many officers hoisted the White Lily. In the Department du Nord the inhabitants were generally supposed to be Royalists. We bivouacked in the fields; the Generals and their Staffs occupied villages, farmhouses etc; but we never experienced want of provisions or forage. Sometimes indeed the troops had barely time to cook their rations. In this essential art the French soldiers are very expert, quickly making their soup with a bit of fat, bread and vegetables.

29th June. Crossed the Oise. Some parts of the country were beautiful enough, but nothing to compare with the richness of Belgium, in cultivation, vegetation or comforts and industry of the inhabitants.

30th June. Entered Chantilly. Spacious stables are the only remains of these once magnificent Royal edifices. As we approached Paris, the work of devastation became more apparent, for the conduct of the Prussians differed widely from that of the British Army.

1st July. We this day had a most severe march, but to the joy of all, Paris was in sight. The Prussians after some skirmishing had established themselves before the French lines under Montmartre, taken the village of Vertrui etc. They received us with hearty cheers. We immediately relieved them, when they filed off to the right. Blücher crossed the Seine, by which movement Paris became invested on two sides, and after some fighting they got possession of Versailles, Sèvres etc. The two blockading Armies were in constant communication.

On the 3rd a cessation of hostilities was agreed upon, and shortly after the Convention of Paris followed. It was reported that at the Battle of Waterloo, the French Lancers, seeing a wounded Prussian, would ride up to him exclaiming, '*Quoi, tu n'est pas mort*' [What, you aren't dead!] and immediately thrust his lance into him. With no less revengeful cruelty did the Prussians often retaliate. Every house was ransacked and plundered: not an inhabitant to be seen. But the moment the British troops appeared, confidence was restored, the wounded French crept out of their hiding places. A singular instance occurred in the Church of Vertrui, where the Prussians had been. One of our Artillery Officers was led there by curiosity. Near where the altar once stood, he perceived something moving in the straw, and a wounded Frenchman with an outstretched hand held up some money, supposing that this offer might save him from the salutation of a Prussian bayonet; but in a faint voice suddenly exclaimed, '*Bon Dieu, vous êtes Anglais!*' [Good God, you're English!] He died that evening.

July 5th. The Convention is signed, and the Duke of Wellington is in Paris. We shall be put in immediate possession of Montmartre, Barriers, etc. The remains of the French Army retire to the Loire, much reduced by desertion. Marched to St Denis.

The hour of retaliation is come, and with whatever feelings of resentment we regard the provocation, when the innocent as well as the guilty must alike suffer, I cannot witness the present wonderful era without some emotion of compassion. At Cambrai Sir C. Colville gave out an unprecedented order, that no Officer should enter the town without a passport. Here he repeated it and the troops were bivouacked outside St Denis. Too severe, for no Army could behave with better order or more discipline. Hardly an instance did I witness, or even hear of, in this severe march. Vegetables alone were taken, and that by authority, and how could it be otherwise, when we were bivouacked in fields and gardens full of them, the Artillery and Cavalry often in cornfields. I never heard of a fowl or duck even having been taken from a farmyard without payment. The word *Barbari* the French could not apply to us. Most fortunate was it that Paris was saved, much to the disappointment of the Prussians and many others. No pen would have been equal to describe the scene had storming been decided on. Fatal are even the consequences often to a victorious army. To an English soldier, who is at all times ruled with the greatest strictness, any relaxation of discipline is particularly dangerous. We had an instance after the storming of Ciudad Rodrigo. Some English soldiers, who commenced plundering, were checked by their officers, and immediately answered, that they had taken the place and had a right to do what they pleased with it.

Grouchy and Vandamme, the former intact, had effected a more regular retreat, and somewhat strengthened by the wrecks of the main body, were ready to defend Paris. But the National Guards refused, and the mock government also very wisely opposed the measure. The Duke of Wellington, in concert with Blücher, was the law-giver. The Russians and Austrians had not yet appeared, but were coming up in great force.

July 6th. Crowds of Parisians, National Guards, etc came out to meet their imbecile – tho' rightful sovereign. They gazed with astonishment at our troops. '*L'Artillerie, la Cavallerie! Ma foi! sont superbes.*' Our Highlanders they termed *Sans Culottes*; but all was gaiety and novelty. For the moment they forgot themselves; but bitter were their feelings on reflection that *La grande nation* was humbled.

52

John Henry and the 35th spent the next two months encamped in the Bois de Boulogne, but enjoying the pleasures of life in Paris combined with racing at St Denis and shooting at Arpajon. He took part in Louis XVIII's processional entry into Paris, and in numerous subsequent reviews of the British and Allied Armies, at which he saw the Emperor Alexander of Russia and the King of Prussia, who arrived in Paris three days after the British and Prussians entered Paris on 7th July. John Henry made some telling comparisons between the armies of the four main Allies. He was under no illusions about the feelings of the French, whatever their superficial signs of welcome to the Bourbon restoration. In many ways he felt more sympathy with the brave soldiers of the defeated army than with the emigrés who now came flocking back behind the Allied armies, clamouring for vengeance on their own compatriots. He could see that men like Colonel Labedoyère, who had taken his whole regiment over to join Napoleon in the Hundred Days, and who had come back to Paris in disguise to see his wife and been denounced by his former valet, should perhaps be made an example of, but he was doubtful about the legality of the trials and executions of the 'White Terror' in Paris after the restoration of the Bourbons, and shocked by the bloodthirsty actions of the Prussian army of occupation, whatever the injuries by the French armies which the Prussians were now revenging.

JHS *7th July.* The Army encamped and bivouacked in the Bois-de-Boulogne, Champs Elysées etc. Here was a gay, glittering scene, formidable and imposing. Anyone having predicted such an event some years ago would have been stamped a madman.

8th July. I rode into Paris this morning, passed by Vendôme. Napoleon's flag was still up. At the Tuileries the National Guards wore the tricoloured cockade, the iron gates were shut. About then Louis entered his Capital by the gate of St Denis. All was as if by magic changed to white. Every house, every window was crowded to excess: white flags with the lily, white handkerchiefs waving: '*Vive le Roi*', '*Vive Wellington*', '*Vive les Anglais*' rent the air. Such apparent joy, such enthusiasm! The streets were passable alone to the procession. I for a long time accompanied the King's carriage. The women held out their hands to me: I saw many in tears. The House-

hold troops and Royalists who had joined him at Ghent formed his escort.
National Guards lined the streets. Many English officers thro' curiosity
joined the procession. No Allied troops assisted, but a tottering throne
indeed must that Monarch sit on, who requires foreign bayonets to place
him on it, and such was the case here. Louis after the battle was generally a
day's march in the rear of the Army.

After a good dinner and a bottle of champagne, returned to my quarters,
meditating on the changes and chances of this mortal life, and the character of the French people. Now will the Allied Sovereigns be convinced that
there was more magnanimity than wisdom or sound policy shewn towards
France last year. 'Tis to be hoped now they will all establish political
matters on a sound basis, beginning by an immense requisition, sufficient
to pay all the expenses of the campaign, exclusive of provisions, forage,
clothing etc.

10th July. The Emperor of Russia and King of Prussia are arrived. Baron
Huffling appointed Governor of Paris. Where is *la gloire nationale* flown
to?

11th July. The French Army ask for terms. All fighting is over, altho' some
places still hold out, refusing to surrender to a foreign force; at the same
time wishing to make peace with their lawful King. The great attachment
of the Army *(to Napoleon)* time alone can eradicate, and very naturally.
They desired not a peaceful King, a Cochon or religious head, as they
called a Bourbon, but war conquest and plunder, to which they had been
accustomed. Nursed from their cradles with military ideas, the youths at
the Lycée were clad in uniforms and cocked hats; word of command and
beat of drum, told them that the profession of arms was the only road to
glory. All public functionaries, custom house, police, etc were military.
Soldiers from the ranks were personally noticed by Bonaparte, and promoted for gallant conduct to commissions. Then came those people who
had purchased confiscated properties of the emigrés, fearful of their restoration to their proper owners, dreading the return of the extravagance and
hauteur of a Bourbon dynasty. The prevalent opinion among the French is
that the English, jealous of the flourishing state of France, a country
always their rival, permitted Bonaparte to quit Elba, well knowing that he
had a strong party at command; and were anxious to foment a civil war,
and so bring down on their heads the whole vengeance of the Allied
Powers.

The Army of the Loire is now disbanded, a grand object gained for the
Royalists, so that we have the French pretty hard in hand, I think. Paris and
the environs form a splendid and formidable scene. Scarcely a day passes
without a review. Thirty or forty thousand men assemble, march and
countermarch, with as much facility as a regiment of Guards in Hyde Park.
The Russians are sturdy fine-looking soldiers, well appointed, not tall,

uniform generally green. The French call them *Cornichons*. Formidable train of artillery: cuirassiers look well. Alexander very fond of military parade and shew. Few Cossacks are seen. They cut a singular figure in sheepskins. These last are nicknamed *Les Cupidons du Nord*.

The Prussians troops are chiefly dressed in blue, younger-looking men, and fair. They disfigure themselves much by drawing their waists tight, and stuffing out their breasts. Many officers they say wear stays. They are now well cloathed (at French expense), and appear in good order when on parade or reviewing, but licentious dogs in quarters or on the march. The Landwehr, or Militia, are the most inveterate. This cannot be wondered at, for they personally suffered the greatest enormities from the French troops in their own country. Blücher, the French tell you, frequents the gambling houses, and if unsuccessful next morning levies an additional contribution.

The Austrian troops are not so numerous. Their operations have been carried on more in the South of France, Italy and Naples. Uniform principally white. The Imperial Guards are fine-looking men. Hungarian Cavalry excellent soldiers: discipline severe, but the Emperor has no objection to his army living at free quarters, and raising a contribution: all fair.

The Duke of Wellington's or British Army includes Belgians, Brunswickers, Nassaus, Hanoverians, German Legion, and Dutch; and the total amount of foreign troops at this moment in France is computed at little short of a million men. We English are more sombre in our looks and manners, honest and just in our dealings, strict in discipline, conscious of our superiority; all of which the French acknowledge, but they do not like us notwithstanding. No wonder, for proud England has worked the engine thro'out. There is not much love lost between us. The Royalists envy us: the Napoleonists execrate us. It is laughable sometimes to hear a fellow cry out, '*Sacré nom de Dieu*', when a sentry or Dragoon pushes him back.

At the Opéra I witnessed great apparent enthusiasm and applause at the presence of the King, and the whole house joined in the national air of '*Vive Henri Quatre*', tho' certainly not with that real patriotic heart and feeling that I have so often heard at one of our own theatres. That old fox Fouché is still employed, little esteemed by Louis. 'Tis now said that when Napoleon landed from Elba, he offered to ensure the King on his throne, and the tranquillity of France, but that his offer was slighted. General Labedoyère has been tried and executed; arrests and trials going on: thought to be a violation of the treaty of Paris. To make a distinction between those who are most guilty, when so much perjury and treachery were publicly manifested, must be difficult indeed, and examples ought to be made. McDonald, Clarke, Lynch etc behaved like men of honour. Having sworn allegiance to Louis last year, refused to follow Napoleon's standard, notwithstanding their long services and attachment to the Emperor; not that I can ever admire the character who quits his native soil to serve a foreigner.

This may seem a surprising comment from a man whose own father had served his whole career in a foreign army. It shows John Henry's ambivalent feelings towards Napoleon's Marshals Jacques Etienne Macdonald, Duke of Taranto, of Scottish Jacobite descent, and Henri Jacques Clarke, Duke of Feltre; these men had given their allegiance to Louis XVIII in 1814 and had therefore not taken Napoleon's part in the Hundred Days, which was honourable in John Henry's eyes; but they were of British origin, and should not have been in Napoleon's army in the first place, so it seemed to John Henry. His father's service in the Portuguese Army, unlike theirs in the French one, was encouraged by the British authorities and was never likely to involve fighting against England, Portugal's oldest ally.

JHS *Aug 1st.* Poor Bony is on board an English Man-of-War, safe in a British Port. That his intention was to make his escape to America there can be no doubt. But he could not elude our cruisers, and made a merit of throwing himself on the generosity and honour of his once most bitter enemy. Indignation and disappointment soon manifested itself, when he was informed that the Island of St Helena was decided upon as his future abode and exile; and most unwillingly did he quit the shores of England, where he cherished a hope and flattered himself to have passed the remainder of his days.

Our time passes away merrily enough, but the vicinity to Paris will not improve our morals. Too many lures thrown out: the French people study amusement and pleasure, I will add, refined vice. The Palais Royal is a sink of iniquity, gambling and licentiousness, from which the Government derive a large revenue. The streets of Paris appear at all times crowded, not altogether business, but industriously plodding and pass time, looking out for novelty and amusement. The Restaurateurs and Cafés always full, men and women, for domestic comforts they are averse to. Theatres filled at an early hour every evening, particularly on Sundays. In fine weather the Tuileries, Boulevards, etc are much frequented. Hundreds of chairs are in readiness, and a gazette for a sou. Tivoli with dancing, quadrilles carried on with much spirit: much taste and elegance: women always neat and well dressed in public, whatever they may be in private. Good order and decorum is kept up, intoxication rare. Exhibitions of painting and statues are safe and respected. 'Tis true that a police and guards are everywhere on the alert. I think the French people generally shew a good-humoured politeness to each other, far different to our own countrymen, although outrageous enough when excited or roused. Europe, the World know that well.

The Bois de Boulogne full of troops presents a grand and busy scene. Owing to the scarcity of tents, the men have cut a quantity of wood for huts, so that if we stay much longer, it may rather be termed Plaine de

Boulogne. I have fortunately got possession of a small room, with a bed but no sheets, a luxury few of us are acquainted with at present. We are near a pretty place called Bagatelle, belonging to the Duc de Berri, who has shewn no kindness whatever to the English, and by his own countrymen generally disliked. Walking in his grounds the other day, a keeper came up to me, and said that no one was permitted to walk there. 'Not an English Officer?' 'No' replied he 'the Duke has given positive orders'. 'Tell the Duke,' said I 'that he may thank the English for being here himself'. I walked on, saw the grounds and gardens and house too.

English troops continue to arrive, many regiments from America; not that there is, I believe, any apprehension of hostilities, but a corresponding force with the Allies give our Ambassador and the Duke weight, which policy probably Lord Castlereagh wanted at the Congress of Vienna. What a fortunate combination of circumstances was the downfall of that foolhardy Murat and peace with America, at such a critical moment as presented itself a few weeks back.

We have established horse racing on the plains of St Denis. Horses rode by Officers, the light genteel carriages, barouches etc belonging to the English, as also the graceful air of our fair countrywomen gracefully riding about, astonish the Parisians, who already imitate them, with a gallant gay Lothario by their side, but only at a walk. The French women are lively and fascinating, tastily dressed, but in point of beauty cannot certainly be compared to the English, for in no country, do I believe, is there so much general beauty as our own. They are sprightly in conversation and manner, much assisted by the many pretty turns of phraseology in the French language; never at a loss for a subject. '*Même sans idée, sans esprit, ils peuvent toujours causer*' [even without ideas, without wit, they can always find something to talk about], recount what they have done, seen, by whom praised, great personages acquainted with, expectations etc. Their feelings at the present moment are naturally severely mortified, and they show it. The Allied Sovereigns, altho' they may thro' policy be attached to the Bourbons, seem determined to make France smart. A restraint and coolness is quite evident.

Contributions of money, provisions, forage, clothing etc are exacted to a great amount, and as a guarantee of future peace and good behaviour the Allies are to keep possession of the strongest fortifications on the frontier. The Prussians wish to destroy all public monuments and emblems of the National glory. They began to blow up the Bridge of Jena, but were prevented by a timely remonstrance. They have already sent off to Berlin several waggons loaded with models of fortified towns etc, and are daily packing up more from the Hôpital des Invalides; paintings from the Louvre, books etc; horses from the arch at the Tuileries. It is reported all will be restored to the rightful owners. I hope with all my heart it may be so.

The boasting French are humbled indeed. Almost unwillingly do even the Royalists thank us for restoring their dynasty, ashamed of their country and conscious of their weakness. An intelligent French gentleman said to me 'Is it not a melancholy and bitter reflection to wish an army of one's own countrymen to be cut down and defeated? Such was the case at Waterloo, when you English gained immortal honour for yourselves. I admired the valour of Napoleon's troops, because they were Frenchmen, but I deprecated their cause, and with a bleeding heart wished them defeat. At Austerlitz, at Marengo, and in innumerable battles they covered themselves with glory. *Napoleon a battu tout le monde; il a fait des choses superbes à Paris. Ah, c'est un grand homme, Notre pays n'a jamais été si grand ni si puissant que sous lui. Mais son ambition l'abîme* [Napoleon defeated the whole world; he did superb things in Paris. Ah, he is a great man. Our country has never been so great or so strong as it was under him. But his ambition ruined him], according to a vulgar phrase'.

This was giving the Devil his due, and just enough. To the Frenchman Paris is everything; the person who has not visited Paris is a *bête*. Bonaparte fully entertained this idea. He spared no expense, no plunder to embellish and beautify it, as the emporium of everything that was grand and scientific: every encouragement given to the arts and sciences, and liberally offered to the public for improvement. The police is good, but they say inferior to Vienna. An officer of our regiment had his watch stolen out of his tent by a soldier. Two days after he recovered his watch, and the broker who had bought it was fined 1000 francs for not ascertaining the person who brought it to him for sale. Under Fouché pretty and artful women were employed in the police and espionage. Tyranny and inquisition were at their height: Napoleon's decree was generally a law: the word glory was in everybody's mouth, honour and honesty in few people's breasts. Defeats and victories were announced and celebrated alike, rejoicings and Te Deums.

We are getting heartily sick of reviews; have had one of the whole British force under our great Captain. It was a grand imposing sight, about 80,000 of all arms. Our line extended some miles, commencing at the Barrière de l'Étoile. We marched by the Sovereigns (not Louis) at the Place Louis XV. The Duke of Wellington, as may be supposed, looked stately and proud, inwardly saying, 'To my victories in Spain may be attributed the entry of the Allies into Paris last year, to the bravery and discipline of these soldiers, the downfall of Bonaparte and restoration of peace to the World'.

A long gazette came out, promotion and honour to the Waterloo heroes. Many a battle had been fought in the Peninsula with as much credit and bravery, but there was a combination of circumstances at Waterloo which gave *éclat irresistible*. Consequently every Officer lamented that he had been deprived of the honour and happiness of getting his head broke. The position of our Brigade was of great importance, as the Duke expected that the enemy, who had thrown forward a large force on their left (a feint) intended to turn his right, and so get between him and Brussels. Had we been moved after the action began, we should have been up and under fire about five o'clock on the evening of the 18th, a critical moment, and rendered essential service. The Duke is said to have expressed much anxiety until the Prussians appeared, altho' fully determined to keep his ground, and confident in his troops in so arduous a conflict. The effect the news of this decisive battle caused in England appeared to throw in the background every former achievement of the British Army. Subscriptions for the wounded, widows etc were raised to a large amount.

Sep 1st. We have now excellent shooting, and are not very particular where we hunt. Partridges and hares are abundant. An Officer the other day brought home 18 hares. It was laughable to see his horse. I have been on a visit to Mr Cotin, son to the authoress, a place called Genbeville, near Arpajon, about twenty miles from Paris. We killed a good deal of game, but found the weather very hot. The French are fond of shooting in the middle of the day, nor do they allow the dogs to range any distance from them. They are very fair shots and use generally double-barrelled guns. Their gunpowder I think inferior to ours. In the evening we had music, billiards and an excellent library, and the family could speak English; so the time passed very pleasantly.

During John Henry's two months in Paris, he watched the return of the Bourbons and the policy of the Allies with a cool sardonic eye, but he was chiefly absorbed in trying to make up his mind about the French. He seems to have remained baffled between his admiration for their courage and efficiency, his slightly shocked but beady-eyed observation of their manners, and his deep distrust of their good faith.

53

John Henry's sister Sophia Walsh and her husband and children had sailed from Ireland to the South of France in September 1814, in the hope that James Walsh's health, much shaken by a business failure, would be restored by a winter in a climate more clement than that of Dublin. This treatment had been successful. James Walsh was now restored to health and he and his family were living in Nantes, where the senior branch of the Walsh family had long been settled. Ardently Jacobite, these Walshes had emigrated to France in 1682 and during the eighteenth century had grown rich as ship-owners at Nantes and been granted the title of Comte de Serraut. They had left Nantes during the French Revolution, and though on their return in 1815 they found that all but one of their town and country houses had been sacked, burnt or appropriated, they still held an influential position in the society of Nantes, and welcomed their distant cousin James and his family. John Henry took the opportunity of his stationing in Paris to go and visit his sister, after his agreeable shooting party at Arpajon.

JHS On return to camp I applied for leave of absence to go to Nantes. Unfortunately on the very morning I obtained it, Mr J Walsh made his appearance, but as it was but for a short period, I set off, and he followed me a week after.

Sept 10th. At 6 o'clock in the morning got into the Diligence, according to the number booked in the office, a good plan; a moving mountain drawn by five horses, three abreast as leaders, driven by one postilion, who with his enormous boots (which are said to have saved many a broken leg) and a long never ceasing cracking whip, rides the near shaft horse. This machine, when contrasted with our light and neat built mail coaches, an Englishman at first gazes at with astonishment, but they are conducted with great regularity. They generally hold twelve inside and three in the cabriolet, including Monsier le Conducteur, a personage of no little consequence. He goes the whole journey, takes charge of your luggage, pays the postilions about one penny a stage for you, and at the end you settle. Very tedious work: stopped to sleep two nights; the third travelled all night. Beds indifferent: meals for three francs abundant; fish, fowl and flesh, vegetables, fruit etc. My fellow travellers were lively and pleasant enough, changing at the different towns. At Chartres we took up some disbanded officers of the Loire army. Politics the eternal subject of conversation, little favourable to the Bourbons of course. These gentlemen warriors soon discovered me to be an English Officer. Military topics then commenced. Napoleon's army was the finest in the World. They had taken Moscow, Madrid, Vienna, Berlin, Rome, Naples, Lisbon, etc. Paris had twice been given up by treachery; Waterloo was lost by treachery; but the English '*se battent comme des diables*', and the Duke of Wellington is a great general. They gave him every credit, and said they had rather make war against the English than any other nation. They were civilized and honourable. Of the Prussians they talked with great contempt and hatred. Poor Louis was abused without mercy; he did wrong to dismiss the Imperial Guard last year. The Maison-du-Roi they ridiculed, and complained much of being disbanded now, after fighting for their country '*comme des braves Militaires*'. Napoleon they spoke of with enthusiasm, and advanced many arguments which common sense would refute; but I opposed them as mildly as possible, if possible avoiding to quarrel, for naturally they were *au désespoir*. Many talked of going to America, and we parted as good friends as might be expected.

We traversed some fine tracts of country, rich in corn, wine and fruit; the plains on the banks of the Loire abounding in cattle and horses; the roads in general good; no appearance of devastation in these parts. In order to see the beautiful winding Loire, I would recommend any person bound from Paris to Nantes at this season of the year to go by land to Orleans, then boating it all the way by Tours etc. The route is delightful.

The family awaiting him at Nantes now ranged in age from William and John, Sophia's eldest sons, who were ten and eight, to the baby Sophia Louisa. The family's means were modest; it was not till twenty years later that James Walsh was able to buy the Château of Port-Hubert on the river Erdre, near Suce which had a Protestant church which the Walshes could attend. In 1815 they were still living in the Royalist quarter of Nantes and leading the simple social life of its impoverished aristocratic inhabitants.

JHS *Sept 16th.* Here I am at Nantes, in my sister Walsh's house. I need not attempt describing the joy we experienced at meeting, and how my nephews and nieces came round Uncle John. The two boys, William and John, had met me on the road, anxious who should first recognize me, and run back to the house to announce my arrival. I felt sincere pleasure at meeting again the family. Mr J Walsh had come to France for his health, which was much improved. They had fortunately remained unmolested during the interregnum of Bonaparte, and I had escaped with a whole skin, once more to enjoy their society. They were comfortably situated, altho' in a strange

land; their fine family around them. To be possessed of too much feeling is
a misfortune; but to be callous to the pure sensations such meetings as
these ought to inspire in every human breast must be a great misfortune,
and my heart was not yet steeled by the horrors of war and the cruel scenes
I had witnessed. It makes my blood shudder when I reflect on the me-
chanical way in which the human race have butchered each other for the
caprice of Kings and tyrants; but such is our nature, and such the decree of
Providence.

Oct 1st. Letters from Paris say that the Allies will soon move from Paris,
that final treaties are ratified. Great murmurs at the removal of pictures
from the Louvre, the statues, horses, etc, and that the encomiums hitherto
bestowed on the English for upright and moderate conduct are now converted to abuse, as the Duke of Wellington is reported to be not only
acquainted with these proceedings (which of course he is) but also acces-
sory to them. This is playing no little compliment to our influence and
power, as if we had a *plein pouvoir*. Whither we shall move is unknown
yet; some say to Belgium, others that the whole of the British Army will
remain in France, as Louis prefers us to any other, and his throne without
foreign aid is tottering.

Five thousand Prussian troops have been at Nantes for twelve days.
They were a heavy burthen on the community; the officers were at free
quarters in private houses, the soldiers in barracks; all ranks provided with
every thing that could make them comfortable, and 'tis but justice to say
that the Prussians behaved well. The Prefect and Mayor treated them as
allies and friends. The Napoleonists here seemed to glory in the many and
heavy contributions exacted from the Royalists. No Prussians were allowed to enter La Vendée, and barriers were erected at the various bridges
to prevent their crossing. I have no doubt that, had they attempted it, the
Vendéans would have opposed them. These faithful, tho' perhaps turbu-
lent Royalists, claimed exemption from contributions. The Prussians are
immoderate eaters, and would frequently arise in the middle of the night
and call for food. A story is told of a Prussian soldier who died. The
Officers suspected that he had been poisoned, and ordered the surgeon to
open the corpse, when not less than eleven pounds of meat were taken out.
At a château near Nantes a Prussian General and his suite drank nine
hundred bottles of wine in five days. My being with my sister at this
moment was lucky, as it prevented an officer and his servant being billeted
on her.

We breathe delightful air in this country. As to society, it is confined;
people generally in moderate circumstances. Among the Royalists my
brother-in-law and family are favourites. The town is spacious, 50,000
souls. At this end live principally the remains of Noblesse, depressed and
poor; the old dynasty pretty well worn away; the new, risen from the

Revolution, courted only by their own party, which is strong. Visits are made of an evening, the same as in Portugal, without the English formality of invitation, except for large or grand entertainments. The ladies bring their work; are musical, and fond of quadrilles and waltzes. *Un thé* and a bunch of grapes satisfies them. Cards generally; whist, Boston, écarté.

An English Brig-of-War came up the river, saying that Bonaparte was safe on board the *Bellerophon*. On the Captain taking the report to the Prefect, a mob of people assembled and asked to see the English Officers, exclaiming '*Oh, mes bons Anglais, tenez bien le coquin là, ne le laissez pas échapper, ne vous enragez pas contre nous un autre fois*'. [Oh, you dear good Englishmen, keep that rascal safely, don't let him escape, don't turn against us all over again.]

This was once a very flourishing commercial city. Large fortunes were made in the slave trade. In the revolution excesses were carried to the highest pitch. I have been shewn a square where it was necessary to have people in readiness to clear away the human blood of the numberless victims sacrificed by the guillotine. The *noyades* were as dreadful, for hundreds were carried away at night, torn from their families, taken off in carts and thrown into the river. A Madame Cornulier, a most amiable lady, whom I often see at my sister's, lost her husband by the guillotine. She herself had mounted the scaffold, her hair cut off, when her husband exclaimed that she was *enceinte*. The barbarians remanded her to prison, where she was delivered, and strange to say escaped.

Every article of living here is most abundant, at this delightful season of the year. Fine fruit, poultry, meat, fish, game etc sold in the public markets; a hare two shillings, brace of partridges fifteeen pence. The French talk of the love of eating in the English. I think certainly John Bull is a coarse feeder; but the one will dine off the one dish and eat again of the same, the other rarely tastes the same dish twice, but if there be a hundred different ones will eat of all. Look at the bill of fare at a Restaurateur's at Paris; what variety, what pains taken to give technical terms to dishes. Cookery is an art, a study. Soup is a matter of course, palatable, though not rich. Finish it by holding up the plate pretty close to your mouth. A glass of wine, which is considered wholesome, *un coup de médicine*. *Vin ordinaire* you drink out of tumblers; superior wine you drink out of a wine-glass. Oysters or bouilli beef, with a slice of melon; boiled fish, a patty in your fingers, as the plate passes. Things are generally overdone, and the dish is handed round. Vegetables eat alone. Roast fish with salad, meat, poultry, game etc, sweet things, cheese etc. You keep the same knife and fork thro'out, tho' your plate is every moment changed. You hand it yourself to the *garçon* or *fille*, clean your knife and fork on your bread, and frequently get up any nice sauce etc with a piece of bread off your plate. 'Tis vulgar to eat twice of the same thing. Everybody has a napkin, which you tuck under your chin, or fix it to your waistcoat. Dinner ended, you roll it up in some fancy form, or in a numbered ring, so as to know it next day. Dessert, coffee, and liqueurs. Ladies and gentlemen all break up together. You frequently see the French pick their teeth with a knife.

I was much amused at playing whist one evening; a missed deal nothing, a revoke nothing. Take back the cards even after two or three rounds, laugh, talk, and change cards. The romantic names of the women in France are Aimée, Felicité, Modeste, Clemence, Fortunée, Desirée, Honorée, Celeste, L'Or, Gracieuses, Agathe, Angelique, Virginie, etc. During my residence at Nantes nothing particular occurred. The Barbin is a fine river or piece of water. We made several excursions up it, pleasant picnics, and concluded the day with drawing a net, to the no small gratification of William and John, who filled their baskets with fish. Many houses in a state of decay and uninhabited, beautifully situated on the banks; splendid chestnut trees. One evening only I went to the theatre with some Vendéan Chiefs. The air of Henri IV was played, amid some hissing.

Among his observations on French table manners and Christian names (the one which he heard as 'L'Or' was presumably 'Laure'), John Henry kept his diary up to date with current events and French public opinion, and copied a proclamation by the Army of the Loire which had retreated from Paris as the Allies entered France. This – unlike Napoleon's proclamations and addresses, of which the fullest documentation exists – is perhaps worth quoting in full (in translation) as a reflection of the uncrushable spirit of Napoleon's soldiers which John Henry could not help admiring, while he detested Napoleon himself.

JHS The following I found one day in the street:- 'Brave Comrades, we are effecting our retreat to the Loire, in conformity with a treaty. In making this sacrifice, so grievous to our glory, we give to our country the highest proof of our obedience. We bear away with us our sharpest regrets at leaving you, brave and generous Citizens of Paris, whose valour and patriotism will forever honour the links of glory and friendship which united us in the defence of our country. May indelible shame be on those cowardly Frenchmen who worked, who are working still, for the defeat of the Nation, and who smile on the successes of foreign armies. Leave them to abase themselves by their cries of servility and joy, they dishonour only themselves, and not their country, which disavows them. Their reward will only be the double contempt of their compatriots and even of our enemies, who know how to respect our glory. Honour to you, brave and generous Citizens, who have made yourselves worthy of that estimable title, by sharing our glorious labours. Defend the national colours, which we have made illustrious by our exploits. These belong to you as well as to us. They belong to the Nation. Preserve, by your noble attitude, your sacred right to our esteem. We will also preserve the same right to yours. Arrived at our destination, we shall return stronger than ever, through the same national temper. Malevolence will no longer have any hold on our reunited arms. If, contrary to our hopes, the promises of an honourable peace which respects our rights to choose our government, and to confer on ourselves a liberal constitution, should not be kept, we shall join with you either in dying to honour once again the name of Frenchmen, or in proving that a nation is always free when it wishes to be. Adieu, brave Comrades, and you Citizens worthy of the name of Frenchmen. On the banks of the Loire, as on those of the Seine, our good wishes will be for the Nation and for you.

Subscribed by Chef des Corps, Officers and Non-Commissioned Officers.'

It was said that on the evening of the 18th of June, when Napoleon lost all hopes, that he held a council of war, and expressed his determination still to head the Army. Talked of going to Suchet, but was dissuaded, one alone agreeing with him, the rest recommending him to go to Paris without loss of time. There is no doubt but that he might still have assembled a large body of troops; but the Allies were pouring in from all quarters and ultimate defeat must have ensued. This was the third time that he had deserted his army (witness Egypt, Russia) and I believe he cared little about his followers, whom he knew well how to retain, provided he could accomplish his ambitious projects. When he entered Paris from Lyons, it was night, and 'tis said two carriages drove up to the Tuileries without lamps, the leading carriage some way in advance, supposed to be his own, containing attendants, probably expecting to be fired at. But the coast being clear, he advanced, as if no such apprehension had been entertained.

54

His leave over, John Henry returned to Paris in mid-October, and ten days later the 35th moved from the encampment in the Bois de Boulogne to cantonments south of Paris, at Marcoussis and Linas on either side of the road to Orléans, between Longjumeau and Arpajon. Here John Henry spent a month in comfort, enjoying his usual good luck over quarters, and expecting to spend the winter there and to have his sister Sophy to stay with him. He had leisure to fill his diary with reflections on what future historians would make of the extraordinary events of 1815, and from there his mind wandered to his own future, to what he would teach his sons if he ever had any, and to picture himself in old age re-reading this diary. His accounts of these last weeks in France are among the liveliest and most readable of the whole diary. Perhaps, in spite of his disclaimer that his laconic soldierly style could never deserve to meet 'the critic's eye', he was tempted at this time to join the busy scribblers who, he foresaw, would soon be rushing into print.

JHS *20th October*. My leave expired. I reluctantly took leave of my dear Sister and family: returned to Paris by the same route, *par Diligence*. At one town the Police wished to detain me, not having any other papers but the Duke of Wellington's leave of absence. However, I was determined, and they allowed me to proceed, recommending me another time to be better provided. My answer was, that I was a British Officer, had my uniform with me, and would travel all over France with the passport of my Commander-in-Chief. This did not please them of course, as the French say we were received as allies, that France never was conquered. On arriving at the Bois de Boulogne, I found matters much *in statu quo*. The Cavalry and some Artillery had already moved into Normandy. The Bois presents one lively scene of camps, huts innumerable, sounding of bugles, bands, drums, parades and marching.

November 1st. The joyful news of going into cantonments arrived. In three days we shall all reach our destination, the greater part of the Army within thirty miles of Paris, and easily collected, in case of need, to any given point. Our brigade march 18 miles on the Orléans road, the 35th stationed at Linas and Marcoussis. The first fortnight I was billeted on the Mayor of Marcoussis, according to his own account a great Royalist. He had an excellent house, gardens, park, etc, but did not hesitate to accept of five francs a day for boarding. I breakfasted in my own room, but dined with the family. His father had a good library, a fine old man. Billiards, shooting etc beguiled the time. On quitting the Mayor, I had a very comfortable house in Linas. The owner being in Paris, I established my own *ménage*. His housekeeper or *Bonne* provided me with everything, furniture, silver, etc and marketed for me. Arpajon being but a few miles off, I frequently visited Madame Jange. However these comforts soon ceased. Sir J. Moore used to say that a soldier has no business with comfort, and I believe he was right.

20th November. The ground covered with snow. The official distribution of the armies reached us. The Allies immediately to file off towards their own countries; the combined Army of Occupation taking possession of the Fortresses etc as stipulated by treaty. It has always, I believe, been the established principle with the Duke of Wellington to keep secret his movements or intentions as much as circumstances would permit, and very necessary it should be so. I was much disappointed at this sudden break up. Away went *ménage* and little comforts. One principal reason of my wishing to stay the winter was my expecting the pleasure of my Sister Sophy coming to see me; as also to get over the bad weather before we commenced our march. Another reason was the anticipation of half pay, the natural consequence of a 2nd Battalion going home at the end of a war. The 35th return to England and proceed to Boulogne, about eighteen days march; a pretty prospect.

December 1st. We daily expect to move and 'tis to be hoped that the arrangements made by the Allies for retaining for a given number of years the strongholds on the frontier of France will secure a lasting peace, as well as prove a salutary lesson to its restless inhabitants. Little equal is my pen to describe at this eventful period so interesting a capital as Paris, much less so singular a nation as the French. Many a busy Author, many a scribbler will ere long publish to the World, the remarkable events, the important era of Napoleon's return to France, an era then big with the fate of Kingdoms. The battle of Waterloo will fill no small amount of sheets in the interesting volumes. For a second time by British valour was the ambitious Bonaparte hurled from his throne, and peace restored to Europe. Proud indeed has every Englishman reason to be who was present on the 18th June 1815.

The short sentenced style of a soldier's narrative generally deserves rather the name of a diary. These few lines, written in a leisure moment for my own amusement will never come under the critic's eye; and should I live to an advanced age, or be a Father of sons, may serve to pass an idle minute, or even tend to impress upon their minds the value of time, and the many advantages to be derived from events and circumstances in early youth, which in my own instance, alas! reflection and experience have too late convinced me of.

I once more visited the Louvre, spoliated of its brightest ornaments, and must confess I felt great satisfaction at pacing this once magnificent gallery; the triumphal car shorn of its brightest ornaments, the horses; the dilapidations among the statues, and models of fortifications at the Invalides is *affreuse*; still it is but retribution. Such treatment strikes home, and has I believe created great indignation and rancour among the Parisians. The extreme moderation of the Allies last year led the French to expect the same this; but thanks to God the day of retaliation was arrived; plunder was restored to its rightful owners, and who has not a right to claim his own property? The English alone found nothing to claim, for they had never lost anything. I regret much that the pillar of Vendôme, bridge of Lodi, and other national monuments have been spared. Long usage of conquest and privilege of pillage had blindfolded the French with an incredible presumption of self right. But now the tide is turned. Few countries but had felt the scourge of war. The French never put in the scale their treatment of other nations when complaining of these hardships. On their own shoulders rests the blame. The general immorality, want of religion, restless, reckless character of the French in these days is notorious. Marshal Ney is under trial. The populous cities, the fertile plains of France, *la belle France*, will long be strangers to smiling Concord and sweet philanthropy.

There was certainly not much smiling concord and sweet philanthropy about Marshal Ney's trial and execution. Like most of the British Army, John Henry deplored the fate of Marshal Ney, next to whom he had sat in Notre Dame at the thanksgiving service eighteen months earlier. Ney had, it was true, turned his coat twice; announcing, as he left Paris when Napoleon landed from Elba, that he would bring the Emperor back in an iron cage, he had then embraced and joined Napoleon. But he had fought bravely and brilliantly at Quatre Bras and Waterloo, and was a hero not only to the French but to many on the Allied side. Louis XVIII himself was reluctant to condemn Ney, but could not or would not intervene to save him from the clamour of the returned emigrés. 'We are going marshal-hunting,' cried the Duc de Berri. Ney was run down, condemned to death, and executed by a firing-squad in the Luxembourg gardens.

JHS *5th December*. Marched early this morning. Had a most uncomfortable day of it. Halted at Bourg la Reine. Well treated by my landlord, who had that morning arrived with his wife from Paris. He had travelled much in Italy, and we conversed chiefly in that language.

6th December. Breakfasted with Sir C. Colville. Rode thro' Paris to overtake the Regiment, not without mixed and strong sensations regarding this capital, the many revolutions it had undergone, the incongruity of its inhabitants, its present state compared with former times. Farewell, farewell, Paris! Slept at St Denis, the famous burial place of the Royal Family of France. Visited the Cathedral, and Institution of the Legion of Honour. Our Battalion was much scattered in the neighbouring villages, as numerous Corps are marching on the same line. My landlord not civil; told me candidly our departure was much more grateful to his feelings than our entrée. I believed him. However the evening passed more pleasantly than I expected, as Mr Tobin of Nantes came out from Paris to dine with me. Ney, the unfortunate Ney, was executed yesterday. He behaved like a veteran, and exclaimed to the firing party, '*Soldats, droit au coeur*' [Soldiers, aim straight at my heart]. If Bonaparte had pledged himself when he retired to Elba never to set foot again on French ground, he was equally dishonourable. Whether so or not, is of course known to higher powers.

7th December. Beaumont. Quartered at a large Château. The family are at Paris, but the servants had everything ready for us, dinner and every requisite prepared. Many families quitted their houses during the *passage de l'armée*. Here was an example, so frequently met with in this country, of a spacious mansion, halls, saloons, billiard room, numerous outbuildings etc out of repair, always better calculated for a summer residence than a winter one, and withal little appearance of comfort.

8th December. Very cold weather. Marched to Noailles; fared well with a rich farmer. There are large farms in Picardy. My landlord has 21 cows, 10 horses, 150 sheep. Ménage rather slovenly; not so neat as our English farms. Country quite open, without hedges or fences. I generally carried my own tea and sugar. On asking the farmer's wife, if she would take a cup, answer, – '*Non, merci. Je ne suis pas malade*' [No, thanks, I'm not ill].

9th December. Heavy snow. On to Marcelles. Quartered at a neighbouring village, called Fontain, at Conte-de-Juigne, a Royalist. His daughter handsome, lately married. We had music and cards in the evening.

12th December. At the village of St Romain, off the main road. At first the old lady on whom I was billeted shewed symptoms of incivility; but a determined aspect soon brought her to her senses, and we parted good friends. In course of conversation I frequently observed much ignorance and many fallacious ideas among the country people; and though generally inimical to Bonaparte, there was always something in his favour.

13th December. Hard frost. Near Arène. 'Tis annoying after you arrive at your supposed quarters, to have the Officers and men scattered about among the neighbouring communes. On our march there was but little variety, and we were all pretty well accustomed to French manners. Mons le Maire was often a low-bred person; generally endeavoured to billet us out of his own parish; so that we sometimes took the liberty of billeting ourselves. Villages often situated in hollows. The roaring of cannon, the inhabitants told us, was distinctly heard here on the 18th of June. When the Battalion assembled of a morning, it was entertaining to hear the Officers (as well as the soldiers' remarks) give an account of the treatment they had received the preceding night. One anecdote this morning made us laugh. An Officer had retired to bed, when a man and a woman came into his room, thinking he was asleep. They quietly began to pull off the quilt. The Officer feigned sleep, and at the moment they thought themselves sure of their prize, he started up and knocked the man out of the door, his hat remaining in the room. The woman fled.

14th December. Rain. Reached Abbeville, a large town said to have been loyal, notwithstanding that a triumphal Arch was erected here, when Napoleon was made first Consul. They say that on his passing thro' Amiens on his way to the Army of England, some wag wrote on a wall in large letters '*La route d'Angleterre, jusqu'à Calais*' [The road to England – as far as Calais].

15th December. Halted. Very well satisfied, for the weather *effroyable*. After dinner, conversing with my landlady on the subject of matrimony and children, she said she preferred girls to boys, for the former afforded more society to a mother; enabled her to obtain money from the father for their dress, amusement etc, and gave opportunities of mixing more in society, as her daughters must naturally be introduced, and brought out in the World, and more, she was enabled by their going abroad to meet her favourites and admirers.

16th December. A dirty day's march. Detached to the village of Quin. Fared well at a farmhouse. The inhabitants in these parts speak a curious dialect. A great number of cart horses are bred about here. They call them *élèves*.

17th December. In the neighbourhood of Crecy. This night at Nampont. *Vide* Sterne's story of the ass.

John Henry was travelling, in the reverse direction, along the route taken by Sterne in his *Sentimental Journey*, and when he reached Nampont he remembered Sterne's story of the encounter there with the old German pilgrim on his way back from Santiago de Compostella, and his piteous laments over his dead ass. Such literary allusions are rare in John Henry's diary; he had hardly had much opportunity to become a well-read man. His education ended when he was sixteen, and he had been living on the move ever since, in billets and garrisons. If he found a volume of Voltaire or Rousseau in a house where he was billeted, as he often did on this march through Northern France, he would pick it up. He could now read and speak French well, and since his Zante days had picked up spoken Italian, though his spelling in both languages, specially of place names, was erratic. His chief interests were in current political and military developments, and to some extent in history and architecture, specially military architecture, a taste perhaps inherited from his ancestor John Slezer, of *Theatrum Scotiae* fame.

JHS *18th December.* To Montreuil, a fortified town; great Napoleonists: *tant pis*; well billeted, *tant mieux*. Thank God, our *promenade militaire* is drawing to a conclusion.

19th December. To Somer. Detached again. Lodged *chez* Mons le Maire. Ordered to halt, the weather having prevented the regular transport of troops. Rode over to Boulogne. I frequently had an Officer or two quartered with me; so we beguiled the bad weather with a pipe or rubber of whist. A volume of Voltaire or Rousseau was generally to be found. I was put to a very trifling expense, being rarely quartered on people who would accept payment. The servants of course always got something.

23rd December. To Boulogne. I need make no comments on this place, and on the ideas of all on marching into a town where the 'Army of England' was assembled. From hence our shores were threatened, at the same time that a boasting enemy kept their boats chained fore and aft. Many English families residing here. In the evening went to a ball, where my fair countrywomen shone conspicuous. Napoleon had commenced a Pyramid to commemorate the height of his ambition, his folly, the downfall of old England. Many people think he never had any intention of making the desperate effort. A French officer, who had served in the Imperial Guard, told me that the invading army consisted of 150,000 men, all French and inspired with the greatest military ardour and confidence in Napoleon, equal, said he, to double the number of the present day. 'That', said I, 'depends on those to whom they may be opposed'. He well understood my meaning, and could not be persuaded that, had they landed in England (which he acknowledged was no easy matter), near a million of men were up in arms, ready to give them a warm reception. Talked lightly of Volunteers, but praised our line troops. '*Ils se battent comme des Diables, et se laissent tuer avec beaucoup de sangfroid*'. [They fight like devils, and meet their death with great coolness.] This said Army of England, he said, made a most astonishing march, and proved to the World their valour at the Battle of Austerlitz. He complained much of the Allies, that they had broken their faith; that after Napoleon and his army were conquered, they ought to have treated France as a friend and an Ally; that they were bound by the Capitulation of Paris to respect *les Propriétés Publiques*. The Allies raised contributions, acted contrary to their Proclamations, interfered with the Government, etc. 'But', answered I, 'supposing you had won the Battle of Waterloo, we should still have been obliged to carry on the War, subjecting ourselves to all the risk, all the expenses, bloodshed, etc. And when not victorious, but the contrary, you expect us tamely to declare ourselves friends and Allies'. Our argument might have lasted all night; for the French possess such a pertinacious loquacity that they will sometimes beat you out of the field by clamour and flow of language. We at last parted as good friends as two persons, holding diametrically opposite views and sentiments, could be supposed to be.

I received every attention in this house, notwithstanding, and must confess that in no instance had I reason to complain seriously of the civility of the French on our march, tho' I have heard many Officers say the contrary. Much depends on oneself on these occasions. There is a *grossiereté* sometimes in the English manners, little congenial to foreigners. I think the lady of the house in a French family is often too servile. She does all the honours of the table; carves, hands your plate, helps you to wine, snuffs the candles, etc, etc. All these attentions shew her good breeding and *aimabilité*.

24th December. To the village of Marquise. Got thoroughly wet. Orders to march to Calais for embarkation.

25th December. Not a very merry Xmas at Wissant. An excellent quarter. Such rank Bonapartists I had not yet encountered. However open enemies are always the safest. Everything was done to make me comfortable. They were candid in their political opinions, which were most freely sported. The French annoy one excessively; so much prevarication and subterfuge, with a great deal of plausibility, blended with insincerity and distrust. They have lost much of that good breeding for which they were once so renowned, and now substitute a degree of ferocity in their demeanour, a brusquerie, the effects, I take it, of revolutions, a long War, and a Military Government. To our glorious constitution and patriotism they solely attribute our power and successes.

28th December. Halted. The news of Lavalette's escape; a concerted business; heroic conduct of his wife. Three of our Countrymen arrested in Paris, concerned in the affair.

The escape of Count Antoine Lavalette from the Conciergerie prison in Paris was a splendidly romantic affair. Lavalette, Napoleon's Postmaster-General, had been condemned to death for having assisted Napoleon's escape from Elba. He was due to be guillotined on 21st December. His wife visited him in prison for a farewell interview, dressed in a red cloak and a plumed velvet hat. In this concealing get-up, and with a handkerchief over his face, Lavalette escaped while his wife remained in the prison. He got clean away from Paris, with false identity papers provided by Sir Robert Wilson and Michael Bruce, Lady Hester Stanhope's lover – both of whom John Henry had met, Wilson in Italy and Bruce in Zante – and Captain Hutchinson of the Guards. Lavalette reached Munich, and lived in Bavaria for years under the protection of Eugène de Beauharnais and under the transparent pseudonym of 'Monsieur Cossar'.

The 35th reached Calais on 27th December. Their last experience of France was one which aroused John Henry's patriotic ire.

JHS *27th December*. On to Calais. No Allied troops had as yet been quartered in the town. By great favour we were allowed to occupy the Barracks within the works. Owing to the pressure of troops we found some difficulty in obtaining quarters, previous to which the Battalion was kept outside the gates under heavy rain for about three hours, and by order of Sir Manly Power we marched in with secured arms, colours cased, no music; a most extraordinary circumstance.

28th December. The weather too bad for embarkation. No civility from the inhabitants. Many speaking broken English, and aping our manners, and evidently shewing a jealous hatred towards us, notwithstanding the thousands and thousands of pounds we spend among them in peace time, whereas in War it is but a miserable fishing town. On the Quay there is a paltry pillar, to commemorate the landing of Louis XVIII, Le Désiré, restored last year to his children. Pretty dutiful children, forsooth! The impression of a foot is imprinted in bronze on the wharf. Frequent quarrels take place between the British and the inhabitants, and I blush to say that our General favours the latter.

29th December. Major McAlister and myself called on the General to remonstrate on the manner in which the Regiment was ordered to march into Calais.

1816. 1st January. A new year. May God Almighty avert revolutions and bloodshed for the future. A most satisfactory letter of reparation and explanation from the Adjutant-General was read on Parade. Everybody was astonished at the imbecility of Sir M. Power in yielding to the humiliating, unjust and illiberal demand of the French Commandant and a few ragged National Guards of Calais, who talked of patriotism, honour, and the rights of a garrison town!!

2nd Jan. Marched for embarkation from the Barracks thro' the Grande Place; band playing, colours flying, bayonets fixed; to the tune of the downfall of Paris. At night stood over with the tide for the white Cliffs of Dover.

55

The last pages of John Henry's diary are clouded with disappointment. His military career was coming to an end, and he had missed the glory and honours that he had hoped for. His service was to finish, as it had begun, in Ireland. He carefully copied into his diary the records of such public recognition as was accorded to the 2nd Battalion of the 35th and his own service with them, but it was not enough to heal his wounded feelings.

JHS *3rd Jan.* Landed at daybreak. With what animation should I have jumped on our dear native land, had the 2/35th Regt been under fire at Waterloo. The numerous questions asked about our killed and wounded, Bonaparte, the French Lancers, etc, could only be answered by a sullen look.

Two days after the Regt landed at Dover, orders were received to re-embark for Ireland, to the great annoyance of everybody. I, however, obtained leave of absence.

6th Jan. Left the Battalion, crowded on board bad transports. Proceeded to London. During the few days I stayed at Dover, I received much attention from Mr Fector the Banker. On my arrival in London, I attended a Levée at the Duke of York's and the next day left with Sir Henry Torrens the following memorial:-

'To Field Marshal His Royal Highness Duke of York, Commander-in-Chief of His Majesty's Forces, etc, etc. London, 24th January, 1816.

The Memorial of Brevet Lieutenant Colonel John Slessor, Major in the 35th Regt, humbly showeth that your Memorialist has been in the Service about twenty-one years, during which time not three years in England. That he served in Ireland during the whole period of the Rebellion; frequently engaged with the rebels; wounded under Colonel Vereker, in the action at Coloaney against the French Army, when his name was publicly made mention of. Served in Gibraltar; in the Island of Jersey, where as Captain he commanded the 1st Battalion of Reserve. In Sicily in the Light Battalion, commanded by Sir James Kempt. In the last Expedition to Egypt; at Rosetta, where the 35th Regt suffered so severely, and were honourably mentioned by the Honble Sir William Stuart. Several times in Calabria. At the taking of the Greek Islands, when he was appointed Civil and Military

Governor of the Island of Zante; which post he held for near three years; received General Sir John Oswald's thanks in public orders, and a sword from the inhabitants. At the capture of the Islands of Lagosta, Corzula and Lessina in the Adriatic, when his name appeared in the Gaz-ette. Served in Dalmatia, Istria and Italy, with a Battalion of Detachments under the command of Colonel Robertson. Attached to the Austrian General, Count Nugent. Repeatedly engaged with the enemy; received Colonel Robert-son's thanks. Served in Belgium and Holland, in Sir Charles Colville's Division at Waterloo; in France, and now under orders for Ireland. Your Memorialist humbly trusts that the above stated services will entitle him to be recommended to His Royal Highness the Prince Regent as a companion of the most honourable military order of the Bath, which is submitted

John Slessor, Major 35th and Lieut Colonel'

The following letter soon reached me, and I felt grieved and hurt at its contents. Indeed at one time I had decided on retiring on half pay, as I can clearly point out Officers who have been made Companions without so strong a claim. Patience.

'Horse Guards. 26th January 1816

Sir

Having laid your memorial of the 24th inst before the Commander-in-Chief, I am commanded to assure you that His Royal Highness has a very favourable opinion of your merits, but your claim to be made a Companion of the most honourable Military order of the Bath does not come within the principle upon which the selection for retrospective services was made.

I have the honour to be

Your obedient humble servant

J Torrens

To Lieut Col Slessor, 35th Regt.'

Here ended my hopes, this war, of honorary reward from my own Sovereign, notwithstanding the zeal I had always shewn in my country's cause. *28th January*. Arrived at Sidmouth. Once more in the domestic society of my dear Mother and Sister. My time passed away very pleasantly here. The country around is pretty, and there are many pleasant families in the place. No orders having as yet been given for the reduction of the 2nd Battalion 35th Regt, I set off to join them on the 2nd of July, route thro' Exeter and Barnstaple to Ilfracombe, where I crossed to Swansea. On to Milford, and took the Packet to Waterford, where the Regiment is quartered. Was agreeably surprised to find that the Waterloo medals had been granted to us. I received mine with satisfaction and pleasure, notwithstanding that I shall ever regret that our Brigade was not in the heat of the action on the 18th June 1815.

Time passed on without any particular circumstance to mark the period, except a most disastrous season. Incessant rain, and every prospect of scarcity. Now and then unpleasant reports of our reduction. From the inhabitants we did not receive any very marked attention.

In *January 1817* I was ordered to take the command of the troops at Wexford, and found it to be a hospitable gay place, most abundant and reasonable in way of living. The neighbourhood good, and a number of resident gentlemen. The lower class in general civil and industrious. One part in particular, a tract of country called Barney Fort, wore the appearance of an English colony.

In February 1817 he received a long-delayed letter from Colonel Robertson, written the previous June and enclosing a gold medal conferred on him by the Emperor of Austria for his service with the Austrian Army in Italy in 1814, together with a letter from the Duke of York, as Commander-in-Chief, authorising him, with the approval of the Prince Regent, to wear this foreign decoration. John Henry wrote a gratified letter to Colonel Robertson, reverting with pleasure to their time together in Lissa and in Italy, and to the Duke of York he wrote

JHS 'Wexford. 21st Febry 1817.
May it please your Royal Highness
I have the honour to acknowledge the receipt of an Austrian Gold Medal forwarded to me by Col Robertson of the 89th Regt, and which reached me two days ago. With pride and satisfaction I receive from the Emperor of Austria this testimony of his Imperial Majesty's approbation of my service in Italy against the French in the campaign of 1814. I beg to express my sincere acknowledgements to his Royal Highness the Prince Regent for having been graciously pleased to approve of my accepting and wearing this honourable badge.
I have the honour to be
Your Royal Highness's
most devoted humble servant
John Slessor, Lt Col 35th Regt'

No doubt John Henry enjoyed making, behind the respectful terms of this letter, the implied reproach that the Emperor of Austria was more grateful in recognising his services than his own Commander-in-Chief who had refused him the CB. A miniature of him done about this time shows him wearing his Waterloo and Austrian medals on his scarlet uniform with epaulettes and yellow facings. He was now all but forty – a rather full-faced man with dark eyes and thick black hair.

Rumours of the imminent disbandment of the 2nd Battalion of the 35th continued to reach Wexford. The 1st Battalion was expected to return to England in the spring of 1817, and then the 2nd Battalion's fate would be sealed.

By 1818, all the second battalions which had been formed during the War for regiments of the line were to disappear. John Henry and his battalion passed the spring of 1817 among the gaieties of Wexford, now – according to John Henry – a scene of peace and goodwill between Catholics and Protestants, in gratifying contrast to the terrible events there during the Irish Rebellion in 1798, when scores of Loyalist prisoners had been piked to death on the bridge by the rebels who controlled the town, as John Henry recalled in his diary.

JHS Wexford in the year of the Rebellion, 1798, was the scene of the greatest atrocities. Religious faction and persecution was carried to its height. Now on the contrary the heroes of that epoch appear to be buried in oblivion. All ranks of both persuasions mixed with cordiality and good faith. Protestants and Catholics shook hands.

In April our suspense was at an end: for the 2nd Battalion was ordered to be disbanded in due form on the 24th by Major-General Doyle: which was done on the Parade in the Barrack Yard, after the Lord Lieutenant's warrant was read. The General in a few words expressed his approbation of the high character the Regiment had always maintained: that, tho' as military men, many among us must regret the dissolution of a regiment so united, and so well disciplined, whereby numbers must feel the inconvenience, still all with reason could boast that their exertions had tended to humble the most inveterate and powerful enemy that England had ever had to cope with. This ceremony being over, the General took his leave, and the 2nd Batt 35th ceased to exist as a Regiment. The Colours were marched down to Lieut Colonel Sir George Berkeley's quarters, the Band playing the British Grenadiers. Here they were cased, after having buffeted about for twelve years, entrusted during that period to a Corps that never would have parted with so dear and sacred a trust of their King and Country but with their lives. On the Adjutant handing them into the house, the Band struck up God Save the King, and many a manly tear was seen to drop at our parting. The men were marched back to Barracks in mournful silence. Those fit for active service were ordered to be detained for the 1st Batt, under officers of the 1st Batt. The remaining were discharged. We had a parting dinner, but by no means a merry one, condolence rather than conviviality. The next day a division of our mess funds, silver utensils, etc took place, a melancholy dissolution. Here ends my military career.

He then quoted the Regimental Orders which Lieut-Colonel Robertson, on behalf of the Duke of Richmond, Colonel of the 35th, issued ten days before the reduction of the 2nd Battalion. These expressed approbation of the 2nd Battalion's 'high state of discipline' and 'gallant and exemplary conduct' in the Netherlands and in France, and gratification that in Ireland 'the Regiment continued to maintain the same high character' by 'their very orderly and quiet conduct in quarters', so that their conduct had been 'universally praised and admired by the inhabitants wherever they have been'. Lieut Colonel Slessor was named as one of the senior officers with whom Robertson 'has long been in the habits of intimacy and friendship. He has experienced from them nothing but the most gracious attention to the performance of their military and public duties, and the most undeviating kindness and assistance from their friendship'.

This, however conventional and customary on such occasions, was some sop to John Henry's feelings, and so was an article in a Wexford newspaper on 28th April which confirms the good behaviour of the battalion while in Wexford.

JHS 'On Thursday the 2nd Batt 35th Regt, quartered in this city, were disembodied, when almost the whole of the men were attached to the 1st Batt, and are to do duty here till further orders as a Detachment from the 1st Battn. We have had frequent occasion to speak of the 2nd Batt of this Regt during their residence here, and always in terms of applause which correct and meritorious conduct deserve. They have been often eminently distinguished in the field of battle, and their behaviour in time of peace has equally added to their reputation. Their duties as soldiers have been discharged with regular and attentive fidelity, and their conduct as members of the community has been equally without reproach. In ceasing to exist as a second Battalion they enjoy the respect and esteem which have been honourably acquired, and which are bestowed without reserve, and with the warmest feelings of approbation'.

John Henry drew a line in his diary under this extract, and then added the last dated entry in the diary.

JHS *1st May.* Having disposed of my military garments, appointments etc, I mounted my horse and started for Dublin, not certainly under the most pleasant reflections, for I felt like a fish out of water, and as if a full stop was put to my professional advancement. In point of pecuniary emolument, a great loser, but my own Master. A round of visits beguiled the time among my friends, Stedalt, Charleville, etc. But I could not divest myself of the idea that I was on leave of absence only, and constantly fancied that I was to join the Regiment again.

He had been in the Army for twenty-three years, the whole of his adult life. For all but two of those years he had been out of England, and his regiment had been his only real home. Now, at nearly forty, he had to start some sort of new life in a much-changed England where he had no roots.

Many years later, as an old man, he added to the front of his diary his matured and resigned reflections on the pattern and meaning of life as he had experienced it.

JHS Few are those whose lives will strictly bear taking a retrospective view of; notwithstanding which much satisfaction may be derived from calling to mind and retracing the scenes and adventures of early days, even should conscience sometimes sting. One person pursues his destined course thro' rugged paths; another thro' smooth; and each arrives at his appointed goal, with various success. One favoured with the smiles of fortune, aided by wordly connections, natural abilities, judgment, disposition, etc; another man ill-fated, experiences the contrary of all these advantages, ever working up against the tide. I say again, few are they who can look back and not wish that they could command the time which they have lost, or recall that which has been done. How changed are our feelings as we advance in life! Our responsibility is increased with each fleeting year. In youth we live but for ourselves; self predominates in everything. In mature age, if we have fulfilled the conditions of our tenure, we feel that we must live for our children. Fortunately increase of years weans us from those selfish and frivolous expenses which youth requires, and we feel it little or no sacrifice to devote to our children the means which before we considered so important to the gratification of our pride and our ambition. Not that we have lost either our pride or our ambition, but they have become centred on other objects dearer to us than ourselves. These we find in the race springing up, to whom we shall leave our names and our worldly possessions. When our own career is closed, worn out with the pursuit of vanity, we pause at a certain age, and come to the conclusion that, in this life, we require but little else than to eat, drink, and prepare for a future existence.

EPILOGUE

The rest of Harriot's and John Henry's lives after 1817 were humdrum in comparison with their adventures and perils during the long war with France. When John Henry's army career came to an end in Ireland, he joined his mother and sister in the house in Spring Gardens, Sidmouth, where they had settled; according to family tradition, they chose Sidmouth because its setting reminded them of Oporto. Sidmouth, comfortably seated in a dip between crimson cliffs on the south coast of Devonshire, was then regarded as a health-restoring seaside resort. Queen Victoria spent a few months of her first year of life there, while her mother, the Duchess of Kent, took warm sea-water baths for her rheumatism; her father the Duke of Kent, on the other hand, caught pneumonia and died there.

The Slessors were not in Sidmouth for this stirring event. In 1817-8 John Henry and Harriot Amelia visited their sister Louisa in Portugal, and in 1819 they and their mother set off to visit the Walshes in Nantes. The two Harriots stayed there for nearly three years, but John Henry was back in England on 9th August 1820 for his marriage to Charlotte Ann Bernard, daughter of the Rector of Crowcombe, Somerset, and of his wife Mary Hawker. It is odd that John Henry's mother and sister did not come back from France for the wedding. There is some slight evidence that with John Henry's marriage, he and his mother and Harriot Amelia began to draw apart. Harriot Amelia, who carried on the family tradition of diary-keeping, mentioned her sister-in-law only once in her rather flat and tedious records of family reunions, and whereas meetings and partings with her 'dear mother' and 'dear sisters' are always accompanied by 'heart-felt joy' or 'heart-breaking sadness', all she has to say about her sister-in-law, who is given neither a 'dear' prefix nor a Christian name, is that she was not at home to meet the two Harriots when they arrived back from their three years in France. It cannot have been altogether easy for such a family group to settle down together. 'So long a lapse of time had naturally made visible alteration in us all,' John Henry had admitted when he saw his mother and sister again in 1814, after an eleven-year separation. There would have been invisible mental alteration too; the link of family affection was still strong, but their minds had grown apart – John Henry's had expanded and left hers behind, Harriot sadly acknowledged. She added a mortified note at the end of her diary, 'but as he never asked to see the journal it would be the last of my

333

thoughts to propose the perusal of it to him. I conclude he would suppose it could not be worth the reading. He is in the right.'

If John Henry never read his mother's diary, he preserved it and passed it on to his descendants. And they all continued to live together in Sidmouth, and to pay visits together to their relations in England – to Aunt Fraser in London, to the old André sisters in Bath, to Girardot cousins at Little Bookham. In 1830, and again in 1833, the Walsh family came over from France on visits, and they all spent many months together in Brighton and in Plymouth. John Henry, by now the father of several children, generally escorted his mother and sister to join the Walshes, but then returned to his family in Sidmouth. A portrait of his mother in her old age shows her with a cloud of snow-white hair, under a frilly cap, surrounding an oval face, long-nosed, firm-lipped, with faded but still acute hazel eyes. Her facial configuration was often to reappear among her descendants. On 12th November 1834, she died. Harriot Amelia recorded the event in her diary with the leaden banality of the nineteenth century obituary style, but nevertheless pathetically revealed the sacrificed life of the spinster daughter at home.

HAS Her dear eyes were closed upon her sorrowing family for ever, calm and free from suffering – but the heart-rending last closing scene has left an indelible impression never to be erased. Nothing is there to regret for her dear sake, for our loss is her gain, she is removed from a World of pain and suffering to one of uninterrupted happiness – and we left to lament a void never to be replaced. To me all now appears a dread waste, and where to look after so long having been permitted, of late years particularly, to look up to her as the source of all my enjoyment, as well as the object of my constant and anxious solicitude. On this sacred Theme I could dwell for hours, but here I close this little narrative with a heart weigh'd down by sad reflections, and thoughts of the past, never to be recalled.

In 1835 Harriot Amelia went to the Walshes at Nantes for two years, then sailed from Nantes to Lisbon for another visit to Louisa Canavaro. There she spent the last four years of her life, and there on 9th April 1841 she died. Louisa wrote at the end of her sister's diary 'Never existed a more noble candid and generous character, ever sacrificing herself for all around her'.

John Henry married late, when he was forty-three, but lost no time in begetting a numerous family. His eldest son, another John Henry, was born nine months and three weeks after his parents' marriage, and Caroline Mary, Agnes Sophia, Charles Hildebrand, Emily Jane, Frederic George, Arthur James (who died as a baby) and Edward Augustus followed. It is possible – though there is no hard evidence for this – that he also had his illegitimate daughter Maria Natalizia within reach. The fact that the baby girl born in Sicily should have been married in 1833 at Honiton, barely ten miles from Sidmouth, could be explained by her having been brought to Devonshire by John Henry, so that he could support and keep an eye on her. Her existence was not known to anyone else in the family, or ever acknowledged by John Henry himself, as far as the records show, but there are references in his diary to the sting of conscience when remembering past events, which nothing in the avowed experiences of his life seems to account for.

In the first years after he retired from the Army, he made efforts to trace his father's family origins in Scotland, getting in touch with his father's old friend Sir Walter Farquhar and his sisters, and through them with various Sangsters and Robertsons in Aberdeenshire, descendants of Janet Robb who was half-sister to John Henry's father. At intervals he also wrote to the War Office, again setting out his claims to a CB, but always without success. On the Army List of officers on half-pay, he moved slowly upwards; he was made a full colonel on 10th January 1837, a major-general on 9th November 1846. He died in Sidmouth on 11th October 1850.

The lives of the great generals, admirals and statesmen who were at the centre of events in the Napoleonic Wars have been depicted many times. The decisive actions in Russia, Spain, Germany, Flanders, at sea, have been studied in detail. John Henry Slessor was never near the centre of the stage for the greatest historic events of the war, or a hero of its most spectacular exploits. He fought in the less often recorded peripheral theatres of the war, and he is a representative of the mainly unsung body of officers – men of good sense, loyalty, reliability, who thoroughly knew their job – on whom the great commanders depended for the sustained effort which, after twenty-two years of war, was to free England and her allies victoriously from a great peril.

In his experiences of war he did not come in for much of the exhilaration of victory and glory. He did not have the knack – which seems like, but perhaps is not, pure luck – of being in the right place at the right time. He arrived on the scene just too late for a series of victorious battles, from the Nile and Maida to Waterloo. His fighting experiences began with a retreat from a skirmish, and ended at one of the great battles of history, but the skirmish gave his side a tactical advantage, while for the great battle he remained disappointedly on the sidelines. This start and finish were characteristic of him; he was never to be at the heart of great historical events, but he was a survivor. His head was grazed by a bullet at Coloney; he was slightly wounded in the leg at Rosetta; those were his only injuries in a quarter of a century of service. Through retreats and delays and muddles, he remained a hard-working resolute part of the great power of national survival that brought England through.

His eldest son became a clergyman, but many of his descendants – English, French, and Portuguese – were soldiers, marines, or airmen. Only one of them, Marshal of the RAF Sir John Slessor, his great-grandson, reached the top. Most of them ended up as Brigadiers, Group-Captains, Colonels, Chefs D'Escadron, Majors. Like John Henry, they and their kind – loyal but independent-minded, steadily rather than spectacularly brave, sagacious without startling brilliance – provided the backbone of their countries' armed services.

SOURCES

Acton, Harold, *The Bourbons of Naples, 1734-1825*. (Methuen, 1950)

Allotte de la Fuye, M., *Le Retour de Sophy Blount, 1846-1897* (Privately printed n.d.)

Anderson, William, *The Scottish Nation, or the Surnames, Literature, Honours and Biographical History of the People of Scotland* (A. Fullerton, Edinburgh, 1880)

Army Lists, 1754-1763, 1794-1850

Arnold, Isaac, *The Life of Benedict Arnold: His Patriotism and His Treason* (J.C. Nimmo & Bain, 1880)

Bunbury, Sir Henry, *Narratives of Some Passages in the Great War with France, 1799-1810* (Peter Davies, 1927)

Cheke, Marcus, *Dictator of Portugal: A Life of the Marquis of Pombal, 1699-1782* (Sidgwick & Jackson, 1938)

Costigan, Arthur William, *Sketches of Society and Manners in Portugal.* 2 vols. (T. Vernor, 1778)

Dalton, Charles. *English Army Lists and Commission Registers, 1661-1714* (Eyre & Spottiswoode, 1892-6)

Delaforce, John, *The Factory House at Oporto* (Christopher Helm, 1990)

Fortescue, Sir John, *History of the British Army*, 13 vols. (Macmillan, 1890)

Francis, David, *Portugal, 1715-1808* (Tamesis Book, 1985)

Galt, John, *Letters from the Levant* (T. Cadell and W. Davies, 1813)

Gwynn, Robin D., *Huguenot Heritage* (Routledge & Kegan Paul, 1985)

Harris, Rifleman, *Recollections of Rifleman Harris* (Peter Davies, 1929)

Haslip, Joan, *Lady Hester Stanhope* (Cobden-Sanderson, 1934)

Historia do Cidade do Porto, (Portucalense Editora, n.d.)

Howard, E., *Memoirs of Admiral Sir Sidney Smith*, 2 vols. (Richard Bentley, 1839)

Jamieson, John, Life of John Slezer in *Theatrum Scotiae* (G. Ramsay, Edinburgh, 1814)

Johnson, Edgar, *Sir Walter Scott. The Great Unknown*, 2 vols. (Hamish Hamilton, 1970)

Longford, Elizabeth, *Wellington: The Years of the Sword* (Weidenfeld & Nicolson, 1969)

Macaulay, Rose, *They Went to Portugal* (Jonathan Cape, 1946)
 – *They Went to Portugal Too* (Carcanet, 1990)
Mackesy, Piers, *The War in the Mediterranean, 1803-1810* (Longmans Green, 1957)
Maycock, F.W.O., *The Invasion of France, 1814* (Allan & Unwin, 1914)
Napier, William, *History of the War in the Peninsula*, 6 vols, (T. & W. Boone, 1832)
Oman, Carola, *Napoleon's Viceroy: Eugène de Beauharnais* (Hodder & Stoughton, 1966)
 – *Sir John Moore* (Hodder & Stoughton, 1953)
Oman, Charles, *A History of the Peninsular War*, 2 vols. (Clarendon Press, 1902)
Pakenham, Thomas, *The Year of Liberty: The Story of the Great Irish Rebellion of 1798* (Hodder & Stoughton, 1969)
Rath, Reuben John, *The Fall of the Napoleonic Kingdom of Italy (1814)* (Columbia University Press, 1941)
 – *The Provisional Austrian Regime in Lombardy-Veneto, 1814-15* (University of Texas Press, Austin, 1969)
Roundell, Mrs Charles, *Lady Hester Stanhope* (John Murray, 1909)
Russell of Liverpool, Lord, *Knight of the Sword: The Life and Letters of Admiral Sir William Sidney Smith, G.C.B.* (Gollancz, 1964)
Sargent, Winthrop, *The Life and Career of Major John André* (Ticknor & Fields, Boston, 1861)
Scott, Sir Walter, *Letters*, 13 vols. ed. H.J.C. Grierson (Constable, 1933)
 – *Life of Napoleon Bonaparte*, 2 vols. (A. & C. Black, Edinburgh, 1878)
 – 'Paul's Letters to His Kinsfolk' in *Miscellaneous Prose Works*, vol.V. (R. Cadell, Edinburgh, 1839)
Sellers, Charles, *Oporto Old and New* (Herbert E. Harper, 1899)
Seward, Anna, *Poetical Works*, 3 vols. (James Ballantyne, Edinburgh, 1810)
Wilson, General Sir Robert, *Private Diary of Travels, Personal Services and Public Events During Mission and Employment with the European Armies in the Campaigns of 1812, 1813, 1814*, 2 vols. (John Murray, 1861)
Woodhouse, C.M., 'Byron and the First Hellenic Tourists' in *Essays by Divers Hands*, vol. XXXVI (Royal Society of Literature, 1970)

Note: all the above published in London unless otherwise stated.

Index